RESPONSIBLE FAITH

RESPONSIBLE FAITH

Christian Theology in the Light of 20th-Century Questions

HANS SCHWARZ

AUGSBURG Publishing House • Minneapolis

RESPONSIBLE FAITH
Christian Theology in the Light of 20th-Century Questions

Copyright © 1986 Augsburg Publishing House

All rights reserved. Except for brief quotations in critical articles or reviews, no part of this book may be reproduced in any manner without prior written permission from the publisher. Write to: Permissions, Augsburg Publishing House, 426 S. Fifth St., Box 1209, Minneapolis MN 55440.

Scripture quotations are from the Revised Standard Version of the Bible, copyright 1946, 1952, and 1971 by the Division of Christian Education of the National Council of Churches.

Library of Congress Cataloging-in-Publication Data

Schwarz, Hans, 1939–
RESPONSIBLE FAITH.

Bibliography: p.
Includes index.
1. Theology, Doctrinal. I. Title.
BT75.2.S43   1986   230   85-26657
ISBN 0-8066-2188-5

Manufactured in the U.S.A.   APH 10-5483

1   2   3   4   5   6   7   8   9   0   1   2   3   4   5   6   7   8   9

CONTENTS

Preface 9
Abbreviations 11

Introduction: A Thoughtful and Thought-Provoking Faith 13

PART 1   PROLEGOMENA **17**

Chapter 1: Theology **18**
A. The birth and development of Christian theology 19
B. Three essential functions of theology 34

Chapter 2: Revelation **40**
A. Signals of transcendence 40
B. Disclosure of a higher dimension 43
C. Exclusiveness of the self-disclosure in Jesus Christ 46
D. The limits of (rational) perception 50

Chapter 3: Scripture **53**
A. The emergence of the New Testament Scriptures 53
B. The formation of the Christian Bible 56
C. The development and function of the canon 58

PART 2   THE GOD WHO ACTS **64**

Chapter 4: God **65**
A. God and the gods 66
B. The limits of our natural knowledge of God 72
C. What God is like 85

Chapter 5: Creation **96**
A. God as creator 97
B. God's relationship to the world 102
C. God's providential activity 114

Chapter 6: Humanity **124**
A. Our creatureliness 124
B. Our administrative task 128
C. Our dialogical structure 134

Chapter 7: Sin **140**
A. The cause of evil 140
B. The power of sin (original and actual sin) 154
C. The extent of corruption 161

PART 3   THE CHRIST WHO SAVES **172**

Chapter 8: Jesus of Nazareth **173**
A. The quest for the historical Jesus 175
B. Jesus of Nazareth 191

Chapter 9: Jesus the Christ **207**
A. The turning point of the resurrection 208
B. Stations of Christological reflection 214
C. The two aspects of Christ 242

PART 4   THE SPIRIT WHO EMPOWERS **259**

Chapter 10: The Holy Spirit **260**
A. The biblical documents 260
B. The early church 265
C. The Reformers and contemporary theologians 270

Chapter 11: The Church **276**
A. The formative period 277
B. The present structure 284
C. The three-pronged potential 317

Chapter 12: The Means of Grace **341**
A. God's Word 341
B. God's sign 352
C. God's presence 362

Chapter 13: The Christian Hope 376
A. Resurrection 380
B. The end of history 393
C. The new world 400

Notes 405
For Further Reading 431
Index of Names 440
Index of Biblical References 442
Index of Subjects 445

PREFACE

Comprehensive presentations of the content of the Christian faith are increasingly written in a team approach. It is virtually impossible for an individual scholar to master the wealth of information and insights offered by ever-advancing reflection and scholarship. Nonetheless, it remains the task of individuals to believe in the Christian faith, i.e., to hold with reasonable confidence that the basis of their trust is indeed trustworthy. Everything else borders on mindless credulity or irrational ideology. This implies that individual believers should "master" the content of the Christian faith, if not in every detail, then at least in its general outline.

The present volume grew out of the concern to present the general content of the Christian faith from one person to another, so to speak, in a comprehensible and comprehensive way, without becoming overly burdened with specialized knowledge. This was facilitated by the fact that in several areas I have previously written monographs which provide a more detailed discussion both of exegetical questions and the historical development of certain themes. The present endeavor also granted me the opportunity to explore the whole content of the Christian doctrine even in areas such as Christology, which I had not yet presented as in-depth studies.

In retrospect—prefaces are customarily written after a work has been concluded—I must confess that I have been astounded at the wealth of Christian doctrine and, had it not been for the stubborn intent to write only one volume, the project would have easily evolved to a multivolumed set. The discerning reader will still find items missing which should have been included. Keeping the desiderata to a minimum, there is for each chapter an appended list of approximately 10 books for further reading. The number has been kept intentionally low, since these specialized monographs themselves provide more exhaustive bibliographies, while the intent of this text is to allow it to speak for itself. Notes have been subjected to the same principle, seldom going beyond the citing of direct quotations.

The intention of this book is not to set forth all the items which one *has* to believe as a Christian. Such fideistic legalism would be more appropriate for an age of authoritarianism than for our present age of personal responsibility. I instead wanted to indicate what Christians today believe, why there are good reasons to believe it, and what difference these beliefs make for the basic outlook on life in today's world. Thus the questions Why? and What difference does it make? are not sacrificed for the sake of the What? The Christian faith is not an exercise in how much one can believe but a wholehearted endeavor to believe in something which is credible and which makes such a difference in one's life that one can venture one's whole life on that belief.

The material contained in this book has been presented many times inside and outside of the classroom in the United States and in West Germany, in a denominational seminary setting and in the brisker air of the university. I owe much to the questions, criticisms, and suggestions I have encountered from colleagues, students, pastors, and laity. My special thanks go to my research assistant, Craig Nessan, who undertook the arduous task of improving my style, bringing the notes into proper form, compiling the bibliographies, and helping with the proofreading and indexes. Diana Sgaslik deserves thanks for checking out numerous references. Bärbel Berger and Barbara Fischer must be thanked for typing the manuscript in its various stages with unfailing patience and accuracy. Finally, I thank my wife for her support as she patiently learns the joys and trials of the life of a teacher and writer. But I would like to dedicate this book to my children, Hans and Krista, as they make the inherited Christian faith more and more their own.

ABBREVIATIONS

ANFa	*The Ante-Nicene Fathers. Translations of the Writings of the Fathers down to A.D. 325.* American Edition. 10 vols. Grand Rapids, Mich.: Eerdmans, 1950–1951.
FaCh	*The Fathers of the Church: A New Translation.* Washington, D.C.: Catholic University of America, 1947–.
LW	*Luther's Works.* American Edition. 56 vols. Edited by Jaroslav Pelikan. St. Louis: Concordia and Philadelphia: Fortress, 1955–.
NPNF (FS)	*A Select Library of the Nicene and Post-Nicene Fathers of the Christian Church.* 14 vols. First Series. Grand Rapids, Mich.: Eerdmans, 1956.
NPNF (SS)	——————. 14 vols. Second Series. Grand Rapids, Mich.: Eerdmans, 1952–1956.
PG	Migne, Jacques-Paul, ed. *Patrologiae Cursus Completus. Series Graeca.* 169 vols. Paris, 1857–1936.
PL	——————. *Patrologiae Cursus Completus. Series Latina.* 221 vols. Paris, 1841-1864.
TDNT	*Theological Dictionary of the New Testament.* 10 vols. Ed. Gerhard Kittel. Trans. G. W. Bromiley. Grand Rapids, Mich.: Eerdmans, 1964–1976.
TDOT	*Theological Dictionary of the Old Testament.* Ed. G. Johannes Botterweck and Helmer Ringgren. Grand Rapids, Mich.: Eerdmans, 1978–.
WA	*D. Martin Luthers Werke. Kritische Gesamtausgabe.* Weimar, 1883–.
WA.TR	——————. *Tischreden.* Weimar, 1912–.

INTRODUCTION: A THOUGHTFUL AND THOUGHT-PROVOKING FAITH

The Christian faith is a thoughtful faith. This is its promise and its handicap. Unlike a meditative religion, such as Buddhism, the Christian faith does not design exercises on how to escape the world and its misery. Unlike a religion of obedience, such as Islam, the Christian faith does not resign itself to the inevitable fate of history. Christians are summoned to accept the challenges of a world in agony and they will not consider anything as a *fait accompli*. The Latin proverb *ora et labora* (pray and work) captures in a nutshell the essence of the Christian faith. For better or for worse, Christian faith and the secular movements it has engendered have changed the face of the earth more than any other movements, religious or otherwise.

The westernization of the world, progressing ever more vigorously during the last few centuries, has perhaps reached its pinnacle in this century. Even the oil-rich Arab countries cannot do without Western hardware and software. The much-maligned multinational corporations, without exception operating from a Western base or from its Eastern offspring, Japan, demonstrate the dominance of the West. Even the so-called mission on six continents is a decidedly Western phenomenon since there are very few Muslim or Buddhist missionaries working in the West. It is rather that Western churches and missionary enterprises farm out missionaries and material support to the ends of the earth. Yet the very success of the Christian faith has also become its greatest problem. Thoughtful people, such as the British historian Arnold Toynbee, have long wondered whether the Christian faith has not advocated more its Western dress than its distinctive message. Certainly, if the Christian message is to transform people it should be expected that the context would not remain untouched. Thus many of the Western ways of life have decidedly Christian roots. Many of our cherished values, such as human dignity, freedom of the individual person, and the sanctity of life, are deeply rooted in, and in fact inseparable from, the Christian faith. We realize that today these values are often advertised as purely rational or humanist ideas. This means that the ideas and movements which the Christian faith has engendered have become largely independent and secular. Most of these ideas we encounter in a totally secular dress. In many ways the dress itself has become the message, proclaiming that humanity does not only live in the world but is itself a worldly phenomenon.

The two main varieties in which modern secularity presents itself are scientific materialism and Marxist dialectic. The first is typical of the attitude in democratic societies, while the latter is characteristic of socialist countries. Both of them are decidedly antimetaphysical and proclaim that today's issues can be addressed and solved only by reference to innerworldly options. This means that the Christian faith, by appealing to a higher power than humanity itself, is more and more considered antiquated.

Since its victory over competing religions in the fourth century, Christianity has been used to decide questions of ultimate values without considering rival options. *Roma locuta, causa finita* (Rome has spoken, the case is settled) was an often-practiced proverb of the Middle Ages. Yet over the centuries the prescribed dogmas of the Christian faith had less and less compelling power for an ever-increasing number of Christian believers. In many instances the initial reaction of the Christian establishment was even stronger coercion and then gradual retreat in the face of overwhelming counterpressure. This strange dialectic of bold advances and hidden disclaimers has not attracted many new members to the Christian fold. Most Christians, too, were somewhere lost in this dialectic process and settled for one side or the other. So we encounter a fundamentalism on the one side, a half-hearted liberalism on the other, and a huge segment of bewildered Christians in the middle. In this situation in which the compelling drive of the Christian message has been replaced by retreat, stubbornness, or bewilderment, we must discover anew the basic thrust and content of the Christian faith. Then we may also realize that it is both a thoughtful and a thought-provoking faith.

Adhering to a thoughtful faith means first of all that we do not merely believe something without considering the ramifications of those beliefs. Nor does it mean we believe merely because we just happened to stumble across an idea that sounded convincing. The biblical mandate not to build upon a foundation of sand addresses the issue clearly. Unless we succumb to credulity we must have reasonable assurance that the ground of our faith (*fides qua creditur*) is trustworthy. Nothing is more detrimental to our witness than an inability to give sound reasons why we are Christians. It simply does not suffice to say that we were born into a Christian family, fortunate as that may be. There must be an intellectual awareness of why we are who we are. Similarly, unless we succumb to credulity, we must have reasonable assurance that the content of our faith (*fides quae creditur*) is trustworthy. It is detrimental to our own witness if we cannot give convincing reasons why we believe what we believe. It does not suffice simply to say that as Christians we believe this or that. With the same "justification" we could state that as humans we believe that the earth is square and refrain from further inquiry. There must be an intellectual tenability to our Christian hope.

Since we have never seen God face to face and since we have not yet seen the resurrection we hope for, there is always an amount of trust involved in our faith. By analogy physicists have also not "seen" an electron or a quantum leap. Yet they do not simply resign themselves to credulity but attempt to verify indirectly the credibility of their hypothesis. Intellectual honesty is absolutely necessary for credibility in our faith. Yet the Christian faith is not just thoughtful in that it requires intellectual rigor but also thought-provoking because it challenges accepted patterns and ideas. The notion that we could neatly pack everything into a drawer and pull out whatever is needed is as unrealistic as the notion that a pastor has learned in seminary everything there is to learn.

Since life is not static but ongoing and dynamic, the answer to life's questions must always be adjusted to new situations. The advances in the sciences continuously pose new ethical problems and our basic faith is not untouched by these new issues. The Christian faith is open to a future for the world, its history, and ourselves. Moreover, since the Christian faith points to a future hoped for, the ground and content of this faith must be continuously reevaluated in the light of God's ongoing history with his world and his people. Such a procedure does not relativize our faith or make it optional. But it shows that even the best faith is in need of growth. Yet before we deal explicitly with the content of the Christian faith, we must delve into some preliminary considerations.

PART 1

PROLEGOMENA

There are many items which could be included under the rubric of preliminary considerations, such as the issues of language, hermeneutics, worldview, authority, etc. Many of these will be touched upon at least implicitly. Yet the items most intrinsic to the Christian faith are: (1) theology, i.e., the attempt to express our faith in a logically coherent and consistent way, as the medium of Christian reflection; (2) revelation, i.e., the way in which God mediates himself to us, as the presupposition of our faith; and (3) Scripture, i.e., the written reflection of God's self-disclosure, as the foundation of the Christian faith.

1

THEOLOGY

As many other concepts of the Christian faith, the term "theology" was borrowed from Greek culture and originally meant poetical (mythical) narratives of the gods. Greek poets, such as Homer and Hesiod, could be called theologians though they only presented mythological narratives about gods. A few centuries later, Aristotle, the most renowned student of Plato, wrote in his *Metaphysics* that the primal philosophy is the science of the first cause for every thing that is. This all-encompassing science he also called theology.

Presumably it was among the Stoics where the change took place from considering theology as belonging to prescientific thinking to assuming it as part of the scientific enterprise. But theology as talk about God did not always live up to this new esteem, not even among Christian theologians. Naturally, one should regard the New Testament writers, such as Paul and the gospel writers, as the first Christian theologians. But the literary output of the New Testament writers cannot be classified as intentional theological literature in the scientific sense. Their purpose has a much more kerygmatic nature, proclaiming the gospel of Jesus Christ. Even the apostolic fathers of the post–New Testament era must be judged in a similar way.

A. The birth and development of Christian theology

The first Christian literature which is intentionally theological in a scientific sense are the writings of the early Christian apologists of the second century. While little attention previously was given to the pagan context in which most of the newly converted Christians lived, at the beginning of the second century more and more people felt that their new faith should be clarified in the context of their former philosophical and religious beliefs. They wanted to make sure that their new faith was sound and reasonable. This was not done out of conceit, but rather, as the church grew, more and more misunderstandings about the new faith arose and malicious gossip was deliberately spread by outsiders. This was also the time when the first persecutions started. In this situation the Christians felt a need to inform the authorities, above all, the emperor, that their new faith contained nothing detrimental to the state, to clear thought, or to desirable morality. The Christian apologetic literature shows that the Christians took seriously the charges they faced and that they were unwilling simply to go into hiding. Their theology contained an appeal to public opinion and it was intended to be widely disseminated. But even the apologists were not without precedent. The Jewish historian Flavius Josephus and the Jewish philosopher Philo of Alexandria had earlier attempted to bridge the gap between their religion and the Hellenistic world. The Christians had learned from them—they were the only ones who preserved Philo's writings—without necessarily using their arguments.

1. *The early church*

The earliest Christian apologists, Quadratus and Aristides, wrote at the beginning of the second century. From Quadratus we have only a small fragment of an apology which he submitted to Emperor Hadrian. The church historian Eusebius of the fourth century tells us that he composed it because "certain wicked men had attempted to trouble the Christians."[1] Eusebius claims that this apology was widely read and that he himself had a copy of it. Yet we do not know either who Quadratus was or the thrust of his apology. We are somewhat better off with Aristides of Athens who, as Eusebius mentions, also directed an apology to Hadrian. Again Eusebius tells us that he still had a copy of it.[2] It was not until 1879, however, that a first fragment of this apology was found. Soon afterwards a complete Syriac translation was even discovered, and other fragments as well, so that we now have a good idea of its contents.

The apology is divided into two parts. In the first part (Chaps. 1–14) Aristides polemicizes against the barbarians and other pagans, while in the second part (Chaps. 15–19) he explains the morals and teachings of the Christians. Aristides claims that the barbarians are wrong since they worship the four elements (fire, water, earth, and air) though they are not divine. The Greeks act wrongly too since they adore immoral and changeable gods in human form. The Jews possess a purer idea of God and are close to the Christians in their morals, but actually worship angels and put too much emphasis on externals such as circumcision and fasting. Only the Christians have a true knowledge of God. In his incarnate Son and in the Holy Spirit the true God who has created and sustains things is recognized. Aristides is not timid about his faith. He sees in the Christians a new race which has the task to lead humanity out of its depravity into new life. The prayers of the Christians he considers the reason for the preservation of the world. His theological reflection, however, is not on the same high plane as his self-assuredness. For instance, he chides the Greeks for worshiping changeable gods while he himself calls Jesus the God who was born, crucified, and resurrected. In this respect the development of the *logos* theology, in which the *logos* represents the immutability of God, was an attempt of later apologists to come to terms with the identification of God and Jesus.

Another of the early apologists who should be mentioned here is *Justin Martyr* (c. 100–c. 165). He wrote two apologies, one about the year A.D. 150 and the other one a little later. He presents the Christian faith as the true philosophy. This claim is supported through the notion of the divine *logos* which indwells completely only in Jesus but can also be seminally present in other persons. Through the presence of the *logos* anything good and benevolent present in pagan observation can be reclaimed as intrinsically Christian. Here also the pagan observation that most of what the Christian faith offers can also be found in paganism can be accounted for. Thus Justin claims:

> We have been taught that Christ is the firstborn of God, and we have declared above that He is the Word [*logos*] of whom every race of

men were partakers; and even those who lived reasonably [i.e., according to the *logos*] are Christians, even though they have been thought atheists; as, among the Greeks, Socrates and Heraclitus, and men like them; and among the barbarians, Abraham, and Ananias, and Azarias, and Misael, and Elias, and many others whose actions and names we now decline to recount, because we know it would be tedious.[3]

Such a notion that the pagans can be saved is quite remarkable. But it also implies that the pagans are accountable for their actions. This was an important argument in the face of the then-threatening persecution.

With Justin's introduction of a seminal *logos* [*logos spermatikos*] the tension between the *logos* both as something divine and as human reasonableness was not yet solved. Do humans act rightly only because of the divine indwelling or is it because they are in tune with the divine? In the latter case the notion of God's salvific activity becomes rather tenuous. If they do so, however, because of the divine indwelling, then human freedom and accountability are severely limited. We encounter here *in nuce* theological problems that will trouble the church for centuries. Yet we admire the courage with which the notion of the seminal *logos* was introduced to Christian theology, a concept which still today pervades Christian theology, as can be seen, for example, in Paul Tillich's distinction between the universal and the incarnate *logos*. When Justin concedes that "each man spoke well in proportion to the share he had of the spermatic word [i.e., seminal *logos*]," he showed appreciation for that which was good and reasonable in a world which the Christian faith set out to conquer.[4] He did not betray the attitude of an anxious, narrow-minded sectarian, but opened the door for dialog.

The one who fostered the dialog more than anyone else in the early church and who stirred up almost unending conflict was the presbyter *Origen* from Alexandria (c. 185–253). His main contribution to apologetics was his *Against Celsus*, directed around A.D. 246 to an eclectic Platonist who in *The True Word* had claimed that a reasonable Christian theology is a contradiction in itself, since Christianity is inherently hostile to all human values. There is no reconciliation possible, Celsus claimed, between Greek reasonableness and the irrational faith of uneducated scum, i.e., the Christians. Small wonder that Celsus' diatribe was not preserved by the Christians. We can only glean its argument from Origen.

Origen attempts to introduce the Christian faith as intellectually credible. Contrary to Celsus' claim, Christians are not inferior to pagans, but at least their equal. In the first part of the apology, Origen attempts to establish the historical credibility of the biblical text. Among other things, he refutes Celsus' idea that Jesus was the illegitimate son of Mary and a Roman soldier named Panthera, objecting that such a birth story does not agree with the noble character of Jesus.[5] He also disclaims the ideas that Jesus was a sorcerer who learned his tricks in Egypt, and that he was not resurrected. Origen chides Celsus especially for the uncritical principle of selection by which he picks and chooses texts from the New Testament and through which he shows his own prejudice. Origen, influenced by neo-Platonic philosophy, admits that there is an affinity between Christian doctrine and Greek philosophy. But that does not mean that his faith becomes syncretistic, since Plato's insights are much more clearly and succinctly stated in the Bible. Plato did not penetrate to the full knowledge of God, and to worship in an inferior way is an insult to God, the only divine being, who governs all things through his providence. Celsus' fear that with the conversion of the Roman Empire to Christianity a catastrophe would ensue is countered by Origen with the claim that it is for the sake of true worship and true prayer that God would give to the empire his protection and blessing. Though Christians do not serve as soldiers and refuse to occupy certain government offices, they do serve the country through their prayers and by teaching people an honest life. Origen succeeded to show with arguments like these that Christians are indeed worthy of dialog and not of contempt.

Yet beyond his contribution to Christian apologetics, with his work *On First Principles* Origen gave the Christian faith its first systematic theology. This tome of four books was perhaps composed between A.D. 212 and 215. He sets the tone in the introduction when he states that the apostles gave us only what is necessary for salvation. Origen adds, however, that there are many other items which still need clarification through clear and logical thought and through the testimony of Scripture. Then he proceeds to do just that. In the first book he covers the doctrine of God, the angels, the creation of the world, the fall, the universal homecoming, and the final fulfillment. In a second book, he deals with the present world and humanity. The third book is devoted to the issues of free will, human sinfulness, and redemption, and in the last volume he writes on Scripture and its (allegorical) interpretation. In four volumes Origen presents the Christian faith as a complete theory of the universe and attempts to remove the intellectual difficulties felt by many Christians concerning the essentials of their faith. Origen was a methodical scholar, trained in Platonic philosophy, and a serious exegete who sought to penetrate the biblical documents for their inner unity in the midst of diversity. He did not want to reach easy compromises between the Hellenistic spirit and the biblical witness, but endeavored to submit the Christian doctrines to the forum of reason. He held the underlying conviction that the Christian faith presented a new and all-encompassing view of the world which was superior to, but not necessarily opposed to, Hellenistic culture. The Christian doctrine evolved for him from the biblical documents in a logical way that maintained inner cohesiveness and consistency. He employs all learned means of his time to present a comprehensive understanding of God and the universe. Without exaggeration we can call him one of the greatest systematic theologians of all time.

What Origen achieved for the whole church, *John of Damascus* (c. 674–c. 749) accomplished five centuries later for the Eastern church in his *Fount of Knowledge*. In contrast to Origen, he was neither a creative theologian nor did he intend to be one. By his own admission he wanted to present the wisdom of the Greeks and, like a bee, to gather salvation from the enemy, i.e., present his dogmatics especially with the aid of Aristotle's philosophical prolegomena. John of Damascus follows primarily Theodoret and Epiphanius in exposing the heresies hated by God. He also adds some of his own comments on Islam. Finally, he exhibits the truth in the words of God-inspired prophets, God-taught fisherman, and God-filled shepherds and teachers in *An Exact Exposition of the Orthodox Faith*. This third part of the *Fount of Knowledge*, often published independently, presents a systematic exposition of the whole theological tradition and obtained almost normative status in the Greek Church. In a first volume he treats the godhead (God and Trinity). In a second volume we read of the created universe (heaven and earth, angels and the devil, humanity, freedom of the will, and divine providence). In a third volume John covers the person of Christ and in a final volume, in which many items are intermixed, we read of the resurrection, the sacraments, eschatology, and such things as church festivals, customs, and morals. Besides Scripture, which he does not allegorize, John uses as his chief authorities Gregory Nanzianzus, Basil, Dionysius the Areopagite, and Leontius. His aim was not to present anything new, but to collect the views of the Fathers in a single treatise covering most of the vital questions of his day. John's work still remains normative for Orthodox doctrine today.

John stands in a line with the apologists by presenting a philosophical picture of God. God is *to ōn* (the being), a concept he claims is innate in humanity. To assert God's existence he uses the cosmological and physico-teleological proofs. With this approach the question soon emerges how his picture of God can be reconciled with a biblical notion of God. This is even more the case since, in his treatment of creation, fall, and eschatology, he exhibits a rather literal understanding of Scripture. It is important to remember, however, that the perception of a tension between philosophical and biblical theology was much more prevalent in the West than in the East.

When we come to the last major figure of the early church in the West, *Augustine* (354–430), bishop of Hippo Regius in North Africa, we encounter an immensely rigorous and prolific writer, yet one who was not really a systematic theologian. Many of his writings are occasional pieces responding to certain controversies, i.e., with the Pelagians, the Donatists, or the Manichaeans. Though Augustine did not write a systematic theology as such, he is practically the father of all Western theology. There is scarcely a single Roman Catholic doctrine that is historically intelligible without reference to his thought. Even the nearly suicidal struggle between pope and emperor at the height of the Middle Ages is deeply influenced, if not shaped, by Augustine's *City of God*, in which he depicts the superiority of the city of God over the earthly city. It hardly needs mentioning how deeply the Lutheran Reformation is indebted to Augustine's insistence on the sole activity of God in human salvation. Similarly, the notion of double predestination prevalent in classical Reformed theology cannot deny its Augustinian roots. Since Augustine was such a prolific writer, it is difficult to single out one work as his main theological treatise. We do better in asking for the central point of his concern.

Augustine shaped the self-understanding of the church as the community of believers and as the only institution through which and in which salvation can be obtained. This devotion to the church did not originate from a love for the institution. But he realized that grace is not a free-floating and privatistic thing. It is a divine event entrusted by God to the community of those who follow him and obey his will. While he sanctioned the church as the institution of salvation, he insisted that the church does not govern itself. It is God who works in and through the church in an act of unconditional love and allegiance to his people. Thus the formal principle of ecclesiastical authority is paired with the material principle of the sole activity of divine grace. This tension between the human institution and the divine agency often led to the danger of one gaining the upper hand over the other. For instance, in Roman Catholicism the human institutional factor was quite often emphasized at the expense of the divine, while in some mystic circles the divine agency was emphasized to the near exclusion of the human institution. Yet it is exactly this bringing together of the church and God's activity which made Augustine's approach to theology so fruitful in spite of its sometimes dangerous interpretations.

2. The medieval period and the Reformation era

After the main roads of theological reflection were laid out in the early church, the Middle Ages were mainly devoted to their solidification and broadening. From the host of prominent figures in this period at least three should be mentioned, one of them more extensively. Chronologically the first in our list is *John Scotus Erigena* (c. 810–?), a man whose life is obscured through the fact that he held no ecclesiastical office and that he lived in turbulent times. Nevertheless, he stands out as one of the most prominent figures in the whole history of philosophy and theology. His great work, *De divisione naturae* (On the Division of Nature) was written around A.D. 867 and is composed as a dialog between a teacher and a pupil. For John Scotus *natura* (nature or, rather, the all-encompassing) is the universal category from which everything proceeds. He divides it into four subcategories: (1) that which creates and is not created

(God); (2) that which creates and is created (the ideas of God); (3) that which is created and does not create (the world); and (4) that which is not created and does not create (God as the end of all things). John Scotus is certainly more a philosopher than a theologian. He marks the beginning of Western philosophy. Even though his is a "baptized philosophy," it becomes a separate discipline, distinct from theology. John Scotus wanted to be true to the teachings of the church. Yet when Jesus is turned into the wellspring of all ideas, the mediator of the development of the world, as well as its origin and destiny, we realize that philosophy has gained the upper hand. It was through his philosophical work that John Scotus finally experienced trouble with the church when, without prior approval, he published his translation of Dionysius the Areopagite (c. A.D. 500). Since then we also know that Dionysius was a disciple of the neo-Platonic philosopher Plotinus and not, as many had then thought, a convert of St. Paul in Athens.

The emphasis on philosophical training is also clearly discernible in the prominent medieval theologian *Anselm of Canterbury* (1033–1109). He is still known today through his three main writings, the *Monologion*, devoted to the problem of theodicy (i.e., how God's wisdom and justice can be reconciled with the evil we see in the world); the *Proslogion*, addressed to God and famous for its ontological proof of God's existence; and the largest, *Cur Deus homo?* (why did God become a human being?) in which he develops the so-called theory of satisfaction (see below, Chap. 9, B-4). In the theory of satisfaction Anselm argues that through his sacrificial death Jesus satisfied God for all our wrongdoings. This theory gradually replaced the earlier notion of deception as promulgated by Origen, Augustine, and many others. In this earlier notion it was advocated that through the fall into sin the devil had obtained a claim on humanity. But because the devil was mistaken in also claiming the innocent Jesus and nailing him on the cross, he once and for all forfeited his claim on us.

Anselm's popularity is shown by the fact that parts of *Cur Deus homo?* were secretly copied and circulated before he could put the final touches on his masterpiece. In some ways Anselm continued the concern of the apologists. Beyond his immediate audience he addressed himself to the skeptical and ignorant who say in their heart that there is no God (Ps. 14:1), and to the Jews and Moslems—he knew these groups from his stay in Italy—for whom the incarnation was blasphemy. Of course, the skeptics of the Old Testament or even of Anselm's time were not the contemporary militant atheists. They were instead practical atheists who saw no compelling reasons for believing in God. Anselm felt that he had to ascertain the content of his own faith in a rational manner so that he could defend it against both skeptics and non-Christians in a rationally persuasive manner. But Anselm was more than an apologist. In his writings, which are deeply theological and not just polemical, he shows compassion for both believer and unbeliever. The thrust of his theology is characterized by the endeavor of *fides quaerens intellectum* (faith seeking understanding) through which faith seeks a reason for its belief independently from Scripture and the teachings of the church. Anselm sums up this goal best in his *Proslogion* where he says: "I give thanks, good Lord, I give thanks to you; since what I believed before through your free gift I now so understand through your illumination."[6] Anselm always presupposes his own faith before he seeks to understand. Nevertheless, he does not want to succumb to a sacrifice of the intellect. For him faith is intrinsically a responsible faith.

When we now turn to *Thomas Aquinas* (1225–1274) we encounter the most respected teacher of the Roman Catholic church. For nearly 10 years he worked on his magnum opus, his *Summa Theologica* (Summary of Theology) in which he systematized in simple and lucid terms the whole of the Christian faith. By the time of Thomas the number of theological problems and the whole field of learning had increased enormously. But Thomas succeeded in welding it into a connected and consistent whole while he constructed and explained the church's doctrine as credible and reasonable. Yet Thomas did not achieve this without outside help. For his philosophical thought-structures, his understanding of the world, and for the frame of his theological system, he was indebted to Aristotle. In short, Aristotelian metaphysics and ethics furnished the main components of Thomas' system. God became the rational cause of the universe and humanity was seen striving after this cause. This frame was then filled with the church's dogma. The work is in three parts: (1) the doctrine of the church, (2) anthropology and ethics, and (3) the person of Christ and the sacraments. The final part on eschatology was never finished, because his death intervened. Yet his work was deemed so significant that the final part was added posthumously from his commentary on Peter Lombard's *Sentences*.

In analogy to Aristotle, Thomas introduces God as the "first cause, himself uncaused" who exists only in act and is therefore without corporality. His essence is pure act and perfection. Then Thomas adduces a fivefold proof of God's existence: God as the first unmoved mover, as the first cause in the chain of causes, as the absolutely necessary being amid all contingent beings, as the absolutely perfect being amid all imperfection, and finally as the rational designer of the world. Thomas also shows in these proofs that humans strive to attain the highest end without ever being able to reach it. He concludes that a new law must be given to humanity and a superadded gift which supplements the limits of human capability so that this highest end can be attained. This superadded grace comes to us through the incarnation of Jesus Christ. Of course, God could have devised other ways to repair human nature, but this was the most suitable. Through the sacraments the essence and power of the soul are perfected and the necessary spiritual effects are attained for the Christian life. The major achievement and the persuasive power of this system lie in the careful argument and the successful synthesis of natural (philosophical) perception and Christian dogma. Similar to many other creative minds, Thomas faced some initial suspicion by the offical church. But he was soon canonized, pronounced a saint (1323), and in 1879 his teachings were even declared normative for the Roman Catholic church. As the rift between the natural and the supernatural, or the physical and the metaphysical, began to become more pronounced in the late Middle Ages the question emerged whether Thomas' elegant synthesis was not too elegant. Is nature really capable of being supplemented by the supernatural? Moreover, is the first unmoved mover still the God of Abraham, Isaac, and Jacob, and the father of Jesus Christ? These were some of the questions that were forcefully posed by Martin Luther, often with direct reference to both Thomas and Aristotle.

Martin Luther (1483–1546) was not a systematic theologian; most of his writings were of an occasional nature. Neither experience (mysticism) nor reason (scholasticism) were the guiding forces in his theological development, but rather the rediscovery of the Bible. Yet he was not a biblicist or literalistic in the narrow sense of the word, since his guiding light in expounding Scripture was Christ. Whatever promotes Christ was acceptable to Luther and whatever detracts from Christ was rejected. This Christocentricity redirected him from a philosophical theology dominated by the First Article of the Creed to a Bible-oriented theology centered on the Second Article. It also led to a concentration on Christ's mission and accomplishments for us. From this emphasis on God's grace, our faithful response followed naturally. The idea was gone that the natural needed only a supernatural addition to return to its original state. The sole activity of God and the radical otherness of God did not allow for such divine-human cooperation.

The theologian who most faithfully brought Luther's ideas into a systematic whole was his co-worker *Philip Melanchthon* (1497-1560). In his *Loci communes rerum theologicarum* (Common Loci of Theological Items), first published in 1521, he placed main emphasis on the doctrine of salvation. The doctrines of God and of creation are only briefly mentioned. The salvational emphasis becomes clear at once when Melanchthon states at the beginning of his treatise that to know Christ means "to know his benefits and not as they teach to perceive his natures and the mode of his incarnation."[7] Then he continues:

> In the epistle to the Romans, when he [Paul] drew up a compendium of Christian doctrine, did Paul the author philosophize about the mysteries of the Trinity, about the mode of the Incarnation or about "active and passive"? On the contrary, what does Paul do? He reasons most certainly about Law, Sin, and Grace. Topics, I say, on which alone the knowledge of Christ depends.

With this verdict he significantly reduced the medieval proliferation of theological items and their often minute distinctions and obscure applications. The crucial criteria for any topic now became whether it is central to the Christian faith and whether it promotes Christ. While the second criterion continues in most quarters influenced by the Reformation, the first one was soon forgotten, especially with the dawn of Orthodoxy.

John Calvin (1509–1564), the self-taught scholar and reluctant Reformer, also led back to a more traditional treatment of the Christian faith. From 1536 to 1559 he several times revised his major exposition of the Christian doctrine, the *Institutes of the Christian Religion*. Initially he followed the traditional disposition of the catechetical material. But in later editions it became more and more an exposition of the apostolic creed and an attempt to treat all theological topics in a strictly systematic manner. The *Institutes* are now divided into four books. In the first, Calvin describes the sources of our knowledge of God, the doctrine of the Trinity, and divine providence. In a second part he deals with Christology, including the unity of the old and new covenants. In a third book we read about new-found faith, which means Christian life, including life eternal. In the last book, which by far exceeds the others in volume, we are introduced to ecclesiology, the sacraments, and temporal authority. Though Calvin quotes Augustine more than any of the other church fathers, he is less restricted than Luther in his Reformation perspective and can also quote classical philosophers with approval. We admire his erudition and his success in bringing together many and often diverse sources into a homogeneous whole. In so doing he stands more in continuity with medieval theology than with the Reformation. His emphasis on the First Article of the Creed especially reveals that. But by insisting on the sovereignty of God, Calvin freed the medieval picture of God from many obscuring ideas. This theocentric approach to theology was not primarily derived from philosophical insight but from the biblical-historical awareness of God's action in history. Thus the history-making God who offers redemption to his chosen people once again becomes dominant for him. Calvin overcomes the pale medieval features of God by connecting him with the biblical history. The culmination of his redemptive action in Jesus Christ then follows naturally.

3. *The present shape of the art*

When we now take a big jump and turn to our present time, we are confronted with so many different trends that at first there seems no common thread discernible. Especially the Protestant representatives leave the impression that there is no consensus at all. But such a surface impression is deceiving.

Our contemporary times, heralded by philosophers such as René Descartes (1596–1650) in France, John Locke (1632–1704) in England, and Immanuel Kant (1724–1804) in Germany, is characterized by an ever-increasing emancipation from ecclesiastical tutelage. In this sense our modern times bear a certain affinity to the period when the Christian faith ventured into the foreign world of Hellenism. Then as now the Christian faith was not the commonly accepted answer to the questions of the day. But there is one decisive difference from this earliest period of Christianity. The Roman emperors such as Decius and Nero, infamous for their ruthless persecution of the Christian faith, were no atheists like their modern counterparts such as Stalin or Idi Amin. Out of allegiance to other religious powers they felt an obligation to stamp out the "Christian blasphemy." But today, any sense of allegiance to powers higher than ourselves is rapidly vanishing. An ever-increasing number of human beings from all ranks feel that they are responsible only to themselves. Thus the persecution of the Christian faith today occurs more under the charges of "superstition and ignorance."

This new situation, in which many people feel they can master life on their own, has deeply shaped the theological discourse of our time. There is first of all the classical approach of *Friedrich D. E. Schleiermacher* (1768–1834). Largely in response to Immanuel Kant's attempt to restrict religion to ethics and to define it within the limits of reason alone, he emphatically claimed in his *On Religion: Speeches to Its Cultured Despisers* that religion is not moralistic legislation or a metaphysical interpretation of the world, but rather a feeling and intuiting of the infinite. Schleiermacher did not want to relegate religion or, what was to him synonymous, the Christian faith to pious feelings nor to rationalistic ethics. As his later elaboration in his masterpiece, *The Christian Faith*, shows, religion is a mode of personal existence, a style of life, within which true self-consciousness of absolute dependence evolves. This self-consciousness is informed by the feeling of being acted upon and by the reciprocal feeling of this action experienced in oneself. The Christian religious self-consciousness emerges from the redemption accomplished by Jesus of Nazareth. In him the feeling of absolute dependence on God was undiminished and therefore it informs and inspires our own feeling of dependence. Schleiermacher's theology is fundamentally Christocentric. But he does not want to destroy its secular enemy through superior arguments because that would only lead to (rational) counterarguments. He shows instead that religion has its own legitimate sphere from which it deeply informs our life attitude.

The concern of Schleiermacher was forcefully picked up by neo-Reformation theology under the leadership of *Karl Barth* (1886–1968). Though Barth sought to overcome Schleiermacher's missing emphasis on God's self-disclosure, he yet remained in many ways dependent on Schleiermacher. Indeed, the arrangement of Barth's *Church Dogmatics* in its division into five parts—Word of God, God, creation, atonement, and redemption—is opposed to Schleiermacher's design in *The Christian Faith* where he started with the religious self-consciousness. Yet Barth too endeavors to show that the Christian faith has its own sphere of existence. For him God is the totally other whom we cannot reach on our own. God's self-disclosure is diametrically opposed to our own idea of God. There is no continuity between the Christian faith and other religions. Religion, we hear, "is a concern . . . of godless man."[8] Even the notion of evolution has nothing whatsoever to do with the Christian faith in God the creator. Important for Barth is the idea of the paradox, the infinite qualitative difference between God and humanity, the total otherness of God, and the impossibility of objectifying God. Revelation is not a category of history but totally of its own kind. For Barth theology is primarily rethinking what has been told to us by God. Theology has to begin and end with God. Small wonder that some have claimed that this theology is only for pious people since it does not even attempt to engage in dialog with the world. Yet this theology grew out of the confrontation with cultural Protestantism and the liberal theology of the late 19th century. It led back to theology's own subject matter and portrayed theology as a science in its own peculiar right.

Paul Tillich (1886–1965), to mention the other pole of contemporary theological reflection, is also indebted to Schleiermacher when he declares: "*The object of theology is what concerns us ultimately. Only those propositions are theological which deal with their object insofar as it can become a matter of ultimate concern for us.*"[9] A human being is ultimately concerned about something and the task of theology is to direct it in such a way that it is concerned about that which is truly ultimate. While Tillich is convinced that theology has its own ground to stand on, he goes beyond Schleiermacher to establish a dialog with all other disciplines. This is the more necessary, since the (secular) analysis of the human situation unearths the existential questions to which faith provides the answer. This method of correlation between the incarnate *logos*, Jesus of Nazareth, and the universal *logos* who is active in the world, picks up on the notion of the *logos spermatikos*, first advanced by the early Christian apologists. In his three-volume *Systematic Theology* Tillich develops a systematic approach to the whole of Christian theology which reminds us very much of the great *summae* of medieval thought, such as of Thomas Aquinas. Tillich's Christian concern shines through on every page and he abhors the idea of eliminating any of the intrinsic Christian tenets. Nevertheless, one gets the impression that the Christian doctrines are more illustrations of his theme, i.e., humanity's existential alienation and its reconciliation with the ultimate, than the actual backbone.

A similar tendency is apparent in the widely popular school of process theology. Its main representatives, such as Norman Pittenger and John B. Cobb, are deeply informed by the Christian faith. In their attempt to secure an intellectually credible and intelligible frame of reference for their theological assertions, they have borrowed their conceptual tools to varying degrees from the philosophies of Alfred North Whitehead and Charles Hartshorne. Especially Whitehead's *Process and Reality* is by some ardent adherents more frequently quoted and more carefully exegeted than Scripture. The main concern of process theology is to provide for contemporary humanity a coherent, intelligible, and unified matrix of human history and existence. The Christian dogma, however, while continuously in the background, has widely lost its normative power and is selectively employed as an illustration for specific items within this matrix.

Another school of thought must be mentioned in which contemporary concerns seem to provide both matrix and authority, the widespread movement of liberation theology. It operates out of a particular geography, such as Asia or Latin America, taking into consideration the abject poverty of the Christian masses and moving toward a praxis-oriented theology. In contrast to the Social Gospel movement at the beginning of this century, it does not herald a democratic liberal Jesus, but nourishes a sometimes uncritical biblical conviction that God in Christ has shown solidarity with the downtrodden and has announced liberation from all kinds of bondage: social, racial, and ideological. Though the Bible provides the major themes for liberation theology, the context often leads to a certain one-sidedness of selection and a repetition of the same issues.

By comparison, Jürgen Moltmann and Wolfhart Pannenberg are approaching the task of theology from quite a different, more European angle. While the former shows Barthian influence by pressing for social involvement, the latter is more interested in defending the Christian faith in the forum of the world. Both develop their theology in an eschatological context from the perspective of the resurrection of Jesus Christ. They have established their systematic starting point by listening to the insights of other areas of theology, most notably those of exegetical studies and the history of culture and dogma. Without losing sight of history and society, they are mindful of Luther's insistence on the primacy of Scripture.

From a biblically informed basis Moltmann and Pannenberg explain the Christian faith, point to the need for that faith in today's heartless and cold world, and dialog with philosophers, scientists, and social theorists. This shows that for the Christian faith to be incisive it can neither afford to pontificate nor to be timid about its tenets. It must proclaim its message to the world while intently listening to the world for its own concerns, arguments, and fears.

B. Three essential functions of theology

We have seen how theology has changed through the centuries. It has reflected the times in which it was thought, spoken, and written and it has reflected its authors from the theoretically minded Anselm of Canterbury to the existentially driven Martin Luther. Yet amid all the necessary changes and diversity, there has been a constancy in its task. In order to maintain a credible and living faith, theology must fulfill and has fulfilled three functions. It must be critical, apologetic, and doxological.

1. *The critical concern for truth*

The critical function of theology is quite often misunderstood. Theology does not criticize and dissect the faith for the sake of being critical. In order to exist truly historically, however, we must be critically aware of our own history. Critical self-reflection is essential to human existence and distinguishes us from animals that live primarily by instinct. It became evident at the Second Vatican Council how important it is for the church to be critical of its own past. There the Roman Catholic church did not discard its past but, as some would do at an annual housecleaning, it critically discussed what could still be maintained in the second half of the 20th century and what had to be said differently. It did not come up with new truth but with the same old truth of God's salvation. However, this truth was said anew and in a vocabulary and conceptual framework that can be understood today.

The critical inquiry into the past will also mean that we consider whether some accents must not be put in different places today than where they were set 100 years ago. If this critical dimension is missing, the church will be in danger of becoming anachronistic, an archaic remnant in a changed world, rather than a beacon beckoning to new shores. Being oblivious to history and the need for critical change is a presumptuous position. It disregards Paul's admonition that "Now we see in a mirror dimly, but then face to face. Now I know in part; then I shall understand fully" (1 Cor. 13:12). We are not yet in heaven enjoying the beatific vision of God. We are on earth, groping and approximating the truth that has been shown to us. Since we are not yet sinless beings, but always prone to fall back to our old ways, we must continuously check ourselves whether we have deviated from the divine path and then assess how we can best pursue it.

The critical dimension of theology should not only be directed inward to assess our own history and the adequacy of our own approach. The inward criticism should also be turned outward, by comparing our own approach with that of other like-minded people. We could discover that there are others on the road with us who strive adequately to interpret God's word for the day. It was one of the big discoveries of the Roman Catholic church at Vatican II when it realized that other Christians also share a deep concern for God's truth and the gospel. When it critically opened its eyes to view the separated brothers and sisters, this church gained many new insights. For instance, it realized anew the importance of reading and studying the Bible and of upgrading the role and function of the laity. Perceiving the value of our common heritage, it felt free to include hymns like "A Mighty Fortress" in its own hymnal.

Especially if we open ourselves to the ecumenical dialog, we need a critical and discerning eye. Ecumenism does not mean surrendering our heritage and position to whomever we engage in dialog. On the contrary, it requires that we develop a discerning faculty and distinguish between those elements in our own tradition which are contrary to the gospel and which prevent its spread from those elements which are worthy of preservation and, perhaps, expansion. The same discriminating approach must also be developed in relation to the partner with whom we dialog.

2. An enlightened apology for the Christian faith

Next to the critical function comes the apologetic function. This term also is prone to misunderstanding. It does not mean that we should apologize for still being around, but it picks up its task from the admonition in 1 Peter 3:15: "Always be prepared to make a defense to anyone who calls you to account for the hope that is in you, yet do it with gentleness and reverence." Apologetic does not mean to throw mud on one other, to badger, or to malign others, but to make clear to anyone who wants to know why we believe what we do. It is a very important task to make our faith intelligible and credible to others, since often others reject faith in Christ out of ignorance or misconceptions. In our apologetic task, we are relating God's self-disclosure to the world. We attempt to explore possible reasons for rejecting it and examine which conceptuality is best fitted for conveying the Christian message. Such a task can never be accomplished once and for all. We have splendid examples for this in the Bible. For instance, next to the Priestly creation account in Genesis 1 there is the Yahwistic account in Genesis 2. Evidently, the account in Genesis 2 no longer sufficed to convey the faith in God the creator and so a new attempt was made to proclaim the same old faith. We should, however, note that Genesis 2 was not thrown out. It still conveyed the message for some. But now another attempt had to be made to recognize the new situation that had emerged.

We still can hear in Genesis 1 the apologetic endeavor to declare to the devout Israelites that there is only one God who created everything that is. The sun, moon, and sidereal gods do not amount to anything. Even if others worship them, they are just dead elements which God has created. The threatening waters of the depth, too, which could so easily devastate coastal areas do not amount to much. God simply trod upon them and he told the waters to part and show forth dry land. We are also told that God is so powerful that he did not have to wrestle with any other powers as the gods did in ancient creation myths. It sufficed that he spoke and thus things happened. In Genesis 2, the situation had been quite different. There the Israelite faith in God the creator did not yet need to be defended against the Babylonian creation myths. The situation was that of the semiarid land and we are told that it is God who causes the rain to fall and who makes everything thrive and blossom. We are also told about our human affinity to the soil. Since we have tanned skin, the reddish soil provides a simile and shows us whence we came and whither we return. It is up to us to take charge of nature, to till the soil and to dominate the animals by naming them. The Yahwistic account speaks to the seminomadic Israelites and explains that everything they enjoy is really God's creation. But drudgery and hard work are the result of their own sinfulness and cannot be blamed on God.

The apologetic function of theology would overstep its possibilities if it wanted to *prove* that God indeed did create the world or created it in one particular way. Apologetics already presupposes a faith commitment, i.e., that God created the world, and wants to explain what that means. Anselm of Canterbury, one of the greatest apologists of all times, expressed this very well when he said: "I do desire to understand your truth a little, that truth that my heart believes and loves. For I do not seek to understand so that I may believe: but I believe so that I may understand."[10] Faith seeking understanding and expression in dialog with others is the deepest reason for apologetics. If we want to reach out to others, we must create an openness for faith in them through dialog and invite them to faith. In so doing we always take seriously where the other person stands so that we can truly be a Jew to the Jews and a Greek to the Greeks. This attention to the situation of the audience is especially prominent in the different New Testament Gospels. Each of the four Gospels has a particular audience in mind and a specific way in which to convey the message. Thus each evangelist transmits the same message, but from a different angle and to different people.

3. Theology as a means to glorify God

Finally, we must mention the doxological task of theology. Like all human enterprise, theology is done to glorify God. We must always be mindful in our theological endeavors that God is not dependent on our performance. He does not need apologists or people who critically assess the past to bring it into line with the promised future. God does not need anybody and he could do everything himself. But out of his free will he takes us into his service to proclaim to others his grandeur and to explain to them our faith in him. We are allowed and even asked to assist God by expressing his self-disclosure in the best possible way. Doxology means joining him as partners and spreading his word. It also means that we use in the best possible way our mental gifts with which he endowed us to glorify him. Theology is adoration of God in word and thought. We do theology not for its own sake or the sake of our self-glorification, but only for God's sake and the gospel's. We owe it to God that we use in his service the gifts he has given us. But even there we must acknowledge that all our endeavors are only preliminary. We do not yet have a full grasp of the truth, but are on the way together with other fellow travelers.

If the task of theology is so intimately concerned with the message which the church proclaims and the faith which it holds, theology cannot be an auxiliary enterprise which the church might either cherish or relegate to secondary status. Theology pervades all the church's life and action, be it liturgy, counseling, or social action. The reason why we do something is not always spelled out or even reflected upon. Sometimes the driving motive is tradition (we have always done it this way), sometimes emotion (I just feel like it), and at other times convenience (it seems the easiest thing to do). Yet in each case our decision has profound theological implications, whether we are cognizant of it or not. This means that the church and each individual Christian always act theologically. They are either in line with God's will or stand against it.

Theological reflection does not bring theology to the church and its activities, but it makes us aware of the theology behind them. Theology is the explicit attempt to raise into consciousness what we are doing. For instance, one can be an excellent Pelagian without ever knowing what a Pelagian is. But once we know what a Pelagian is and what is wrong with this line of thought, we at least are able to discern how close we come to advocating this ancient and still so modern heresy. If we are open to theological reflection, it will not always mean that our actions will be automatically better—the old Adam is still part of us—but at least our actions will be better informed. If we make mistakes and sin, at least we are able to discern them and can ask for forgiveness and amend our ways. Here is the big difference between secular people and true theologians. Secular people are mostly unaware of their own sinful lives and God's offer of forgiveness. Christians (theologians), however, know who they truly are (sinners) and, therefore, ask God for help. Theological reflection brings into consciousness what we do and how we do it. To those who are aware, it permeates all facets of the church's life and of our own. It makes the difference between being a habitual or a conscious Christian. Yet theology remains a lifeless structure without revelation as its content and norm. Is the notion of revelation, however, still tenable in today's rationally minded world?

2

REVELATION

In today's factual world the term *revelation* sounds dubious. Though this word carries with it the notion of surprise, it is elusive once we ask about its otherworldly content. Revelation claims to tell us in this-worldly language something about that which is not of this world. This connection between the this-worldly and the otherworldly is the crucial point and at the same time the problem in talking about revelation. Three major questions must be addressed regarding revelation: (1) How can we speak today of revelation without resorting to a language which has no reference point in the space-time continuum in which we live? (2) Does revelation add anything to our knowledge which could not be attained otherwise? (3) On what basis can we assert that there should be preference given to the revelation in Jesus Christ?

A. Signals of transcendence

In the strict sense revelation is never disclosure by someone about something (propositional revelation). Even when I say, "This was a revelation to me," we actually mean that something disclosed itself to me, i.e., it showed itself to me for what it really is (existential revelation). Revelation then is self-mediation or self-disclosure of something or someone. The use of the word *revelation* for the sharing of a secret or the sharing about a future plan does not deserve the designation of revelation unless it is at the same time a disclosure of oneself. When we talk about divine revelation, we do not talk about self-disclosure or self-mediation of just anything or anyone, but divine self-disclosure and the self-mediation of God. Yet God is by very definition that which is not confined to our space-time continuum. God is not a phenomenon of space, time, and matter, and hence is withdrawn from our sense experience. How is it then possible that we get hold of something that does not pertain to our realm?

In analogy to the general and special knowledge of God, classical theology distinguished between a general and special revelation. Martin Luther, for instance, conceded that there is a knowledge of God outside the biblical revelation. This was attested to him through non-Christian religions and through pagan philosophers such as Cicero. The worship of gods in other religions presupposes a notion of God and a recognition of God's attributes. Even atheists, who deny God, have the voice of their own conscience which attests to God in spite of their own intentions. This general revelation does not just comprise the notion that God is omnipotent and omniscient, but is the giver of all good things, is gracious and benevolent, and will help people in their need if they call on him. For Luther, this general notion of God is attested by Paul, who says about the human species, "What can be known about God is plain to them . . . . Ever since the creation of the world his invisible nature, namely, his eternal power and deity, has been clearly perceived in the things that have been made" (Rom. 1:19f.). But Luther sees two limitations of this general revelation: (1) Although through reason one can know everything about God, there is no certainty involved about what is known. Reason can speak of revelation only in terms of probabilities. (2) Reason knows that God *is*, but it lacks the capacity to know *who* God is. We are always confronted with a multitude of claims for ultimacy and it is empirically impossible to decide in favor of one or another.

The Lutheran systematician Paul Althaus (1888–1966) followed Martin Luther in claiming a primal revelation (*Uroffenbarung*). According to Althaus God disclosed himself outside of and prior to Christ in his true being. Though it was not a full disclosure, it did leave one with a certain experience of God. This self-attestation of

God can be found in human existence and destiny, in history, in nature, and in the human knowledge of truth. Althaus does not deny the tragic sides of human existence, history, and nature. But he is convinced that there is a certain order which we can experience in their arrangement and structure. Althaus goes one step further than Luther by distinguishing primal revelation from natural theology. Natural theology is based on the human capability of knowing God on one's own. Primal revelation, on the other hand, is the general experience of God from which no one completely escapes. This primal revelation is important for Althaus, since it provides the point of contact at which the transition can be made to the revelation in Jesus Christ. It also allows for a positive evaluation of other religions. They are phenomena expressive of God's presence.

Karl Barth in particular reacted very strongly against the assumption of a primal revelation. He claimed that apart from Jesus Christ we know absolutely nothing of God. While in his revelation in Jesus Christ God manifests himself to us and wants to reconcile us to himself, religion is *our* attempt to come to terms with life and to justify ourselves. In short, religion is the business of godless humanity. Barth thus collapsed primal revelation and natural theology into one and rejected both. This move is understandable when we consider that Barth reacted against a liberal theology which had molded itself into a kind of cultural Protestantism which welded together culture and religion, a religion for which the enlightened reason of the late 19th century was the sole criterion.

Long before these 20th-century debates, Gotthold Ephraim Lessing (1729–1781) had claimed in *The Education of the Human Race* (1780) that revelation does not give a person anything one might not have derived from "within oneself." Instead one merely obtains it more quickly and more easily. Revelation, in other words, does not add anything to our knowledge or insight which in principle we could not have known otherwise. When we listen to the tone of other publications of that period, mainly from the British Isles, such as of John Toland, *Christianity Not Mysterious* (1696) or Matthew Tindal, *Christianity as Old as Creation or the Gospel, a Republication of the Religion of Nature* (1730), we notice that a significant change had occurred long before liberal theology emerged at the end of the Enlightenment period. General revelation had become the norm for special revelation and was understood to occur only within the boundaries of natural theology. Yet a natural theology, if it really means an attempt to speak about God on the basis of our own possibilities, is actually a contradiction in itself. If such speech is an extension of oneself then it cannot reach God; or if it is not just an extension of oneself, then it must be facilitated by something or someone beyond one's own self. Looming behind a natural theology which is not just an extension of ourselves and even behind a general revelation is the so-called *praeparatio evangelica*, i.e., the preparation of the gospel. In order to understand God's word of grace, it is necessary to have some prior understanding of that term.

Karl Barth emphatically claimed that it is impossible to have an understanding of God's word prior to God disclosing himself to us. Not even God's law was considered as a teacher preparing the way for Christ, since, as Barth insisted, nobody understands the law and the gravity of our deviation from it without first experiencing how gracious God is to us. Most other theologians, however, pursued the notion that since the world is God's creation, he makes his presence felt in it. This presence is actually perceived by us no matter how feeble that perception may be. God provides his own point of contact, not in his special revelation, but through his preserving and sustaining activity. Whether we think of humanity's infinite openness to the world (Pannenberg), its insatiable thirst for knowledge (Lonergan), its personhood (Emil Brunner), or its paradoxical character of existence (Gilkey), all these "signals of transcendence" (Peter L. Berger) serve as an indication of God's presence in the world. Special revelation then creates a deepened awareness of who God really is—the one who created the world and preserves it.

B. Disclosure of a higher dimension

It is interesting that when religious traditions talk about revelation they do not want to leave the impression that revelation is only the discovery of something which I already knew, or something which was hidden within me. They talk about a new and surprising experience beyond our own possibilities. Strictly speaking they never admit the possibility of a natural knowledge of God but they relate a making known to us of that which is not at our disposal (e.g., God). This making known or disclosing does not take place in a transcendental realm but rather in our world, in our space-time continuum. For instance, when the Old Testament talks about Yahweh's epiphanies, it mentions his appearance in material objects, in a burning bush, a pillar of cloud, in fire, or in the tent of meeting. Revelation is the appearing of that which is not of space and time within the space-time continuum. God's self-disclosure occurs always in our world.

The assertion of such self-disclosure immediately calls for rational scrutiny. How can something that is neither caused nor conditioned by us, or by the world accessible to us, disclose itself in our world? Ludwig Feuerbach rightly cautioned that such self-disclosure might only be the result of wishful thinking or of a pious projection of our desires. Have not many discerning people admonished us that humanity must learn to assume adulthood and walk without metaphysical crutches? Indeed, whenever we talk about revelation, the possibility of a projection or of a piously disguised self-deception looms on the horizon. Moreover, the history of religion is tarnished with fraud and self-deception. The claim of a revelation must always be carefully analyzed. This caveat pertains as much to the content of revelation as to its very occurrence.

If revelation means disclosure of something or someone not contained in space and time, it would traditionally mean that revelation is a divine action and not a human possibility. God who is not of this sphere of life discloses himself in our space-time continuum. Such an event could become comprehensible if we see it in analogy to something (or someone) occupying a higher dimension disclosing itself in a lower dimension. This means that our space-time continuum presents one dimension and the realm of God another and higher one. A higher dimension (e.g., a cube) possesses all the possibilities of a lower dimension (e.g., a plane) as well as the additional ones of the higher dimension. God could then present himself in the lower dimension as a part of that dimension as well as disclosing for us new and unprecedented possibilities that otherwise are not present in the lower dimension (e.g., a bush which does not burn, or a human being walking on water). While we must concede the new character of such phenomena, we are by the limitations of our nature unable to perceive these phenomena as being caused by another dimension. We can only think in and perceive our own dimension. Thus we attempt to explain these phenomena on the basis of our available experience. This means that the transition from the other dimension to ours—and even its very existence—can never be ascertained with absolute empirical certainty. Once the transition to our dimension has been made, the self-disclosing subject becomes an object within our own dimension and is subject to treatment as an object within our dimension. This does not mean, however, that revelation is relegated to the realm of fantasy.

In his antinomies (contradictions) of pure reason Immanuel Kant (1724–1804) convincingly demonstrated that a two-dimensional view of the world is a logical possibility. He showed that one can logically assert both that the world has a beginning in space and time and that it does not have one, that there is a smallest unit which can no longer be divided and that there is no such unit, that there is a necessary cause for the world's existence and that there is none. With these antinomies between two statements, he showed the limits of human reason and indicated that since human reason is the measure of all things, it cannot extend itself beyond the boundaries of *things*. This means there is a fundamental twofoldness built into the way we are able to perceive one world. We cannot look at the world from the outside and verify that it is really the way it appears to be. Most scientists have long ago recognized this and no longer pose the question regarding what the objects of their investigation, e.g., particles, waves, life, etc., really are, but rather how they function. While the "nature" of things is withdrawn from our investigation, there is still a contact maintained between the object matter and the investigator. Even scientists cannot existentially divorce themselves from the object matter they investigate. There always occurs an interaction between the scientists and their object matter which prevents a strictly neutral investigation.

By analogy, as soon as God discloses himself to us, we must become cognizant of the relation between this "objective past" and the attempt to coordinate this disclosive phenomenon with other phenomena within our dimension of space, time, and causal nexus. Once we have integrated the phenomenon into one world of experience, we must remind ourselves that our one-dimensional interpretation need not be exclusive. It may very well be that a higher dimension may also be involved in this occurrence. Thus a God-disclosive phenomenon, e.g., Jesus walking on water (providing that it did actually occur) asks us whether we want to consider it as more than a parapsychologically explainable phenomenon such as levitation or whether God wants to tell us something with this episode about the nature of the new world to come. Scripture has shown in many places that the occurrence of revelation demands and results in our existential response of indifference, acceptance, or rejection. For instance, when Jesus, as God's self-disclosure, began his mission, he confronted his audience with the words, "The time is fulfilled, and the kingdom of God is at hand; repent and believe in the gospel" (Mark 1:15). But we do not eliminate reason, once we begin to trust that this is indeed God's self-disclosure. For instance, Anselm of Canterbury explicitly employed reason in order to understand what he believed. Once the initial decision of accepting or rejecting a higher dimension is made, one must delineate the reasonable implications of such a decision lest one ends up in credulity. Yet it would be wrong to assume that the decision of accepting or rejecting the actuality of revelation (though not its possibility) is already based on a strictly rational argument. Reason can investigate the phenomenon of revelation as such but it cannot verify the claim that it is indeed revelation.

C. Exclusiveness of the self-disclosure in Jesus Christ

The issue becomes even more complicated when we consider the validity of the New Testament claim that God's revelation in Jesus Christ is of an exclusive character. For instance, according to John, Jesus says to his disciples: "I am the way, and the truth, and the life; no one comes to the Father, but by me" (John 14:6). In other words, Jesus provides the only access to God. This does not mean that we can approach God through the historical Jesus of Nazareth. It means that God disclosed himself to us in Jesus and thus this historical figure provides the avenue to God.

The encounter with Jesus becomes normative for our knowledge of God or for our "being in truth," as John prefers to say (John 3:18). Similarly, Peter emphasizes, "And there is salvation in no one else, for there is no other name under heaven given among men by which we must be saved" (Acts 4:12). The name of Jesus provides salvation and brings us again in tune with God. But given the Jewish background of this assertion the name alluded to by Peter must have been at one time the name of Yahweh. That Jesus and Yahweh have become interchangeable again attests to Yahweh's self-disclosure in Jesus. Since the New Testament writers are convinced that Yahweh identified himself with Jesus of Nazareth, who reciprocally identified himself with God, they concluded that this self-disclosure of God had insurpassable character. In Jesus occurs an actual self-mediation of God in the best communicable form for us, i.e., in another human being. Such self-disclosure is insurpassable, since one cannot communicate to humans better than through a human being.

But the question is whether such self-mediation is exclusive. It might be that in the course of history God has identified himself totally with other human beings too. Thus the existence of other redeemers might be a distinct possibility. If we reflect upon the rest of the universe beyond our globe God might even have made other covenants with other sentient beings similar to the covenant which the Christian community has experienced. But the fears which such assumptions raise are unwarranted. Through the very structure of God's self-disclosure in Jesus Christ such conclusions, if proven valid, could not invalidate the exclusiveness of this self-disclosure. The opening sentence of the Letter to the Hebrews, for instance, reads: "In many and various ways God spoke of old to our fathers by the prophets; but in these last days he has spoken to us by a Son, whom he appointed the heir of all things, through whom he also created the world" (Heb. 1:1f.). The writer explicitly mentions that in various ways God disclosed himself in Old Testament times, through such means as dreams, visions, and auditions, through angels and through animals. Yet now things are different, we hear, since God has spoken in an eschatological time. Jesus is now the decisive factor because he speaks as an eschatological figure in an eschatological time and preaches an eschatological message.

In the apocalyptic time of the early first century A.D. there were many with whom eschatological expectations were connected, such as John the Baptist, Judas the Galilean, and, above all, Bar Kochba. Only in the life and destiny of Jesus, however, can we recognize that the long-awaited eschaton has already begun. For example, Jesus claimed that through him "the blind receive their sight, the lame walk, lepers are cleansed, and the deaf hear, the dead are raised up, the poor have good news preached to them" (Luke 7:22). Every alert Jew knew that with this reference Jesus applied to himself the Old Testament images that were associated with the time of salvation (Isa. 35:5f.). Jesus introduced himself as the one in whose actions salvation became manifest. The same is true for his proclamation. When he mentioned that new wine should not be poured into old wine skins (Matt. 9:17), he wanted to emphasize that the old time is past and the time of salvation has been initiated. Once Jesus stated it even more clearly: "But if it is by the finger of God that I cast out demons, then the kingdom of God has come upon you" (Luke 11:20).

With Jesus the kingdom of God has already begun. What had been expected for centuries and so often projected into the future or into the present has now started. The kingdom of God is in the midst of you, said Jesus. He did not call for an immediate decision because he was such an important preacher or because he had such an important message. The kingdom of God had been realized with his very appearance and thus it was fulfilled time, decisive time. The coming of Jesus is the turning point of history. Moreover, the emerging Christian community did not simply preserve Jesus' message and the record of his actions. Instead, under the impression of the Easter event the proclaimer suddenly became the proclaimed and therewith the focal point of the Christian gospel. This radical change becomes understandable in the context of the apocalyptic expectations that were shared by Jesus, his disciples, and part of the Jewish community. According to these expectations the resurrection of the dead is an important part of the final eschatological drama. Sharing these hopes and expectations the disciples could now recognize that Jesus actually was who he said he was, the initiator of the eschaton which God had brought about through Christ's resurrection as a proleptic sign.

But Christ's resurrection was not understood as a mere confirmation of prevalent apocalyptic ideas. When Paul, for instance, refers to Christ's resurrection he does not simply refer to him as the validation of the apocalyptic hope for a resurrection. He understands Christ's resurrection as the presupposition of our own resurrection. Through the resurrection of Jesus Christ the apocalyptic *idea* of a common resurrection is modified to the Christian *hope* in the resurrection, because of Christ and because of his resurrection. Christ is not only the turning point or focal point of history, he is also the goal of history, a goal which he proleptically anticipated in his own resurrection. Each Christian can and will participate in this anticipation because, as Paul said, "If any one is in Christ, he is a new creation; the old has passed away, behold, the new has come" (2 Cor. 5:17). This does not mean that Christians are no longer subject to the conditions and limitations of this phenomenal world. Insofar as they identify themselves with Christ, however, their ultimate destiny is not identical with that of this world but with that of Christ.

Thus the idea of an ongoing revelation apart from Jesus Christ and his destiny, or even beyond it, would contradict his anticipatory character. A revelation of the God who provided this world with its foundation, its present course, and its ultimate destiny cannot be thought of apart from Jesus Christ. Of course, the question must be posed here whether the emphasis on the exclusiveness of God's self-disclosure would contradict the God-disclosive status of non-Christian religions.

We have observed that the revelatory history of God starting with the people of Israel and culminating in the life and destiny of Jesus the Christ is basically a history of God's initiative or, in other words, the history of a great invitation. The religious history apart from this invitation is neither just an expression of human sinfulness nor a history simply leading up to Christ. It is the history of humanity being moved from its existential separation from its creator to a glimpse of the one who has created and does sustain it. While some religious manifestations express the misconception that finite humanity can heal its existential separation from God on its own, this view conveys the notion that only God can reconcile the world with himself.

The emphasis on the exclusiveness of God's self-disclosure in Jesus Christ might imply in the minds of some a rejection of non-Christian religions. This should not be the case. Although the Christian proclamation is a decisional proclamation and, as far as we know, the response of those encountered by it will have eternal significance, with regard to non-Christian religions our conclusions must be of a more differentiated nature. Since God disclosed himself in Jesus Christ in an insurpassable way, God has been experienced in an insurpassable way as a God of holiness and compassion. From this experience we confidently hope that those who were never able fully to experience God's complete self-disclosure in Jesus Christ will not be eternally separated from him. The God-disclosive history of the Judeo-Christian tradition then becomes a source of hope for all people and a source of clarity in understanding God. If we want to ask why God's self-disclosure in Jesus Christ is exclusive and insurpassable, we cannot ultimately cite any convincing empirical reason. We can only refer to God's primacy in the revelatory process and acknowledge that "it pleased God" to disclose himself in that way.

D. The limits of (rational) perception

Again we have been confronted with a structural boundary in adducing proofs for the finality of God's self-disclosure. We remember that we also had to acknowledge a boundary when we attempted to prove the veracity of revelation. We will see this limitation especially clearly when we review the so-called Christological controversies in which the emerging church attempted to ascertain how God was present in the human being Jesus of Nazareth. After several generations of intensive spiritual and political struggle it became evident that the issue could not be easily settled. The church understood Christ to be both identical with God and still a fully human being, i.e. truly God and truly man. At the Ecumencial Council of Chalcedon (A.D. 451) the church recognized the limits of human reason and arrived at a decision in which the divine-human being of Jesus Christ was defined in a delimitating way. The council fathers plainly stated that Jesus is truly God and truly a human being. They restrained from defining descriptively how both natures are related to each other in Jesus Christ while at the same time insisting on their actual presence and inextricable togetherness. Thus they preserved the concept of the unity of the person of Jesus Christ and also the humanity of Jesus.

The church refused to distort God's ultimate self-disclosure by making it into a timeless philosophical truth. It stated that Jesus as Jesus of Nazareth is a person like us living in space and time. At the same time it affirmed that Jesus as the Christ is not someone totally available or accessible in the space-time continuum. If both "natures" were accessible in our space-time continuum, there would be no reason why the church could not rationally define how God's self-disclosure in Jesus is related to another phenomenon of space and time, namely Jesus' human nature. But empirical research can never come up with an affirmation like "Jesus was God's self-disclosure." Even biblical exegesis can only unearth bits of historical information about a truly human being called Jesus of Nazareth. If empirical research arrived at assertions about Jesus' divine nature, it would leave its empirical ground and enter either the realm of faith or of speculation.

Naturally, such conclusions must affect our understanding of Jesus Christ as the God-disclosive event. We have seen before that the significance of Jesus can only be appropriately understood in the context of Israel's history of promise and expectation. In the contextual history of Israel it is not as an isolated event that the Christ event reveals the Godhead of Yahweh. But the history of Israel is not a special kind of history whose course, culminating in the Christ event, makes God's self-disclosure unmistakably evident. On the other hand, through historical events both Israel and the Christian community gained insight that transcends empirical verification. In other words, the history of Israel and the Christ event seem to have God-disclosive power. How can God then be disclosed in such events if, as the Chalcedonian confession recognized, he is neither an additional component of the historical process nor separable from it? The only solution is to consider this process as a paradox.

Though every cause and component of Judeo-Christian salvation history (*Heilsgeschichte*) can be explained within a strictly empirical reference system as being part of our space-time continuum, it must at the same time be understood as a totally God-wrought process, i.e., as being part of God's dimension. Observing the paradox, the Christian faith affirms that Jesus' proclamation, action, and destiny are not the result of a religious fanatic, but a disclosure of God's demand and promise. The paradox then asserts that through Jesus of Nazareth, a fully human being, God becomes transparent. Since we always perceive God's ultimate pronouncement and action through an anthropomorphic veil, we have no direct access to God's dimension but perceive it only in our dimension in its approximate, anthropomorphic form. Therefore this ultimate self-disclosure of God is still a disclosure in approximation, God becoming communicable in human form.

The necessary approximation through which God enters our own dimension results both in the paradox of Jesus being true God and a truly human being and, therefore, in the decision-demanding character of God's self-disclosure in Jesus Christ. Since the Judeo-Christian *Heilsgeschichte* confronts the listener with the claim that it is the God-disclosive history, he cannot escape from making a choice. But the choice to accept Jesus as God's ultimate self-disclosure does not simply result as the option between two possibilities. Since the Judeo-Christian history of salvation has the power to convince the skeptic as well as to withhold its other-dimensional character from the seeker, the believer affirms that God himself is involved in the decision-making process. Once we have recognized that in Jesus another dimension is present, the approximation character of the self-disclosure allows for increasingly deeper investigation into this disclosive process. The result will be an ever deeper understanding of God's self-disclosure contained in the human form of Jesus of Nazareth. This growth in the understanding of God's self-disclosure can best be attained through the study of Scripture, the written reflection upon this self-disclosure.

3

SCRIPTURE

Scripture, Bible, or Holy Writ is the body of writings which gained normative status within the Christian community and is the source from which this community nourishes its faith. While there are rather diverse styles of writings, such as poetry, letters, legal prescriptions, and narrative, they all are essentially reflections of and witnesses to God's self-disclosure in history.

A. The emergence of the New Testament Scriptures

Though commonly known, it is good to be reminded that in the New Testament the word *Scripture* means the Hebrew Scriptures. Besides the Hebrew Scriptures there were two other authorities for the New Testament community, the apostles as the eyewitnesses of Jesus (Gal. 1:8) and the Lord Jesus Christ (1 Cor. 7:10). He is their ultimate authority and endows both the Hebrew Scriptures and the apostles' teachings with authority (1 Cor. 7:10). All three witness to the Word of God. But Jesus Christ is not only the witness to the Word; he himself is the Word (John 1:1ff.). Jesus is not only the origin and originator of the New Testament but also its essential content. Thus the proclaimer, Jesus of Nazareth, became the proclaimed, Jesus Christ.

The important question, however, is to what extent the New Testament preserves the proclamation of Jesus of Nazareth. Those relying very heavily on form criticism contend that only some features of his proclamation and his death are historically verifiable. The Christian community was primarily interested to use the Jesus material as an illustration for their faith in the Lord. Other scholars, however, assert that the words and deeds of Jesus were carefully handed down as a holy word. In either case, there is no doubt that Jesus is the ultimate reference point both as the origin of the Christian Scriptures and as their central focus.

At the beginning of the development of the New Testament stood an oral tradition initially consisting only of small units, such as miracles and dialogs in the case of the later gospels, or individual letters as with regard to the Pauline corpus. While it is evident that the letters were read in communal gatherings, i.e., in worship services, there is uncertainty about the primary use of the Gospels. That they were only kerygma (missionary appeal) seems unlikely. It is much more probable that the words of Jesus and the accounts of his deeds and life were soon conceived of as the new Torah, God's Word of the new, eschatological covenant. Not incidentally do the terms *word* (*logos*) and *Word of God* (*logos theou*) correspond with the names current in Judaism for "Holy Scripture." How exactly the Holy Scripture of the Christian faith finally was formed is one of the most difficult questions of early church history. But we may not be wrong in assuming that the collection of the sayings of Jesus which scholars identify today as the source Q is the first trace of a process which resulted in the New Testament canon. It is probably too simple to assume that the New Testament canon, i.e., the limitation of the New Testament to 27 books, was merely the result of the church's stand against the heresies of the Gnostics, Marcionites, and Montanists. We should rather perceive the present canon as the end product of a long process.

The earliest Christianity had already an authoritative canon to which they referred quite often, the Jewish collection of the Law and the Prophets, i.e., the Old Testament. Jesus himself set a precedent when he acknowledged the validity of the Law and the Prophets (Matt. 5:17). But, at the same time, he authoritatively decided that it should be interpreted in the light of God's will (Matt. 5: 21f.). The Christian community followed the example set by Jesus. For instance, it was significant for Paul that "Christ died for our sins in accordance with the scriptures, that he was buried, that he was raised on the third day in accordance with the scriptures" (1 Cor. 15:3f.). Paul could explain the significance of Jesus' death and resurrection by referring to the authority of the Old Testament. Yet the Hebrew Scriptures did not have for him unrivaled authority. This becomes clear when he claims that the Christians, being endowed with the Spirit, can perceive the pointers toward Christ in the Old Testament while the Jews lack this insight.

Next to the Old Testament comes the authority of the Lord (1 Cor. 7:10). Following the example that Jesus had set, it was an authority higher than the Old Testament. There is also the authority of the apostles (1 Cor. 7:25) as the ones who have the Spirit, an authority to be set alongside the Old Testament. Yet Paul, for instance, gives no indication that he would consider his letters on a level equal with that of the Old Testament. For him they were only occasional writings. The decisive battle over the place, value, and interpretation of the Old Testament was fought when the Christians attempted to convince the Jews that the Christians alone had the correct interpretation of Scripture which for them meant a Christological interpretation (Acts 17:2f.). Jesus was the final self-disclosure of God (Heb. 1:1) and thus he was considered authoritative for the interpretation of the Hebrew Scriptures. In this way the Hebrew Scriptures then became the Old Testament over against the New Testament.

Initially the New Testament consisted mainly of the living tradition of the Lord and of writings of apostolic authors, such as Paul or Luke, who were also accepted as authorities. In the postapostolic time Clement still puts the words of the Lord next to the Old Testament Scriptures but not above them (1 Clem. 13:1f.). The apostles at that time, appear as the mediators of the commands of the Lord (2 Peter 3:2). In 2 Clem. 14:2 we read the phrase "that the books and the apostles teach." This means that at that time, approximately the middle of the second century, the apostolic writings, while on the same level as the Old Testament, were not yet accessible in book form. Once the oral tradition ceased with the death of the eyewitnesses, the necessity gradually emerged to entrust the living tradition to written memory and to codify it.

When 2 Clement refers to the sayings of the Lord as "another Scripture" (2 Clem. 2:4), it indicates that the words of Jesus are to be treated as the Old Testament Scripture. In 2 Peter 3:15-16, we read concerning Paul and his letters of "the wisdom given him" and also of "the other scriptures," without being told what these scriptures include. This, the last letter of the New Testament, was perhaps written around the same time as 2 Clement. Both letters seem to indicate that something like New Testament Scriptures were known to their writers at that time. This development of the New Testament Scriptures was certainly furthered through the collection of Pauline letters to which Paul himself refers (Col. 4:16). During the middle of the second century Papias compares the Gospels of Mark and Matthew, showing that he knows more than just one Gospel. Yet he still prefers the old tradition claiming "what was to be gotten from the books would not profit me as much as what came from the living and abiding voice."[1] About the same time Tatian synoptically merged the four then extant Gospels into one in his *Diatessaron*. Justin Martyr tells us in his *First Apology* that during the Sunday worship "the memoirs of the apostles or the writings of the prophets are read," thereby indicating that the Gospels (memoirs of the apostles) have the same rank as the Old Testament writings.[2]

B. The formation of the Christian Bible

Around the year A.D. 144 Marcion founded his own church, starting from metropolitan Rome. He introduced his own version of the canon consisting of a shortened and amended Gospel according to Luke and 10 likewise revised letters of Paul. It is difficult to determine whether Marcion employed an already-existing canon which he modified or whether he created his own canon without relying on a prior source. Yet we are sure that there were already collections of New Testament writings at his time and that his attempt to present his own canon facilitated and speeded up the formation of the church's own canon.

By the end of the second century we encounter almost the same collection of New Testament writings which we have today. But not all the congregations and regions arrived at exactly the same understanding regarding which writings were to be considered canonical. For instance, some congregations accepted Paul's Letter to Laodicea, a letter which originated under Marcionite influence, and, around A.D. 170, opponents of Montanism rejected as Gnostic the

Gospel according to John and the Book of Revelation. The Acts of the Apostles was not mentioned anywhere before the close of the second century. At the end of the second century the Muratorian Canon presents us for the first time with a clearly defined canon. But this fragment does not mention 3 John, James, and 1 and 2 Peter, and it includes the Apocalypse of Peter (though mentioning that some do not want to read it in church). This shows that the canon was not produced by an authoritative decree. It gradually developed through the congregational use of certain Christian writings. In this process the presumed or actual apostolic authorship of these documents undoubtedly facilitated their reception.

The New Testament canon precisely as we have it is first listed in A.D. 367 by Athanasius in his 39th Easter Letter. The only variation from today is that Hebrews is counted as a letter of Paul. Augustine acccepted the canon of Athanasius, and in 405 Pope Innocent also mentioned a canon consisting of 27 books. Most of the Orthodox churches followed this precedent. Even into the fifth century, however, the Syriac church used as canonical the *Diatessaron* of Tatian; it also took that church longer to accept the more peripheral writings of the New Testament.

Once the validity of a common canon was accepted, the theological problem of the canon emerged. The very term *New Testament* denoting a collection of explicitly Christian books is clearly a theological assertion. It confesses that next to an Old Testament there is a new. As the New Testament insists, it means that God had made a new covenant which replaced the old one (2 Cor. 3:6). This new covenant was established through the blood of Christ (Mark 14:24). Since the Christian church did not reject the Hebrew Scriptures but used them as its Old Testament, it affirmed the covenant with Israel as its predecessor covenant. Thereby it saw itself as the new Israel and the new covenant community standing in continuity with the old covenant.

This feeling of continuity shows itself clearly in the hermeneutical principles with which the Hebrew Scriptures were read and used. The Christians claimed that these Scriptures witness to Christ (John 5:39; Acts 10:43). In contrast to the Jews, the Christians did not read the Hebrew Scriptures as a community waiting and hoping for the Messiah but as people who knew that they were pointing to Jesus as God's Messiah. This also helps to explain why some of the allusions to Christ's redemptive work which they found in the Hebrew Scriptures we can hardly recognize as such today (cf. Gal. 4:22-31). If we are to show the continuity between the old Israel and the new Israel we cannot abandon the term *Old Testament* and call this body of literature "Hebrew Scriptures." Such a move would leave unexplainable why the explicitly Christian part of the Bible is called "New Testament." To continue in this line of reasoning and rename the New Testament "Christian Scriptures" would concede the possibility of several covenants which stand alongside each other as equals instead of in succession. This succession, however, allows for the progression of salvation history and intensifies the hope for final redemption. By claiming the Hebrew Scriptures for its own use as the Christian Old Testament, the Christian church escaped the danger of becoming an alternative to the Jewish faith or a rival organization. Following the proclamation of Jesus and recognizing him as the Messiah, the Christian church dared to take over the promises to the Israel of old and perceive itself standing in continuity with Israel and its promissory history. The repeated attempts to rid the Christian church of its Old Testament (cf. Marcion in the second century and Adolf von Harnack in the 19th century) were doomed to failure. They would have robbed the Christian faith of its roots and its dynamic structure.

C. The development and function of the canon

The next theological issue, though a more contemporary one, is that of relating Scripture and tradition. Tradition was constitutive for the first Christian community and initially was largely identical with the kerygma or the gospel of Jesus Christ. Modern exegesis has shown more and more convincingly that there are not two authoritative sources of revelation, Scripture and tradition, but that both are inextricably intertwined. It is now commonly recognized that the earliest tradition precedes the first written documents. We have seen that, far into the second century A.D., the living tradition was preferred to the written "memories." How important the living tradition was is shown by Paul when he refers to tradition, both in the case of the institution of the Lord's Supper and concerning the Lord's resurrection (1 Cor. 11:23ff. and 1 Cor. 15:3). Though he claims that he has received the tradition from the Lord, it is evident that the tradition was handed on by human beings. Ultimately, however, tradition is always from the Lord. The tradition which is from the Lord is so authoritative that even Paul or "an angel from heaven" (Gal. 1:8) could not carry more authority.

Exactly in that period during which the living tradition was gathered in the canon, another aspect of tradition gained increasing significance. It was tied to the bishops as the successors of the apostles and was used to combat allegedly secret traditions introduced by the Gnostics. The Christian community defended its teachings by claiming an unbroken line of tradition. As Clement, for instance, argues: "The gospel was preached to the apostles on our behalf by the Lord Jesus Christ; Jesus Christ was sent out from God. Christ therefore came from God, and the apostles from Christ. Both these appointments, then, were made in an orderly way according to the will of God" (1 Clem. 42). Appeal to the tradition meant the assurance that no novelty was introduced and that in some way or another continuity was preserved. In a classical way Vincent of Lérins formulated in A.D. 434 in his *Commonitorium* the principle of tradition: "All possible care must be taken that we hold that faith which has been believed everywhere, always, by all."[3] While this does not exclude growth and advancement, it disallows for one-sided growth. Throughout the Middle Ages the tradition remained, at least officially, subordinated to Scripture.

In combating the Reformation, the Council of Trent stated that the unwritten traditions which have come to us from Christ, and the Holy Scripture handed on through the apostles, would enjoy equal honor and affection.[4] Thus tradition has again been accorded equality with the written word. The possible results of this equality can be seen from the dogmatic definition of the Assumption of Mary into heaven, where we read that "all these arguments and considerations of the Holy Fathers and of the theologians are based on the Holy Scriptures as their ultimate foundation."[5] The primary basis for this dogma was not Scripture but the Fathers and theologians, albeit in accordance with Scripture.

At the Second Vatican Council we hear that the gospel "is the source of all saving truth and moral teaching."[6] This affirmation of the priority of the gospel, however, is severely mitigated when we read: "It is not from sacred Scripture alone that the Church draws the certainty about everything which has been revealed. Therefore both sacred tradition and sacred Scripture are to be accepted and venerated with the same sense of devotion and reverence."[7] Here the formulation of Trent is repeated and reference is made again to two strands of revelation. However, an additional step is taken when we hear that both sacred tradition and sacred Scripture flow "from the same divine well-spring, and in a certain way merge into a unity and tend toward the same end."[8] This statement would allow for the notion that all revelation is in some way, though perhaps obscurely, contained in Scripture. Tradition, however, would give us only a mediated understanding of Scripture, since in some way or another it is always enriched through popular piety and harnessed through the teaching office.

We must affirm that the church understands and interprets Scripture always in the light of the continuous tradition. Even individual Christians are unable to extricate themselves from the impact of tradition. But the interpretations of tradition hardly ever coincide with each other and therefore do not eliminate divergence. They are always interpretations from a peculiar angle. Even the most comprehensive dogmatic definitions do not mute or replace theological reflection; rather they stimulate them. Yet there are degrees of reflection which no longer recognize the common tradition and pose the question of apostasy. This has happened several times during the course of the church's history: at the earliest councils in the case of the Nestorians and Monophysites, at the height of the Middle Ages with the Eastern Church, and at the beginning of modernity with the different strands of the Reformation. Each time one side claimed that the other had left the common tradition. Thus the appeal to tradition can be at times divisive just as a common interpretation of tradition has proven at times to be a unifying rallying point for those who attempted to combat apostasy. At the same time, ignoring tradition is certainly no remedy for maintaining unity—as we have seen over and over in the case of certain sects and denominations that intentionally ignore tradition, including credal statments, and go back to the "simple Word of God" contained in Scripture. Yet ignoring tradition usually does not lead to greater unity. Virtually all of these sects and denominations lead a separate existence, maintain their own idiosyncracies, and jealously safeguard their scriptural insights against "infidels."

Martin Luther can show us a more tenable approach. While he insisted on the sufficiency of the *sola scriptura* (Scripture alone), he accepted the work of the early church fathers and the creeds of the church. Even his predilection for Augustine and his distrust of Aristotle were not simply personal bias. While he insisted that the church of his time had fallen away from the truth, he was not blind to the truth still present in the church of his time. He distinguished between what was acceptable within tradition and what was not. For him, the decisive criterion for acceptable tradition was that it did not contradict Scripture. This saved him from a narrow biblicism which would have allowed only that which was explicitly stated by Scripture.

But does not such an implicit Scriptural attestation of components of tradition allow for many marginal beliefs, including, for instance, the dogma of the Assumption of Mary? Luther would hardly agree, because for him Scripture itself can not be treated indiscriminately. Though at that time not much was known about the formation of the canon, Luther wisely distinguished between center and periphery in Scripture, both in Scripture as a whole and among the individual writings. For instance, Luther remarked that he preferred that Philip Melanchthon's *Loci Communes*, the first Lutheran dogmatic, be included in the canon rather than the "Judaizing" Letter of James. He also had severe doubts about the canonical value of the book of Revelation. Only when he regarded it as a book about the history of the church was he willing to accept it. On the other hand, he valued highly the Gospel according to St. John and Paul's Letter to the Romans. The reason for these discriminations was not personal preference but the deep theological conviction that Scripture bears witness to Christ. Whatever most clearly proclaims Christ was central for Luther, and whatever obscures or neglects him is moved to the periphery.

But the mere presence of Christ as the central character in a writing is not sufficient to assure its canonicity. The apocryphal gospel in which Jesus is portrayed as a miracle worker who is quite oblivious to the needs of others shows this to be true. Thus, decisive for canonicity is the proclamation of the central thrust of Jesus' mission, Jesus portraying and accomplishing God's grace towards us. This means that the *solus Christus* (Christ alone) must be interpreted in the direction of the *sola gratia* (through grace alone).

Whatever advocates the graciousness of God in Jesus Christ is central to Scripture. We encounter in it the *viva vox evangelii,* the living voice of the gospel.

One might wonder whether in such hermeneutical considerations the Old Testament has any place or value. Luther would answer with an emphatic yes, for at least two reasons. (1) The Old Testament is the cradle and the diapers in which the Christ child was laid. One must therefore know the Old Testament in order to understand Christ. Through its promissory history the Old Testament also points to Christ, with Yahweh being the father of Jesus Christ. Thus the sameness of God provides a strong continuity between both testaments. (2) There is also much gospel in the Old Testament. A Christocentric criterion for establishing canonicity subjects the Old Testament to a critique similar to that applied to the new. The Mosaic Law, for instance, is seen as the law of the Jews, with no binding value for us. Not even the Ten Commandments are obligatory for us, since they were clearly given through Moses to the Israelites. We hear from Luther that we are free to draw up our own commandments which should then correspond with God's will for us. Since the Ten Commandments, however, were directly given by God through Moses, Luther admits that they contain God's will much more clearly than anything else we might devise. Hence we notice their lasting value. But, as Luther has shown in his Small Catechism, they must be adapted to the new (Christian) situation.

We should finally mention that though Luther consistently interpreted Scripture in a Christocentric way, he did not want to interpret it allegorically. We should always attempt to discover the literal sense. If God speaks through Scripture, he does not do so in an allegorical way, but in a literal, i.e., straightforward way. Luther always insisted on the *sensus literalis,* the literal meaning of a passage. To unearth this meaning Luther wanted people to be able to read Scripture in the original languages so that they would not be swayed by later interpretive translations and might come as close as possible to the original meaning of the text. It is not without significance that in today's ecumenical dialog the growing together of the different traditions is greatly facilitated through reading and comparing the respective traditions in the light of the gospel. The amazing progress made in these dialogs within a relatively short period of time is the best witness to the efficacy of the hermeneutical key which says that our Christian faith and witness must be continuously guided, checked, and corrected by the biblical witness to God's gracious action in Jesus Christ.

This does not mean that we are ever without tradition or even should be. Rather it means that all tradition must flow from and be brought into line with its source, the biblical witness to God's gracious self-disclosure. Since Scripture is the primary material source of God's self-disclosure to us, it must be accredited with normative authority or, as the Lutheran *Book of Concord* says, be "the sole rule and norm of all doctrine."[9] Scripture is sufficient in what it communicates for our salvation. As a historical book it contains many other items which are peripheral and not necessary for salvation. Yet what is necessary for salvation Scripture does contain in a clear and concise manner. It is our primary access to what God has done for us and our salvation.

In addition, we should always remember that each piece of Scripture was written in a specific context and tradition and is read by us in a specific context. To hear this word most effectively, we must be aware of the context then and the context now. We must also be aware that we always have a prior understanding of what Scripture wants to say to us. The question, however, is to what extent we allow for a correction of our prior understanding. If such willingness is not present, the text becomes a pretext for pious self-justification. In other words, we hear what we want to hear. But it is exactly the surprise-causing effect of Scripture which allows us to hear God speaking through it. We perceive his will and accept his word of grace. While Scripture must be seen both in its original and its present context, neither one should become dominant. Scripture itself should be allowed to speak to us so that we can hear the Word in the words. This does not mean that there is a special way in which Scripture should be read which differs from the reading of other literature. There is also no special way of interpreting Scripture which differs from the way of interpreting other literature. The only difference lies in the content. Since Scripture is the primary reflection of God's self-disclosure in Jesus Christ, it should be read and interpreted with the expectation that this reflection will draw me into its reflective process, i.e., that it open my eyes so that I can perceive the one to whom it witnesses.

PART 2
THE GOD WHO ACTS

After these preliminary, though necessary considerations, we must now move to the subject of God, the focal point of all theology. When we talk about God within the Judeo-Christian tradition we are immediately confronted with the conviction that God is not a distant or remote power but rather a being who is intimately connected with people. The primary confession is that God is actively involved in the affairs of the world. After initial reflections upon who it is whom we call God, we must deal with God's activity as creator and sustainer of both world and humanity and attempt to determine their relationship to God. Finally, we must mention human sinfulness which separates us from God.

4

GOD

Phrases such as "an act of God" or "God wanted it this way" attest to the fact that, at one time at least, God was conceived of as the answer to virtually everything and especially to things for which we did not know the answer. In many ways we still use this "God of the gaps" to fill in for our ignorance. Yet as our knowledge about the natural context continuously expanded, the need to resort to God as an answer that fills in for our ignorance became less and less. As Dietrich Bonhoeffer claimed, God has literally been edged out of the world and relegated to inactivity. Instead of functioning as the answer, God became the problem. Correspondingly, God has lost a meaningful place in our everyday language and is now referred to in predominantly meaningless phrases, such as "Oh, God!" or "for God's sake."

This demise of the "Christian" God was unintentionally furthered by the decision that God should no longer be referred to with the proper (Jewish) name *Yahweh*. Since he is the only God he should rather be addressed by the generic term *theos* (God). By universalizing the name, God's universal significance was properly expressed. Yet at the same time God's peculiar relation to a special part of history, the God-disclosive history of Israel with which the name *Yahweh* is inseparably connected, was more and more attenuated. Consequently the danger emerged, increasingly actualized through the centuries, that one talked about a universal God with less and less specificity as to who this God really was. This dilemma shows itself in the modern speechlessness about God as well as in the growing inability meaningfully to distinguish between God and the gods.

A. God and the gods

In its spiritual conquest of the Roman Empire the Christian faith always had to defend its faith in God against the belief in other gods. In more recent times the question how the Christian God is related to other gods again emerged during the Crusades.

1. *The recent encounter*

In their journeys to Palestine the crusaders and, in turn, many others came in contact with Islam and its claim that there is only one God, Allah. Since the Moslems proved to be rather skilled in defending themselves against the Christian crusaders, the ideological result was often skepticism about the truth of one's own Christian faith, or at least the tacit concession that one might not have grasp of the whole truth.

Centuries later Gotthold Ephraim Lessing (1729–1781) summed up this sentiment very eloquently in his *Parable of the Rings*. This parable, contained in the dramatic poem *Nathan the Wise* (1779), states that a father once had three sons. He wanted to give them a precious ring, but since he did not want to prefer one son above the others, he made exact duplicates of the original ring. Lessing then poses the question of who has the original ring. The only criterion is the way the three sons act. But, Lessing concludes, perhaps none of the three sons, Islam, Christianity, and Judaism, has the original ring. It might well be that the true ring has been lost. Underlying this religious relativism or skepticism is the motif of the three imposters, Moses, Jesus, and Mohammed, which was already contained, though in slightly different way, in Giovanni Boccaccio's *The Decameron* (The Ten Days' Work, c. 1350).

While in the Middle Ages it was the Near East which caused bewilderment, it is now the Far East with its temples and rituals which casts its spell upon us. Through TV programs and increasing travel the whole world is practically at our fingertips; many of us are confronted with a number of colorful and unusual-looking religious edifices and practices. Though we usually just admire the fascinating and foreign splendor that goes with these religions, we cannot escape noticing that other people believe in other gods and that they take them at least as seriously as we take our God. The frequently heard claim, "we all believe in the same God anyhow," sums up the conclusion drawn by many who feel that it really does not make any difference in what kind of God we believe, since Allah, God, or Vishnu are only different names for the same entity.

If it were true that we all worship the same God under different names, it should make us wonder that the same God is perceived and worshiped in such entirely different ways. While the saying goes that there are *many* ways leading to Rome, perhaps not *all* the ways lead there. Perhaps some of this "God talk" addresses someone else than the one whom we usually call God. This at least was the conviction of the Israelites of Old Testament times.

2. Israel's struggle

For the Israelites the encounter with other gods is as old as their faith in Yahweh. The Old Testament does not even hide the fact that Israel's ancestors have not always known Yahweh. Though the Yahwist claims that the worship of Yahweh is the primal religion of all humanity (Gen. 4:26), the more recent priestly writer specifies that God did not reveal himself to the patriarchs with his proper name *Yahweh*. For instance, in Gen. 17:1 we read: "When Abram was ninety-nine years old the Lord [Yahweh] appeared to Abram and said to him, 'I am God Almighty [El Shaddai]; walk before me, and be blameless.' " Similarly, according to Exod. 6:2f., Moses is told, "I am the Lord [Yahweh]. I appeared to Abram, to Isaac, and to Jacob, as God Almighty [El Shaddai], but by my name the Lord [Yahweh] I did not make myself known to them." This confirms that the proper name for God, Yahweh, is of later date in the Israelite religion and its appearance is closely connected with Moses. Yet there was no doubt for the Israelites that whomever the patriarchs worshiped was in fact Yahweh. Most important for Israel, however, was not some myth about Yahweh (for instance about his genealogy or about the children he spawned or how he was superior to all other gods) but instead central was the Israelite confession that Yahweh rescued them from Egypt and led them to the promised land. So we read in the creed of Deut. 26:5-9:

> A wandering Aramean was my father; and he went down into Egypt and sojourned there, few in number; and there he became a nation, great, mighty, and populous. And the Egyptians treated us harshly, and afflicted us, and laid upon us hard bondage. Then we cried to the Lord the God of our fathers, and the Lord heard our voice, and saw our affliction, our toil, and our oppression; and the Lord brought us out of Egypt with a mighty hand and an outstretched arm, with great terror, with signs and wonders; and he brought us into this place and gave us this land, a land flowing with milk and honey.

A problem, however, emerged once the Israelites had settled in Palestine. There is no doubt that the so-called God of the Fathers was essentially conceived as a nomadic God. When the groups connected with the patriarchs moved into Canaanite territory, they did not, however, abandon their God and adopt gods more akin to a settled agrarian existence. Instead they kept allegiance to their God and, though using pagan sanctuaries, gradually even connected these with their own God. Some of the former etiologies of the Canaanite cult were reinterpreted and even used in such a way that the local gods were equated with the God of the Fathers. Especially the God El seems to have been identified with the God of the Fathers without even changing his name. Consequently, we still find narratives in the Old Testament with the names El Olam (Gen. 21:33) or El Bethel (Gen. 28:10-22) or Peniel (Gen. 32:25-32). Of course, this was not mere equation. It meant that the specific elements of the God of the Fathers were introduced into these narratives, while at the same time allowing for considerable influx of Canaanite ideas into the Israelite understanding of God. But in the long run it proved to be an effective means not only for conquering Palestinian territory but for making any exclusive worship of Canaanite gods in the conquered territory impossible.

When those Israelites around Moses entered the promised land they easily identified Yahweh with the God of the Fathers. But could they also equate Yahweh with the gods of Canaan? Once the Israelites abandoned their nomadic existence and settled down in the more cultured land, these gods were a great temptation for them. After all, customs and language of the cultured land deeply reflected the intrinsic connection between an agrarian way of life and the acceptance of these powers. There was also no doubt that these other gods were actual powers and masters over other nations (cf. 1 Kings 11:7f.). The statement in Deut. 32:17, dating from the 11th century B.C., "They sacrificed to demons which were no gods, to gods they had never known, to new gods that had come in of late, whom your fathers had never dreaded," portrays the magnitude of the spiritual struggle taking place during the first centuries after Israel had entered the promised land.

Gideon may serve as a prime example of the internal strife within the emerging Israelite community (Judges 6–8). He himself was a strong supporter of Yahweh who destroyed an altar of Baal in his native town of Ophrah and cut down the sacred Asherah (a cultic pole dedicated to the fertility goddess, Asherah). But Gideon's stand for Yahweh is almost surprising in view of the fact that he is also called Jerubbaal (Judg. 7:1), a composite form of Baal, the name of a Canaanite deity. Further illustrating the competing religious loyalties is the fact that the name of Gideon's father, Joash, was still a composite form of Yahweh, the God of Israel. We also hear that Gideon's own Israelite people were enraged about his destructive acts against Canaanite sanctuaries. But then we are told that even Gideon himself set up a golden ephod in Ophrah. As far as we know, an ephod is a rich costume covered with gold or silver and studded with stars and other cosmic symbols. The Israelites who adhered to the strict Mosaic traditions could easily interpret it as an idol, like Canaanite statues of gods. But in the official Yahwist cult of the day it could also be understood as the visible symbol of the invisible deity. The story of Gideon gives us some idea of the kind of absorption, adaption, and rejection that took place in those first centuries after Israel settled down in the promised land.

We have noticed that the Israelites sensed no difficulty identifying the Canaanite El first with the God of the Fathers and later also with Yahweh. But the story was different as far as the Canaanite fertility god Baal is concerned. Initially, some Israelites may have equated Baal with Yahweh or venerated him along with Yahweh. Even some of his characteristics may have been conferred upon Yahweh. For instance, we find names that are composites of the name Baal, such as Ishbaal, the son of Saul, and we see that, in analogy to Aleyan Baal, the god of thunder, Yahweh was praised as the one "who rides upon the clouds" (Ps. 68:4). However, the constant battle of the prophets against the worship under trees and in high places—and sometimes even against the whole sacrificial cult (Amos 5:21-27)—shows us the prevailing trend of thought. Deuteronomy, reflecting upon the situation after Israel had entered Palestine, makes the point clear:

> When you come into the land which the Lord your God gives you, you shall not learn to follow the abominable practices of those nations. There shall not be found among you any one who burns his son or his daughter as an offering, any one who practices divination, a soothsayer, or an augur, or a sorcerer, or a charmer, or a medium, or a wizard, or a necromancer. For whoever does these things is an abomination to the Lord; and because of these abominable practices the Lord your God is driving them out before you. You shall be blameless before the Lord your God. For these nations, which you are about to dispossess, give heed to soothsayers and to diviners; but as for you, the Lord your God has not allowed you so to do (Deut. 18:9-14).

We are not confronted here with monotheism in the modern sense of the word. The actuality of other powers besides Yahweh is recognized, though they are rejected as unworthy of adoration. There is also no doubt that guidance and help come only from Yahweh, who offers assistance and who demands their allegiance.

3. *The Christian discernment*

In the New Testament the allegiance to Yahweh, the Father of Jesus Christ, is continued. But now also a clue is offered as to why there is such a plurality of deities. Paul writes:

> For the wrath of God is revealed from heaven against all ungodliness and wickedness of men who by their wickedness suppress the truth. For what can be known about God is plain to them, because God has shown it to them. Ever since the creation of the world his invisible nature, namely, his eternal power and deity, has been clearly perceived in the things that have been made. So they are without excuse; for although they knew God they did not honor him as God or give thanks to him, but they became futile in their thinking and their senseless minds were darkened. Claiming to be wise, they became fools, and

exchanged the glory of the immortal God for images resembling mortal man or birds or animals or reptiles (Rom. 1:18-23).

God is actually known to all people. However, they have exchanged the true knowledge of God for their own ideas about God and have constructed idols and false deities.

In his monumental 12-volume work *Der Ursprung der Gottesidee* (The Origin of the Idea of God, 1912–1955) the Roman Catholic priest, missionary, and ethnologist Wilhelm Schmidt expanded this assertion claiming that the belief in an all-powerful highest being stood at the beginning of all religious development. Through a process of degeneration this belief was lost and humanity developed a mythology with many gods and spirits. Schmidt claims that the belief in this highest god can still be traced in primal religions. Australian aborigines, African bushmen, Mongols, and many other tribes continue to believe in a highest god. Today, however, most historians of religion reject the thesis of the existence of an original monotheism as having been gleaned more from certain biblical passages than from careful field studies. It was not, however, the intention of Paul to propose an original monotheism. He is rather interested to show that, ideally at least, everyone could have a sufficient knowledge of the one supreme God who disclosed himself in an insurpassable way in Jesus Christ. But through human sinfulness, or arrogance, this knowledge has been perverted into the worship of gods according to our own desires.

In this context the sharp distinction made by Karl Barth between religion and the Christian faith is relevant. Barth concluded that all religion is a human fabrication in which we humans do the talking and fashion a god according to our wishes. In the Christian faith, however, God talks to us and we listen. Barth concedes that Ludwig Feuerbach's thesis, that humanity projects its own desires upon the sky and then worships them as gods, is an accurate description of the religious scene. However, it does not begin to touch that which transpired in the Christian faith and which is built on God's initiative.

Barth's condemning approach to the religious scene is seldom continued today. But he had a point. We must admit that under the guise of popular piety even the Christian faith has been corrupted by superstition and outright idolatry. For instance, Buddha made his way into the Roman Catholic calendar of saints as Barlaam and Josaphat. Moreover, the Roman Brumalia (December 25), preceded by the Saturnalia (December 17–24), having been celebrated as the shortest day of the year, the emergence of the "new sun," and the lengthening of days, made such inroads into the Christian celebration of Christmas that the Christians of Mesopotamia accused their Western brothers and sisters of idolatry and sun worship for adopting this pagan festival. This shows that the Christian faith in God is not the distillate of pure religion while all other religions are contaminated by human sinfulness.

Initially the Judeo-Christian tradition simply recognized the existence of other divine powers next to Yahweh. But the belief in Yahweh excluded the veneration of other gods. The worship of Yahweh increased the sense of belonging together. It was usually defended as the expressed will of God (First Commandment) and through the belief that other gods did not measure up to Yahweh. Once the Israelite God, Yahweh, lost his proper name within the Judeo-Christian tradition and was referred to by the generic designation *God,* the one and only God had to render obsolete all other gods. This meant that these other gods either were considered irrelevant for true faith in God or that any of their characteristics deemed compatible with Christian faith in God had to be considered as a manifestation of the one and only God. God's self-disclosure within the Judeo-Christian tradition thus provided the criterion of what to accept or to reject from other notions of God.

B. The limits of our natural knowledge of God

If the one God is encountered in varying degrees and in a multitude of ways, the question arises to what extent human reason can gain adequate knowledge of God. A natural knowledge of God has only been disputed in more recent times. The Psalmist confidently asserts, "The fool says in his heart, 'There is no God' " (Ps. 14:1). In antiquity, individuals who denied the existence of God were not taken seriously. They were considered as fools and treated as such. The apologists of early Christianity argued for the universal presence of the *logos spermatikos* or seminal *logos* through which all people have a notion of God.

Martin Luther was at times critical of natural reason. He even called it a whore, implying that it would side with any argument.

But he was confident that all people knew about God. With reference to Paul, Luther asserted that "this light and understanding is in the hearts of all men and can be neither suppressed nor put out."[1] All people know that God is omnipotent and omniscient, the giver of all good, that God is kind and gracious, and willing to help a person who calls upon him in time of need. While reason knows many things about God, it has no certainty in its knowledge, since it perceives God only from the outside and does not know God's heart. Luther expressly distinguishes between the general and proper knowledge about God. The former knows that God is, that God created the world and sustains it, that he is righteous and judges us. But general knowledge does not know that God wants to save us nor is it clear that our notion of God coincides with his reality. This latter knowledge can only be given to us through God's self-disclosure in Jesus Christ.

It is exactly this natural knowledge which has attracted and continues to attract the minds of many. From the earliest times the most prominent theologians and many other curious inquirers spent considerable efforts to demonstrate through the power of human reason that God does exist. There are especially five proofs which have gained prime importance in these endeavors.

1. The search for a necessary being (ontological argument)

Anselm of Canterbury, the great theorist of early scholasticism, proposed the ontological argument in a manner still fascinating today. He wrote his *Proslogion* or *Address* from the point of view of one who is "seeking to understand what he believes."[2] Anselm did not start with a blank, gradually working himself up to the notion of God. The question which fascinated him is not that of the existence of God, but just who the one is whom we call God. Anselm arrived at an answer by asserting that God is "something than which nothing greater can be thought."[3] Proceeding from this definition he claimed that such a being cannot exist in the understanding alone. It must also exist in reality or else it would not be the most perfect being. It is at this point that Anselm's argument has received most criticism. Anselm seemed to consider existence (in reality) as a property of God in analogy to other properties, thus belonging by definition to the idea of the most perfect being.

In his *Critique of Pure Reason* (1781) Immanuel Kant (1724–1804) strongly objected to this kind of method, stating that logical and real predicates are being confused in the ontological argument. Unlike omnipotence or omniscience, being is not a real predicate and the transition from existence in thought to existence in reality cannot be accomplished by simply adding another predicate, that of being, to make God perfect. Kant illustrated this with the example of a hundred thalers. "A hundred real thalers do not contain the least coin more than a hundred possible thalers," but "my financial position is, however, affected very differently by a hundred real thalers than it is by the mere concept of them (that is, of their possibility)."[4] The actual existence of the thalers is thus not contained in their thought but has to be added to their thought. However, Kant did not seem to have listened to the rest of Anselm's argument.

Anselm was well aware that God's existence in reality is different from the existence in reality of a hundred thalers. God's existence is not of a possible but of a necessary kind. Anselm argued that there are things which can be conceived of as either existing or not existing. But since these things exist, they would be of higher quality than God and he would not be "that than which nothing greater can be thought." Anselm therefore affirmed: "You exist so truly, Lord my God, that You cannot even be thought not to exist. And this is as it should be, for if some intelligence could think of something better than You, the creature would be above its creator—and that is completely absurd."[5] Anselm did not consider his line of argument as an actual proof of God's existence, because he leaves open the possibility that one can deny God's existence in reality. He realized that people differ considerably in their understandings of God and thus the notion of God can be understood inadequately. For a person with an inadequate understanding of God it does not naturally follow that God exists also in reality. But he who thoroughly understands that God is that than which nothing greater can be conceived "understands clearly that this same being so exists that not even in thought can it not exist."[6] Since he felt that he was one of those, he concluded his investigation by saying, "I give thanks, good Lord, I give thanks to You; since what I believed before through Your free gift I now so understand through Your illumination."[7] It becomes evident that Anselm's argument is not a proof in the traditional sense of the word, since it presupposes already a stand of faith concerning God's very existence and nature. The question, however, must be asked whether the presupposition of the Christian God that Anselm assumed is actually necessary for the ontological argument. In other words, need one be a Christian in order to understand who it is whom we call God?

The French philosopher René Descartes (1596–1650) seems to have omitted the Christian presupposition of the ontological argument and proceeds on strictly philosophical grounds. In his *Meditations on First Philosophy* (1641) he outlines two ways of arriving at God. In the third *Meditation* he first wonders why we have the idea of God. He is sure that this idea cannot proceed from ourselves. The word *God* implies a substance that is infinite, immutable, independent, all-knowing, all-powerful, and by which I myself and everything else have been created. Descartes assumes that "all those attributes are so great and so eminent, that the more attentively I consider them the less does it seem possible that they can have proceeded from myself alone; and thus . . . we have no option save to conclude that God exists."[8] Of course, Descartes remembers that he defines God as infinite substance. Since he considers a human being as a finite substance, humans could have apprehended the idea of the infinite substance by negating the finite. But Descartes disclaims that one could arrive at an adequate understanding of an infinite substance through such negative causal inference. Descartes suggests that "there is manifestly more reality in the infinite substance than in the finite substance, and my awareness of the infinite must therefore be in some way prior to my awareness of the finite, that is to say my awareness of God must be prior to that of myself."[9] Only through God's perfect and infinite nature do I realize my imperfection and my finitude. Thus the idea of God is the most completely true, clear, and distinct of all ideas that are in me.

In his fifth *Meditation* Descartes follows even more closely Anselm's argument, yet without reference to him. He argues that though one cannot think of a mountain without a valley it does not follow that valleys and mountains must be in existence. Our thinking only indicates that mountain and valley, whether existent or nonexistent are inseparably conjoined with each other. However,

Descartes asserts, in thinking of God as sovereignly perfect, we "cannot think Him save as existing; and it therefore follows that existence is inseparable from Him, and that He therefore really exists."[10] Of course, Descartes knows that God's necessary existence might be brought about by my thinking it as necessary. But the surprising thing is, we hear Descartes say, that we cannot think of God as lacking existence, i.e., to think of this sovereignly perfect being as devoid of complete perfection. Descartes admits that one cannot think a triangle either except to think that the sum of its three angles are not greater than two right angles and that its greatest side subtends its greatest angle. But these necessary assertions of its essence leave the question open as to whether a triangle exists at all. This, however, is different with God. Though we think of God and his essence as clearly and distinctly as of the said triangle, Descartes asserts that he "cannot think of anything, save God alone, to the very essence of which existence pertains."[11] Thus there is nothing more evident than that there is a God, that is to say, a sovereign being, and that of all beings God alone has existence as appertaining to essence. Descartes does not suggest that at all times we must conceive of the idea of God. Yet each time we allow it to occupy the mind, we find ourselves necessarily constrained to ascribe to God all perfections, including that of existence. This conclusion is the weak point in Descartes' argument.

In recent times fewer and fewer people seem to feel compelled to hold the idea of God, because for more and more people the world makes good sense without reference to God. Descartes was not yet aware of this rapidly growing sentiment. For Descartes God still served as the guarantor of our reality and that of the world. Yet at least since Isaac Newton scientists became more and more used to explaining nature's phenomena without reference to God. For Newton the laws of nature no longer have humanity or God as their starting point. They describe relations between specific natural phenomena that have been generalized as mathematical concepts and are applied to explain other natural phenomena. Does it follow from this autonomy of science that not only Descartes' ontological argument, but also the traditional cosmological argument, which we will discuss next, are no longer valid?

2. The search for a first cause (cosmological argument)

The cosmological argument starts with the observation that there seems to be no effect without a cause. But to assume from the possibility of an infinite regress that there is always a cause prior to an effect seems to be unsatisfying. Thus many philosophers and theologians postulate a first uncaused cause by concluding from the existence of the world to the cause of its existence.

While Plato (427–347 B.C.) in his *Laws* argued that the first source of change and movement has set itself into motion and in turn sets into motion a second thing, and this second thing still a third and so on, Aristotle (384–322 B.C.) changed the idea of such a self-originated motion. Considering the problem of how motion came into being, Aristotle rejected Plato's idea of a world soul that moves itself and then in turn moves other objects. He regarded such a world soul as secondary, since it would claim the actuality of motion as secondary to potency. Thus that which is moved and also moves other things cannot be primary but must be intermediate. Only that which moves without being moved can be the true prime cause or the unmoved first mover. Such first cause will be something eternal, since it is actuality and not a potentiality which at some point was not yet actualized, and it is substance, because "everything that changes is something and is changed by something and into something."[12] To avoid the conclusion that there might be a reaction from the moved back to the first mover, Aristotle assumed that there is no physical contact between both. The first kind of spatial motion which the first mover produces is engendered by the heavens which are first moved by the object of thought and desire. Since the heavens and the world of nature depend on such a first principle of motion, the first mover exists by necessity, and its mode of being is good as far as it exists by this necessity.

Thomas Aquinas not only wrote an extensive commentary on Aristotle's *Metaphysics* (*Commentary on the Metaphysics of Aristotle*), but in his *Summa Theologica* (1266–1273) he adopted Aristotle's cosmological argument with some significant modifications. Four of his five ways to prove the existence of God are devoted to the cosmological argument. The first and most obvious way according to Thomas is based on change. We observe that some things in the world are in process of change. Anything that is in process of change is being changed by something else. If it could change itself, it would already contain actually and potentially within itself that toward which it moves. Since it is still moving toward something, it can only potentially contain the goal toward which it moves, and the actuality must be caused by something outside. Though we can push back the chain reaction of cause and effect further and further, we must stop somewhere, otherwise there would be "no first cause of change, and, as a result, no subsequent causes."[13] If we exclude the possibility of a first cause of change, which is not changed by anything else, there would be no intermediate causes, which are caused by something prior to them and, in turn, cause something subsequent to them. Thomas now postulates such a first cause and identifies it with God.

The second way in Thomas's argument concerning the existence of God goes very much like the first one and is based on the nature of causation. The third way in Thomas's argument is somewhat different and is based on the distinction between what must be by necessity and what need not necessarily be. Thomas observes that in our experience things can be or cannot be; there is no necessity about their existence. Yet if everything were like this—springing up and then dying—then once upon a time there would have been nothing. "But if that were true there would be nothing even now, because something that does not exist can only be brought into being by something already existing."[14] From the fact that there are things now Thomas concludes that not everything is of the quality that it could be or could not be. In other words, "there has got to be something that must be."[15] It cannot owe the necessity of its existence to something else, but owes it to itself and thus in turn causes other things to be. Again Thomas equated this first necessary cause of existence with God.

The fourth way in Thomas's argument again is somewhat different and is based on the gradation observed in things. Thomas states that some things are found to be more good, more true, more noble, and so on, and other things less. All these comparative terms describe approximations to a superlative, the best, the truest, the noblest, and so on. The things which contain all these superlatives are the things most fully in being. We might expect that Thomas would now employ the ontological argument and claim that the one thing most perfect must by necessity exist. But he again uses a cosmological argument and works with the assumption of a first cause. When many things possess a common property (e.g., varying degrees of goodness), then the one most fully possessing it can cause others to participate in it. If such causative superlative would not exist, there would not be these properties. Therefore Thomas concludes that there is something "which causes in all other things their being, their goodness, or whatever other perfection they have. And this we call 'God.' "[16]

All these cosmological "proofs" of the existence of God boil down to the observation that no finite being thus far observed has the cause of its existence in itself. Therefore the conclusion is reached that there must be an infinite being which is the cause of all finite beings and of itself. Yet is such a conclusion justified on logical or phenomenal grounds? Immanuel Kant, one of the keenest critics of all proofs of God's existence, answered with an emphatic no! But he rightly called the cosmological argument the most natural and "the most convincing not only for common sense but even for speculative understanding."[17] Kant demonstrated the limits of the cosmological argument in his fourth antinomy of pure reason. He showed that neither on the basis of experience nor on the basis of pure reason alone can it be decided whether there is a supreme cause of the world or whether such a cause is nonexistent.

In his actual criticism of the cosmological argument Kant again affirms that to infer a cause from observing the contingent only applies to the observable world but it has no meaning whatsoever outside this world. Kant emphasizes that our experience and logic are confined to the realm in which we live, to our space-time continuum. There is no way logically to transcend this realm and attain any degree of certainty. Kant also reminds us of the dilemma which we have faced with the ontological argument when he states that the logical necessity of a prime cause does not necessitate its reality.

3. The argument from design (teleological argument)

The human mind thought of still other ways to "prove" God. There is for instance the teleological argument which to some extent runs like the cosmological argument, though in the opposite direction. From the beauty, harmony, and expediency of the world the conclusion is reached that there must be a highest intelligence that once arranged the world so perfectly and still governs it this way. The harmony within the world can best be observed in the growing organism or in the ecological harmony of the animate and inanimate world.

In Greek antiquity the observation of nature led philosophers such as Anaxagoras (c. 500–428 B.C.) to the assertion that there must be a world intelligence that functions as the ordering power of the universe. Even the skeptic Cicero of ancient Rome could not but praise the beauty of the world and the marvelous regularity of its motions. Centuries later the German biologist and neovitalistic philosopher Hans Driesch (1867–1940) still assumed a causality within the organic world which works to make things whole. This entelechy, as he called it, is not contained in space and time but acts in it. It works teleologically in transforming a mere sum of equipotentialities into the wholeness of a mature organism. Similarly, it leads to restitution in lower animals, for instance, when the tail of a salamander grows back after it has been cut off. In plants the same entelechy leads to adaptation. When plants are removed from a warm climate and are placed into a cooler environment they protect themselves with a hairy film. Hans Driesch considered each living organism in its indisputable wholeness as the most obvious result of this entelechy.

Before agreeing too readily with Driesch we should also remember Charles Darwin's assessment of natural adaptation when he said, "I cannot think that the world, as we see it, is the result of chance; yet I cannot look at each separate thing as the result of Design."[18] Perceiving design and beauty in nature is only half of the truth. Immanuel Kant again seems right in his evaluation of the teleological argument. He asserted that this proof which presents the world to us as an immeasurable stage of variety, order, purposiveness, and beauty, must be mentioned with respect. "It is the oldest, the clearest, and the most accordant with the common reason of mankind. It enlivens the study of nature, just as it itself derives its existence and gains ever new vigor from that source."[19] In talking about harmony, purposiveness, and harmonious adaptation, however, this physico-theological proof, as Kant called it, refers only to the form of the world and not to its substance. Thus, Kant suggests, by analogy to our observing a human artist who shapes beautiful artifacts out of raw materials, we could at best arrive at an architect of the world, but not at its creator. If we want to prove the existence of an all-sufficient primordial being, according to Kant, we would then have to resort to the cosmological argument. Since we have already noticed that he reduces the cosmological argument to its ontological presuppositon, we are not surprised when he arrives at the conclusion that the teleological argument serves only as an introduction to the ontological argument.

Kant not only demonstrated the interdependence of the three arguments for the existence of God thus far reviewed, but he also pointed to a dangerous moment in the teleological argument, namely, that the God proved through this argument would only be a world architect. This idea of a world architect received hardly any attention in the Middle Ages. Thomas Aquinas, for instance, only in his fifth and last way to prove the existence of God emphasized the goal-directedness and orderliness of nature. In the period of the Enlightenment, however, the teleologial argument led not only to the assumption of a world architect, but even more mechanically to that of a divine watchmaker.

For example, the Christian apologist and Archdeacon of Carlisle, William Paley (1743–1805), a contemporary of Kant, ventures to compare the works of nature with a watch, though he asserts that "the contrivances of nature surpass the contrivances of art, in the complexity, subtlety, and curiosity of the mechanism."[20] It is only too tempting for minds less bound to the Christian tradition to interpret the world on a totally mechanistic basis and relegate God to the once important but now irrelevant position of divine watchmaker. This shows us that in order to arrive at a proof of the existence of God, theologians have unintentionally furthered the argument that the world no longer needs an active God.

4. *The voice from within (moral argument)*

The moral argument for the existence of God has gained new importance through Kant. Unlike the English empiricist David Hume a generation before him, Kant not only criticized traditional arguments for the existence of God, but advanced his own argument, that of the moral necessity of God. Kant was not the first philosopher to resort to the moral argument. The Spanish physician, philosopher, and theologian Raymond of Sebonde earlier advocated it in his *Theologia Naturalis Sive Liber Creaturarum* (1434-1436). According to Raymond humans are reasonable beings. Yet they can neither reward nor punish themselves. Thus there must be a higher authority who assumes the role of distributing rewards and punishment. If such ultimate retribution did not exist, human life would make no sense, since in the lives of individuals good and bad would not balance out.

In concluding his *Critique of Practical Reason* Kant touches the same issue when he confesses, "Two things fill the mind with ever new and increasing admiration and awe, the oftener and more steadily they are reflected on: the starry heavens above me and the moral law within me."[21] While the starry heavens show us the magnitude of the universe and our own smallness, the moral law within us endows us with dignity and personal worth. The moral law impels us to strive for the highest good in the world. But no rational being in this world can conform at any time to the moral law. Kant claims that such perfection can only be attained through infinite progress beyond this life in life eternal. If we assume we could attain it already in this life, we either bend the moral law according to our own inclinations, or we indulge in fanatical dreams which completely contradict our real knowledge of ourselves.

Kant proceeds to show that both immortality and God must be postulated by pure practical reason. Conformity with the moral law, which is to bring about true happiness, rests on the assumption that a harmony can be obtained between nature, our own destiny, and the moral law within us. The latter two might be able to conform, provided that we are the author of both of them. But how can they conform with the world around us? Kant observed that since man is not the cause of nature "his will cannot by its own strength bring nature, as it touches on his happiness, into complete harmony with his practical principles."[22] If, however, there is a supreme cause of nature which has a causality corresponding to our moral intention, such conformity could be reached. Consequently, Kant assumes the existence of God as the necessary presupposition for achieving the highest good. If there is no God, as ultimate author and coordinator of our moral drive and of nature's innate possibilities, it would not make sense for us to strive for the (then unattainable) ultimate harmony. Kant readily admits that the notion of God is derived from a practical need and "it can be called *faith* and even *rational faith*, because pure reason alone (by its theoretical as well as practical employment) is the source from which it springs."[23] This argument for God, as the purposive integrator of our yearning and the cause of the world, also shows that we are "the final purpose of creation," and that nature will eventually harmonize with our happiness. Kant even asserts that without us "the whole creation would be a mere waste, in vain, and without final purpose."[24]

Johann Gottlieb Fichte (1762-1814), deeply influenced by Kant, again emphasized a moral order of the world. He claimed that everyone experiences a call to duty, which is related in its content to that of everyone else's call. The originator of this call and of its unity with all other calls endows our life with direction and also guarantees the final victory of the good. While Kant still maintained that God as the purposive integrator must be perceived as a personal agent, Fichte's idealistic notion of God is clearly pantheistic. It is similar to Friedrich Schiller's comment that the world's history is the world's judgment. God is equated with the driving forces of the world. God is no longer the unconditioned conditioner but the unexplainable way the world processes present themselves. Such a notion, however, indicates that the moral argument for God's existence can easily divorce itself from the Judeo-Christian faith, for the support of which it was once developed, and result in a pessimistic or at least skeptical outlook on the world processes.

5. By common consent (historical argument)

The last argument we want to mention is the historical argument or the argument from common consent. Its basic assertion is a phenomenological one, namely, that all nations at all times revered a god or gods. It is an argument which hardly indicates in its outset that it wants to lead up to the God of Judeo-Christian faith. Having observed that all peoples at all times worship deities or higher beings of some kind, the conclusion is drawn that there must be a reality behind this common human attitude.

Though this argument might have sufficed in centuries passed, it is no longer applicable to our own time. The clearly increasing number of people who either unintentionally or deliberately reject the notion of God or of any gods is one of the most bewildering phenomena of our time. In our contemporary situation the historical argument is a very dangerous one. It is dangerous because it could lead to the assumption that up to a certain point in time humanity worshiped metaphysical powers, but through a process of maturation dissolved the metaphysical world into the physical and has no longer a need for belief in divine agents.

We must ask ourselves what all these arguments actually prove. First, they prove that since the beginning of logical thought the most brilliant representatives of the human race endeavored to argue on a rational basis for the existence of God. The very fact of this enterprise should make us stop and think, if we are tempted to discard the question of God altogether. Beyond this point the opinions are divided. Official Catholic doctrine still holds that God's existence can be proved. As recently at 1950 Pope Pius XII pronounced in his encyclical *Humani Generis* that "human reason ... by its natural powers and light can in fact arrive at true and certain knowledge of one personal God who in His providence guards and directs the world, and also of the natural law infused into our souls by the Creator."[25] This is in line with the statement of Vatican I "that God, the beginning and end of all things, can be known with certitude by the natural light of human reason from created things."[26]

On the Protestant side, however, Kant's criticism of the proofs of God's existence left an undeniable impact. Most Protestant theologians are very hesitant to ascribe to human reason such a high power. But already a generation before Kant, the German pietist, philosopher, and mystic, Johann Georg Hamann, had pointed out that a God whom we can grasp with our reason and whom we can penetrate with our mind is no God. Any proof of God's existence would mean either that God is on equal basis with us, i.e., part of our world, or that we are on an equal basis with him, i.e., not confined to our world. Though Hamann's observation is basically right, he forgets that whenever we speak of God we are unable to grasp God completely. However, this inability does not make us refrain from using approximations or anthropomorphisms in our God-language. For instance, we believe in God's self-disclosure to us in human form in Jesus Christ. Yet would it not be feasible that God has also disclosed himself to some extent to all people outside of Jesus Christ? Is Vatican I wrong when, upholding the natural knowledge of God, it quotes Paul's Letter to the Romans saying; "For the invisible things of him, from the creation of the world, are clearly seen, being understood by the things that are made"?[27] Even Paul seems to concede at this point that God can be known to some degree by natural reason.

Of course, one could refer to Søren Kierkegaard who claimed that "to prove the existence of one who is present is the most shameless affront, since it is an attempt to make him ridiculous."[28] However, such a rejection of the "proofs" of God's existence seems to result from a misunderstanding of their function. The "proofs" serve either a doxological function in glorifying God through the means of reason, or they serve an apologetic function in attempting to convince doubters or unbelievers of the reality of God. They are hardly ever intended as a means of confirming whether God is really there. This means that they always imply a prior faith decision, even if it is one of "pure rational faith" as in Kant's moral argument. The one who sets out to "prove" is already convinced that there is "someone" to prove. If we want to confine ourselves to a neutral ground prior to faith or prior to unbelief, then Kant's critique of the first three arguments must be heeded and our result would be the ambivalent position of Kant's antinomies of pure reason. It is there that he demonstrated that as soon as we leave the ground of faith or unfaith and argue about something beyond sense experience (e.g., God, immortality, etc.) we can "prove" both the pros and the cons of the argument with equal validity.

C. What God is like

When we address the question of what God is like, we again encounter an external way of talking about God through reason and an internal way of perceiving God in faith through his self-disclosure. Especially Søren Kierkegaard (1813–1855) underscored the difficulty of talking appropriately about God when he pointed out that there is an infinite qualitative difference between God and humanity. Karl Barth too cautioned us of this difficulty when he pondered:

> As ministers we ought to speak of God. We are human, however, and so cannot speak of God. We ought therefore to recognize both, our obligation and our inability *and by that very recognition give God the glory*. This is our perplexity. The rest of our task fades into insignificance in comparison.[29]

In their attempt to talk about God many philosophers and theologians have followed the path outlined by Pseudo-Dionysius (c. A.D. 500). He was a disciple of the neo-Platonic philosopher Plotinus but wrote under the pseudonym Dionysius the Areopagite, a convert of St. Paul in Athens, and consequently gained almost apostolic authority. In his treatise *The Divine Names* he outlined his methodology:

> Furthermore, we must ask how it is that we know God when He cannot be perceived by the mind or the senses and is not a particular Being. Perhaps 'tis true to say that we know not God by His Nature (for this is unknowable and beyond the reach of all Reason and Intuition), yet by means of that ordering of all things which (being as it were projected out of Him) possesses certain images and semblances of His Divine Exemplars, we mount upwards (so far as our feet can tread that ordered path), advancing through the Negation and Transcendence of all things and through a conception of a Universal Cause, towards That Which is beyond all things.[30]

Pseudo-Dionysius advocated here a threefold way to arrive at a notion of the likeness of God, the *via negativa*, or the negative way, the *via eminentiae*, or the superlative way, and the *via causalitatis*, or the way of causal inference. We attribute to God adjectives like infinite, immortal, incomprehensible according to the negative way by trying to negate attributes that are usually assigned to human beings, such as finite, mortal, and comprehensible. We confer upon God adjectives such as omnipotent, omniscient, or omnipresent according to the superlative way by attempting to surpass attributes that are usually associated with human beings, such as potency, knowledge, or presence. Finally God is referred to as the first uncaused cause or the creator of all things according to the way of causal inference. Even statements such as "God as the moral order of the world" (Kant) or "the holy" (Otto) or "the pure act" (scholasticism) are ultimately related to one of the three ways which Pseudo-Dionysius outlined.

Process thought, in its attempt to construct an intelligible idea of God, proceeds along similar lines. When Alfred North Whitehead (1861–1947) calls God the "eminently real" we are confronted with the *via eminentiae*.[31] And when Charles Hartshorne calls God "the unsurpassably interacting, loving, presiding genius, and companion of all existence," we detect features of the *via eminentiae*.[32] At the same time, however, we hear of the "fellow sufferer who understands," and notice that God is perceived almost as one of us, perhaps indicating that the process notion of God is not just a philosophical construct but has also gleaned from the Christian conviction that God has become human.

It is also important to note that the attributes of God are hardly ever described as direct descriptions of God. Their essentially symbolic character, however, does not mean that they have little value but that they participate in the reality of that for which they stand. Of course they are used as philosophical constructs, delineating certain qualities which should be met if God indeed did exist. That God is really this way, quite naturally, hinges on the premise that God is eminently real. Yet on strictly philosophical grounds the existence of God can be ascertained only as a distinct possibility and not as a necessity. This ambivalent situation does not change in favor of more certainty once we proceed to the question of what God is like.

There is, however, another avenue possible which allows for more certainty. Friedrich Schleiermacher alluded to it when he wrote: "*All attributes which we ascribe to God are to be taken as denoting not something special in God, but only something special in the manner in which the feeling of absolute dependence is to be related to Him.*"[33] God's attributes result from our attempt to express how we have experienced God's relationship to us. This means they are neither descriptive of God nor do they originate from human fantasy. If they are a true expression of our experience of God's relationship to us they disclose something of God. They are not descriptions of God's divine "essence" but of the way in which we encounter God. Since a true encounter always discloses something of the essence of that which is encountered, we can be confident that true attributes always disclose something of the divine essence to which they point.

It is, however, difficult to obtain such attributes apart from our encounter with God, i.e., apart from God's self-disclosure. Martin Luther pointed this out very dramatically when he said in his picturesque manner:

> It is therefore insane to argue about God and the divine nature without the word or any covering.... Whoever desires to be saved and to be safe when he deals with such great matters, let him simply hold to the form, the signs, and the coverings of the Godhead, such as His Word and His works. For in His Word and in His works He shows Himself to us.[34]

God's self-disclosive history is the avenue along which we can approach the so-called attributes of God.

1. The classical attributes of God

The so-called classical attributes of God, such as aseity, omnipresence, omniscience, omnipotence, and eternity, are philosophical concepts which are not mentioned in the Bible. This does not mean, however, that their content is missing in the biblical documents. We read, for instance, in the Bible that God created "the ends of the earth" (Isa. 40:28) and therewith the whole universe. This point can then lead to the assertion of God's eternity. Similarly, the Psalmist confesses, "Before the mountains were brought forth, or ever thou hadst formed the earth and the world, from everlasting to everlasting thou art God" (Ps. 90:2). He is before and after all time, and his "years have no end" (Ps. 102:27).

Since time is a measure of change and God does not age nor grow weary, God is not subject to change. God is, however, present in each moment of time without being confined to such a moment. Thus eternity also denotes eternal presence. As Immanuel Kant reminded us, time is a means by which we conceptualize objects. In order to define an object we need to use the categories of space and time. For example, we define a chair by saying that a certain chair is at a certain moment in a certain place. Since God, however, is no object, all time distinctions are meaningless concerning God. For him there is no sooner or later but only eternal presence. This caused the German historian Leopold von Ranke (1795–1886) to say that each time period is equidistant to eternity, i.e., to God. Everything is equally close to God and nothing is without God's presence. This leads to the assertion of God's omnipresence. The meaning of the concept of *omnipresence* is again expressed eloquently by the psalmist when he says:

Whither shall I go from thy Spirit? Or whither shall I flee from thy presence? If I ascend to heaven, thou are there! If I make my bed in Sheol, thou art there! If I take the wings of the morning and dwell in the uttermost parts of the sea, even there thy hand shall lead me, and thy right hand shall hold me (Ps. 139:7-10).

God is not confined in time and he is analogously omnipresent in space. He is everywhere and at the same time active and present. Since he is everywhere present, this omnipresence can easily lead to the assertion of a pantheistic God who is synonymous with everything and everyone. In his speech at the Areopagus Paul alluded to this by quoting popular Greek philosophy of his time saying, "in him [i.e. God] we live and move and have our being" (Acts 17:28). Yet he did not promote pantheism but rather proposed a panentheistic stance, in which everything is enclosed by God. When Martin Luther asserted that "nothing is so small, God is smaller, nothing is so big, God is bigger," he too wanted to escape from the dangerous road of pantheism and propose a specific personal presence of God, namely, the divine presence in the sacraments.[35] This assertion of a personal omnipresence excludes a deification of nature and people and allows for the possibility of grasping the divine through its own condescension in a specific object, i.e., the elements of the sacrament.

The affirmation of divine omnipresence leads to the affirmation of God's *omniscience*. Since God is omnipresent with regard to space and time, there is nothing hidden from him. Jesus expressed this conviction when he said in the Sermon on the Mount, "Your Father knows what you need before you ask him" (Matt 6:8). In a similar way we read in the Letter to the Hebrews, "And before him no creature is hidden, but all are open and laid bare to the eyes of him with whom we have to do" (Heb. 4:13). God's omniscience does away with the notion of events happening through an irrational fate. Yet it also seems to exclude human freedom, since God has foreknowledge of everything. If this foreknowledge were coupled with the idea of the divinely predestinating will, it would simply replace fate with God. To escape this consequence and still maintain God's ordering will, Gottfried Wilhelm Leibniz (1646–1716) suggested in his monadology that the whole world consists of blind monads (i.e., entities) which have different degrees of perception and which are all arranged in one grandiose and preestablished harmony. While this would allow for God's ordering activity, it bears the danger of a deistic concept of God. God could then be relegated to the role of an original world designer or a world mechanic who has long since receded into inactivity. Yet the above quote of Jesus from the Sermon on the Mount suggests an active God who interacts with his creation.

The notion of God's omniscience is most important in order to affirm God's creating and sustaining power. Nothing comes into being without God's knowledge and will, and nothing is sustained and preserved without them. Some things are beyond our knowledge but not beyond God's. Everything that is, has been, and will be is the outcome of God's will. These assertions, however, again touch on the issue of freedom, since an absolute determinism would turn God into a tyrant and humans into mere puppets. It is especially process thought that has attacked this kind of thinking and instead introduced the hyperbole of divine persuasion. Though this concept differs from biblical references to the ease with which God does his work, it rejects the idea that God is an impassionate onlooker or a merciless tyrant. We admit that nothing happens without God's knowledge and permission, but we cannot admit that everything happens according to God's desires. Yet such considerations dare not result in the admission of God's partial impotence or in his permitting or allowing evil things to happen, since this would imply God's complicity with evil.

The question of theodicy, how so much evil can occur in God's world if God is a benevolent force, cannot be answered to our satisfaction if we consider our present world alone. There is a certain degree of freedom within God's creation. Though God knows everything that happens and foreknows everything that will happen, God does not predetermine everything. God's predetermination is important only when we consider God's concern for the ultimate benefit of humanity, i.e., for salvation. While many things may and do indeed happen against God's desires, nothing can invalidate God's salvific plan. Everything will eventually participate in his redemptive activity. Yet we are at a loss to say why God does not change the plots of the wicked nor eliminate evil. We can only surmise that a life of automatic goodness would rob something of human freedom and also of the dangerous risks which such freedom involves.

At almost every point at which we recognize God's omniscience we implicitly acknowledge God's *omnipotence*. While the biblical witnesses are convinced that God can do whatever he pleases, there is no speculative interest in God's omnipotence. When it is asserted, it is to demonstrate that God can indeed follow through on his promises of salvation. For instance, when the disciples wondered who could be saved by living up to God's commandments, Jesus responded: "With men this is impossible, but with God all things are possible" (Matt. 19:26). Similarly, when Sarah questioned whether she could still give birth to the promised offspring she was asked, "Is anything too hard for the Lord?" (Gen. 18:14). Likewise, at the announcement of her pregnancy the angel confronted Mary with the assurance, "For with God nothing will be impossible" (Luke 1:37).

The facetious question as to whether God can create a stone so heavy that he cannot move it does not touch the reality of God. Omnipotence does not mean arbitrariness or license but the assurance that God will remain the one whom he promised to be. God's omnipotence assures us that we can trust his promises. This is also what Dietrich Bonhoeffer had in mind when he wrote from the Nazi prison, "God does not give us everything we want, but he does fulfil all his promises."[36] Omnipotence does not entail a theory which investigates how far-reaching God's power is but rather conveys the assurance that God's power is strong enough so that his words will not return empty.

In our deliberations on the attributes of God, we have frequently cited biblical references. This betrays a fundamental necessity. If we would attempt to arrive at these attributes by purely rational reflection, we would need external criteria by which to judge whether these attributes are corroborated by our experience of God. But if we deduce them from reflection on God's self-disclosure as attested by a peculiar tradition of faith, then the reference to historical experiences is already demonstrated and our primary task remains only to ask for the logical consistency of such attributes. Either way, we cannot divorce these attributes from the criterion of God's self-disclosure. Consequently, we attempted to illuminate them by referring to the Judeo-Christian tradition.

2. God as person

Valid and important as the classical attributes of aseity, eternity, omnipresence, omniscience, and omnipotence are, the main tenor of the biblical authors goes in a different direction. Since these authors witness to a God who is involved in history, the most important feature they stress is God's intensely personal nature. This immediately sets God apart from an impersonal fate or a primordial principle. It also assures the unity of God against any kind of polytheism and theistic or deistic pluralism. In early Hebrew history the reality of other gods was not disputed. But it was gradually realized that Yahweh was the only God and all other gods were at the most surrogates. Thus everything divine was centered in the one God who was experienced as an addressing and addressable God who was active in the whole world. Martin Buber rightly asserts:

> The description of God as a Person is indispensable for everyone who like myself means by God not a principle (although mystics like Eckhart sometimes identify him with "Being") and like myself means by "God" not an idea (although philosophers like Plato at times could hold that he was this): but who rather means by "God," as I do, him who—whatever else he may be—enters into direct relation with us men in creative, revealing and redeeming acts, and thus makes it possible for us to enter into a direct relation with him.[37]

When God encounters us as a Thou, we are encouraged to address God in like fashion as a person. Through our awareness of God as personal and as *the* person we become persons in the true sense and are encouraged to recognize other individuals as persons. While God is of intensely personal nature, it would be wrong to consider God as a person like other persons. God is rather *the* person from whom we receive our personal qualities. To some extent this is expressed when we talk about humans as religious beings. If the religious dimension is missing, that is, if there is no cognizant relationship with God, then something is also missing in our human dimension. To be a person means to be in some way or other related to *the* person, to God.

When we consider God as *the* person, any labels of gender characteristics or physical residency would only diminish such a notion. Each generation must express God's supreme personhood with the presently available conceptual tools. For instance, Israel did not deny certain man-like features to Yahweh. Yet the idea of Yahweh's sexual differentiation is not of interest, since Yahweh was vehemently opposed to any fertility cult. Similarly, as long as the temple in Jerusalem was the central sanctuary, Yahweh was understood to be present in his temple. At the same time we hear Solomon say, "But will God indeed dwell on the earth? Behold, heaven and the highest heaven cannot contain thee; how much less this house which I have built!" (1 Kings 8:27). In other words, God is not limited to a physical abode.

3. Compassion and holiness

When we ask what characterizes the personal nature of God, we are confronted with the polarity of compassion and holiness. God's compassion for his people is the pervasive theme of the whole Old Testament and God's compassion is the actual *raison d'etre* for the New Testament. The holiness of God mitigates against his compassion being understood as sentimentality or softheartedness. God is God and as such he is holy. We could further describe God's compassion with the terms love, faithfulness, and covenant. Only in a few cases are we told that God loves individuals (cf. 2 Sam. 12:24; Neh. 13:26). Usually, however, love denotes God's relationship to his people who are then enabled and encouraged to love God. In Deut. 7:9 we read, "Know therefore that the Lord your God is God, the faithful God who keeps covenant and steadfast love with those who love him and keep his commandments, to a thousand generations." This passage explains in a nutshell how God was experienced by the Israelites. God shows faithfulness to Israel by making a covenant with them. This love is not infatuation or sporadic but something one can trust. God's very mode of dealing with his people is free from capriciousness. What God is like is not described in terms of being but derives from a certain action.

When we read in Mic. 6:8, "He [Yahweh] has showed you, O man, what is good; and what does the Lord require of you but to do justice, and love steadfast love, and to walk humbly with your God?" (RSV alt.), we gather that these attributes of faithfulness and love have not originated in the human mind and been in turn projected upon God. Quite the opposite, they are derived from the way

God relates to humanity and become human possibilities through humanity modeling itself after God. But Israel can recognize from the trail of broken covenants, broken by Israel and renewed by God, that God's compassion also extends into the future. The people long for an "everlasting covenant" (Isa. 55:3). The Christians claim that this longing found its fulfillment when Jesus, the Messiah of God, established on God's behalf "the new covenant" with his blood (Mark 14:24). Since the Christian community understands itself in succession with God's chosen people, his compassion assumes a prominent place in the New Testament.

When we now quickly look at God's holiness, the other component which characterizes God's personal nature, we must first note that holiness is a basic concept of religion, closely related to *mana* and *tabu*. We notice that holiness in the Old Testament is occasionally understood in a way similar to these religious concepts. For instance, Uzzah had to die because he touched the ark, the place of God's presence, and had come in contact with the holy (2 Sam. 6:6f.). Yet the essential aspect of holiness in the biblical documents is that of power. It is power in the service of the God who uses all things to make his kingdom triumph. Unlike *tabu* it is no longer the prohibitive aspect of holiness which is decisive, but the aspect of communion which bestows life. When we hear of the Lord, "consecrate yourselves therefore, and be holy, for I am holy" (Lev. 11:44), we notice that the Israelites are encouraged to model themselves after God. Through his holiness God gathered and preserved Israel in the face of all other nations and inspired them to become a holy and God-dedicated nation.

Closely connected with holiness is God's righteousness. Again the punitive, distributive, and justificatory connotations recede to the background and the main emphasis is on conformity to a norm which manifests itself in a certain way of acting. Again we hear, "For the Lord is righteous, he loves righteous deeds; the upright shall behold his face" (Ps. 11:7). God is not a primordial tyrant, but recognizes the good and punishes wickedness.

In the New Testament this notion is continued when we hear of God's righteous judgment which will occur at the parousia of Christ (Acts 17:31) and of God's righteousness which guides the activity of the Christian community (2 Peter 1:1). Yet there is also a new moment in the New Testament understanding of righteousness, which is especially prominent in the Pauline writings. Righteousness is God's alone and we are taken up into God's righteousness and set in it. Righteousness is a conjunction of judgment and grace which God enjoys and demonstrates. Ultimately, it is a pardoning by which God draws us into a new life in his kingdom and which will be fully manifested at the last judgment (cf. Rom. 1:16f.). This means that righteousness that establishes fellowship with God is solely God's doing. It has been brought about through God's sovereign, gracious, and decisive intervention in Jesus the Christ (Rom. 3:25f.).

When we finally mention God's wrath, a close concomitant to God's holiness, we notice first the conviction that it is God's prerogative to show power and wrath, even if nothing has provoked it (cf. 2 Sam. 24:1). Yet soon Israel realized that God's wrath is not just a demonstration of power and sovereignty. God is a jealous God, we hear, and his wrath will be upon those who neglect his laws. Though the day of the Lord is a day of wrath which looms high over Israel, we hear the psalmist say, "For his anger is but for a moment, and his favor is for lifetime" (Ps. 30:5). It seems that God's wrath has as its ultimate goal not destruction and punishment but the success of his promises, the salvation of humanity. But even in the New Testament God's wrath is still to be feared, since "it is a fearful thing to fall into the hands of the living God" (Heb. 10:31). Yet for those who accept God's compassion as shown in Jesus Christ, the time of the wrath has passed away and something new has come. "In Christ God was reconciling the world to himself" (2 Cor. 5:19). The polarity of compassion and holiness is finally brought together as the ultimate redemptive event in Jesus Christ.

Our consideration of what God is like centered on God's disclosure in history. In talking about history we almost never ventured beyond the God-disclosive history presented in the Judeo-Christian tradition. Yet to stay within this boundary would be a severe shortcoming. It would not allow us to focus on an equally important facet of God's holiness, his universal creative and history-making activity.

5

CREATION

When we talk about creation, we cannot do so without referring to God's relation to the world and his governance of the created. In the 20th century any talk about creation would also be meaningless without at least recognizing the *scientific theories* of the origin of the universe. There are three main theories: (1) The theory of the cosmic egg, also called the big bang theory, starts with a primordial explosion of an immensely dense mass; (2) the theory of a hyperbolic or of a pulsating universe which entails the notion of a continuous expansion and subsequent contraction process; and (3) the steady state theory, now largely abandoned, which presented the notion of a continuous creation.

These theories have in common several decisive points: (1) They attempt to delineate the "prehistory" of our universe without mentioning God. This deliberate atheism in theory, which is characteristic and necessary for the modern scientific enterprise, must always be remembered lest it leads to an atheism in principle which would assume that the scientific enterprise provides the proof that God is nowhere present. As any mathematician or computer programmer knows, what has not been considered in the input cannot be expected as output. (2) Each theory starts with a given (mass, matter, or energy field) and proceeds from its starting point to delineate a possible development of our universe. (3) Although each of these theories contains a higher or lesser degree of plausibility, they are not facts. Since they concern themselves with something that is in principle removed from observation, the beginning and development of the universe, they will always remain theories.

Any conflict of these theories with the Christian faith in God the creator cannot stem from the Christian conviction that God created the world. It could not even stem from the insistence on a creation out of nothing, since this is not the object of scientific investigation. At most it would originate from a dispute about details, i.e., how the universe obtained its present shape.

Yet there is another, much more fundamental question: what difference does it make when we say that God created the world instead of saying that it evolved by itself through some kind of primordial big bang? In order to understand what the Christian belief in God the creator actually means, we must now delineate this belief.

A. God as creator

Like virtually all other religions, the Judeo-Christian tradition treasures stories of the creation of the world which connect the beginning of the world with its present state. But the first affirmation in the Judeo-Christian tradition is not that God created the world. The present arrangement in the Bible in which Chapters 1-11 of Genesis precede all other biblical documents is of rather late date. Even in the Apostles' Creed the first affirmation is the belief in "God the *Father* almighty," and then follows "creator of heaven and earth." The affirmation that God is someone who has a special relation to his people (as a father to his children) echoes the first and great conviction of the Israelite faith: Yahweh has a special relation to Israel. "He has freed us from the land of Egypt, from the house of bondage" (cf. Exod. 20:2; Deut. 5:6; 6:21; etc.).

God is primarily a God who acts in history. The belief in God the creator must then necessarily come in second place. Gerhard von Rad has pointed out very precisely that the doctrine of creation "has always been related to something else, and subordinated to the interests and content of the doctrine of redemption."[1] It is only in the wisdom literature of Israel where we encounter unequivocal, self-contained statements of the belief in creation. The point becomes clear when we consider Psalms 33; 74; 136; 148; etc. After rejoicing in God as the creator who spoke and it came to be, who commanded and it stood forth, the psalmist immediately connects this assertion with the confession of God's activity in history. "The Lord brings the council of the nations to nought; he frustrates the plans of the peoples. The council of the Lord stands forever, the thoughts of his heart to all generations. Blessed is the nation whose God is the Lord" (Ps. 33:10ff.).

The belief in God the creator is not, however, just a cosmic backdrop against which the soteriological pronouncements gain in persuasiveness. For instance, in wisdom literature we have seemingly self-contained statements of the belief in God the creator. Yet the "cosmic" orderliness witnesses to God's continual activity and reinforces the trustworthiness of God's promises. This means that God's creative and redemptive activity belong together and are to be seen in continuity with each other. The idea that as a result of the fouling of God's good creation somehow God was forced to change his plans is totally foreign to the biblical witnesses. God's activity, including its results, can never go so wrong that he would have to replace his creative activity through a redemptive rescue operation.

Next to the creation Psalms, 8; 19; and 104, and Job 38–42, the primary witness to God the creator is found in the first chapters of Genesis, specifically the priestly account in Genesis: 1:1—2:4a and the Yahwistic account in Genesis 2:4b-25. These two accounts hardly date back beyond the 7th or 8th century B.C. This relatively late date may not be surprising when we keep in mind that no religion prior to the period from 800 to 500 B.C. was more than a tribal religion. Only from that era on, which Karl Jaspers called the pivotal age of history, can we trace the emergence of universal religions beyond their original tribal forms. The growing awareness of the universality of God's activity at this time led to an expansion of the scope of history in two ways: history was pushed back to its earliest beginning at the point of creation (Gen. 1:1ff.) and was expanded to include all nations in God's salvific work (Isa. 2:2f.; 49:6). The insight that God created the world is not to be misunderstood as a hypothesis about a prime cause or a prime mover of the world. It is the corporate existential confession that the God who is presently at work in the world is none other than the one who brought the world into existence and who will bring it to completion.

When we briefly look at the *priestly account* of creation we are first puzzled that God's creative activity is described as taking place on six "days." Speculative minds have often attempted to determine just how long each of these days might have been. By connecting them with the genealogies which follow the creation accounts, many have attempted to calculate how many years have lapsed since the creation of the world. Yet such endeavors miss the point of the narrative. It was not written with the purpose of providing a scientific chronology in the modern sense of the word. Even the attempt to harmonize Genesis 1 and 2 with scientific theories of the emergence of the universe misses the message of these narratives. They do not primarily seek to explain how our world began. When we find, especially in the priestly account, remarkable similarity to the evolutionary sequence of which science tells us today, we are rightly amazed about the insights people possessed millennia ago. But such affinities would hardly tell us anything about the truthfulness of the theological message contained in these accounts.

Even the idea that the seven days of creation foreshadow a six-day workweek with the seventh day as Sabbath somehow misses the thrust of the narrative. Certainly, the introduction of a day of rest for God appears to be a justification for instituting the Sabbath. That may indeed have been implied. But the mention of specific days in the priestly creation account and the connecting of these through genealogies with our present history seeks first of all to show that these events are no longer part of the timeless mythological context from which much of the imagery was borrowed. The biblical creation accounts are no longer stories about gods, such as the Babylonian creation myth, *Enuma elish*. Genesis 1–2 tells us that God's creative activity in the beginning did not take place in some kind of prehistory or suprahistory. God's creative activity made history possible, and at the same time is part of the historical process.

Since the priestly creation account contains several other decisive differences from the Babylonian creation myth, we might not be wrong in assuming that it was composed in polemical contradistinction to that myth. This would not be surprising given its probable age, approximately the time of the Babylonian exile (c. 6th century B.C.). In the exile the Israelites had lost their homeland and were confronted both with a culture much more advanced than theirs and with splendid religious cults. In this environment the Israelites rightly wondered whether their faith in Yahweh still had any validity. It was important for them to hear that their God was even in this foreign land, as Ezekiel's vision disclosed (Ezekiel 1).

In contradistinction to the Babylonian gods the priestly account declared the Israelite God to be the creator of the whole universe. We can see this apologetic tendency in many places, among them: (1) The deep (*tehom*) over which the spirit of God hovers resembles the mythological chaos-dragon, Tiamat. But, the priestly writer declares that *tehom* has no power of its own. There is no power struggle between two cosmic principles, God and the deep. *Tehom* is only mentioned because the creative will of God is above it. (2) Similarly, there is no need for the God of Israel to engage in a struggle in order to carry out his creative work. God speaks and so it is. God's mighty words suffice. Only God can create. The word *bara* used to denote God's creative activity has no analogy in the works of humanity. God creates the world with extreme ease. (3) In an almost ironic way we hear that "God called the light Day and the darkness he called Night" (Gen. 1:5). After separating light from the threatening darkness he gives each its proper name. By naming them he puts them under his authority. The same course is followed with the heavens, the earth, and the sea. When we come to the sun, the moon, and the stars the procedure is somewhat different. God simply made them and told the sun and moon to rule over day and night respectively. Remembering the elevated status which the heavens, earth, sea, light, darkness, and the celestial elements enjoyed in neighboring religions we understand how revolutionary these statements were. The elements of nature were robbed of their divine power and the Israelites emphasized that the heavens, the earth, and all that is within them were only creations of their God.

God's creative acts are accompanied with the statement "and God saw that it was good" (Gen. 1:4, 10, 12, 18, 21, 25). At the conclusion the assertion is given that everything God had made was *very* good (Gen. 1:31). It is also mentioned that God finished the work he had started. There is no unfinished business, nothing that somehow by accident was left undone. The affirmation of the world as "very good" means that the creation is endowed with God's approval. It is God's good world.

When we now take a brief look at the preexilic *Yahwistic creation account*, we notice a different way of describing God's activity. In the priestly account it seemed that God created one level after another until finally humanity was created as the pinnacle of creation. In the Yahwistic account God's creative activity seems to occur in concentric circles. It is again asserted that God created the earth and the heavens. But only the more immediate environment receives more extensive attention. In place of the cosmic vision of the priestly writer, the Yahwist's approach is much more limited to the earth. Instead of the threatening waters of sea we are introduced here to the waterless desert in which nothing will grow until God gives the life-enabling rain. But this approach is as important as the one in the priestly account. The Yahwist represents the view of a people who can say: "Look around you; God has made all this just for you."

We have omitted so far one important theological question, the issue of a *creation out of nothing* (*creatio ex nihilo*). It is implied by the opening line in the priestly account where it states, "In the beginning God created the heavens and the earth" (Gen. 1:1). It is here not explicitly stated that God started without anything when he began to create the world. We might also speculate why God had first created a formless, watery, abysmal, and nocturnal chaos before he created day and night, and the heavens and the earth. Of course the *tehom* (chaos) could be interpreted here as something which God used to create the world. But it could also be argued that the *tehom* is no self-subsisting entity. It too owes its existence to God. We obtain help in solving the issue of creation out of nothing when we consider the conceptual horizon of the priestly writer. At that time the idea of a state in which one thing was not clearly distinguishable from another, such as in chaos, was considered as not yet having been created. In order to assert that God created out of nothing the priestly writer claimed tht God created out of chaos. A similar mode of thought occurs in the Yahwistic account. There the dry, barren ground is a parallel to the chaos of Genesis 1. For us today chaos already represents something, though in a disordered state. Therefore we have trouble understanding the exact intention of this ancient text. Yet the message should be clear. God created without any given, without any precondition. There is nothing which is not intentionally created by God. Thus any accidental by-products of creation are excluded. The creation accounts are thus a confession of the unity of God. There are no other givens besides God. Everything that is owes its existence to God. This has also important implications for God's relationship to the world.

B. God's relationship to the world.

God's relationship to the world has become more and more elusive even for those who have previously taken God for granted. This homelessness of God is not only due to the relatively recent shift from a geocentric worldview to a heliocentric one. It is also furthered by our ever-increasing assertion of autonomy. As life and nature become more and more calculable, God becomes more and more a fringe phenomenon.

1. Defining the undefinable

There are two main lines of thought which have historically evolved to define God's relationship to the universe, namely, pantheism and deism or theism. While deism or theism attained prominence in the 17th and 18th centuries, pantheism is historically older and was known to the pre-Socratic philosophers, such as Xenophanes, as well as to the Upanishad texts of ancient India. This kind of pantheism seems to have arisen as a critique of the polytheism prevailing at that time, emphasizing the one in the many. Western pantheism, however, reacting against a monarchial notion of one supreme being, seems to emphasize the opposite, namely, the assertion of the manifold presence of the same God. Representatives of this kind of thinking are Giordano Bruno, Baruch Spinoza, and Georg Wilhelm Friedrich Hegel.

a. The pantheistic approach: Giordano Bruno (1548–1600) radicalized Copernicus' idea of a heliocentric worldview to such an extent that for him all points of orientation vanished. He did not want to identify the finite world with God nor did he want to draw a strict distinction between the two. He concluded that God is

> completely infinite because he can be associated with no boundary and his every attribute is one and infinite. And I say that God is all-comprehensive infinity because the whole of him pervadeth the whole world and every part therof comprehensively and to infinity.

That is unlike the infinity of the universe, which is comprehensively in the whole but not comprehensively in those parts which we can distinguish within the whole.[2]

While God remains the interpretive and sustaining power of the universe, it is difficult to locate such a universal God and receive guidance from him. But then Bruno found other surrogates for God, for instance, when he mentioned that "our earth, the divine mother, who has given birth to us, doth nourish us and moreover will receive us back."[3] Once the reference to a personal transcendent God has been lost, the need arises to locate this God in a more immanent fashion. While the Roman Catholic church deemed Bruno's thoughts dangerous enough to burn him at the stake in 1600, his ideas could not be that easily extinguished. Pantheistic ideas were promoted throughout the centuries up to the present. We could cite here the mystic Jacob Boehme, a close contemporary of Bruno, or John Toland, who first used the term "pantheist" in 1705 in his *Socinianism Truly Stated*, or Arthur Schopenhauer in the 19th century, influenced as he was by Eastern thought.

The Dutch philosopher Baruch Spinoza (1632–1677) did not cite Bruno directly but seems to have been familiar with his central ideas. Spinoza in turn influenced such thinkers as Goethe, Lessing, and Schleiermacher. The problematic nature of Spinoza's attempt to relate God and creation derives from his overarching concept of substance. In *Deus sive natura* (God or the World) he made clear that there was only one substance and not a multiplicity thereof. But then he distinguished in nature between *natura naturans* (active nature) and *natura naturata* (nature as a passive product). Since he considered God as creative and self-sustaining, he could distinguish between created nature and God as its imminent cause. Spinoza stated that the modes or creations "have been from all eternity, and to all eternity will remain immutable. A work truly as great as becomes the greatness of the workmaster."[4] With such an assertion it is easy to wonder to what extent God is still involved in the creative process. Since God is no longer the overarching principle but nature itself, Spinoza must resort to nature's innate principles to account for creation, sustenance, and direction.

Do nature's own possibilities suffice to account for the difference between being and nothingness and between void and creation? It is necessary to be concerned that God is not divorced from creation. We should not go to the extreme of collapsing the distinction between the two. The result might easily become an atheistic materialism, although Spinoza would never admit to it in his own system.

The most prominent representative of pantheistic thought, albeit of a very different and much more promising kind, is Georg Wilhelm Friedrich Hegel (1770–1831). Hegel wanted to witness to the living God in his philosophical system because he was convinced that the whole universe stems from and witnesses to the living God. To accomplish his task Hegel drew philosophy and religion closely together. For him God is the absolute Spirit which permeates art, religion, and philosophy. In these three forms the absolute Spirit attains its true nature. The absolute Spirit must be distinguished from the subjective spirit in individual human beings and the objective spirit of the human community. The absolute Spirit is the eternal, in itself same Spirit that becomes another and recognizes the other as itself.

Through the dialectic movement of the Spirit Hegel found it easy to assert that the world is created. The Spirit "becomes an other to itself: it enters existence. . . .It creates a World."[5] For Hegel the creation of the world is not something accidental or arbitrary, something that might or might not be. Creation pertains necessarily to the concept of God as absolute Spirit, since it is a part of God's true infinity to posit a finite world. This dialectic process excluded the possibility of the creation of the world from some kind of primordial matter. The absolute Spirit demands that apart from God there is no eternal, self-subsisting matter, not even a chaos. God creates the world out of nothing. As God posits the world over himself as another, he wills a finite world. The world has no independent existence apart from God's creative activity and must be continually posited by God.

Unlike Spinoza, Hegel did not dissolve God into nature, and unlike panentheists he also did not dissolve nature into God. Yet in his universal metaphysical system the whole universe becomes a justification for God and vice versa. Contrary to Kant's emphatic claim that for reason God is at the most a logical possibility and a moral necessity, in Hegel God again becomes a logical necessity. If there is God, there must a world and vice versa, since both are indissolubly related. Hegel's approach is deeply informed and shaped by biblical insights. But he failed to take sufficient notice of them on two accounts. He did not clearly enough indicate that the world is fallen and, secondly, he did not realize that there was no necessity for God to create the world. Both omissions increased the divine character of the world and tended to obliterate the distinction between the creator and the created. As a result, many of his less biblically interested followers again collapsed God and the world and advocated atheistic materialism. For Hegel, as for pantheism in general, the gravest danger stems from the highest achievement, the close relation between God and the world. Perhaps Schopenhauer was right, when he once quipped, "Pantheism is only a euphemism for atheism."[6]

(b) Between theism and deism: Theism, the other prominent possibility of relating God and the world, clearly distinguishes between God and world. Theism as a historically evolved term developed in gradual opposition to deism and pantheism. At first deism and theism were used almost synonymously. But they drifted farther and farther apart until theism was most attached to orthodox talk about God and deism acquired a connotation of religious unorthodoxy. Theism usually stands for the belief in a personal God who is beyond and above the world, a God who has created the world out of nothing and preserves and governs it. Often characteristic of theism is the belief in a personal God who is seen in radical contradistinction to the world but who is creatively and preservingly active in it. Judged by this preliminary definition many, if not most, Western philosophers and theologians could be classified as theists. Yet we want to mention only those who most significantly advanced a theistic understanding of the relationship between God and the world.

In his treatise *The True Intellectual System of the Universe* (1678) Ralph Cudworth (1617–1688) uses the term "theism" for the first time in European history of thought. Though leaning heavily on René Descartes, he rejects Descartes' mechanistic theism and his skepticism about our ability to discern God's purpose in nature. For Cudworth there is also no dichotomy between the spiritual and the material worlds, because God, as the eternal divine spirit, endows all being in all its gradations with living harmony and order.

Reality allows for discerning the presence of its spiritual basis. The spiritual basis comes from God and points towards him who manifests himself as the living and present one. Cudworth's *System* was soon recognized as the standard text for the refutation of materialism and atheism. The harmonious relationship between God and world which Cudworth assumed to be discernible in the world led him to believe in a harmony between reason, religion, and revelation. But this harmony was largely based on reason which, as Martin Luther cautioned long before, is a whore and can go in whichever direction it is led. As reason became more and more autonomous, the relationship between revelation, reason, and religion soon crumbled. This can already be seen in Anthony Ashley Cooper, third earl of Shaftesbury.

Anthony, third earl of Shaftesbury (1671-1713), defended the apologetic method of Cudworth and praised him for depicting the position of the atheists with their own arguments before he refuted them. But the earl had no real place for revelation in his own system. Reason suffices to discern God as the creative genius in nature. Even the distinction between God and nature is not always clearly maintained since "God has created Nature and has endowed her with creative powers so that she might carry on the work of providence."[7] But once our understanding of the relationship between God and nature is no longer informed by divine revelation and we assume that nature carries on God's work of providence on its own, God is bound to be relegated to an increasingly inactive status. Thus the transition from theism to deism is a fluid one, as Immanuel Kant pointedly noted when he said, "The *deist* believes in a God, the *theist* in a *living God*."[8]

When we look at François Marie Arouet, commonly called Voltaire (1694-1778), who was deeply influenced by English deism and Newtonian mechanics during his three years of exile in England (1726-1729), we notice that the world has come of age. In Voltaire God is divorced from the world. God is relegated to inactivity and regarded as the "primordial and final cause of all."[9] Once God is pushed away from the world, then, in contrast to biblical understanding, the only task remaining for God is the creation in the beginning. God is no longer involved in the ongoing process of guidance and sustenance. In this view the world will sooner or later lose its sense of purpose and direction unless it can find it from within.

Yet within the world only finitude and relativity can be encountered. We are confronted then with a plurality of purposes and directions all claiming for allegiance in the marketplace of values. But they all bear the mark of penultimacy and therefore of arbitrariness. This is the situation, once we confront modernity.

To bring God back into the world, process thought advocates a "theism of the second type."[10] God should not be conceived of as a primordial tyrant at whose fiat everything occurs. In God's primordial nature lies "the unlimited conceptual realization of the absolute wealth of potentiality"[11] and in his consequent nature God "shares with every new creation its actual world."[12] Both God and the world are instruments of novelty for each other.

> What is done in the world is transformed into a reality in heaven, and the reality in heaven passes back into the world. By reason of this reciprocal relation, the love in the world passes into the love in heaven, and floods back into the world. In this sense God is the great companion—the fellow-sufferer who understands.[13]

Charles Hartshorne built upon these insights of his former teacher Alfred North Whitehead, and conceded that this God is not indeed the entire actual God whom we meet in worship. Yet it is a sufficient concept to understand how God and the world are related and interact with each other. Hartshorne claims that the ultimate ideal of knowledge and of action remains this:

> To deal with the world as the body of a God of love, whose generosity of interest is equal to our contrasts, however gigantic, between mind and mind, and to whom all individuals are numbered, each with its own life history and each with its own qualitative—enjoying and suffering, more or less elaborately remembering and anticipating, sensing and spontaneously reacting—natures.[14]

To talk about God not as absolutely infinite, but to conceive of God with process thought as one who is in some respects finite, is a genuine biblical insight, because God's self-limitation enables his self-disclosure. He has to become finite in order to mediate himself to humans who have a finite conceptuality. The concern for divine compassion is also a genuinely Judeo-Christian insight. Process thought is thus superior to classical theism, traditional deism, and popular pantheism in its attempt effectively to relate God and the world. God is not "the transcendental snob," nor is he distant from the world nor synonymous with it. The deficiency of process thought, however, comes from its tendency toward pantheism. When the world becomes "the body of a God of love" (Hartshorne) and when creation out of nothing is rejected, we are confronted with a God who strongly resembles Einstein's view of the universe. He is finite, though in itself infinite. Such a God, however, cannot give the world a genuinely new turn but can only rearrange its given ways in ever-novel turns. Charles Hartshorne may have unintentionally given us a clue as to why even the process approach must be insufficient when he conceded that process thought does not portray the entire actual God whom we meet in worship. We remember that in the Judeo-Christian tradition God the creator cannot be separated from the God of history. Perhaps God's relationship to creation simply cannot be satisfactorily treated without considering God's activity in history.

2. God as the maker of history

Characteristic for Israel's understanding of God's activity in history is the introduction of the Decalogue. We read in Exod. 20:2: "I am the Lord your God, who brought you out of the land of Egypt, out of the house of bondage." These mighty deeds in history are constitutive for Israel's faith in Yahweh. These deeds are recalled when the farmer brings his gifts to the sanctuary (Deut. 26:5-11) and they are mentioned when the father initiates his son in the meaning of the Commandments (Deut. 6:20ff.). Even the prophet Ezekiel reminds the Israelites that they came from Egypt and that there they became God's people (Ezek. 20:5). When the Israelites remember these events, they assure themselves of the continued presence of the mighty God who made events such as the exodus possible. Israel does not trust in history but in the God who makes history possible. The emphasis on God as the maker of history becomes especially evident in the creed of Deut. 26:5-9. Here the main events of the salvation history are recapitulated, beginning with the time of the patriarchs and concluding with the conquest of the promised land:

> A wandering Aramean was my father; and he went down into Egypt and sojourned there, few in number; and there he became a nation,

great, mighty, and populous. And the Egyptians treated us harshly, and afflicted us, and laid upon us hard bondage. Then we cried to the Lord the God of our fathers, and the Lord heard our voice, and saw our affliction, our toil, and our oppression; and the Lord brought us out of Egypt with a mighty hand and an outstretched arm, with great terror, with signs and wonders; and he brought us into this place and gave us this land, a land flowing with milk and honey.

Though the passage cited does not just contain objective facts, we nevertheless notice a close concentration on objective facts. The general outline of Israel's history is perceived in the light of God's actions. In other words, the biblical events in this creed and in most other parts of the Old Testament are a concentration and sometimes even distillation of historical events, events that are at the same time interpreted as God's action.

The Old Testament presents the course of history as a kind of salvation history. The continual and progressive reinterpretation of the traditions of Israel are necessitated through ever new historical occurrences which are in turn incorporated as part of that tradition. This means that the older promises are never abandoned or superseded by the actual progression of history but are incorporated into it in a fulfilled, modified, and expanded way. The tension between promise and fulfillment was not overcome by the simple advance of Israel's history but was strongly creative of Israel's historical self-understanding.

Israel's perception of salvation history was not only expanded toward the future, it was also expanded into transnational and transhuman terms. The prophets already understood other nations to be included in God's plan for Israel and vice versa (cf. Isa. 2:2-4; Amos 1:6-8; etc.). Especially in apocalyptic literature it was not just the world of individuals and nations but the whole cosmos that was understood to be involved in God's salvation history. This historicizing of the whole cosmos in terms of a universal salvation history is of tremendous importance for theology. Jürgen Moltmann rightly pointed out that without apocalyptic Israelite salvation history would have been "bogged down in the ethnic history of men or the existential history of the individual."[15] Having started with the patriarchs, God's salvation history eventually included all Israel and all nations. All of history was understood as the working out of God's purposes or simply as salvation history.

It is difficult to decide whether this perspective of a universal salvation history was continued in the New Testament. Only a few passages in Luke-Acts and some brief references in the Epistles imply a cosmic dimension of salvation. In most cases, however, we are confronted with the history of just one person, Jesus of Nazareth, and not with the history of a people or of a community. But the early Christian community perceived the history of Jesus to be intimately connected with the history of God with his people. For instance, the Letter to the Hebrews opens with the telling words, "In many and various ways God spoke of old to our fathers by the prophets; but in these last days he has spoken to us by a Son" (Heb. 1:1f.).

The history of Jesus, however, is not simply a continuation of the history of God with his people. It is the history of the "last days." This is underscored by Paul when he says that God sent his Son "when the time had fully come" (Gal. 4:4). Rudolf Bultmann captured this new situation very appropriately when he observed that the emerging church

> understood Jesus as the one whom God by the resurrection has made Messiah, and that they awaited him as the coming Son of Man. For it is apparent that in that very fact they understood his sending as God's decisive act. In expecting him as the Coming One they understood themselves as the Congregation of the end of days called by him. For them factually—no matter to what degree it may have been clearly conscious—the old had passed away and the world had become new.[16]

History and salvation history have reached their goal and thereby "history is swallowed up in eschatology."[17] Does this mean a return to the earlier Israelite understanding of God's history which considered only God's particular history with his people while it ignored the larger historical context?

3. *The tension between history and salvation history*

Bultmann makes a strict distinction if not separation between history and salvation history. He asserts that contrary to New Testament expectations "history did not come to an end, and, as every schoolboy knows, it will continue to run its course."[18] Yet Bultmann suggests that especially Paul and the Gospel of John did not expect the eschatological event as a dramatic cosmic catastrophe but as happening within history, "beginning with the appearance of Jesus Christ and in continuity with this occurring again and again in history, but not as the kind of historical development which can be confirmed by any historian."[19] Consequently, the meaning and future development of history becomes secondary for a Christian. Decisive is the confrontation with the eschatological event, Jesus Christ, in the proclamation of the church. This proclamation demands a decision from us and enables us to understand ourselves as free from the world and its historical process while still a part of this process.

Many of Bultmann's students share his strictly dialetic view of history. Other theologians, however, are more reluctant in divorcing God's saving event from history. Karl Barth, for instance, claims in his *Church Dogmatics* that "the history of salvation is *the* history" which encloses all other history and to which in some way all other history belongs as its illustration and reflection.[20] Barth understands salvation history as "the nexus of the particular speech and action of God for the reconciliation of the world with Himself which at its center and climax is the history of Jesus Christ."[21]

Oscar Cullmann, too, emphasized the importance of salvation history for our understanding of history in general. According to Cullmann the coming of Jesus is the midpoint of history: the whole New Testament holds the view that the midpoint of time lies no longer in the future but in the past. In the light of the Christ event as the midpoint of history the whole Old Testament history is seen as a preparatory history moving toward this midpoint. This view is especially dominant in the Gospel according to Matthew in which Jesus is depicted fulfilling a multitude of Old Testament promises and bearing a large number of Old Testament messianic titles. The history of salvation after this midpoint is described in the New Testament as an unfolding of the Christ event. The first Christian community regarded the Christ event together with its New Testament interpretation as the revelation of the divine plan according to which salvation history will continue to develop up to the end.

Cullmann is aware that secular historians would not describe the history of Israel, including the emergence of Christianity, as salvation history but as interwoven with the histories of other peoples. However, Cullmann claims that salvation history rests on "the *di-*

vine selection of events within the whole of history."[22] It forms a very narrow line which continues on "for the salvation of all mankind, leading ultimately to a funneling of all history into this line, in other words, a merging of secular history with salvation history."[23] Since all history finally merges into salvation history, Cullmann would find it exciting to show the hidden ways in which, in the light of the biblical revelation, the preparation for salvation was made in the history of the Gentiles and their religions. But Cullmann refrains from attempting a historical proof of the factuality of salvation history, knowing that the events of salvation history are experienced as divine revelation in such a way that they can be perceived and fully interpreted as *God's* actions only through faith. With this concession, Cullmann admits that salvation history does not consist of pure historical facts but of an interpretation based upon these facts which is attributed to God's self-disclosure.

Wolfhart Pannenberg is dissatisfied with an approach that connects God's saving activity with historical occurrences but which ultimately also requires God's faith-empowering action to make us aware of God's self-disclosure contained in them. Pannenberg does not want to distinguish between a special salvation history and the rest of history because "God's redemptive deed took place within the universal correlative connections of human history and not in a ghetto of redemptive history."[24] Consequently, Pannenberg postulates, "In contradistinction to special appearances of the Godhead, revelation in history is open to everyone. It has universal character."[25] The Holy Spirit and faith are not necessary to recognize God's self-disclosure in the events attested to in the Bible. These events have convincing power when perceived in their historical context because they speak the language of facts, and God's self-disclosure is in that language.

Pannenberg, is however, also aware that mere acknowledgment of history is not enough. History, and this means especially the history of Jesus, must be grasped as an event that has bearing on one's existence. "*Mere* historical faith, which is satisfied with the establishment that the event happened and does not allow itself to be grasped by this event, thus has precisely not understood aright the inherent meaning of this history, but has diminished it."[26] Yet Pannenberg realizes that not everyone accepts the Christ event as something that touches one's own existence. Thus an illumination is necessary for someone to apprehend psychologically the significance of the Christ event.

Pannenberg has convincingly elaborated the dynamic thrust of the Christ event. He has also pointed out that to recover the meaning of the Christ event one has to perceive it in its historical context, i.e., Jewish apocalyptic. Yet we need more than a rational proof if we are to recognize that this part of history, starting with ancient Israel and culminating in the Christ event, is not just a piece of Near Eastern history but instead the history from which all other history receives its illumination, direction, and judgment. Notwithstanding his immense effort to show the intelligibility of this history, Pannenberg has to concede that we need illumination to accept this history's decisiveness for our own future. Ultimately, it is God's own doing that opens our eyes to perceive the significance of this little piece of history called salvation history for the understanding of all other history, including our own.

In mentioning that salvation history, culminating in the Christ event, illuminates, directs, and judges all other history, we do not want to convey the impression that only salvation history is wrought by God. All history is God's history, while salvation history is like a red thread which guides us on our way through history. When God is introduced as the one for whom nothing is impossible and who determines the course of history, we are not confronted with a God who runs the whole of world history according to his preconceived plan, but we are confronted with a God who will bring his plan of salvation to completion (Gen. 18:14 and Luke 1:37). The mighty acts of God serve as a constant reminder that God is at work in the whole world for the penultimate and ultimate benefit of humanity. They show us that God's plan of salvation will eventually prevail even over the most adverse obstructions.

How, then is God related to the world? We have seen that the deistic inactive mode is no satisfying model. Neither is the pantheistic identification of God with the world. Even the Christian positioning of God over against the world as its governing agent leaves much to be desired, especially if such involvement should be made rationally self-evident. Perhaps the spatial model of correlation which these concepts imply is inadequate, for the simple reason that in the Judeo-Christian tradition God is primarily conceived of as the Lord of history. Yet it would be wrong simply to abandon a spatial model in favor of the historical or chronological one (e.g., if we would speak of the God ahead of us instead of the God above us). If God is indeed the originator of our space-time continuum, he cannot be *described* with the categories he created. God can only be related to them as the one who is superior to them. This superiority includes both that God is not part of the structures he created and that he is able to work within them. The working within them shows itself both in God's involvement in history as his plan of salvation is advanced, and in the process of divine providence, as stability is expressed and dangerous situations are conquered.

C. God's providential activity

God's providence expresses itself primarily in two ways: in a general way in nature, morals, and history, and in a special way in miracles.

1. Trustworthiness through general providence

Being faced with an inhuman world dictated by the impersonal printout of a computer screen and perceiving themselves as "mere technological necessities," more and more people ask themselves today: Does anybody care? Similarly in a time when even experts are hard pressed to tell us with assurance what the future has in store and in a time in which more and more dark and threatening clouds appear on the horizon, the question naturally emerges: Is there any meaningful future ahead of us? Keeping in mind that God is the Lord of history, we will not fall into the trap of becoming fatalists who resign ourselves to whatever will come, hoping in Stoic modesty to be able to find an ecological niche in which we can live relatively unhampered by the inescapable consequences of fate. We will also not fall prey to astrological attempts to rescue the future through observing the stellar constellations or manipulating lucky numbers, amulets, or magic rites. While these items play an important role in the lives of many, we are convinced that God alone has ultimate control of the future.

(a) Order in nature: When we turn to God's general providence we are first confronted with God's work in the processes of inanimate and animate nature. This kind of providence is envisioned in

God's covenant with Noah when God assured him, "While the earth remains, seedtime and harvest, cold and heat, summer and winter, day and night, shall not cease" (Gen. 8:22). Through the orders of preservation God maintains nature and provides stability and predictability. The Old Testament understanding of *ruah* (spirit) serves to illustrate these sustaining and maintaining processes. When God gives his Spirit, something becomes alive and it lives as long as God leaves his Spirit with it. But when he takes back his Spirit, the living creature is destined to perish. Thus the Old Testament people cry to Yahweh, "Cast me not away from thy presence, and take not thy holy Spirit from me" (Ps. 51:11).

When God is perceived as being behind all events and is ascertained as the one without whom nothing can occur, then this excludes the idea that God is responsible only for good things, while Satan or some anti-Godly power is responsible for adverse events. The biblical writers asserted that though there are adverse powers at work in the world, ultimately it is God who is behind everything. There is a certain degree of openness in history and in nature which can result in what we call good or bad and which can lead to a devastating earthquake or a fatal heart attack, as well as to a beautiful sunset. These bewildering areas of freedom cannot and do not impede God's overarching rule which will ultimately make his kingdom triumph. We could question whether it is not a capricious or careless God who allows for such openness. Yet the alternative would be the automatic goodness of puppets which would rob humanity of its responsibility and creativity.

Our lives are safeguarded by several kinds of dependabilities which allow for orderly development and long-range planning: (1) One is represented in the cycles of day and night and of the seasons. They are a basic factor in the development of life on earth and, to our knowledge, they are completely reliable and dependable. Though the laws of nature which they depict are never 100% foolproof, the probability for alternative natural occurrences is virtually zero. (2) A different form of dependability arises in the realm of biological, chemical, and physical processes. We encounter this, for instance, in chemical and nuclear reactions or in cellular functions. Without the dependability of these powers there would be no life on earth and no human history. But the biblical witnesses remind us that God provides this kind of dependability. Jesus tells his disciples that no sparrow falls to the ground without God's permission, and that all their hairs on their head are numbered (Matt. 10:29f.). (3) There is still a third kind of dependability which we encounter primarily in the evolutionary process of the universe and of life itself.

As far as the first two kinds of dependabilities are concerned and the structure of things they involve, the universe could have gone in many other directions. But once the initial steps were taken all other possibilities were gone and lost forever. The whole evolutionary process, especially the development and sustenance of life on earth, is so uncalled-for that the American vertebrate paleontologist George G. Simpson claimed, "There is no automatism that will carry [humankind] upward without choice or effort and there is no trend solely in the right direction. Evolution has no purpose."[27] The evolutionary process is not proceeding along predetermined lines. But once certain choices are made, certain steps are necessitated. Thus Jacques Monod could rightly talk of chance and necessity. We are confronted here with a kind of dependability that on the one hand tells us that the evolutionary process is ongoing and therefore dependable. But at the same time it is open and undetermined. This openness does not mean that we could bend the process according to our own desires. Though we interfere with the evolutionary process by the very fact of being involved in it, we are also subject to the process. For instance, we are caught by surprise when "nature" reacts to the way we treat it.

With regard to the third kind of dependability we also discern a peculiar kind of divine involvement. First we hear in the creation account that God spoke and it was so (Gen. 1:6f. *et al.*). Then we are told that humanity is commanded to assume a certain responsibility within the created order (Gen.1:28). Finally we hear that God takes protective care of humanity by making for Adam and his wife garments of skins and clothing them (Gen. 3:21). These passages indicate neither that the originally created order itself nor humanity's role within these processes suffices to insure humanity's survival. God also has to abide with his creation. Martin Luther expressed this in a very picturesque way when he said: God "has not created the world like a carpenter builds a house and then leaves it and lets it be the way it is, but he stays with it and sustains it the way he has made it, otherwise it would not remain."[28] God is with his whole creation, guiding and sustaining it.

(b) Moral norms: God's providential activity becomes especially prominent in the moral process. While in the natural process of inanimate and animate nature the aspect of God's continuous creation is dominant, in the moral process God's preserving action rules supreme. We have seen that God guides and maintains his creation. In a similar way he endows humanity with moral orders by which it can proceed and which may aid it in finding its proper place within creation.

The moral process is frequently aided by the human conscience. While people often appeal to the conscience, this court of appeal differs considerably among humans, depending on the extent and way the underlying moral norms are perceived. The moral norms have often been equated with the so-called natural law. While the laws of nature are expressive of the dependability in inanimate and animate nature, the natural law witnesses to the dependability of moral norms. In recent years the so-called natural law has been called more and more into question, especially because it was understood as something unalterably given. Since John Locke, however, more and more people have joined the empiricist camp and conceived of human nature as a *tabula rasa* which acquires its norms through sense perception. Only lately, since ethological research has pointed out that human moral behavior is not as unspecified as one might believe, has opinion changed. Arnold W. Ravin expressed this very well when he said:

> Every culture has a concept of murder, that is a specification of conditions under which homicide is unjustifiable. Every culture has a taboo upon incest and usually other regulations upon sexual behavior. Similarly, all cultures hold untruth to be abhorrent, at least under most conditions. Finally, all have a notion of reciprocal obligations between parents and their children. These universal or near-universal ethics . . . do indicate some profound and fundamental needs in all men to behave within certain limits of ethical boundaries.[29]

To be a human being means to act according to certain norms which enable us to live together and further our own species.

The explicit form which these norms assume, however, depends on the environment in which the social behavior takes place. If these forms are not developed in accordance with the changes we encounter and inaugurate, we will become victims of our environmental conditions instead of guiding ourselves through the use of these norms. For instance, unless we realize that the right of a United States citizen to possess all kinds of firearms in order to be armed against a possible tyranny is long outmoded, we will become more and more victims of crimes with guns, whether they be those which individuals store at home or those bought for the explicit purpose of murder or extortion.

The need for continuous reevaluation of the explicit form of moral norms also affects our understanding of the so-called theology of orders. Since we do not live in a static pre-fall state, there are no orders of creation. The moral norms which guide us are goal oriented, intended to preserve humanity against possible self-destruction. For Christians there are no static God-given orders which maintain the status quo. Instead there are orders of preservation which are intended to preserve us in the light of Christ. In this light we must reappraise the Ten Commandments. Basically, they are guidelines for the preservation of our humanity. Whenever a significant number of people disregards one or several of them (e.g., the commandment against stealing or lying) our humanity is in jeopardy and chaos threatens. The acknowledgment of certain moral norms is a necessary precondition for human existence as such. Atheists can recognize them as partly inborn and partly handed on by tradition. In the light of God's self-disclosure in Jesus Christ, however, Christians perceive in these norms the preserving activity of God. He is preserving the human community from its self-destruction and against the seductive and destructive tendencies of the anti-Godly powers. Martin Luther expressed this once very descriptively when he said, "If God would withdraw his protective hand you would become blind, or an adulterer and murderer like David, you would fall and break your leg and drown."[30]

Through God's self-disclosure in Jesus Christ we are reminded of the trustworthy, yet transitory character of the moral process. It will find its fulfillment and completion in the eschatological new creation when the moral norms will be clear and self-evident. Then our moral behavior will be characterized by complete harmony with God.

(c) Meaning in history: From this discussion of the moral process it is only a small step to begin to consider God's providential involvement in the historical process. Yet this step is a very difficult one to take, since historical survival of nations and their increase of power has often been identified with divine providence.

How differently the role of God can be adduced from the same historical event can be seen by using the example of the devastation of Rome in A.D. 410 by the Gothic hordes of Alaric. Many people interpreted this event as signaling the wrath of the ancient gods, since the people had forsaken the ancient cults and adopted Christianity. The church father Augustine, however, endeavored to show in his book *The City of God* that the decline and fall of Rome was due to the moral depravity of paganism. A generation later the presbyter Salvianus of Marseilles explained the devastation of Rome as a judgment on the Christians, since their unrighteousness in church and society had led to the fall of Rome as God's punishment. We can learn from this example that to interpret an historical event as the result of divine providence can easily become a piously disguised form of self-justification.

We should refrain from conceiving divine providence atomistically as a fragmentary demonstration of God's power. We should rather trust that through his providential action, even in the historical process, God's kingdom will finally triumph. But we are unable to claim with Friedrich Schiller that world history is world judgment.[31] It is also difficult for us to agree with the attempt of G. W. F. Hegel to conceive of world history as a theodicy in which the thinking spirit is reconciled with evil.[32] Since we are unable to justify God's providence by pointing to individual historical events or to equate in deterministic fashion the whole historical process with God's providence, a criterion to assess the trustworthiness of God's providential activity in the historical process must be gained from other sources.

It is important to remember that God is introduced in Scripture as the one for whom nothing is impossible and who determines the course of history. Yet it is even more important to recall that this is done to express the conviction that God will bring his plan of salvation to completion (Gen. 18:14 and Luke 1:37), but not to impress on us the notion that the whole history runs according to God's preconceived plan. When Jesus was asked for a theological interpretation of the death of the Galileans whom Pilate had slain or of the 18 men who were killed by the tower which collapsed at Siloam (Luke 13:1-5), he deliberately refused to equate history with God's judgment. The same was true when his disciples asked him why a certain man was born blind (John 9:3). At the same time Jesus did not simply shrug his shoulders and declare that history is without meaning. In the first two instances he answered in existential fashion that events like these remind us of our own mortality and sinfulness. In the last case he commented, according to the evangelist, that it served to manifest the works of God.

In other words, historical events are not an end in themselves. They are also not just part of the larger context of world history. Ultimately, historical events have eschatological significance. While asserting that the historical process will find its fulfillment and completion in the eschaton, we must refrain from the temptation to identify God with *one* of the causes of the historical process or with *the* cause. We should rather side with Friedrich Gogarten when he reminds us that, by accepting us as his own, God has granted us the freedom to lead our lives responsibly without again interfering through divine providence.[33] God wants us to be his governors in the world. A governor without freedom and responsibility would be a mere puppet and not a responsive and responsible being. Yet responsibility does not exclude divine providence. Rather, it necessitates providence. We should be God's governors, and precisely because of this God-given responsibilty we need God's assistance and guiding providence.

While God in his general providence "provides both order and grace as the matrix of existence,"[34] human existence is not a self-contained phenomenon. It is open toward the future which is foreshadowed in the Christ event as the promise and as the proleptic anticipation of a new creation. But once we touch upon a new creation, we are actually talking about God's special providence.

2. Direction through special providence

In granting order for existence God primarily sanctions the natural configurations already prevailing in our world. Yet in God's involvement with nature we notice that there are both constancy and surprise. When we turn to God's self-disclosure as it culminated in

Jesus Christ we noticed the same. On the one hand God's involvement with humanity developed along certain lines (e.g., covenant, promise and fulfillment, law and gospel, etc.). At the same time there are events which were totally unpredicted, such as the crossing of the Red Sea, the election of David, and the miracles of the Messiah. The unexpected is quite often a feature of God's activity. When we talk about God's special providence, we do not only say that God is able to give things an unprecedented turn, but that this new turn of events foreshadows something of the new quality of life promised in the eschaton. While God's general providence guides the way toward the eschaton, his special providence gives us a glimpse of the new eschatological reality.

When we consider miracles, which usually fall under the rubric of special providence, many potential misunderstandings must be avoided. A miracle is not just something unusual or a demonstration of God's power. It is a foreshadowing of a new divine order. At the same time we must insist that a miracle is an exception. Something which occurs every day may still cause us to marvel but it is not a miracle. Augustine stated this very succinctly with reference to the feeding of the 5000: "For certainly the government of the whole world is a greater miracle than the satisfying of the five thousand men with five loaves; and yet no man wonders at the former; but the latter men wonder at, not because it is greater, but because it is rare."[35]

Since a miracle is an exception to the usual way things happen, the question emerges how such events are possible. The idea emerged that a miracle had occurred when natural causes do not suffice for a total explanation of an event. This means that God as the additional supernatural cause makes a miracle possible through bypassing the natural sequence of events. Since scientific progress discovers more and more natural causes, such a line of thought would bring miracles to the brink of extinction. Furthermore, the biblical writers did not conceive of God as a *deus ex machina*, appearing in certain cases to rescue impossible situations, but as the one who is ultimately behind all events. When we look at some important biblical miracles, such as the crossing of the Red Sea, we are told that this was a perfectly natural event, since a mighty wind made the waters recede. The "miraculous" point, however, was that the wind commenced at the right moment to allow the safe passage of the Israelites, and stopped at the right moment to prohibit the Egyptians from pursuing them. Even many of the healing miracles which Jesus performed, modern medicine tells us, are highly unlikely but not impossible.

Such unusual events are of course not restricted to the Bible or to the Judeo-Christian tradition. We also hear of highly unusual events in other contexts. Yet in the biblical tradition they take on special significance because of their Judeo-Christian context and the promissory history connected with it. For instance, when John the Baptist wondered whether Jesus was actually the Messiah, Jesus told the disciples whom John had sent: "Go and tell John what you hear and see: the blind receive their sight and the lame walk, lepers are cleansed and the deaf hear, and the dead are raised up, and the poor have good news preached to them "(Matt. 11:4f.). Speech and action go together and interpret each other. Jesus' actions are explained as signs of the messianic age. They are symbols of the new age when the distortions of the present age, such as disease and death, will no longer reign.

Yet all miracles have only temporary validity. Though the destructive anti-Godly powers may be overcome at one point in history, sickness and death soon reign again. In this light Jesus' own resurrection assumes prime importance. Jesus was not resuscitated to die again at some later date. As Paul victoriously exclaimed, in Jesus' resurrection death was overcome through a new, imperishable form of life (1 Cor. 15:55ff.). In him the barrier of death was removed and a new form of life permanently emerged. From the destiny of Jesus we can then hope that the other miraculous signs of a new creation will one day be endowed with permanence. The promised transformation of the whole cosmos which has commenced in Jesus Christ will one day be universalized. Miracles indicate that this present world has no permanence but is on the way to its fulfillment.

In this context the impact of prayer must at least be mentioned. The New Testament, especially, is full of exhortations to pray and to ask God for anything that we need. But prayer is not a means by which we put God in a corner so that he has no choice but to comply with the content of our prayers. Prayer is also not a frivolous attempt to see how far-reaching God's power might be. Though God encourages us to dialog with him, petitional prayers, especially if their fulfillment would involve God's special providence, must be seen in the eschatological context. Dietrich Bonhoeffer reminded us that "God does not give us everything we want, but he does fulfill all his promises."[36] We should also remember that Jesus did not heal all the sick persons he encountered in Palestine—for instance, he never conducted healing services— but healed only a few to illustrate his message. While a prayer will never go unheard, it will not always be fulfilled according to our wishes. Yet, remembering the life and destiny of Jesus Christ, we are even then assured that God's compassionate activity will ultimately prevail.

6

HUMANITY

In our previous discussions we made only implicit mention of humanity. Now we want to deal with it explicitly and to elaborate briefly on three of humanity's most important facets: our creatureliness, our administrative task, and our dialogical structure.

A. Our creatureliness

Science has discovered more and more details about the gradual evolvement of the tree of life which includes humanity. This fact does not diminish the basic Judeo-Christian assertion that humanity in general and each human being in particular are the result of the express will of God and not simply of genetic causes. In his creation account the priestly writer devotes four verses to the relationship between God and humans. Three times we hear in Gen. 1:27 that God *created* humanity, as if to emphasize that humans are definitely creatures of God—not more and not less. It is almost frightening, however, to see how closely humans are associated with animals. No special day of creation is reserved for them. They are created on the same day as the land animals. Like the fish and the birds, they are blessed and given the command to be fruitful and multiply. They are even supposed to share the same food with the land animals.

The Hebrew word *adam* which is used to denote a human being is actually a collective word meaning humankind. To insure that it is not misunderstood as depicting some kind of archetypal primal androgynous being, the immediate qualification is added that God created "them" male and female. Humans are not created for a life in solitary existence, but are called to be a *thou* to one other. The full meaning of being human cannot be realized in monological existence, nor in the communal existence of men or of women alone, but in the encounter between men and women. It also means that our sexual differentiation is not a human achievement but a constitution given with our creation as such. We know each other only as sexual beings, since every person is either a she or a he, but not an it.

When we turn to the Yahwistic creation account, we notice again the emphasis on our total dependence on God. Humans are cared for by God in many ways and do not have life on their own. "The Lord God formed man of dust from the ground, and breathed into his nostrils the breath of life; and man became a living being" (Gen. 2:7). This is one of the classical insights of Old Testament anthropology, as Gerhard von Rad rightly observed.[1] In reading this biblical quote we might wonder why no mention is made of the soul as an entity separate from the body. Though the distinction between body and soul, or body, soul, and spirit is frequently made in the Bible, a human being is always conceived of as a unity. There is no higher (divine) soul which animates an inferior body. A human being with body and soul is enlivened through God's life-giving Spirit alone. As long as God's Spirit abides with us we are alive and healthy. When he takes his Spirit away, however, we are like those "in the pit"; we are dead. What makes Gen. 2:7 so peculiar is the intimate connection between *adam* (man) and *adamah* (earth). Humans are made of dust. "You are dust and to dust you shall return" (Gen. 3:19), we hear again toward the end of the temptation story. Humans and nature form a unity. Humans are taken from nature and return to it.

In contrast to the priestly writer, the Yahwist does not say that God simply commanded the earth to bring forth humans, as God did with other living creatures. God breathes life into a human being and it becomes a living being. Human life cannot be taken for granted; it is a gift of God. We receive our human existence through participation in God's life-giving spirit. Perhaps today when we are wondering whether the human family will survive the threatening effects of environmental pollution, overpopulation, and a scarcity of natural resources, this insight into the nature of human life as a gift to be used responsively assumes renewed importance.

It is not, however, just the life of the human family in general that is understood as a gift from God. The creator of the human family is at the same time creator of each individual human being. The psalmist confesses God's creative activity in this way: "Thou didst form my inward parts, thou didst knit me together in my mother's womb. I praise thee, for thou art fearful and wonderful. Wonderful are thy works!" (Ps. 139:13f.). It is similar in the book of Job:

> Thy hands fashioned and made me; and now thou dost turn about and destroy me. Remember that thou hast made me of clay; and wilt thou turn me to dust again? Didst thou not pour me out like milk and curdle me like cheese? Thou didst clothe me with skin and flesh, and knit me together with bones and sinews. Thou hast granted me life and steadfast love; and thy care has preserved my spirit (Job 10:8-12).

Though the writer knows about the procreative process, that the semen is ejected into the female organism and the solid embryonic body is formed ("Didst thou not pour me out like milk and curdle me like cheese?"), this whole process is at the same time understood as a work solely wrought by God. It is beyond the imagination of the Old Testament writers that the process of nature should be separated from the activity of God.

Luther captured very well the biblical understanding of the dependence of human life upon God when he said that God "could easily create children without man and woman. But he does not want to do it. He joins together man and wife so that it seems as if man and wife would do it, but nevertheless he does it hidden under such masks."[2] Each human being is totally God's work regardless of his or her line of descent. The question whether life evolved "naturally" (unaided) from inanimate matter, though scientifically very significant, is theologically secondary. Both inanimate nature and the living creatures are God's creation. Whenever and wherever human life appears, it is a gift of God.

In the Yahwistic creation story our creaturely position is indicated not only by the statement that humans are taken from dust and created through God's life-giving Spirit; surely the reddish-brown skin of the Israelites reminded the author of the reddish-brown dust of the earth. The creaturely position is also emphasized when he points out humanity's close relationship with the animals. Like humans they are created from dust and we find it almost embarrassing that it is the animals which are first created as "a helper fit for him" (Gen. 2:18). Yet the idea that humans and animals could be on equal level is rejected. Instead we hear that the animals are brought to Adam so that he could name them and exercise authority over them.

When we come to the creation of woman, we notice that God's creative activity does not tolerate any spectators. Adam falls in a deep sleep when Eve, i.e., "the mother of all living," is created. We are allowed to view God's creation only retrospectively. Though Eve is created last, she is not an afterthought; she is the final act in God's original creation. It may sound strange for us that Eve is taken from a rib of Adam. Originally this figurative speech may have arisen from the observation that most of the vital human organs are enclosed within the ribs except for part of the abdomen. But for the Yahwist this image has taken on a different meaning. It affirms that Eve is not on the level of the animals; she is not made merely from dust. She is from the same kind of "ensouled material" as Adam. Man (*ish*) notices this immediately and calls her woman (*isha*, similar to the Old English meaning of woman, i.e., female man). Again we cannot escape the notion that man and woman belong together; they are created for each other.

Next comes the interesting statement in the Yahwistic account that "a man leaves his father and his mother and cleaves to his wife, and they become one flesh" (Gen. 2:24). Contrary to Israelite custom and perhaps reflecting an earlier matriarchal culture, it is the man who leaves his family, not the woman. But this statement no longer describes a custom, it now describes a natural drive. Just as they were once one flesh and woman is taken from man, their natural drive is to reattain this unity.

We must admit that although they contain many differences in detail, both the priestly writer and the Yahwist are unanimous in emphasizing humans as creatures—creatures living in proximity to the realm of animals but yet created distinctively different from the animal world, and in the basic twofoldness of man and woman.

When we now consider the biblical understanding of humans as God's administrators we will again notice that the human position has to be guarded against two temptations: reducing a human being to the highest developed animal or elevating it to the position of God.

B. Our administrative task

When we consider our task as administrators of God's creation, the question soon emerges regarding that which enables us to administer God's creation and also toward which end it should be administered.

1. Made in God's image

Our position as God's administrators seems to stem from the claim that humans were created in the image of God. "Let us make man in our image, after our likeness," commences the priestly account of the creation of humanity; then it concludes, "So God created man in his own image, in the image of God he created him" (Gen. 1:26f.). This plural form "let us make" may suggest that the priestly writer felt uncomfortable with the daring statement that God created humans in his own image; it implies that humans are created in the image of both God and all the heavenly beings associated with God. This sentiment coincides with the observation in one of the creation psalms that God has made humanity "little less than God" (Ps. 8:5). Again with reference to God and his heavenly court, *Elohim*, the plural form for God, is used (the notion of a heavenly court is not uncommon in the Old Testament; cf. Job 1 and Isaiah 6). But what does it mean that humans are created in the image of God?

The assertion that we are created in the image of God does not refer just to characteristics which we regard as specifically human, such as our ability for moral decision, our dignity as persons, or our inalienable rights. It does not mean that humans are a replica of God, though this thought might be inferred. The priestly writer is not even much interested in defining what the image of God entails, but rather emphasizes the purpose for which this image is given. When God created humans, he destined them to have a special relationship with the animals. Similarly the Yahwist, who does not mention that humans are created in the image of God, knows that

God conferred upon humans certain responsibilities (Gen. 2:15-17) and that he wants them to make certain decisions regarding the creation (Gen. 2:19f.; cf. the significance of naming somebody or something). Humans are placed in a special position within God's creation. Since they are called to have dominion over the animals, to subdue the earth, to till the garden, and to name the animals, they have a special relationship with God.

Perhaps we can more clearly understand in which respect humans ought to function in God's image when we consider the Near Eastern custom of erecting images of earthly rulers. In the ancient Near East the setting up of a picture or a statue of a king always indicated that the area in which his replica was erected was under his dominion (Dan. 3:1-6). If humans are introduced into God's creation as being created in the image of God or as God's image, this could mean that humanity exercises and symbolizes God's dominion over the world. Humanity's dominion over the world reminds everyone that God is in control of creation and it reminds us that we exercise our authority on God's behalf.

One might wonder what kind of people can fulfill the demand to have authority over God's creation. Do the creation accounts envision absolute rulers who have a special gift for exercising authority? The answer is surprising when we consider that the idea of dominion is always connected with the plural, "let *them* have dominion" (Gen. 1:26, 28). The focus is not on a charismatic leader but on the human community. Each one of us is asked to act as God's administrator. The psalmist reaffirms that the administration of God's creation is not delegated only to exceptional people. For instance, in Psalm 8 he rejoices that God has given us dominion over the works of his hands. But then he continues by asking, "What is man that thou art mindful of him?" (Ps. 8:4). The created image of God in humans is not explained as an inherent quality coming to expression only in exceptional people. It is simply God's will that we be his administrators.

For our assessment of the human position it is significant that the statement "So God created man in his own image, in the image of God he created him" is immediately followed in the creation accounts by the remark "male and female he created them." Neither the physical strength of a man nor the reproductive faculty of a woman better signifies the human position of being created in

God's image. In representing the human community men and women together exercise the privilege and obligation which this position entails. Very appropriately Gerhard von Rad observed: "The idea of man, according to P [i.e., the priestly writer], finds its full meaning not in the male alone but in man and woman."[3] This would mean that neither a man nor a woman can obtain his or her full personhood without the other. It would be wrong, however, to understand this as an emphasis on sexuality or procreation. God's blessing on man and woman and his command to be fruitful and multiply is referred to separately. It is not given simultaneously with humanity's creation in God's image and with the sexual differentiation between male and female. The procreative faculty is thus not a consequence of being created in the image of God; it is rather a gift of God to be used responsibly. Emil Brunner was right when he observed that the statement "So God created man in his own image, in the image of God he created him; male and female he created them" is such a simple assertion "that we hardly realize that with it a vast world of myth and Gnostic speculation, of cynicism and asceticism, of the deification of sexuality and fear of sex completely disappears."[4]

Most animals are attracted to their sexual partners only for copulation and the procreative process, and after the young ones mature the "marriage" is dissolved. Humans, however, live always consciously in the context of sexual differentiation. Once they reach their adult stage, they are never oblivious of their sexual status. We have noticed that some behavioral psychologists emphasize that the peculiarity of this differentiation is not just a biological and physiological differentiation, but one that finds expression in the spiritual and attitudinal realms as well. Cultural imprinting can either reinforce this differentiation by relegating most men and women to clearly defined occupational and behavioral patterns, or it can seek to obliterate the differentiation by attempting to overcome them. On the one hand, attempts to reinforce this differentiation often segregate men and women and therefore make the realization of full personhood through mutual interdependence more difficult. On the other hand, tendencies to obliterate the differentiation regard men and women not as equal but as identical, consequently depriving man and woman of the mutual enrichment through which they become fully human. While efforts to reinforce sexual differentiation are often attributed to a male-dominated culture, tendencies to obliterate the differentiation are sometimes attributed to the women's liberation movement. This women's liberation movement, however, is much too multifaceted to arrive at such a simple equation; to some extent it is only a countermovement to a male-dominated culture.

2. Administration in jeopardy

We have seen that the insight that humans are created in God's image can be realized only in the mutuality of the man-woman encounter. When they join together to approach their own being and the world that surrounds them, they can best exercise the dominion to which they are called. Yet there are certain phenomena that can raise doubts as to whether humans are actually fit to be God's administrators. We might question whether the understanding that humans were created in the image of God does not overestimate their potential. While humans can discern between good and evil, their knowledge and will often seem to go separate ways from their reflection and action. The Old Testament history already is a narration of human disobedience and seems to belie the assumption that humans were created in God's image. Similarly, the sacrifice of Jesus would be unthinkable without human disobedience.

When we consider major issues which confront us today, the validity of the claim that humans, created in God's image, are to have dominion over the earth becomes even more questionable. We are confronted with potential or actual overpopulation in many parts of the world, with the rapid depletion of our natural resources, and with a tremendous ecological imbalance. How, then, can we still take seriously the commission to be "fruitful and multiply, and fill the earth and subdue it"? Many responsible people today claim emphatically that our number one priority is comprehensive and total population control. But the priestly writer seems to demand the exact opposite. Furthermore, discerning people point out that the Genesis accounts elevate humans above the rest of creation and, as a result, humanity and nature were destined for a collision course. Lynn White, for instance, observes:

> Especially in its Western form, Christianity is the most anthropocentric religion the world has seen . . . .Man shares, in great measure,

God's transcendence of nature. Christianity, in absolute contrast to ancient paganism and Asia's religions (except, perhaps, Zoroastrianism), not only established a dualism of man and nature but also insisted that it is God's will that man exploit nature for his proper ends.[5]

Could we object to this charge by saying that the Judeo-Christian tradition bears not much influence on today's "post-Christian" world? Lynn White rightly counters that our daily habits of action

> are dominated by an implicit faith in perpetual progress which was unknown either to Greco-Roman antiquity or to the Orient. It is rooted in, and is indefensible apart from, Judeo-Christian teleology. The fact that Communists share it merely helps to show what can be demonstrated on many other grounds; that Marxism, like Islam, is a Judeo-Christian heresy.[6]

We must indeed agree that there is some truth in these charges. Too often Christians have been poor stewards both of their own gifts and of the gift of nature entrusted to them. The biblical understanding that humans are created in the image of God led in many quarters to an unjustified ethical optimism. Today this attitude finds its continuity in a historical optimism which claims that history will continuously evolve and will necessarily evolve toward the better. The basically optimistic assessment of human potential in both Eastern communism and Western capitalism also largely arose from within the Judeo-Christian context.

Lynn White and many others, therefore, demand that we abandon our preferred position and perceive ourselves as fully integrated into the context of nature. The Great Chain of Being flowing from the highest to the lowest members of the universe would then once again be whole. While we agree fully with the diagnosis of the problem—our exploitative and self-glorifying attitude—we must disagree with the proposed solution which advances a pantheistic worldview, and therefore a divinization of nature, together with our integration into the context of nature.

Since animate and inanimate nature are intrinsically interrelated, solipsistic beings cannot sustain themselves. We are doomed if we try to live as if we are gods created in our own image. Yet today's problems cannot be solved if we go to the other extreme and resign ourselves to the natural. Our existence is vitally related to nature and its structures as the wellspring which make our existence possible. But, as many behavioral scientists point out, our instinctive drives are not strong enough to dominate our behavior and guide us in our complex industrial society. We are reasonable beings, no longer fundamentally driven by instinct. At this point it is crucial to remember Hegel's assertion that we link the eternal with the accidental in our thinking. There is something eternal that comes to expression in us. The Old Testament refers to this phenomenon when it tells us that we receive our existence as human beings through participation in God's life-giving Spirit. It would be wrong to limit the Spirit only to its animating function. It is also the Spirit of all wisdom and truth, as the Bible amply attests. Since we depend with our whole existence on our participation in the Spirit, the Old Testament rightly understood humanity as theomorphic, created in God's image. This means that the cause for today's uncertainty and bewilderment lies in our secular spirit. We have abandoned our position as being created in the image of God. Therefore we have weakened our participation in God's Spirit both in terms of right judgment and full participation in (divine) life.

At this point the biblical understanding of humans as persons becomes crucial. Persons live both in conformity to God and as his representatives. This notion evolved into the characteristic Judeo-Christian and, in its turn, Western idea of freedom to govern the world and to regulate the affairs of society and interhuman relationships. Freedom, however, is not "to do as you please." It carries with it the obligation to exercise dominion in accordance with God's life-giving spirit, to further the good, true, and beautiful, and to help to alleviate and eliminate what is distorted and self-centered.

Since we always discover the meaning of our existence through that which we serve, there are basically two possibilities for us to acquire such meaning: (1) If we serve God as his administrators, our existence gains meaning from God and our actions are done to glorify God. Glorification of God through overpopulation (Gen. 1:28 reads, "fill the earth," not "overpopulate it"), exploitation of natural resources, and global pollution is self-contradictory. Rather, our experience of God as faithful and compassionate should become normative for the way in which we, as his administrators, are experienced by others. Being created in God's image thus calls for a life-style of authority, yet in humility; of determination, yet with compassion; of faithfulness, yet in dignity.

(2) If we, on the other hand, serve as our own administrators, our existence must gain meaning from ourselves and our actions serve only to glorify ourselves. We become driven to perform heroic deeds and continuously to triumph over nature and over our own kind. Nature and other people become means for obtaining short-term advantages for ourselves. Solitary humanity, as it emerges more and more today, serves as a warning of the consequences if we abandon our position as God's administrators. Neglecting our responsibility to foster and cultivate God's creation, we consider it our own dominion and destroy its natural context. Acid rain and climatic changes, overpopulation with certain animals and extinction of others, and epidemics for humans, animals, and plants are some of the consequences. In attempting to secure the world for ourselves we are about to lose it.

C. Our dialogical structure

The Greek historian Herodotus tells us of the Egyptian King Psamtik (Psammetichus) II who wanted to discover what language children would speak if they grew up in total isolation. He commanded foster mothers to feed a group of infants, bathe and dress them, but forbade them to fondle them or talk with them. This experiment, however, was not successful. Gradually all the children died. This tragic phenomenon is today well researched. Behavioral psychologists even tell us that if after its second month the infant cannot establish a lasting relationship with a caring person, severe developmental disturbances, called hospitalism, will occur. A human being cannot forever live in solitary isolation.

1. A necessary interaction

Our human constitution as such necessitates that we continuously interact with our environment. While animals are highly specialized creatures who have adapted themselves to a specific environment, humans are by nature not adapted to most environmental situations. A polar bear can live comfortably in the arctic cold and a camel in the desert heat. But humans cannot live comfortably in most environments without creating an artificial environment of clothes and housing which they will vary in response to the given situation. They dress warmly and heat their homes in cold climates, while in warm climates they dress lightly and attempt to cool their homes. By their high degree of specialization most animals are much more restricted in their living habitat than humans, who can always modify their environment to fit their needs. This means that humans interact with their environment much more strongly than do animals. A certain openness to new experiences aids humans in their vital pursuit of environmental adaptation.

Human senses are much less specialized than those of most animals. We do not share the excellent eyesight of eagles, we do not have the strength of elephants, and we do not have the hearing and smell of dogs. But what animal is there that can climb a 10-foot fence, jump 12 feet in distance, dive 10 feet deep, or see and hear another person 300 feet away? We are by nature much more versatile than most animals. Moreover, while very highly developed animals show only rudimentary signs of planned interaction with the environment through the use of simple tools, humans have developed numerous highly complex tools through which they can experience and manipulate the environment. In this they are like no other created being. Finally, humans can approach their environment with perspective and this perspective can vary at will. For an animal, by contrast, the perspective of perception is largely determined by instinctive behavior. When a female dog meets another female, a fight will result, the result of the instinctive safeguarding of one's offspring and the sensing of a potential rival for the male. But when humans encounter one another they can perceive each other in many different ways, largely depending on the circumstances, e.g., as the parent of the child's friend, as a neighbor and friend, or as a rival for the other's spouse. This means that we are not bound to a certain way of looking at the things we encounter but are always open for new insights into our interaction with persons and things.

While the behavior pattern of animals is usually established once adulthood is reached, adult humans remain open to the world. This fundamental and significant characteristic of humans—their continuous, creative, and active discourse with the environment—can therefore be classified as a phenomenon of neoteny, of being mature while still growing up. Humans always retain some of their "immature" characteristics into adulthood; they are always becoming and never definitely set in their ways. This allows for a freedom of action which is peculiarly human, uninhibited by rigid structures and norms for action and reaction. Humans can dialogically interact with their environment and become reasoning beings.

An interesting point is that humans are never satisfied with the presently available. They always strive beyond that which is at hand. There is a continuous emphasis on growth, maturing, and learning. Besides the undoubted benefits that this attitude has brought about through the advancement of knowledge and technological know-how, it has also had some rather undesirable effects. Every advancement brings with it a "leaving behind" and the pain involved with that departure. If change occurs very rapidly, the question arises regarding an appropriate point of orientation, since what we formerly depended upon is rather quickly outmoded. When we consider that most of the knowledge we acquire in school is obsolete within a few years and that in many scientific disciplines one of the most difficult problems is how to keep abreast of the steadily increasing flood of information, we wonder whether it is meaningful continuously to reach out to the new and unprecedented. We should consider the increasing strain that this drive toward progress puts on our rapidly diminishing natural resources and also question the nomadic character of a modern "throwaway," get-up-and-go society.

2. Increasing dissatisfaction

While the phoenomena of growth and of reaching out beyond the presently available are intrinsic to human existence, the rapid acceleration of "progress" is a rather recent phenomenon. Why is there no satisfaction from having attained a certain goal and why must attained goals be ever more rapidly superseded? Perhaps this mood stems from a growing dissatisfaction with what is at hand (and therefore potentially available). But even more it may stem from a growing sense of alienation from that which provides a stable frame of reference beyond all change. Our dissatisfaction with the world may witness to our need to be related to more than the world, i.e., to God as the world's foundation and direction.

As humanity divorced itself more and more from God and began to assert its autonomy, it needed something or someone else capable of endowing its finitude with infinite value. Thus humanity has searched more and more frantically for a point of orientation and meaning for its life. Yet such a reference point does not seem to be attainable within the realm of the finite. A rediscovery of the ultimate relationship would not entail the human spirit resigning itself to passivity. Instead it could assume a more relaxed posture and slow down its search, since then even finite things and persons would be regarded as having a touch of infinity. They become reminders of God instead of surrogates which need to be discarded ever more rapidly in the vain attempt to secure the infinite from the finite. Once the ultimate relationship with God is rediscovered, we would also notice that dialog with God frees us from bondage to things and from the need to acquire ever new gratification. We would realize once more that we belong to a God who guides and protects us and who holds us accountable for what we do or leave undone.

3. The dialog of prayer

The ability to flee to the God who invited us to come to him in the time of trouble is very different from interhuman relationships which are mostly carried out under the conditions of mutual benefit. As a caring and loving God he discloses to us the meaning of our life—meaning found not in self-justification nor solitary existence but in communion with God. This is nowhere better expressed than in prayer. Martin Luther rightly stated that God's order or command and the prayers of the Christians are the two pillars which support the entire world and without which the world would disintegrate.[7] God promised to consider the content of our prayers in his preserving, sustaining, and creative activity. Through our prayers we are on God's side, cooperating and dialoging with him concerning the future of the world.

Prayer can have a variety of content. (1) There is adoration and praise. Again it is Luther who reminds us that we should not call upon God only when we are in trouble. We should also thank him for his help and rescue, remember his acts of kindness, and praise him for them, because "he is the Creator, the Benefactor, the Promiser, and the Savior."[8] A life without prayer is no longer in tune with God as the creative source of all life; it mistakenly presumes that our world is self-sufficient. Prayer serves here as a reminder of the one from whom we have everything that is. Therefore we should ask God even for things that we usually take for granted, such as good weather or daily food.

(2) With this statement we have already touched upon the second category, that of petitional prayers, which probably form the main content of most prayers. Georgia Harkness rightly prioritizes the wide variety of petitions when she says that "to seek God's forgiveness for past and present sin, and thus to find hope for the future, is an essential part of the Christian prayer."[9] If we do not include in our prayers the plea for forgiveness of sin, our dialog with God will always be disturbed. Then both in our prayers and in our prayer expectations we will act out of our own sinful and selfish interest, but not out of conformity with God. Petitions are therefore first concerned with inner strength and renewal. Of course, this will include more than just forgiveness. It will also be a prayer for inner peace in time of conflict, for clarity of outlook and new strength in moments of fatigue, and for power to cope with the daily demands of life. A stanza from the gospel hymn "What a Friend We Have in Jesus" seems to express this attitude very appropriately:

> *Have we trials and temptations?*
> *Is there trouble anywhere?*
> *We should never be discouraged—*
> *Take it to the Lord in prayer.*
> *Can we find a friend so faithful*
> *Who will all our sorrows share?*
> *Jesus knows our ev'ry weakness—*
> *Take it to the Lord in prayer.*[10]

From the acknowledgment of God's benevolent activity in Jesus Christ, new strength and peace of mind can be gained. God as the ruler of the universe cares about us small, unimportant beings so much that he comes to us in the human form of Jesus Christ. This God who cares is also the one who gives strength to the weary and lifts up those who are in low esteem (Luke 1:52).

In our petitional prayers, we dare not forget frequent petitions for physical health and healing. Since prayers are not intended to be a substitute for work, petitions for recovery from physical illness should never replace appropriate medical care. However, the two are not mutually exclusive. The same insight must guide our attitude toward so-called faith healing. We should remember that God usually acts in a mediated way through the usual course of events, i.e., medical attention and gradual recovery. Only in rare exceptions does God direct events in an unusual way, i.e., miraculously. We should also not expect that the dialog with God in true prayer is followed by an automatic granting of our petitions. A dialog is not a demand for surrender but a true give-and-take. We are encouraged to turn to God in all our troubles but we are not guaranteed that all our petitions will be fulfilled. If we take seriously the dialogical character of prayers, we must also be ready for God's noncompliance with our petitions.

Finally, in petitions concerning events in nature we must bear in mind that this is primarily the realm where we need to affirm the natural protective order of God. But as God's administrators we can also remind him of those who are especially exposed to danger in the natural world, such as miners, travelers, pilots, and sailors. Again, prayers are not intended to replace protective measures but are to accompany them. Similarly, it is our prerogative and duty to pray in the midst of adverse conditions, such as storms, floods, and other disasters, that their impact will be softened or averted. Since a prayer is never uttered in selfish interest, we will keep in mind not only the well-being of ourselves but also of others. This means that the same adoration, praise, and petitions we extend on our own behalf we extend also on behalf of others.

In all our prayers we always conclude with the same expressed or tacit admission which Jesus made in Gethsemane as he concluded the most fervent prayer ever uttered, "Nevertheless, not as I will, but as thou wilt" (Matt. 26:39). A Christian prayer is not a demand for God's surrender, but rather the privilege of a dialog with the one who has formed the earth and the whole universe, and who has been our dwelling place in all generations (Ps. 90:1f.).

7

SIN

Though God's existence, or at least his interaction with our world, is frequently questioned, human sinfulness is an almost universally accepted fact. In most cases, however, the analysis of the human situation does not end in despair but in the conviction that we might well be able to extricate ourselves from this predicament, given the right insight and the proper procedure. Thus treatises on "five easy steps toward self-improvement" are almost as frequently written as analyses of our dire predicament. It is, therefore, important to see whether the human predicament can indeed be solved by our own efforts or whether other forces, stronger than humanity, must intervene and save us from the evil in which we entangle ourselves.

A. The cause of evil

If the cause of our sinful actions is located within the human sphere, we might be able to eliminate it, perhaps through reeducation, genetic engineering, or preventative means. If the cause, however, is external to us, it could easily be too big for us to handle. With some significant modifications the Judeo-Christian tradition tells us that the cause of evil is not something that is superimposed on us, making us mere victims of outside forces.

1. The intrinsic nature of evil

The cause of evil is inherent in the structure of human existence. We notice this as soon as we turn our attention to the Old Testament.

(a) The Old Testament outlook: We find the first account of the Fall in Genesis 3, a passage conspicuously isolated from the rest of the Old Testament. The story of the Fall is not developed by the psalmists, the prophets, or other writers in the Old Testament. But we dare not treat it as though it expresses an isolated incident. It forms part of humanity's history and is the first link in a whole sequence of sinful events. It is immediately followed by the story of Cain slaying his brother (Gen. 4:1ff.), by the vindicative attitude of Lamech (Gen. 4:17ff.), the marriage between the sons of God and the daughters of humans (Gen. 6:1-4), the flood (Gen. 6-9), and finally the construction of the tower of Babel (Gen. 11:1-9).

The event depicted in Genesis 3, however, is not just one among many. It is the first sinful event which occurred to the first woman, Eve, and to the first man, Adam, whose names are understood as proper names in the latter part of Genesis 3. By talking about Adam and Eve as specific human beings, the Yahwist wants to show the exemplary character of this event. The sin committed in Genesis 3 is not simply a violation of God's command not to eat from the tree of the knowledge of good and evil. Rather, distrust of God is at the center of the Fall account. While the condition depicted in the Yahwistic creation account is characterized by innocence, a childlike relationship with God and also between man and woman, the harmony between God and human beings is now broken. The intention of the Yahwist in connecting creation and Fall so intimately is perhaps not so much to show how the once-good creation became corrupted, but to demonstrate the reason for our present human predicament.

Often the disruption of the initial harmony has been perceived as actually beneficial because it allegedly leads to the actualization of the human potential. Hegel, for instance, understood sin as the logical necessity to recognize the good, since if man "does not know about evil, he also does not know about good."[1] He characterized the Fall "as the eternal myth of man through which he becomes man."[2] The German philosopher Friedrich Schiller thought along similar lines and concluded that the alleged disobedience against God's command was actually

> the fall of man from his instinct, which brought moral evil into creation, but only to enable the moral good within creation. Therefore without doubt it is the happiest and greatest event in human history. From this moment onward his freedom is inscribed, here the first and remote foundation was laid for his morality.[3]

This idealistic notion of human sinfulness has also been affirmed by many psychoanalysts. For instance, Erich Fromm claimed, "This first act of disobedience is man's first step toward freedom." Man was expelled from paradise and is now able "to make his own history, to develop his human powers, and to attain a new harmony with man and nature as a fully developed individual instead of the former harmony in which he was *not yet* an individual."[4] Carl Gustav Jung showed more the ambivalence of this step when he wrote, "There is deep doctrine in the legend of the fall: it is the expression of a dim presentiment that the emancipation of the ego-consciousness was a Luciferian deed."[5] Pursuing a different perspective, Pierre Teilhard de Chardin came close to an idealistic perception when he asserted that evil is a necessary by-product of evolution through which in manifold errors and trials nature progresses on its evolutionary course.[6]

The idealistic interpretations of the Fall are based on the assumption of an evolutionary process in which a later stage of the process is perceived as more highly developed and therefore better. But it is difficult to assert, on strictly biological grounds, that an evolutionary development toward a higher stage is necessarily better.

The eruption of sinfulness in Genesis 3 also cannot be deduced by causal inference from God's good creation. When Adam is questioned by God about his behavior he tries such a causal inference, saying, "The woman whom thou gavest to be with me, she gave me fruit of the tree, and I ate" (Gen. 3:12). He wants to excuse himself by blaming the cause of evil on God. The woman tries a similar causal inference when she replies to God, "The serpent beguiled me, and I ate" (Gen. 3:13). Again the excuse is made that the cause of evil comes from outside. Yet none of these attempts suffices before God to account for the gravity of the situation. There is also no causal connection between this first sin and the emergence of subsequent sins, though the Yahwist demonstrates in the chapters following the account of the Fall that evil spread like a forest fire. But he nowhere mentions that the emergence of new sin is connected with prior sin in such a way as to be able to excuse the significance of each particular case.

Evil came into the world with the first appearance of man and woman; it erupted again with every subsequent appearance of man and woman. But the emergence of evil cannot be compared with a fateful decree against which humanity has no choice. The essence of human beings was not sinful from the beginning. The temptation had to come from the outside. Yet the cause of evil is not an anti-Godly principle outside of God's creation, such as in Gnostic thought. The serpent is explicitly introduced as an animal and as part of God's creation. Why this part of God's good creation becomes the tempter is beyond the interest of the Yahwist since an answer to this question does not contribute anything to the description of human sinfulness. Two items, however, still need clarification: (1) Who or what was it that tempted humans and (2) what were the consequences for them once they succumbed to sin?

The first couple, we hear, was tempted to be like God, knowing good and evil. It is difficult to assume that God has created something which is to become his potential challenger. While it is also absurd for the Yahwist to surmise that anybody could be like Yahweh, it is much easier for him to suggest that a human being wanted to become divine like the *elohim*, the heavenly beings. When humanity was tempted to know good and evil, it was not just tempted to know the distinction between good and evil, but to know everything about good and evil. Human temptation was then and is now the desire to know everything and to know it better. This attitude should not be confused with the emergence of humanity's inquisitive spirit. It is rather the destructive desire to disallow for any "thous" who have their own sphere, and to treat them as "its" without concern for their individuality. This human hubris effectively destroyed humanity's relationship with God.

God did not, however, respond to humanity's sinful pride like an insulted tyrant. Admittedly, the harmonious unity with God was destroyed and the couple was exiled from the garden. Once they had sinned, however, the threat that the day they eat from the tree of knowledge of good and evil they would die (Gen. 2:17) was not actualized. They were only reassured that they would return to dust from which they were taken (Gen. 2:7; 3:19). Almost as if in defiance of the original threat, Adam now dares to call his wife Eve, i.e., the mother of all living. Not even the obligation to work can be understood as the actual curse of the Fall (cf. Gen. 2:15). However, once the harmonious relationship with God was broken, the harmonious relationship between humanity and nature, and between man and woman, had disappeared too. Life now, confesses the Yahwist, became a drudgery, filled with hatred and passion and longing for harmony. Yet life did not come to an end, because "the Lord God made for Adam and for his wife garments of skins, and clothed them" (Gen. 3:21). Instead of lamenting evil, the Yahwist points to signs of grace that were given to the first couple on their wanderings through life, the coats of skins and God's help in clothing the couple. This compassionate act of God, rather than the verdict that there would be constant animosity between the snake and humanity (Gen. 3:15), can well be viewed as the first intimation of the gospel.

When we try to determine the cause of evil according to other Old Testament scources, we arrive at the following conclusions: Initially God was indiscriminately understood as the source of both good and evil. There was, however, a growing tendency to restrict God's involvement in the cause of evil to the act of punishing humanity for its wrongdoings. This meant that the cause for humanity's evil doings had to be found outside God, first in the temptation taking place through someone within God's good creation, later in the image of a heavenly accuser (cf. Job), and finally in the growingly independent status of a (the) pernicious Satan (1 Chron. 21:1). This meant that the Israelite understanding of God was gradually clarified. This process is reflected in God's ongoing self-disclosure, culminating in his full self-disclosure in Jesus Christ. While this process of clarification is reinforced in the New Testament, we must remember one decisive point: Regardless of the question of the cause of evil in a particular incident, the Old Testament unanimously agrees that the existence of an evil tempter outside of humans does not diminish humans' accountability for their own actions. Even when temptation appears to be irresistible, human responsibility for their actions remains unchanged. We can see this very plainly even in the Chronicler's version of David's temptation when David confesses, "Was it not I who gave the command to number the people? It is I who have sinned and done very wickedly" (1 Chron. 21:17).

(b) Extrabiblical and intertestamental materials: Since the primary references to Satan (Zech. 3:1; Job 1:6ff.) do not appear until the early postexilic era, Babylonian and Iranian influences could easily have shaped Israel's understanding of Satan. Indeed there is a close parallel between the biblical book of Job and the so-called Babylonian Job or the "Poem of the Righteous Sufferer."[7] This poem tells about a pursuer who inflicts diseases upon a righteous man. While this Babylonian pursuer or demon of sickness bears resemblance to the disease-inflicting function of Satan, we remember that this is just one feature of Satan in Job. Furthermore, the Babylonian demon of sickness is opposed and finally overcome by the good god, while we hear in the book of Job that Satan acts with God's permission. While we recognize definite textual parallels between the Babylonian and the biblical narratives, we notice that at decisive points their theological implications are diametrically opposed.

In another interesting way Babylonia becomes important for our understanding of Satan. When Satan's actions are described in the Old Testament they often resemble the divine court procedures recorded in Babylonia. According to Babylonian mythology the relationship between God and the people runs like the ordinary court procedures. In these procedures between God and the people an accuser appears, a royal official, traveling around the country and representing "the Eyes of the King."[8] This concept of "Eyes of the King" is also known in Media, Persia, and Egypt. We need not be surprised then to find its traces in the accuser function of Satan in Job 1:6ff., and in Zech. 3:1ff.

Of much greater significance than these Babylonian parallels is the influence of Zoroaster's (Zarathustra's) teachings on the Old Testament understanding of Satan. In the center of Zoroaster's teachings is Ahura Mazda, the one supreme god, who governs the whole development of the world (Yasna 31:8). Since Zoroaster excludes anything evil in his understanding of Ahura Mazda, he refers to him only indirectly as the father of twin gods, Ahra Mainyu (evil spirit) and Spenta Mainyu (holy spirit) (Yasna 30:3f.). The original monotheism is thus paired with a strict dualism and Ahura Mazda contains in himself the inclination towards both good and evil.

There is an apparent similarity between some of Zoroaster's teachings and the gradual realization by the Israelites that the cause of evil must be excluded from their understanding of God and be attributed to causes outside God. We will also notice that some of the characteristics associated with Ahra Mainyu gain prominence in the New Testament understanding of Satan. But the emphasis that the Old Testament places on God as both maker of history and creator of the world and the careful attention that it gives to Satan as part of God's ultimate domain show the fundamental difference between the thoroughgoing Old Testament monotheism and the basically cosmic-ethical dualism of Zoroaster. Unlike Zoroaster, the Old Testament writers never dared to imply that Yahweh was the father of Satan. While it was essential for the Israelites to assert that Yahweh was the Lord of history, they had no interest in seeking to establish a causal connection between God and Satan. This does not diminish the strong possibility of the catalytic influence of Zoroastrianism upon the Judeo-Christian tradition through which its understanding of Satan was furthered and clarified.

In the intertestamental period, which in many ways prepares the stage for the New Testament message, Satan is commonly understood as the one who wants to destroy the relationship between God and humanity, and especially between God and his people. In some ways, however, Satan here functions still very much as in the Old Testament. The *Similitudes of Enoch* (1 Enoch 37-71), for instance, tell us that a number of Satans are ruled by Satan (1 Enoch 53:3). They usually have access to heaven and are able to appear before the Lord of the Spirits (1 Enoch 40:7). Their function is threefold: (1) they accuse people before God (40:7); (2) they tempt people to do evil (69:6); and (3) they act as angels of punishment (53:3; 56:1).

In other places we hear that while humanity is responsible for its own sins, sin can be traced back to Adam's Fall (Apoc. Abr.23 and 26). Yet the Fall, whether of angels or of Adam, is not the cause of sin, it is only its historical background. This is clearly expressed in 2 Bar. 54:15, 19:

> For though Adam first sinned and brought untimely death upon all, yet of those who were born from him each one of them has prepared

for his own soul torment to come, and again each one of them has chosen for himself glories to come . . . . Adam is therefore not the cause, save only of his own soul, but each of us has been the Adam of his own soul.

We hear in this text that through Adam's Fall physical death came into the world, an understanding which is taken up by Paul in the New Testament. But the Fall is not yet seen as the cause of spiritual death. This latter idea is only occasionally mentioned in the intertestamental period (cf. 2 Bar. 48:42f.; 4 Ezra 3:21).

The main tenor of the intertestamental period, however, is expressed in the admonition, "Know, therefore, my children, that two spirits wait upon man—the spirit of truth and the spirit of deceit" (T. Judah 20:1). Humanity must choose between light and darkness, between the Law of the Lord and the works of Beliar (T. Levi 19:1). In the Qumran writings the command for a personal decision takes on cosmic dimensions. World history is perceived as a battle between light and darkness.[9] There is no neutral ground between the sons of light and the sons of darkness who fight in this world for the ultimate victory. But humanity does not become a tool in the struggle between the two "spirits." It receives its destiny from the hands of God. In the intertestamental period Satan, Beliar, Mastema, or Azazel—as the evil one is variously called—is understood as raging against God and rivaling his dignity. Being confronted with a time of immense political and spiritual crisis, the perspective of the intertestamental writers was certainly appropriate. But they did not simply surrender the world to an indefinite dualistic struggle. They still held God to be in control. Through the catalytic influence of Zoroaster's Parsiism they were able to make sense of an antagonistic world and its history without compromising their Israelite faith in one God. They arrived at a dynamic ethical dualism, the basis for which had already been laid in the Old Testament. This "modified dualism," as W. F. Albright called it, deeply influenced Christianity.[10]

(c) The New Testament understanding: In the New Testament we encounter an absolute and irreconcilable opposition between God and Satan intensified by the presence of the kingdom of God in Jesus Christ. Jesus' whole mission can be understood as a continuous confrontation with Satan. He appears at the decisive points of Je-

sus' life and destiny—at the beginning of his ministry in the story of the temptation (Mark 1:12f.), and at the end of his ministry through the betrayal of Judas Iscariot (Luke 22:3). The episode of Beelzebub (Mark 3:22-27) indicates that the whole demonic realm is understood as being under the control and supervision of Satan. Whenever Jesus casts out demons it is a manifestation of the greater work of casting out Satan. This leads us to the peculiarly ambiguous position of Satan in the New Testament.

(1) On the one hand, the synoptic writers tell us that Satan has as his goal the total destruction of humanity and especially of Jesus of Nazareth, the bringer of the salvific reign of God. This destructive power of Satan cannot be underestimated. He is the one who causes evil in the world. But the New Testament writers refute the idea that every personal calamity is due to some corresponding personal sin (cf. Luke 13:1-3). They are not interested in establishing a causal connection between one's sinfulness and subsequent "punishment" through diseases or other kinds of suffering, as was popularly believed among the people of their time. The New Testament writers are much more interested in pointing out the salvational purpose of these evil occurrences.

(2) On the other hand, the New Testament writers tell us also of Satan's defeat through Jesus Christ. In the story of Beelzebub (Mark 3:27) it is clearly expressed that Satan has found his victor and this is reaffirmed with each subsequent deed of Jesus, concluding in his sacrificial death (1 Cor. 15:57). Satan still wants to accuse people before God, but Jesus intercedes for them so that their faith "may not fail" (Luke 22:32). Satan has even lost his preferred position and access to heaven, because Jesus affirms, "I saw Satan fall like lightning from heaven" (Luke 10:18). This coincides with the observation in the book of Revelation that "the accuser of our brethren has been thrown down, who accuses them day and night before our God" (Rev. 12:10). Because Satan is overcome we are not surprised that the disciples are promised that they can "tread upon serpents," which means that they have authority over the evil and seductive anti-Godly powers (Luke 10:19).

The tendency to divide the world into two spheres of influence, one in which Christ rules and one which Satan rules, is clearly advanced in the Johannine writings. But we do not find a cosmological dualism introduced in the Johannine writings. According to

John the world is still God's creation, created through the *logos*. The world is not divided in Gnostic fashion into an evil cosmos, the domain of Satan, and a celestial heaven, the heaven of all believers in which the father in heaven rules. A new birth is still possible for everyone (John 3:3), because "God sent the Son into the world, not to condemn the world, but that the world might be saved through him" (John 3:17). When we have "overcome the evil one" (1 John 2:13) through faith in Christ we are not lifted up into another sphere. We still live in this world and therefore the caution is still necessary, "Do not love the world or the things in the world" (1 John 2:15). Thus Rudolf Bultmann is right when he observes, "Each man is, or once was, confronted with deciding for or against God; and he is confronted anew with this decision by the revelation of God in Jesus. The cosmological dualism of Gnosticism has become in John a *dualism of decision*."[11] But this dualism will not continue forever. "The world passes away, and the lust of it; but he who does the will of God abides for ever" (1 John 2:17). This is the hope which undergirds New Testament faith.

All of this shows that there is a growing awareness in the biblical writings that the cause of evil cannot simply be attributed to God. Especially during the political turmoil of the postexilic period, trust in God as the giver of all good things could not be reconciled with God as the source of good and evil. From the very beginning, however, the power of evil was understood to be of so great a magnitude that it could not just be conceived of as stemming from humanity itself, individually or corporately conceived. The need to relegate the cause of evil to an outside force, however, never diminished the individual or corporate accountability for evildoing. Since God has always been understood as the creator of everything that is, the cause of evil had to come from within God's good creation.

To find out why a part of God's good creation denied its own originator may be interesting for speculative minds, but it is unimportant for the biblical writers. It is also beyond the interest of the biblical writers to define clearly what is meant by evil. Though evil is often understood as that which impairs the life-enhancing process, it is most frequently conceived of as something that obstructs the furthering of God's kingdom. Even biological impairments such as diseases or physical disturbances such as earthquakes can be included under the category of evil. The reason for not distinguishing the so-called "natural evils" and the "spiritual evil" seems to lie in the biblical conviction that the world cannot be dualistically divided into two primordial principles, God as the cause of all good, and Satan as the cause of all evil. The biblical witnesses are convinced that ultimately—and occasionally even penultimately—the cause of evil cannot but glorify God (John 9:3).

2. The anti-Godly reality

When we now consider the issue of the personification of the cause of evil we certainly do not want to revert to a pagan polydemonism such as the one that made fateful inroads into medieval Christianity and resulted in witch-hunts and mass neuroses. Yet we find it impossible to locate the cause of evil strictly in the human sphere or to consider it as just part of the natural process. We should not forget that at the height of the Enlightenment even Immanuel Kant in a book with the significant title *Religion within the Limits of Reason Alone* (1793) insisted on the existence of a radical evil. Kant almost seems to have anticipated Konrad Lorenz's behavioral findings when he said: That man is evil cannot mean anything but that "he is conscious of the moral law, but has nevertheless adopted into his maxim the (occasional) deviation therefrom."[12] It is not humanity's constitutive nature that makes it bad but rather something for which humanity is accountable. It is a radical evil working in every human being.

There are two ways, according to Kant, in which we could account for this radical evil in humanity.[13] First, it could stem from human *sensuality*. But to relegate the cause of evil to the sphere of their senses would degrade humans to mere animals, indicating that they are not actually accountable for the evil which they do. Second, it could stem from our *intellect*. If human depravity, however, as kind of malignant reason would stem from our intellect, we would be the incorporation of the diabolic itself and would no longer act in true freedom. Thus Kant concludes that to seek the origin of evil in human sensuality would be too restricting, while extending it to the intellect would be too all-embracing to account for the radical evil in humanity. For Kant, rather, evil is a natural inclination that we freely follow.[14]

If we assume a cause of evil outside humanity, do we then not just push the causal nexus one step further without sufficient grounds? We might be inclined to think so. But even psychoanalysis does not explain the phenomenon of evil by referring only to humanity. With reference to destructive forces Sigmund Freud talks about the (ambivalent) *superego* and Carl Gustav Jung about the (ambivalent) archetypes and a person's shadow. In their destructive tendencies these phenomena are explained as a kind of haunting memory within the individual or within the whole of humanity. As psychoanalysis wants to stay within the objectively given (i.e., humanity), it cannot provide any further explanation for these destructive forces, unless it assumes a constitutive depravity of humanity. But this notion had already been rejected by Kant.

Another possibility to account for evil would be to assume "meta"-physical forces outside humanity. However, such an explanation would necessarily exceed the possibilities of science and philosophy. To assume such a possibility for the origin of evil, however, might not be far-fetched. We are not content either with scientific cosmogonies or their objectively given (matter or energy) in explaining the emergence of the universe. Nor are we content with paleontology and its objectively given (the prehuman biological realm) to account for the emergence of humanity. So it might be legitimate that we go beyond psychoanalysis and its objectively given (the human psyche) to probe the depth of evil.

When we say "Satan" we do not want to revert to a primitive mythological figure but we want to express "that there is a principle or force of evil antecedent to any evil human action."[15] We must caution, however, against the assumption that we could now easily distinguish between the works of Satan and of God. Three concerns are involved in this caution:

(1) Though God's creation is good, the ongoing process of God's redemptive history reminds us that it is not yet redeemed and perfected. This allows for the occurrence of many "natural" phenomena which we know will not be part of the new creation. One of these phenomena is the necessity of death of one form of life in order to sustain and further other forms of life. We could call them "natural evil" to indicate that they are not anti-Godly constellations but part of God's continuing creative and redemptive process. Gordon Kaufmann rightly calls "natural evil" a "somewhat inaccurate way of referring to this fact that God's hand cannot always be

seen—that men often are, indeed, engulfed in what appears to be the very denial of loving purpose."[16]

(2) This leads to a second point, that God works through the appearance of the opposite. Especially Luther emphasized this by saying that God works like someone who is using a rusty and rough hatchet. "Even though the worker is a good craftsman, the hatchet leaves bad, jagged and ugly gashes. So it is when God works through us."[17]

(3) The most bothersome concern, however, expressed especially forcefully in Luther's *The Bondage of the Will* (1525), is that God works in evil people toward evil purposes. Though this reaffirms the biblical conviction that God can use Satan ultimately to achieve his purpose, even Luther was bothered by this statement and asked himself: "But why does he [God] not at the same time change the evil wills that he moves?" Luther does not indulge in speculations at this point. He simply admits: "This belongs to the secrets of his majesty, where his judgments are incomprehensible. It is not our business to ask this question, but to adore these mysteries."[18]

The great question of philosophy is why there is something and not just nothing and the great issue of theology is why there is not just good but also evil. Satan is the ultimate referent in our search for the cause of evil. Insisting that God works evil in evil people, Luther did not dare to say in *The Bondage of the Will* that God is the cause of evil. On the contrary, Luther affirms in the same treatise that humanity is either ridden by God or by the devil.[19] This shows us the paradox involved in our search for the cause of evil. While we must affirm that ultimately everything comes from God, we are aware of the powers of darkness which are both integral to and contrary to God's redemptive history.

The powers of darkness have their limit in God and they are not equal to him. If we cannot affirm God's infinite superiority over all demonic or satanic powers, our trust in the ultimate triumph of God's kingdom is impaired. We would have to doubt the fact that nothing is impossible for God. We would also constantly be afraid that we were associated with part of the creative process that either is not under God's dominion or that cannot be redeemed. To avoid this dilemma of faith we must affirm with Luther that God is also the God of Satan.[20] In classifying Satan as nothingness Karl Barth has picked up this emphasis on the sub-Godly aspect of Satan. Barth affirms:

> Nothingness is that from which God separated Himself and in face of which He asserts Himself and exerts His positive will.... As God is Lord on the left hand as well, He is the basis and Lord of nothingness too. Consequently it is not adventitious. It is not a second God, nor self-created. It has no power save that which it is allowed by God.... Even on His left hand the activity of God is not in vain.[21]

When Barth continues that God's not wanting and not willing also has consequences because God is active even in his not working and not willing, he comes close to denying the equally important insight that must be maintained together with the sub-Godly aspect of Satan, namely, the noncreational aspect. We do not know to whom Satan "owes" his being. Karl Barth seems to neglect this when he indicates that at least indirectly the "nothingness" owes its being to God's inactivity. Though he rejects the notion that nothingness is created by God, his line of argument comes very close to making the existence of nothingness dependent on God.[22]

Besides the sub-Godly limitation and the noncreated origin there is also Satan's anti-Godly tendency. Without neglecting the other two features, this aspect received prominence in the biblical story of the life and destiny of Jesus. Here God and Satan encountered each other on the same plane. Karl Barth therefore is right when he stresses that the battle with Satan is primarily and actually God's own affair.[23] Luther, in his hymn "A Mighty Fortress Is Our God," also warned us that "our ancient foe doth seek to work us woe." If we consider such abysmal attacks of the demonic as occurred at Auschwitz and Hiroshima and those which continue to occur today in subtler ways, we cannot escape the threatening character of the utter destructiveness and perversity of these powers.

This destructiveness and perversity surfaces prominently in the New Testament, when Satan is called the father of lies and a murderer from the very beginning (John 8:44). Here our observation is reinforced that these powers do not operate on our finite human level. They are in constant rebellion against God, fighting against him on an equal level. Humanity's subsequent rebellion, however, though not to be taken lightly, is not an act of innate perversity or predetermined necessity. Humanity is willingly drawn into this battle, following the path of these forces. Like them, humanity challenges God's authority and attempts to set itself up as a new god in full autonomy.

In the story of Jesus' temptation we see both the power and the intention of these forces (Matt. 4:1-11). They attempt to win human allegiance so that they are worshiped instead of God, and in turn they promise us unbounded influence. Through the Christ event, however, we know, as Martin Luther affirmed in "A Mighty Fortress Is Our God," that "one little word [Christ] shall fell him." As these powers recognized, Christ had come to destroy them and their influence (Mark 5:7; 1 Cor. 15:57). Claiming Christ to be on our side, we can join his victory over these powers.

It has become clear that these destructive powers do not confront us like an impersonal *it*, but like a persuasive and overpowering *thou*. A personification of these powers clarifies our perception of them. Since, however, neither Old nor New Testament has a consistent name for them, often leaving the impression that there are a multitude of anti-Godly powers, it is appropriate to refer to them by their common intentionality as anti-Godly powers. The term anti-Godly powers would also relieve us of the possible misunderstanding that we are talking here about a devil or a satan in analogy to myths or to fairy tales.

B. The power of sin (original and actual sin)

After trying to determine the location and magnitude of the cause of evil, we must now delineate how evil manifests itself in our human nature and to what extent we are still free to follow our own deliberations. Though we do not want to take Genesis 3 lightly and belittle the magnitude of humanity's fallen nature, we realize that the Fall did not undo God's creation. Even under the spell of the Fall we are created in the image of God and remain God's administrators. When we describe and evaluate the biblical and the church's understanding of human sinfulness, we do this with reference to our actual nature, our responsibility, and our having been created in God's image. While we must distinguish between actual sins and original sin (which is reaffirmed by every subsequent actual sin), we will soon see that for the biblical witnesses the intention and structure of both actual and original sin point in the same direction. Both are understood as aversion from God, implying that sinfulness is humanity's unnatural nature.

1. Aversion from God

The biblical witnesses use a multitude of expressions to describe sin. In all cases, however, sin is foremost aversion from God. This is illustrated, for example, in the picturesque account of the first sin. Adam replied to God's inquiry about why he was hiding himself, "I heard the sound of thee in the garden, and I was afraid, because I was naked; and I hid myself" (Gen. 3:10). Humanity breaks away from its close relationship with God and then experiences a basic insecurity in its subsequent encounter with God.

Whether humanity trespasses against required norms, whether it attempts to reject all norms, or whether it is simply in error, in each case its activity is considered a sin against God. For instance, David transgressed against the Hittite Uriah in the most blatant way when he had Uriah sent on a fatal military mission so that David could take Uriah's wife, Bathsheba, as his own. It was only after David was confronted with God through the prophet Nathan that he recognized, "I have sinned against the Lord" (2 Sam. 12:13). God demands conformity with his will, but humanity becomes sinful and, by avoiding God because of its sins, implicitly attests to the legitimacy of the will of God.

Sin is everything which does not proceed from a trusting relationship with God. Paul puts this understanding of sin very precisely when he says, "Whatever does not proceed from faith is sin" (Rom. 14:23). Since sin is always defined by relating an action or its result to our ultimate destiny as found in God, sin as such is not accessible to phenomenological investigation. The people in Sodom and Gomorrah, for instance, did not perceive their perversity as sinful. Only in the sight of Yahweh was their conduct understood as grave sin (Gen. 18:20). If sin is aversion from God, we are not surprised to hear that a person who sins shall die (Ezek. 18:4). To turn away from the giver of life has implications for this life and beyond.

Sin is primarily a theological term, indicating the disruption of the life-giving and life-sustaining relationship between God and humanity. By contrast, evil usually denotes a phenomenological and evaluative description of that which is bad or harmful. Unless grace intervenes, sin will always have ultimate consequences. Life cannot be indefinitely sustained or newly created without the continuing relationship with God, the source of all life. But not all sinful acts manifest themselves immediately in evil consequences. As finite beings we are unable to assess accurately the long-range effects of each individual act. Moreover, often something is considered good even though it may have evil results after the plans are carried through (cf. the proliferation of nuclear energy to aid underprivileged countries). Frequently also good and bad components are intermixed in a human action so that one is at a loss to assess its propriety (cf. the dynamic leader who ruthlessly uses nonpeaceful means to achieve the good of the community). This dilemma shows the urgency for humanity to act in conformity to God's life-giving Spirit to avoid ultimately and often penultimately disastrous results. Reference to God, however, means to view an action in the light of ultimacy and universality. We attempt to discern whether an action contributes or distracts from the promised goal of a new creation and to examine whether the chosen methods for action are analogous to that of God's own action embodied in Jesus of Nazareth.

In Judaism one distinguished between "mortal" sins, such as idolatry, licentiousness, and bloodshed, and "venial" sins that were committed unknowingly. For the former it was thought that satisfaction could only be attained through death, while for the latter it was assumed that one could atone through rites of purification, good works, and sufferings. Sin was mainly understood as transgressing the divine law, behind which God was still discernible.

In the New Testament the distinction between degrees of sinfulness was abolished and human sinfulness was once again directly related to our attitude toward God. The Sermon on the Mount, for example, shows us Jesus' deep awareness of the extent to which each person is hopelessly entangled in sinfulness. Jesus did not just acknowledge humanity's sinfulness; rather, he tackled sin in an unprecedented way. His whole ministry must be understood as a continuous battle against the anti-Godly powers. His victories over the anti-Godly powers were manifestations that the time of salvation had commenced and that the destruction of these powers had begun. This means that Jesus emphasized humanity's thoroughgoing sinfulness and, through his ministry, proleptically eliminated the very cause of sin by checking the anti-Godly powers that tempt to sin.

As the bringer of the kingdom of God, Jesus also established table fellowship with sinners and pronounced forgiveness of sin (Mark 2:15-16). He did not separate himself from sinners but, as the one who stands in the place of God, established a new communion with them. These acts signaled the beginning and foreshadowing of the eschatological communion of God with his people when he will no longer hold their sins against them. In Jesus, therefore, it becomes true what the servant of Yahweh had promised: "I, I am He who blots out your transgressions for my own sake, and I will not remember your sins" (Isa. 43:25). The forgiving of sins constitutes an eschatological moment; the new creation in which everyone will be in communion with God is anticipated proleptically. Even so, the proclamation of the kingdom of God and the forgiving of sins should not be taken lightly. They demand a response and ask for acceptance. Those who reject God's Holy Spirit as present in Jesus' life and destiny have forfeited their chance to return to God. They have brought judgment upon themselves and committed an unforgivable sin (Matt. 12:31f.).

The life and destiny of Jesus is the great crisis for sin, as especially the Gospel of John indicates. Here Jesus confronts the people with his words and deeds. They realize in this confrontation that they are sinners and are offered the chance to return to God. "If I had not come and spoken to them," we hear, "they would not have sin; but now they have no excuse for their sin" (John 15:22). In the confrontation with Jesus occurs the separation between those accepting him and thereby accepting God and those who reject him. By rejecting God in Christ the latter are judged and their sins stand against them. Therefore, we encounter the threatening, and at the same time comforting, pronouncement, "He who believes in the Son has eternal life; he who does not obey the Son shall not see life, but the wrath of God rests upon him" (John 3:36).

2. Our second nature

In the context of the Noachian blessing we read the devastating words, "The imagination of man's heart is evil from his youth" (Gen. 8:21). This same statement that once brought judgment upon humanity (Gen. 6:5) now constitutes the premise for the pronouncement of God's grace. Human beings are sinful from birth to death. The psalmist goes one step further when he exclaims, "Behold, I was brought forth in iniquity, and in sin did my mother conceive me" (Ps. 51:5). As exegetes caution, the psalmist does not introduce a traducianistic understanding of sin. Such a theory was not developed until Tertullian. Yet he admits the sinful context into which he was born, speaking of the "mother" Israel, in analogy to Isa. 54:1-5, alluding to the historic origin of Israel from her patriarchal ancestors (cf. Isa. 43:27). This means that sinfulness accompanies not only the history of individuals but also the corporate history of Israel.

In following this kind of Jewish reasoning Paul extends our perception of sin by saying that "sin came into the world through one man and death through sin, and so death spread to all men because all men sinned" (Rom. 5:12). Adam is the "gate" through which sin came into the world and sin is the "gate" through which death reached all people. Paul does not want to put the blame on Adam for the emergence of sin and death. Sin for Paul (*he hamartia*) assumes anthropomorphic features, personifying the anti-Godly destructive powers that found their way into our human world through this first human being. Paul, however, talks about the emergence of the age of death not just in a biological way. Symbolically this age had its beginning in Adam who is the antitype to Christ, the head of the age of life and the bearer of the new aeon.

Many Western theologians concluded from Paul's remarks that humanity had once been in an integer or original state, in which it had the possibility of not sinning and consequently of not dying.[24] Death, sorrow, and pain were thought to have come into the world through human sinfulness. Only those outside the confines of orthodox faith dared to assert that already the first human being would have died, whether or not he or she had sinned.[25] Today most theologians rightly refrain from speculations about a premortal, original state of humanity. Yet they too acknowledge that there is something peculiar about human death. Unlike the death of an animal, human death is not only a biological phenomenon.

Why do humans make death one of their primary concerns? Why was the issue of death from the earliest times of philosophical speculation one of the primal concerns? Does this not indicate that

Paul was correct when he asserted that the first human being was the gate through which sin and death-awareness entered the human world? Once humanity had alienated itself from its primordial conformity with its creator, death, as God's condemnation of this sinful life-style, threatened humanity and reminded human beings of their ultimate dependency which they had tried to reject.

Like us, Paul is not so much interested in the condition of the first human being. Instead he wants to say that we are born into the sinful context which was initiated by the first human being ever to live on this earth. Nobody starts fresh from the beginning. We are all influenced by the sins of the human family. This is what Paul means when he says, "By one man's disobedience many were made sinners" and "one man's trespass led to condemnation for all men" (Rom. 5:18f.). Indeed, we must talk here about sin as a hereditary affliction. At the same time, however, Paul appeals to personal accountability because we also know how we should conduct our lives. Everyone knows about God's will. Even the pagans, who do not have the (Old Testament) Law, have the law written on their hearts and they have a conscience which speaks to them (Rom. 2:14f.). We are reminded here of Luther's insight that there is not a special law for Christians, but that the same "natural" law applies to both Christians and non-Christians.[26] We have seen that the existence of common basic norms for human behavior is reaffirmed by the findings of ethological research.

It is significant how humanity expresses its sinful existence. Paul asserts that sinful humanity exchanges the truth about God for a lie and worships and serves the creature rather than the Creator (Rom. 1:25). This means that at the center of human sinfulness lies the abandoning of humanity's administrative position. The human family abandoned its position as God's administrators of the world and wanted to rule the world in autonomy. To gain complete autonomy, humanity attempts to overcome its inescapable finitude. In an attitude of boasting self-glorification, humanity tries to expand its dominion over the world to ever-broader horizons. Since the world, however, is finite and since human expansionism will sooner or later reach its limits, humanity must ultimately surrender itself to the finite things by which it is surrounded. Thus this behavior leads to religious idolatry.

This shows that humanity is deceiving itself in its struggle for autonomy. As a finite entity it can never be in full control of its own situation. Instead of trusting the infinite God, an attitude which would enable it to have dominion over the world as God's administrator, it wants to have dominion over life as a whole and consequently trusts the finite world. Thus humanity wants to dominate what it should trust, and trusts what it should dominate. We wonder whether this perverse and sinful attitude results from humanity's own choice and why it lives by its own intentions contrary to the way it ought to live.

In Chapter 7 of his Letter to the Romans Paul leaves the impression that sin has demonic character. In confrontation with God's law, nascent desires are awakened (Rom. 7:5). These desires or passions are not primarily sensual desires but include the whole gamut of sinfulness, from the original sin of pride to actual individual sins. In its unnatural (fallen) state human freedom is reduced to that of a slave (Rom. 7:14). Remembering his own situation prior to his conversion, Paul can identify with human sinfulness and exclaim:

> I do not understand my own actions. For I do not do what I want, but I do the very thing I hate.... So then it is no longer I that do it, but sin which dwells within me. For I know that nothing good dwells within me, that is, in my flesh (Rom. 7:15-18).

Unlike later Manichean teachings, Paul does not identify flesh and sin but only insists that human existence in the flesh is also an existence in sin. The human sphere of the flesh is dominated by sin. We can even draw the conclusion that humanity, living according to and in the human sphere, is enslaved by sin. Though humanity knows what to do and intends to do it, it cannot accomplish it. This should not come as a surprise, since we have just noted that as long as humanity lives in and from itself it lives in pride and sin, turned away from God. That it still wants and wills the good attests to the unnatural status of this behavior. Thus even though human nature has not been changed, humanity lives in a totally unnatural way, with its back turned to God.

It is evident that humanity's unnatural attitude need not effect the penultimate quality of its actions. Very often we find high moral standards among pagans and among deliberate atheists. But already Augustine observed that the virtues "are rather vices than virtues so long as there is no reference to God in the matter."[27] The relationship to God is the deciding factor which determines not phenomenologically but theologically between a virtue and a vice. As soon as this relationship is broken, human action is sin against God regardless of how "good" it is. Sin is aversion from God and must always be measured against this background.

Paul knows, however, that we are not condemned to live according to the flesh; we can also live according to the Spirit. Right after the admission, "Wretched man that I am! Who will deliver me from this body of death?" Paul exclaims, "Thanks be to God through Jesus Christ our Lord!" (Rom. 7:24f.). The Christ event liberates us from the bondage of sin (Rom. 5:21). Living according to the Spirit means that we no longer live on our own and for ourselves. Paul can therefore say that we are no longer on our own (1 Cor. 6:19). We are Christ's and belong to Christ. In the trusting relationship with Christ, enabled through the Spirit, the basic alienation is overcome. As was the case with the basic sinfulness of natural humanity, however, this new status does not bring about a biological or genetic change. It is achieved through God's grace. Therefore it is open to false interpretations and Paul constantly summons us to realize that which we already are. Sin no longer has dominion over us. But we still fight it in daily battles, battles which also know defeats, but which can and do foreshadow Christ's victory over sin.

C. The extent of corruption

When we now cast a glance at how the church wrestled with the understanding of sin, we soon notice that the basic issue was and still is whether there remains some goodness in humanity or whether it is now a totally corrupt entity. We want to deal with the question under the three headings under which it gained most prominence in the church, namely the issues of freedom and responsibility, of humanity as God's shattered image, and the corporate dimension of sin.

1. Freedom and responsibility

The issue of freedom and responsibility twice gained unprecedented prominence in the history of the church, once in the formative years of Western theology climaxing in the struggle between

Augustine and Pelagius, and then again in the emergence of the Protestant Reformation. Shortly before A.D. 400, an ascetic Christian named Pelagius had moved from Great Britain to metropolitan Rome. Revulsed by the laxity of morals in Rome, he admonished the people to lead a good life and appealed to their natural possibilities. In Rome he found an eloquent follower in the prominent lawyer Coelestius, and even Bishop Julian of Eclanum stood at his side. Pelagius argued that if God has commanded us to do the good, we must be able to do it. Indeed humanity is free, he concluded, to decide to do the good or the bad, since it has freedom to do either of them. As a reasonable creature a human being has had this possibility since the beginning of creation, because God endowed it with a free will and gave it the ability of free judgment. So humanity was by nature capable of doing good or bad. Though human freedom comes from God, it is up to humanity whether it wants to do good or bad.[28]

Pelagius understood by freedom primarily psychological freedom through which humanity freely decides what it wants to do. While this assessment of human freedom would not present any theological problems, Pelagius then equated this freedom of choice with moral freedom. In so doing, he ignored that moral life is not the resultant of individual acts but of a whole life attitude, that is, whether one lives in conformity with God or not. However, he argued that there can be no sinful attitude or sinful "nature," because if there were, what we call sin would then not be sin. Rather, it would be a fateful state of affairs for which God could not hold us personally accountable and punish us.

Pelagius did not hold that humanity was without sin, but he insisted that it could still be sinless. Since sin consists only of separate acts of the will, the idea of its propagation by the act of generation was, to Pelagius, absurd. Adam was the first sinner, but there is no demonstrable connection between his sins and ours. Newborn infants are therefore declared sinless and do not need Baptism for the forgiveness of their sins.

It would be easy to classify the position of Pelagius and his followers as self-redemptive moralism. They believed in the inherent goodness of humanity and actually did not need Christ's salvific deed to be able to return to God. When we consider Pelagius' assertions, however, in the context of classical antiquity, his position becomes more understandable. In the environment in which fatalism and determinism ruled supreme, most theologians emphasized personal responsibility rather than the inevitability of sin. For instance, Theodore of Mopsuestia could assert very much like Pelagius "that it is only *nature* which can be inherited, not sin, which is the disobedience of the free and unconstrained will."[29] But Augustine thought this kind of reasoning to be very dangerous.

Augustine points out that with divine assistance the first human being could have remained good and that God could have changed his possibility of not sinning and not dying to the impossibility of sinning and dying. But Adam did not stay this way; he sinned and since all people are joined together in him, all people sinned through him (Rom. 5:12). Therefore in Adam the whole human family became a corrupt entity.

Unlike Pelagius, for Augustine sin is not handed on through contact or imitation but through procreation. Sexual concupiscence expressed in the act makes the newborn child a victim of sin, although the procreative act in itself is not a sin for the reborn. Yet Augustine asserts that even as sinners we are "capable of good actions and of evil ones."[30] The inherited concupiscence is not determinative but becomes sin through "willing consent."[31] Humanity can even at times avoid concupiscence and grave sins and instead select virtues of wisdom and fortitude.

Augustine would fully agree with Pelagius that a human being has the possibility to choose between virtues and vices. But he differs from Pelagius when he insists: "But this will, which is free in evil things because it takes pleasure in evil, is not free in good things, for the reason that it has not been made free . . . . Nobody has a free will to do the good without the assistance of God."[32] In other words, goodness before God does not just consist of individual, morally good acts. It is the result of a life attitude which is in conformity with God. Therefore, the "virtues of the pagans are splendid vices." Once humanity revolts against God, the creator and sustainer, it destroys the natural order and it cannot remake this order on its own through benevolent actions. For Augustine, sin is not merely doing what is morally wrong, as Pelagius insisted, but he recognizes that it has much larger dimensions which are shown by our presumptuous attitude of attempting to take control of our own life. Sin is revolt against God; it is aversion from God and so also pride and self-love.

Augustine makes it clear that for each individual act people still need God's grace so that they do not succumb to their sinful inclinations. We might wonder, however, whether Augustine does not eliminate personal responsibility for sin when he emphasizes God's predetermining will. Though Augustine talks primarily about God's predetermining will toward salvation, he also talks about predestination toward damnation. But he remains rather silent concerning the reason for this double predestination. He refers to God's will and to the mystery of grace because "he who is delivered has good ground for thankfulness, he who is condemned has no ground for finding fault."[33] In other words we have no right to expect that God would accept us. We can expect only that he reject us. All else is undeserved grace.

Perhaps the church was wise when at the Synod of Orange in A.D. 529 it reaffirmed Augustine's insight in humanity's total dependence upon God while at the same time passing over Augustine's idea of double predestination in silence. Humans are free to choose between good and bad. We hear this from both Augustine and Pelagius as well as from representatives of the life sciences. Their opinions differ, however, once they attempt to assess this occasional but persistent deviation from the good. In our time Konrad Lorenz concluded that "man is not so evil from his youth, he is just *not quite good enough* for the demands of life in modern society."[34] In Augustine's time Pelagius made a similar remark with regard to the demands of life in urban Rome. Yet what might be excusable for a scientist is not excusable for a theologian, that is, the failure to recognize that wrongdoing, once committed, cannot be undone. Even if one forgives the evildoer and he or she attempts restitution, the sinful act itself cannot be taken back.

Today we notice this in an especially painful way when we examine our exploitative attitude toward nature. Once we have squandered natural resources we cannot put them back into the ground. Only a truly creative power can accomplish what is naturally impossible. This is what Augustine meant when he insisted on the necessity of the relationship between God and humanity in order for us to live a genuinely good life. Our real freedom does not come from the inherent possibility for us to choose between good and bad. It rather lies in the freedom for us to become children of God and to live in communion with the power that promised to make all things news.

A thousand years after the Pelagian controversy the same issues were discussed once more, again with similar arguments. In 1524 Erasmus of Rotterdam wrote his diatribe *On the Freedom of the Will* in which he attacked the restrictions which Luther made upon humanity's free choice. He observed that "after his battle with Pelagius, Augustine became less just toward free choice than he had been before. Luther, on the other hand, who had previously allowed something to free choice, is now carried so far in the heat of his defense as to destroy it entirely."[35] Erasmus questioned the point of the biblical admonitions and precepts if indeed we can do nothing and God does everything. Similarly, he noticed that we often read in Scripture of godly people, full of good works, who walked in the presence of the Lord. Again their good deeds cannot be simply sin. Of course he conceded all good works are due to God, without whom we can do nothing. But at the same time he emphasized that even if the contribution of free choice itself is part of the divine gift, "we can turn our souls to those things pertaining to salvation, or work together with grace."[36]

Martin Luther was shocked by Erasmus' trust in the human potential of working together with God toward one's salvation. He responded in 1525 with his treatise *The Bondage of the Will* in which he flatly renounced the idea that a human being had free will. Luther asserted that, like the Pelagians, Erasmus wanted to replace Christ as redeemer with our free will, since according to Erasmus the free will can fulfill God's commandments. As Augustine had done before him, Luther emphasized that humanity does not just commit individual sins but that its whole attitude is determined by sin. The source for this sinful desire is original sin which is inherited by everyone.

With Augustine, Luther understands sin also as concupiscence, a drive that for Luther, however, is not primarily sexual. Humanity's procreative faculty is a divine gift, though polluted through human lust. While Luther is more appreciative of human sexuality than Augustine, he agrees with Augustine that original sin is handed on through the procreative process. One could ask whether it is then not simply a fateful decree that all subsequent generations are sinful. Luther responds that humanity is never forced to sin but does evil voluntarily. Moreover, God is not a demon who causes good or evil according to his wishes. "God cannot act evilly although he does evil through evil men, because one who is himself good cannot act evilly."[37]

According to Luther the free will of the sinner is an empty phrase. True freedom existed only in paradise and will again exist only through grace. Without grace, Luther says with Augustine, the human family is a corrupt entity, turned away from God. Again sinfulness does not diminish humanity's moral choice. "The Ten Commandments," Luther asserts, "are inscribed in the hearts of all men."[38] There is wisdom in humanity and a drive toward the good. We can build houses, found families, educate children, and establish good and just order in economy, commerce, and government. But none of these activities makes us more pleasing to God, they only enable us to be more pleasing toward each other. While emphasizing the total depravity of humanity insofar as it might provide a natural ability to live in relationship with God, both Augustine and Luther agree with their opponents that there is still a possibility for moral goodness in humanity.

2. Humanity's shattered image

We have heard that humanity is a corrupt entity whose members can hardly be conceived as living up to the image of God. The question must now be raised of the extent this changes the claim that humanity was created in the image of God. Irenaeus (?– c. 190) was one of the first to distinguish between *image* and *similitude* (or *likeness*) to affirm both humanity's sinfulness and its status as God's special creature.[39] This distinction goes back to Gen. 1:26, in which two different Hebrew words (*zelem* and *demut*) are used to express that humanity is created in God's image. The two Hebrew words are not synonymous. The second one tries to qualify the idea that an image could mean a replica. Some of Irenaeus' dogmatic conclusions, however, drawn from the different use of words go beyond their scriptural basis. Irenaeus claimed that through Adam's Fall the God-intended development of humanity, through which it was to become immortal, was interrupted. Humanity lost its similitude, i.e., its relationship with God, while it retained the image, being a reasonable and morally free creature. This distinction enabled Irenaeus to affirm that humanity did not change physically but only relationally once it had become a sinner.

The distinction between similitude and image, however, could easily be interpreted to mean that sinfulness affected only part of humanity while the rest remained in a state of original integrity. This train of thought could lead to the notion that humanity needs only to improve in order to be no longer sinful. This hazard is already unintentionally there in Augustine when he uses neo-Platonic terminology and talks about evil as a deficiency of the good that results from a deficient cause or from a defect.

In late medieval theology the aspect of sin as deficiency gained theological prominence. Thomas Aquinas, for instance, stated that "original sin in its material sense is indeed concupiscence, while in its formal sense it is certainly a defect of the original justice."[40] This "corrupt disposition," namely, the privation of original justice, is now called original sin.[41] But it can be corrected through a supernatural gift which achieves a sublimation of humanity beyond its sinful nature.[42] Human nature no longer needed a conversion but an addition or a sublimation. Grace was now understood as something supernatural in humanity, a supernatural quality.

To perceive grace as a supernatural addition to humanity's natural state is as dangerous as the idea that a human being is not a totally corrupt and sinful entity, but only lacks the supernatural gifts of the similitude, i.e., original justice and integrity. The church thought differently and decided at the Council of Trent in the Decree on Justification that through God's grace humanity can assent, cooperate, and dispose itself to God's salvific activity.[43] This meant that the church did not hold that humanity's nature was really changed. Its properties as an image of God were still thought to be extant so that the lost similitude could be restored through a supernatural addition.

The Reformers, however, discarded the distinction between image and similitude. "Man must be an image," we hear Luther say, "either of God or of the devil, because according to whom he directs his life, him he resembles."[44] A human being is perceived as a unity and if it is sinful, the whole being is sinful. This is underscored by Luther's statement in *The Bondage of the Will* that a human being resembles an animal that is driven either by God or by the devil.[45]

John Calvin, though asserting that there is nothing left in humanity of which it could boast, claimed that there are "some remaining traces of the image of God which distinguish the entire human race from the other creatures."[46] This was the line of thinking that Lutheran Orthodoxy—perhaps even more cautiously—took. Johann Gerhard, for instance, maintains that "with regard to these most minute particles . . . the image of God was not utterly lost."[47] These "most minute particles," however, are inborn moral principles, humanity's dominion over other creatures, its intelligence, and its free will concerning the things which are under its control. Something important was emphasized here, but with inadequate conceptuality. Humanity did not suddenly become stupid, lazy, and unreliable once it was drawn into universal sinfulness. Even as sinner a human being is still God's creature and related to God.

Genesis 1:26 does not talk about an ideal state in the distant past. Still today humans are called to be God's administrators. To fulfill this task they are still endowed with the same gifts they always possessed. This does not mean Luther was wrong when he stated that humanity has totally lost its status as being created in the image of God. Luther attacked with this statement the idea that some features in humanity were still integral while others were contaminated by sinfulness. Thus he insisted that the total human being was a corrupt entity.

Today most Roman Catholic theologians have abandoned an ontological understanding of humanity being created in the image of God which so easily leads to the misunderstanding that part of a human being is still intact while the other part is corrupt. Michael Schmaus, for instance, mentions that the Genesis statement that humanity is created in God's image should be understood in a functional way.[48] Humans are called to exercise dominion over the world. Only with regard to the new creation in the eschaton should we talk about an ontological understanding of the image of God brought about through our full participation in Christ (cf. Rom. 8: 29; 2 Cor. 3:18). Schmaus also mentions that according to the Fathers the statement that we are created in the image of God means that God is reflected in us.[49] This implies that we can realize ourselves only if we realize ourselves as being created in the image of

God. But instead of reflecting God, we want to be like God. We misuse the creation instead of exercising dominion over it and managing it in thankfulness to God. We search for ourselves in the creation instead of looking there for the "footprints" of our creator. Therefore, in trying to discover the cosmos, we lose ourselves to the cosmos. Our world begins to resemble more and more a kingdom of sin rather than the kingdom of God.

3. The social dimension of sin

In the Gospel of John we hear the conviction expressed that the cosmos is ruled by the prince of this world. It was not until Augustine's classic *The City of God*, however, that the kingdom was systematically described. Augustine speaks of two cities, the city of God and the city of the world. One city "consists of those who wish to live after the flesh, the other of those who wish to live after the spirit, and when they severally achieve what they wish, they live in peace, each after their kind."[50] The two cities are not neatly separated. The city of God lives like an alien in the city of the world. The two cities or societies have been formed by two kinds of love, "the earthly by the love of self, even to the contempt of God, the heavenly by the love of God, even to the contempt of self. The former, in a word, glories in itself, the latter in the Lord."[51] The decisive difference between the two cities lies in the intentionality of their actions, whether one "lives according to himself" or according to God.[52] In the earthly city the possessions and comforts of this life tend to twist and block the way to God, whereas in the city of God they help to ease the burden of our life. Thus the believers are looking forward to judgment day when the city of this world will be dissolved and the kingdom of God will emerge.

Sin is here understood as having a social dimension. It serves the self-glorification of humanity and is, at least potentially, self-destructive. We should not forget that Augustine wrote *The City of God* under the impact of the devastation of Rome by the Gothic hordes of Alaric in A.D. 410. Human history, as a history of the city of the world, is seen as bringing upon itself its own judgment, which is at the same time part of God's judgment. Thus the city of God serves as a reminder and a corrective for the city of the world.

In the late 19th century, Albrecht Ritschl (1822–1889) reintroduced the distinction between the kingdom of sin and the kingdom of God, to some extent closely resembling Augustine's distinction and to some extent in deliberate opposition to it. This becomes evident when he writes:

> Sin, which alike as a mode of action and as a habitual propensity extends over the whole human race, is, in the Christian view of the world, estimated as the opposite of reverence and trust towards God, as also the opposite of the Kingdom of God—in the latter respect forming the kingdom of sin, which possesses no necessary ground either in the Divine world-order or in man's natural endowment of freedom, but unites all men with one another by means of the countless interrelations of sinful conduct.[53]

Ritschl rejected Pelagius' individualistic notion of sin, since he realized that the subject of sin is *"humanity as the sum of all individuals"* and that it leads to an association of individuals in common evil.[54]

As a strict follower of Kant, Ritschl abandoned the understanding of original sin as something inherited and instead emphasized humanity's own choice. The sinful desire and action of each individual "has its sufficient ground in the self-determination of the individual will."[55] Ritschl even asserts human freedom so far as to argue that there exists in each child "a general, though still indeterminate, impulse toward the good, which just falls short of being guided by complete insight into the good, and has not yet been tested in the particular relationships of life."[56] Does Ritschl really imply here that each child can be educated toward the good? Perhaps we get a clue to this question when we consider how Ritschl defines sin.

"Sin is the opposite of the good, so far as it is selfishness springing from indifference or mistrust of God, and directs itself to goods of subordinate rank without keeping in view their subordination to the highest good."[57] The Augustinian, Neoplatonic notion of sin as a deficiency of the good is present here as well as the understanding of God as the highest good. Since for Ritschl sin ultimately rests with humanity, both individually and corporately conceived, the Pelagian touch of his theory cannot be overlooked. With his concept of the kingdom of sin, however, Ritschl rightly emphasized and reminded us of each human being's individual responsibility and sin's corporate dimension.

Ritschl's emphasis of both aspects of sin, individual responsibility and corporate structure, was picked up by Walter Rauschenbusch (1861–1918) in his delineation of the kingdom of evil, and later also by Reinhold Niebuhr. Rauschenbusch claimed that "the doctrine of original sin has directed attention to the biological channels for the transmission of general sinfulness from generation to generation, but has neglected and diverted attention from the transmission and perpetuation of specific evils through the channels of social tradition."[58] Unlike Ritschl, however, he does not want to give up the hereditary notion of sin or the supernatural power of evil behind all sinful human action. If we abandon one in favor of the other he is afraid that our perception of sin will become much more superficial and will be mainly concerned with the transient acts and vices of individuals.

Rauschenbusch is convinced that the idea of the kingdom of evil gives to our modern mind an adequate sense of solidarity and a sufficient grasp of the historical and social realities of sin. Since the life of humanity is intimately interwoven, we cannot just talk about individual sins. "The evils of one generation are caused by the wrongs of the generations that preceded, and will in turn condition the sufferings and temptations of those who come after."[59] We are all bound together by the yoke of evil and suffering. "When the social group is evil, evil is over all."[60] But Rauschenbusch does not stop with the recognition of the corporate dimension of evil. Rauschenbusch also knows of a kingdom of God. Yet a conversion from the kingdom of evil to the kingdom of God cannot be confined to our inner self and our personal interests. Conversion is both a break with our own sinful past and with the sinful past of our social group.

Rauschenbush convincingly demonstrates that, just as committing a sin is not just a matter of our own private decision, conversion from our sinful existence is not solely something which occurs privately between the individual and God. Conversion has interpersonal consequences and—what Rauschenbusch did not recognize at his time—consequences for our relationship to our natural world as well. Sin as aversion from God affects our attitude toward ourselves, other people, and nature; in short, it affects our whole person.

PART 3

THE CHRIST WHO SAVES

When we now turn our attention to the Christ who saves we can do so only from the background of the God who acts. Jesus Christ is the decisive action of God as indicated in the opening lines of the Letter to the Hebrews: "In many and various ways God spoke of old to our fathers by the prophets; but in these last days he has spoken to us by a Son." In order to properly understand Jesus, we must see him against the Hebrew background out of which he emerged and, in order to grasp his significance, we must remember the human condition as described in the previous chapter. Humanity, being created in the image of God, continuously falls short of being God's administrator in this world. As a result of humanity's repeated and willful failures we could only expect that God would abandon it and leave it to its own demise. Yet God does not act as we would naturally expect. In his infinite patience and graciousness God devises one way after another to prod humanity to return to the right way. When all else fails God finally sends his Son to us to accomplish what we are unable and unwilling to accomplish for ourselves and at the same time to act as our source of inspiration and guidance. Yet who is this Son, this Jesus Christ? If nothing else, he was a human being who lived among us. Whether he was more than a human being is not just one problem among others; it is the crucial point of God's salvific plan.

8

JESUS OF NAZARETH

None of the "founders" of the world religions is as contested concerning his message and person as Jesus of Nazareth. There is hardly any debate regarding whether Mohammed lived and what he taught. It is commonly accepted that he regarded himself as Allah's prophet and that he made known to the people Allah's revelation which he claimed he had received through an angel. Similarly, we know approximately when Buddha lived, who his parents were, and the major tenets of his teaching. But with Jesus the story is different. Occasionally some people still doubt that he ever lived and call the New Testament a purely literary invention. But even among the vast majority of scholars who agree on Jesus' historicity, there is neither a consensus on his significance nor on the content of his teachings. The reason for this dilemma is twofold.

(1) While Islam stresses obedience and while Buddhism emphasizes contemplation, the Christian faith invites understanding. When Philip was summoned to join the minister of Queen Candace and heard the minister read from the prophet Isaiah, he did not ask him whether he had the right insight or whether he had obeyed all the precepts of the prophet. His question was: "Do you understand what you are reading?" (Acts 8:30). The Christian faith invites discerning reflection.

(2) The other reason for our dilemma stems from the fact that Jesus is the founder of the Christian faith only in a very limited sense. Though Jesus had some followers during his lifetime, it was only after his death that a rapidly growing group emerged who in some way or other considered him to be the Christ. Rudolf Bultmann rightly claimed: "He who formerly had been the *bearer* of the message was drawn into it and became its essential *content. The proclaimer became the proclaimed*—but the central question is, in what sense?"[1] The question then arises whether Jesus should be considered to be part of the Christian faith or whether he is only its presupposition. Again Bultmann is right when he asserted that "*the message of Jesus* is a presupposition for the theology of the New Testament rather than a part of that theology itself.*"*[2] Without the message of Jesus, there would be no New Testament theology. But New Testament theology is more a reflection on Jesus than it is a collection of his sayings.

Not even the Gospels present an account of Jesus' teachings. This becomes immediately evident when we consider how they begin. Mark's opening words are: "The beginning of the gospel of Jesus Christ, the Son of God" (Mark 1:1). Similarly, Matthew starts with the announcement, "The book of the genealogy of Jesus Christ" (Matt. 1:1). Only Luke seems to go a different route when he claims that he attempted "to write an orderly account" (Luke 1:3). Even there the intention of the account is not biographical or historical but to "know the truth" of the faith (Luke 1:4). We have no document that exists solely for the purpose of telling us about Jesus.

Skeptical minds might conclude that the reason for this missing factual information is that Jesus' mission ended in failure. At the end of Jesus' life stands the cross. Why should anybody want to tell about a person who did not succeed unless one rejoices in utter negativity? Such conjectures, however, have no basis in the New Testament. Its starting point is not defeat but victory. Two of the synoptic writers begin their narration as "the gospel of Jesus Christ." The recognition that Jesus was the Christ led to the deemphasizing of the human person Jesus and an attempt to perceive this person as the Christ. Skeptics might still object that the move to recognize Jesus as the Christ was the great cover-up by which his early followers wanted to ignore the fact that Jesus' mission had failed.

After listening to this objection, we could in effect ignore it and continue to proclaim Jesus as the Christ, as the church has quite often done. Such an approach would, however, ignore the validity of the objection and simply affirm the need for faith in a doubting world. At the same time, however, it would neither attempt to persuade the skeptic nor engage him or her in dialog. Our unwillingness to listen to his charges could be interpreted as a sign of bad conscience. The other possible avenue, the one we want to take, is to ascertain—as far as this is possible—that the affirmation of Jesus as the Christ rests on the proclamation, person, and destiny of Jesus of Nazareth. This means that we want to show that our faith in Jesus as Lord and Savior is not a deception and, if not a logical consequence, at least a legitimate possibility ensuing from the Jesus event.

This option confronts us immediately with the issue of continuity. To what extent is there a continuity between Jesus of Nazareth and the Christ portrayed in the biblical documents? To what extent is there continuity between the biblical Christ and the Christ of the dogma of the church, such as the trinitarian and Christological dogmas? If it is possible, at least in outline form, to ascertain this kind of continuity, then we can go on to contemplate the significance of Christ for today. Before we venture into our specific task, however, we must briefly review the main results of the search for the object of our investigation, Jesus of Nazareth. Had not Albert Schweitzer claimed that the search for Jesus ended with a big question mark? Perhaps there is no criterion by which to delineate the one with whom Jesus Christ, the focus of the Christian faith, could have continuity. In this situation it is even more necessary to pay careful attention to the so-called lives of Jesus and the kind of research or presuppositions which motivated them.

A. The quest for the historical Jesus

In his famous study *The Quest of the Historical Jesus: A Critical Study of Its Progress from Reimarus to Wrede* (1906), Albert Schweitzer defined perceptively the starting point for the inquiry into the historical Jesus. Up to the time of the Reformation the New Testament served as the unquestioned basis for the dogma of the church. The quest for Jesus was thought to be identical with the quest for Jesus Christ. In the Lutheran Reformation the emphasis was on the works of Christ and not on his person. This becomes evident from Luther's explanation of the Second Article of the Apostles' Creed when he affirmed Christ's divine and human natures and then immediately delineated what Christ has done for us. Similarly Philip Melanchthon declared in his *Loci Communes* (1521) that to know Christ properly is "to know his benefits and not . . . to perceive his nature and the mode of his incarnation."³ Through the emergence of an increasingly critical historical consciousness the distinction was made between the Jesus of history and the Christ of the New Testament.

1. *"In many and various ways"*

The quest for Jesus is the result of the use of autonomous reason in a way that seeks to investigate the history which led to the formation of the New Testament and which senses that there is a difference between the narration of these documents and the actual course of events. Since reason is thought to be a reliable guide in historical matters, this endeavor results in a rationalistic interpretation of Jesus. The rationalistic interpretation of Jesus is initially characterized by a critical animosity toward the New Testament documents that only gradually changes into a more constructive approach. This initial hostility was not always totally the fault of the new investigators, but to a large measure also that of the theological and ecclesiastical establishment. As occurs in any tradition of long order, this establishment was skeptical of new approaches. The first part of this pilgrimage virtually coincides with the onset of the Enlightenment of the 18th century and is delimited by Reimarus at its beginning and Semler at its end.

Hermann Samuel Reimarus (1694–1768), professor of oriental languages at the Gymnasium Johanneum in Hamburg, influenced more than anybody else during the Enlightenment period the approach to the scriptural documents. During his lifetime he was known as a pious and devout Christian. Yet in the midst of his studies doubts occurred to him about the biblical documents, doubts which he entrusted to his pen in hope of finding evidence to refute them. But his doubts grew and finally resulted in a lengthy manuscript of which one part is entitled *On the Goal of Jesus and His Dis-*

ciples. This last part was heavily edited and and published by Gotthold Ephraim Lessing in 1778. While Reimarus never doubted the historicity of Jesus, he wanted to distinguish between the writings of the apostles and what Jesus actually said and did. Reimarus pointed out that the whole content of Jesus' proclamation can be reduced to the summons, "Repent, for the Kingdom of Heaven is at hand" (Matt. 3:2).

Reimarus suggested that until his death the disciples considered Jesus to be a secular, powerful savior of the people of Israel. Only when their hopes collapsed through his unexpected and premature death "did the apostles build the system of a spiritual suffering savior for the whole human race."[4] This shift depended heavily on their claim that Jesus rose from the dead and ascended to heaven. It is important for Reimarus that the resurrection appearances were witnessed only by Jesus' disciples but not by the Sanhedrin or other leading Jews in Jerusalem. Reimarus finds credible the claim that the disciples came secretly by night, stole the corpse, and went around saying he had risen. This means that the Christian faith is based on a deliberate fraud. Reimarus even suggests that the disciples waited 50 days before they publicly announced Jesus' resurrection. By then the body was so badly decomposed that nobody could have recognized him even if the stolen corpse had been found. For Reimarus the idea of Christ's return in power has no basis in the sayings of Jesus. The disciples set it far enough into the future that they could not be confronted with contrary evidence if it did not arrive at the predicted time.

Reimarus' objections have been repeated throughout the centuries in various forms. But they have not gained in credibility. No serious scholar today would claim that the transition from Jesus of Nazareth to Jesus the Christ occurred by deliberate fraud. Yet several of his points are still noteworthy today. Reimarus convincingly showed that there is a difference between the Jesus of history and the Christ of faith. He also perceived correctly that the Gospels were written under the influence of the Easter events and therefore are not biographies in the strict sense. They were composed to facilitate the proclamation of Jesus Christ. Reimarus also noticed that Christ's resurrection and parousia are central to the Christian faith. But he failed to realize that these central tenets of the Christian faith are indeed fully anchored in the life and destiny of Jesus.

Like many contemporaries Johann Salomo Semler (1725–1791), professor of theology in Halle, had rejected Reimarus' approach. In his four-volume treatise the *Free Investigation of the Canon* (1771–1775), he claimed that the Word of God and Holy Scripture are not identical. While proposing a rigorously historical analysis of the Bible, he did not want to act destructively. His theory of accommodation, which dates back to the Greek Fathers and which had gained renewed attention in the 19th century, was helpful in reconciling biblical criticism with the Christian faith. Semler proposed that the biblical writers shared with their contemporaries the same understanding of nature. Jesus and his disciples used certain figures of speech and religious concepts as an accommodation to the more limited intellectual horizon of their audience. Semler sees this substantiated when Jesus talks directly to his disciples while he uses parables in his disourse with other people. Similarly, Jesus' insistence on the nearness of the parousia was an accommodation to Jewish apocalyptic expectations. Jesus' real message, however, was the presence of salvation and of the kingdom. Contrary to Jewish expectations Jesus did not proclaim a visible, political kingdom, but an invisible, internal, and spiritual kingdom which is accessible to everyone and which can be realized in the hearts of all people. With his emphasis on the interiorization of the Christian faith Semler went beyond the shallow rationalism of Reimarus. Yet when Semler discarded most of the external forms with which Jesus proclaimed his message as accomodation to his listeners, Semler showed that he himself was a child of his time, a child of the Enlightenment. Semler nevertheless realized that at the center of Jesus' proclamation stood the kingdom of God and its coming.

The 19th century marks the high point of the life-of-Jesus literature. In part this was facilitated through a greater awareness of the different strata which make up the New Testament. Although there had already been numerous books on the life of Jesus, Friedrich D.E. Schleiermacher was the first theologian to lecture on this topic, doing so in 1819 and four times afterwards. Now the life of Jesus had become a distinct part of academic studies. Schleiermacher attempted to perceive Jesus in the context of his time and also in his own right. He was convinced that the Christian faith is well-founded only when it can ascertain its foundation, Jesus of Nazareth. With this conviction in mind and also knowing that he could not present a life of Jesus in detail, he attempted to sketch out Jesus' life and ministry.

One of the problems which Schleiermacher attempted to solve was the contradiction between historical investigation, which can conceive of Christ only in human terms, and faith, which associated with him the divine. According to Schleiermacher Jesus knew about his messiahship through the claims made by others and through its confirmation by his own self-consciousness. This self-consciousness gradually developed in him until it assumed the definite form of oneness with his Father's will. Central to Jesus was the idea of the kingdom of God which arose out of his self-consciousness and his perception of sin.

It is important for Schleiermacher that Jesus emerged from the context of Israelite history. He recognized a process of adaptation through which Jesus took over ideas from the religious history of Israel and adapted them to his own mission. Schleiermacher concludes: "*What the men of God of the old covenant wished and expected as their hopes and as divine promises was fulfilled in Christ.*"[5] In other words, Jesus was the fulfillment of the Old Testament covenant. Important for Schleiermacher is also the total dependence of Jesus on God, which attests to Jesus' divinity. "*He attributes everything to the constancy of his relationship to God, to the constant, uninterrupted vitality of his consciousness of God.*"[6] When we come to the end of Jesus' earthly life we notice that Schleiermacher attributes little significance to Jesus' resurrection. He calls the resurrection a revivification after which Jesus continued his work on earth as he had done before. Jesus himself saw his resurrection only as a temporary affair which should have concluded with his ascension. The ascension is also seen as unnecessary for Jesus' salvific efficacy. Though Schleiermacher recognizes that Jesus stands in continuity with the Old Testament covenant, providing its fulfillment, he overlooks the eschatological significance of Jesus' life and work. Since he consistently says "Christ" instead of "Jesus" one gets the impression—perhaps a correct one—that he introduced more a dogmatic Christ than the Jesus of history.

David Friedrich Strauss (1808–1874) was familiar with Schleiermacher's lectures on the life of Jesus when he wrote his two-volume *Life of Jesus* in 1835–1836. His approach is much more radical than that of Schleiermacher and can be summarized in the following statements. Birth, infancy, and childhood narratives are discarded as largely mythical and devoid of historical value. Jesus was influenced by John the Baptist and continued John's proclamation of the coming messianic kingdom once John was imprisoned. Strauss will even go so far as to say that "Jesus held and expressed the conviction that he was the Messiah; this is an indisputable fact."[7] Jesus also thought that he would make a visible second advent on the clouds of heaven as the messianic Son of man and conclude the existing dispensation. At first Jesus assumed that he would be glorified without suffering and dying but later he realized that suffering and death was a necessary part of his messianic mission. The critical approach of Strauss' *Life of Jesus* set off a storm of attacks. Strauss even was released from his tutorship in Tübingen and transferred to a less visible position.

Several years later he attempted to write a positive assessment of the life of Jesus for more popular circulation. But again he was unable to bridge the chasm between the Christ of faith and the Jesus of history. In this *New Life of Jesus* (1864) Strauss described gospel texts reflecting apocalyptic eschatology as predictions and ascribed them to the early church rather than to Jesus himself. With regard to the resurrection Strauss posed the following alternative: "Either Jesus was not really dead, or he did not really rise again."[8] According to Strauss rationalism favored the first option, while he was convinced that historical evidence must lead to the second option. The empty tomb narratives are the product of a legend and the appearances of the crucified Jesus are subjective visions or hallucinations engendered by the disciples' enthusiasm. The ascension too is declared a myth.

Unlike Schleiermacher Strauss attempted to found Christology on the Jesus event and not on a Christ idea. But he encountered the problem that "the New Testament authors have an idea of the person and the life of Jesus which cannot be harmonized with our concept of human life and the laws of nature."[9] The stringent causal and mechanistic worldview of the 19th century eliminated for Strauss most of the New Testament witness to Jesus as the Christ. The mechanistically interpreted laws of nature became the criterion of what was credible. For example, Strauss could not admit the union of the human and the divine in the person of Jesus. Moreover he thought this was not necessary, since it was much more plausible that the union with the divine took place in humanity as a whole instead of in a single human being. This semi-Hegelian option has again been advocated more than a century later by Thomas J. J. Altizer, a representative of the so-called death-of-God theology. Thus Strauss proposed the divinization of humanity and in turn regarded Jesus as a mere human being who had essentially failed. This latter conclusion was again proposed with much vigor by Albert Schweitzer. But before we turn to Schweitzer, we should first listen to two other seminal scholars who stand at the turn of the century and who represent the approach of liberal theology.

In the winter semester of 1899–1900 Adolf von Harnack (1851–1930), the great German church historian, gave a series of lectures at the University of Berlin before nearly 600 students on the topic "What Is Christianity?" While Strauss thought he had almost entirely destroyed the historical credibility of the Gospels, Harnack contended that two generations of historical criticism had succeeded in restoring their credibility in their main outlines. The biblical materials

> offer us a plain picture of Jesus' teaching, in regard both to its main features and to its individual application; in the second place they tell us how his life issued in the service of his vocation; and in the third place, they describe for us the impression which he made upon his disciples, and which he transmitted.[10]

Harnack was also much more open to the factuality of Jesus' miracles than Strauss. He realized that science again allowed for the feasibility of many of them. "In our present state of knowledge we have become more careful, more hesitating in our judgment in regard to the stories of the miraculous which we have received from antiquity."[11]

Since Jesus searched out sinners and ate with them, Harnack concluded that Jesus could not have been part of a separatist ascetic community. Yet Jesus lived in the Jewish world and his life and his discourses do not show any affinity to the Greek spirit. Only after his death were his thoughts Hellenized. We notice a romantic tinge when Harnack suggested that Jesus is "possessed of a quiet, uniform, collected demeanor, with everything directed to one goal . . . his eye and ear are open to any impression of the life around him" and "*his eye rests kindly upon the flowers and the children, on the lily on the field.*"[12]

Jesus' teaching, according to Harnack, can be summarized in three points:

> ... firstly the Kingdom of God and its coming.
> Secondly, God the father and the infinite value of the human soul.
> Thirdly, the higher righteousness and the commandment of love.[13]

While Harnack realized the centrality of the kingdom in Jesus' proclamation he had not yet developed a sense of eschatological realism. He asserted that "Jesus simply shared with his contemporaries" the idea of the kingdom of God and the kingdom of the devil and of the last eschatological battle at which the kingdom of the devil is defeated.[14] Jesus grew into this view and retained it. The other view, however, that the kingdom does not come with outward signs but is already here, was his own. Harnack further spiritualized eschatology when he contended that the kingdom of God is "a still and mighty power in the hearts of men."[15]

"In the combination of these ideas—God the father, providence, the position of men as God's children, the infinite value of the human soul—the whole gospel is expressed."[16] For Harnack Jesus is not the central focus of the gospel, but only God himself to whom Jesus points. Harnack made this clear when he said: "The gospel, as Jesus proclaimed it, has to do with the father only and not with the son."[17] Jesus "*is the way to the father, and as he is the appointed of the father, so he is the judge as well.*"[18] Jesus resembles John the Baptist in Grünewald's painting of the Isenheim Altar. He points to God and restores our trust in God. Jesus knows God both as the Father and as his father. "Jesus is convinced that he knows God but in a way in which no one knew him before, and he knows that it is his vocation to communicate this knowledge of God to others by word and by deed—and with it the knowledge that men are God's children."[19] With this last statement Harnack anticipated the whole program of the Social Gospel movement, the recognition of the fatherhood of God and the subsequent acknowledgment of human solidarity through the brotherhood of men.

Although not the central focus of the gospel, Harnack was convinced that Jesus was more than just an ordinary human being. Jesus knew himself to be the Messiah and he acted accordingly. Consequently his influence is still being felt. "The certainty of the resurrection and of a life eternal which is bound up with the grave in Joseph's garden has not perished and on the conviction that *Jesus lives* we still base those hopes of citizenship in an Eternal City which make our earthly life worth living and tolerable."[20] Harnack did not attempt to prove the facticity of the resurrection. He was aware that it is both a matter of faith and the bedrock of the Christian faith. Harnack was cognizant of the eschatological context of Jesus and his proclamation. But in his attempt to show the singularity of Jesus, he overlooked the fact that Jesus could not be divorced from this context. Instead Jesus was its decisive center. In classical liberal fashion Harnack distinguished between those things which we can no longer believe and those which we still accept, judging the former to be nonessential elements in Jesus' message and pointing to the latter as the actual core.

When we now turn to the understanding of Jesus in the Social Gospel movement, we encounter a genuinely American phenomenon, responding to the rapid industrialization and the influx of hundreds of thousands of immigrants. It is related to the increased social consciousness of late 19th-century British theology and is influenced by German liberal theology. It shows an amazing affinity to certain strands of liberation theology of our own day. Whether we turn to Washington Gladden, Henry Churchill King, Shailer Mathews, Francis Greenwood Peabody, or Walter Rauschenbusch, the understanding of Jesus is remarkably similar.

By way of illustration let us turn here to Shailer Mathews (1863–1941), for many years professor of New Testament history and interpretation and later dean at the Divinity School of the University of Chicago. In 1897 he wrote a book with the significant title, *The Social Teachings of Jesus: An Essay in Christian Sociology*. In this book he discusses the silence of Jesus with regard to politics, the interest of Jesus in economic life, the doctrine of equality, the doctrine of nonresistance and the transformation of society in general, to name just a few topics. We hear that "inevitably Jesus touched upon economics"[21] and that "wealth must be used for the establishment of the ideal social order whose life is that of brothers—the kingdom of God."[22] Jesus "was neither socialist nor individualist .... He calls the poor man to sacrifice as well as the rich man. He was the Son of Man, not the son of a class of men."[23]

Mathews' central category for understanding Jesus is the idea of the kingdom. The kingdom is neither a merely political kingdom, a theocratic state, a subjective state of the individual, nor exclusively eschatological. "Jesus thought of the kingdom as a concrete reality rather than an idea . . . [and] this reality was not to be left as an unattainable ideal, but was to be progressively realized, perhaps evolved."[24] The notion of an evolutionary progression looms high on Mathews' agenda. "By the kingdom of God Jesus meant *an ideal* (though progressively approximated) *social order in which the relation of men to God is that of sons and* (therefore) *to each other, that of brothers.*"[25] An understanding of sonship towards God and brotherhood within the community are the propelling forces of social amelioration and the means by which the kingdom will be brought about. For Mathews, however, the kingdom is not wrought solely through our own efforts. At one point—we do not know when—the growth of the kingdom will be supplemented by a divine cataclysm. Then the new social order will triumph and offenders of this order will be isolated. "Individual and institutional life will no longer testify to the reign of even an enlightened selfishness. The world, by virtue of man's endeavor and God's regenerating power, will have been transformed into the kingdom."[26] This means that the kingdom is the result of our cooperation with God as his sons and among ourselves as brothers.

In a later book, *Jesus on Social Institutions* (1928), a revision of his earlier life of Jesus, only subtle changes are made. But Jesus is placed into the context of the revolutionary spirit which Mathews discovered in his research on the French revolution. He starts with chapters on "The Revolutionary Spirit in the Time of Jesus" and "The Social Gospel of Jesus." He points to the revolutionary naturalism of Jesus' time and its general mood of instability. We hear that "Jesus not only adopted the messianic-revolutionary technique, but he also adopted what might be called the revolutionary technique and, like John, formed his group (*ecclesia*) of sympathizers."[27] Such a statement strikes us as amazingly modern and shows a striking affinity for the present-day concern of liberation theology.

Jesus the agitator was not primarily an agitator of social change, or one who discussed morals in general. His teaching was intended for the active soul and it was carried on by the church. "The true descendants of the original group about Jesus will be those who possess something of the revolutionary attitude."[28] Yet a revolutionary spirit does not imply violence, bloodshed, and war. Instead it is the realization "that God is love and that brotherliness rather than coercion is the true basis for human relations."[29] The optimism which is entailed in such an approach becomes evident when Mathews declares that "Jesus teaches that goodwill is a practicable basis upon which to build human society."[30] We hear nothing of the immensity of human depravity or of the inbreaking of the kingdom of God. Mathews rather presents an evolutionary vision resulting in human and global betterment.

Mathews did not realize that the original reason for relativizing all present value structures and for the emergence of a new community was the nearness of the kingdom and the eschatological figure of Jesus. Rather he emphasized the present implications of the imminent end of history. This approach is very different from the one taken by Albert Schweitzer who stands representatively for the rediscovery of the eschatological context of Jesus and his mission which have dominated 20th-century discussions of Jesus.

2. A new struggle with history

When we come to the beginning of the 20th century we not only encounter critical reason which investigates the New Testament documents but reason which has become critical of itself. Does reason really wrestle with these documents, as had been thought, or does reason simply arrange the documents to fit its own predelictions? In this way a new and much more self-critical dialog with history commences.

Albert Schweitzer, famous Bach interpreter, medical doctor in tropical equatorial Africa, and New Testament scholar, published in 1901 a book entitled *The Mystery of the Kingdom of God: The Secret of Jesus' Messiahship and Passion*. In his life of Jesus Schweitzer did not want to start with the beginning of Jesus' life, but with its center, with his messiahship. To some extent he still carried out the legacy of Strauss when he asked:

> If Jesus really regarded himself as Messiah, how comes it that he acted as if he were not Messiah? How is it to be explained that his office and dignity seem to have nothing to do with his public activity?

> ... On the other hand, if one assumes that he did not take himself to be the Messiah, it must be explained how he came to be made Messiah after his death."[31]

Schweitzer wanted to pose the alternative: either Jesus took himself to be the Messiah, or this position was first ascribed to him by the early church. Contrary to Reimarus, Schweitzer does not opt for the latter literary solution. Like Harnack, he was convinced that Jesus knew himself to be the Messiah. But in contrast to Strauss and Harnack, the clue to the whole phenomenon of Jesus rested for Schweitzer in eschatology. While Jesus' earlier development lies in the dark,

> at his baptism the secret of his existence was disclosed to him, — namely, that he was the one whom God had destined to be the Messiah. With this revelation he was complete, and underwent no further development. For he is now assured that, until the near coming of the messianic age which was to reveal his glorious dignity, he has to labor for the kingdom as the unrecognized and hidden Messiah, and must approve and purify himself together with his friends in the final affliction. The idea of suffering was thus included in his messianic consciousness, just as the notion of the pre-messianic affliction was indissolubly connected with the expectation of the kingdom.[32]

Jesus' message was similar to that of John the Baptist: Repent and attain righteousness, because the kingdom of God is close at hand. In contrast to John, Jesus performed miracles as well. But Jesus' preaching did not yield much success even though he tried hard. This was his first disappointment. The coming of the kingdom was thus delayed, even though all the necessary signs were present. As one of the most significant signs of the coming kingdom Jesus had discovered that John the Baptist was Elijah reincarnate. When John was beheaded and the kingdom still did not come, Jesus was once again disappointed and realized that he too had to suffer death. Thus he turned with his disciples to Jerusalem and there claimed to be the Messiah. The Jewish authorities, who had always been suspicious of him, accused him of blasphemy and put him to death. He died, but nothing happened.

Schweitzer concluded his book with the hope that his critics will find no fault with his aim, "to depict the figure of Jesus in its *overwhelming heroic greatness and to impress it upon the modern age and upon the modern theology.*"³³ This was the first significant attempt to explain Jesus' mission in completely eschatological terms, a mission founded on an idea that had proved to be wrong. Although this booklet contained enough dynamite to shatter many of the cherished thoughts of both conservatives and liberals, it received hardly any attention.

A different reception greeted Schweitzer's next book, *The Quest of the Historical Jesus: A Critical Study of Its Progress from Reimarus to Wrede* (1906). It was the first massive and conscientious assessment of the search for the historical Jesus. Schweitzer's verdict was radical and negative. Each generation—rationalism, liberalism, modern theology, etc.—tore down the picture of Jesus erected in the preceding generation and attempted to build its own. Yet none of them realized that each new edifice reflected more its own aspirations and desires than those of the Jesus who had actually walked this earth. While these lives were written with utmost sincerity, Schweitzer concluded that "Jesus as a concrete historical personality remains a stranger to our time."³⁴ Schweitzer, however, does not give up in despair. The two people mentioned in his title, Reimarus and Wrede, circumscribe his program. Reimarus was one of the first to provide an eschatological picture of Jesus, though he claimed that it was based on fraud. William Wrede also asserted that the noneschatological picture of Jesus was untenable. But he claimed that the eschatological element in the Gospels was a literary construction. Schweitzer then proceeded to propose again the alternative contained in his earlier book:

> There is, on the one hand, the eschatological solution, which at one stroke raises the Marcan account as it stands, with all its disconnectedness and inconsistencies, into genuine history; and there is, on the other hand, the literary solution, which regards the incongruous dogmatic element as interpolated by the earliest Evangelist into the tradition and therefore strikes out the Messianic claim altogether from the historical Life of Jesus. *Tertium non datur.*³⁵

Schweitzer took a clear stand for a thoroughgoing eschatological interpretation of Jesus. He declared that Jesus' ethics were interim ethics which aimed to prepare for the kingdom of God. Since the kingdom had not come when Jesus expected it, our ethics cannot be derived from Jesus' ethics. Nevertheless, Jesus' demands for a denial of the world and a perfection of personality are still valid for us, though they are in contrast to our ethics of reason. Schweitzer concluded that we need more persons like Jesus. His enthusiasm and heroism are important for us because they derived from a choosing of the kingdom of God and from a faith in this kingdom which was strengthened by his encounter with obstacles.

> In the knowledge that He is the coming Son of Man [Jesus] lays hold of the wheel of the world to set it moving on that last revolution which is to bring all ordinary history to a close. It refuses to turn, and He throws Himself upon it. Then it does turn; and crushes Him. Instead of bringing in the eschatological conditions, He has destroyed them. The wheel rolls onward, and the mangled body of the one immeasurably great Man, who was strong enough to think of Himself as the spiritual ruler of mankind and to bend history to His purpose is hanging upon it still. That is His victory and His reign.[36]

It is relatively unimportant for Schweitzer that Jesus was actually mistaken in his eschatological expectations. Decisive was his attitude toward history and toward the obstacles he had to overcome in accomplishing his goal.

With this publication Schweitzer started an immense uproar. The liberals could tolerate Schweitzer's portrayal of Jesus as a kind of religious fanatic who was misled by his own ideas. But they rebuked him for reducing Jesus' ethics to mere interim ethics. Regardless of how critical liberalism had been toward the Jesus of the New Testament it continued to cherish his ethical ideals. Now Schweitzer had declared that it is impossible to separate Jesus' ethics from his eschatological proclamation. This meant that the attempt of liberal theology to eliminate the eschatological dimension of Jesus' proclamation and to confine itself to the "timeless" validity of his ethical teachings (e.g., Harnack) found no basis in the historical Jesus.

Using his own argument against him, conservative scholars claimed that Schweitzer too had projected his own image of Jesus upon the New Testament in trying to write a life of Jesus. They concluded that the true historical Jesus could not be found by strictly historical investigation but only through faith. Indeed, Schweitzer's approach did bear the marks of his time. He attempted to exempt the historical Jesus from the constantly changing results of historical research when he claimed: "Jesus means something to our world because a mighty spiritual force streams forth from him and flows through our time also. This fact can neither be shaken nor confirmed by historical discovery. It is the solid foundation of Christianity."[37] While we cannot lay our hands on Jesus as a historical reality, Schweitzer affirmed that his spirit is still alive and active among us. With this conclusion the foundation of the Christian faith is turned into a spiritualized and therefore timeless truth. This meant that even Schweitzer employed one of the basic ideas of liberal theology, the timelessness of Jesus. But here we should not overlook Schweitzer's contribution: he showed that the Gospels are not merely literary products but are grounded in the life and mission of Jesus. This life and mission, moreover, must be understood in thoroughly eschatological terms.

Dialectic or neo-Reformation theology at the beginning of this century picked up the concern of Albert Schweitzer in a surprisingly positive fashion. Rudolf Bultmann (1884–1976), for instance, claimed that "the 'Christ after the flesh' is no concern of ours. How things looked in the heart of Jesus I do not know and do not want to know."[38] The reason for this is twofold. (1) A historical reconstruction of Jesus of Nazareth can be of only relative validity, subject to later refutation, amendment, or confirmation. As Lessing had claimed 150 years before, the accidental truth of history cannot become the foundation of faith. (2) Though Jesus is a historical fact in history, it is not his personal qualities, such as the eternal value of his message, the depth of his soul, or the genius of his personality that is important but rather the fact that God had acted decisively through him. Important is what he intended, what can also become a demand for us.

According to Bultmann, Jesus wanted to confront his audience with the demand for a decision for or against God, which at the same time entailed salvation or judgment. For Bultmann what is amazing is that God had acted in the human form of Jesus and that in being confronted with Jesus' call we are confronted with God. Since the encounter with God is decisive, Jesus as a historical person becomes almost irrelevant. Without hesitation Bultmann can assert that Jesus did not hold himself to be the Messiah, that most of the miracles attributed to Jesus never occurred, that he was deceived in assuming that the world would soon come to an end, etc.

Although he labels most of the New Testament events in the life of Jesus as mythological, this does not conceal his positive concern. Bultmann was convinced that these mythological elements needed to be interpreted existentially, i.e., they describe for us a certain understanding of existence and place before us the decision as to whether or not we will understand our existence in like manner.

Even Karl Barth, who initially agreed with Bultmann's method as a way of escaping from the strictures of historical research, questioned whether Bultmann did not restrict the scope of the New Testament by exclusively insisting on the character of its messsage as appeal. It is strange, moreover, that Bultmann, having disclaimed the relevance of Jesus of Nazareth for our faith, nevertheless in his *New Testament Theology* devoted a whole chapter to the proclamation of Jesus. We read here about Jesus' idea of God, and the question of his messianic consciousness. Following similar lines, Bultmann also wrote a book on Jesus of Nazareth, devoted primarily to Jesus' proclamation. Bultmann realized that without Jesus there would be no New Testament proclamation. Yet for him Jesus is not part of the New Testament proclamation; he is simply its presupposition and is treated as such.

James M. Robinson in his seminal book, *A New Quest of the Historical Jesus,* cautioned that if the New Testament proclamation is completely divorced from the historical Jesus, it will become a symbolized principle or a timeless myth. This means it will become exactly that from which Bultmann sought to rescue it. To avoid this pitfall, Robinson argues that we must ask whether the understanding of existence contained in Jesus' life and destiny is congruent with the kerygmatic understanding of Jesus' existence.[39] In other words, if we do not want to end up with a fictitious kerygma, we must pose the old question of Reimarus: Is there a continuity between what Jesus himself stood for and what the New Testament authors claimed that Jesus stood for? If Jesus did and said one thing and the New Testament authors turned it into something completely different, then either Jesus misunderstood himself or they misunderstood him. If we comply with Robinson's demand we would not go so far as to prove the veracity of the New Testament proclamation. We would, however, show the extent of its continuity with its raison d'être, Jesus of Nazareth.

Neither Robinson nor most other New Testament scholars who are convinced that there is a theological necessity to show the continuity between Jesus of history and the Christ of the New Testament hold that it is possible to write a new life of Jesus. In order to do so we would have to have knowledge of both the internal and external development of Jesus. While the former is hardly discernible at all, the latter is available only in the most general outline. We know most about Jesus' proclamation. Ernst Fuchs picked up on this situation and suggested that if Jesus' word and action point in the same direction, we can be certain that we are confronted with an authentic witness to Jesus. Yet, to develop a persuasive criterion for discerning authentic Jesus materials is the most difficult task in New Testament research. Each criterion implies certain presuppositions which influence the outcome of research. This difficulty, however, also has its comforting aspect. Since the New Testament writers did not endeavor to distinguish between their own interpretation of Jesus' message and his own words, they implicitly affirmed that they stood in continuity with the message of Jesus. This does not mean that they simply continued his message. But they saw no actual discrepancy between the two.

B. Jesus of Nazareth

Our rapid review of the quest for the historical Jesus has shown us how difficult it is to penetrate beyond the reflection of the first Christian community and the New Testament authors back to the Jesus of history. The many shared results of the quest have also shown us that the task of penetrating to the Jesus of history is not impossible. Yet Jesus alone is not what matters in the Christian faith. If the Jesus of history were our sole concern, then the New Testament writers would have missed their mark, since they neither provide nor want to provide us with a biography of Jesus of Nazareth. It is of fundamental theological relevance, however, how the historical Jesus is reflected in the New Testament.

Jesus is the starting point and the focus of the New Testament proclamation. Without an adequate understanding of him we cannot arrive at an adequate interpretation of the New Testament kerygma. Without a basic knowledge of Jesus and his message we would also be unable to determine whether the New Testament proclamation is in continuity or in discontinuity with Jesus' own teaching. Without entering into biographical detail we want to illustrate the figure of Jesus by using two important coordinates, his Jewishness and his eschatological significance. The former is quite often forgotten, since we habitually attempt to remake Jesus in our own image. But Jesus was a Jew and can be understood only in the context of the Judaism of his time. He lived and taught from the Hebrew Bible—then composed of the Pentateuch and the prophetic books—and had discourse with Pharisees, Sadducees, scribes, etc. It was especially the question of his continuity with the Jewish tradition which led to his trial and finally to rejection by the religious authorities of his time. The second point, his eschatological significance, is much more familiar to us, since it has dominated the theological discussion for a good part of this century. Yet, quite often in this discussion eschatology has been almost divorced from Jesus himself and has been treated primarily as a literary topic of certain New Testament authors.

1. The Jewishness of Jesus

The childhood narratives convincingly demonstrate that Jesus was brought up to be a faithful Jew. He was circumcised and instructed in the law, and was obedient to his parents. He also must have taken the movements of his time very seriously, since he insisted that John baptize him and prepare him for the imminent advent of the eschaton. Perhaps Jesus had heard of John and sought him out in order to hear his message. In all likelihood Jesus also talked with John and his disciples before he was baptized. Since Jesus' public ministry began without any reported preparations, we may assume that his baptism itself had a catalytic impact, similar to that of the Old Testament call experiences. Though Jesus may have already been conscious of his unique relation to God, it was not until after his baptism that he assumed a public ministry. For some time the public ministries of Jesus and John the Baptist ran parallel to each other. Then John was imprisoned and beheaded. His disciples buried him "and they went and told Jesus" (Matt. 14:12), an act which shows that they felt close enough to Jesus to share with him their sad news. From that moment on Jesus' ministry begins its independent and unique path.

Since Jesus began his work in such close proximity to John the Baptist, we may wonder whether Jesus' ministry bore such originality. Indeed, Jesus and John the Baptist agreed at many points. They were both dissatisfied with the current trends in Jewish thought and practice (Matt. 3:10 and 12:34), they shared fervent eschatological expectations (Matt. 3:10 and 7:19), and they were convinced of the necessity of an immediate decision to repent and to dedicate oneself wholly to the service of God (Matt. 3:8 and Mark 1:15).

There were also decisive differences between John and Jesus. While John was an ascetic, Jesus was not. Unlike John, Jesus did not stay in the desert but traveled throughout the country and even entered the house of notorious sinners (Luke 19:7). Jesus' messsage did not exclusively carry the somber tone of the impending judgment. For him the time of salvation had already come (Luke 11:20), while for John it was still impending. John was pointing to a mightier one who would come after him and who would baptize with the Holy Spirit (Matt. 3:11). Evidence for the changed tone of Jesus' message can be discovered in his actions which he interpreted in the light of the Old Testament imagery of the time of salvation (Matt. 11:4f.; Isa. 35:5). Jesus had great praise for John when he said, "Truly I say to you, among those born of women there has risen no one greater than John the Baptist" (Matt. 11:11). Yet Jesus also kept John in the proper perspective when he added, "Yet he who is least in the kingdom of heaven is greater than he . . . . For all the prophets . . . prophesied until John" (Matt. 11:11, 13). While John signified the conclusion of the Old Testament, with the coming of Jesus something novel had happened. But what was so new about Jesus?

Until his death Jesus attempted to be a faithful member of the Jewish community. He did not start a new religion as did Mohammed or Buddha. To many he appeared to be a Jewish scribe or a teacher. So we hear at the beginning of his ministry that "on the sabbath he entered the synagogue and taught" (Mark 1:21). More than once Jesus is called teacher (Mark 5:35; 12:19) and his more intimate followers are consequently "students" (*mathetai*), somewhat incorrectly translated as "disciples" (Mark 3:7). Jesus teaches his disciples (Mark 8:31) who in turn instruct others (Mark 6:30). It is significant that the original New Testament term for the gospel tradition was not *euangelion* (evangel), but rather *logos* (word) or *logos theou* (word of God), terms which show a correspondence to the Jewish terminology for "Holy Scripture."[40]

Thus Jesus may be seen in close connection with the rabbinic tradition. Indeed this may also account for the fact that in the New Testament the term *logos* is used to denote the gospel which tells us of Jesus and his sayings. Consequently, we should not assume that Jesus taught indiscriminately or continually. As the Swedish New Testament scholar Harald Riesenfeld has pointed out, "He imposed certain limitations on his preaching as he did in the case of his miracles. And what was essential to his message he taught his disciples, that is, he made them learn it by heart."[41] Jesus taught not like other rabbis. He also accompanied his teachings with miracles (cf. Mark 2:9), which rabbis usually did not do. Therefore the people remarked that "he taught them as one who had authority, and not as the scribes" (Mark 1:22) and assumed that he was a prophet (Mark 8:28).[42] His enemies, however, told the Roman authorities that he was a zealot rebel and Pilate later convicted him as such.

When we look at the ethnic and geographic boundaries of Jesus' activity, the impression is reinforced that he was a faithful Jew. If the sparse references in the synoptics are geographically reliable, Jesus stayed within Jewish territory unless he had to flee from his enemies (Mark 8:27). His activity was confined to the Jewish people; when he helped non-Jewish people he clearly marked this an exception (cf. Mark 7:24-30). Since the later church was very interested in missionary activity among non-Jewish people, we may be sure they would have emphasized Jesus' outreach among these people if there would have been a historical basis for it. Yet even the rabbis at the time of Jesus did not seem to show the same inhibitions as did Jesus. They "traverse sea and land to make a single proselyte" (Matt. 23:15). Jesus, however, understood himself as sent only to Israel.

Jesus was not a narrow sectarian. He was in touch with the important people and events of his time. Jesus' main partners in dialog, and the ones who finally caused his death, were the Pharisees, the leading religious group at his time. Their prime concern was to fulfill the demands of the Torah as interpreted by the tradition. Jesus too had no intention of revolting against the law. "Whoever then relaxes one of the least of these commandments and teaches men so, shall be called least in the kingdom of heaven; but he who does them and teaches them shall be called great in the kingdom of heaven," we hear Jesus say, according to Matt. 5:19. With such an attitude he should have had nothing to fear from the Pharisees or scribes, who largely followed this rabbinic emphasis on the law. These groups should have felt comfortable with Jesus.

The situation is somewhat different when Jesus claimed, "I have not come to abolish them [the law and the prophets] but to fulfill them" (Matt. 5:17), and, "For I tell you, unless your righteousness exceeds that of the scribes and the Pharisees, you will never enter the kingdom of heaven" (Matt. 5:20). What is more, we even hear Jesus say, "The law and the prophets were until John; since then the good news of the kingdom of God is preached" (Luke 16:16). But even such radicalism was not unknown in Judaism. The scribes and the Pharisees could have heard similar statements from John the Baptist, who did not allow for any kind of religious security and who called everyone to repentance. In fact, much of the radical interpretation of the law as we encounter it in the Sermon on the Mount could have been preached by John. Thus his calling all Israel to repentance, while painful to the pious Pharisees and scribes who attempted to meet the demands of the law to the letter, should not have caused grave problems for Jesus.

We notice, however, from the above-mentioned passages that Jesus not only radicalized the law and its demands but also claimed that with him the time of salvation had come and the law had been fulfilled! This claim, to be the one who ushers in the kingdom and who brings about the fulfillment of the promissory history of Israel, caused the controversy with the Jewish leaders. Even at Jesus' trial the high priest inquired, "Are you the Christ, the Son of the Blessed?" (Mark 14:61). If Jesus had clearly shown messianic qualities in word and deed, his claims should not have caused his ultimate rejection. In order to understand this reaction, it is important to remember that in the Jewish calendar the year 5000 had awakened messianic hopes in many people, since the Messiah was supposed to usher in the sixth millennium, the age of the kingdom of God.[43] Thus in the second quarter of the first century A.D. messianic expectations were especially fervent. For instance, there was the prophet Theudas, who was put to death by the Roman procurator in A.D. 44. There was an Egyptian prophet who arose a few years later and who together with his followers attempted to take over Jerusalem. Again the Roman authorities defeated the *coup d'état*. Josephus also mentions that a band of other "deceivers and imposters, under the pretense of divine inspiration fostering revolutionary changes, they persuaded the multitude [in Jerusalem] to act like madmen, and led them out into the desert under the belief that God would there give them tokens of deliverance."[44]

The messianic hope usually implied the overthrow of the Roman power in Palestine. It was commonly expected that the Messiah would redeem Israel from exile and servitude, and even redeem the whole world from oppression, suffering, war, and, above all, from heathenism. Along with the redemption of humanity from evil, the Messiah was expected to save humanity from evil in nature. The messianic age would also bring about great material prosperity. The earth would bring forth an abundance of grain and fruit which humanity would be able to enjoy without excessive toil.

When we review these expectations, we must agree with Rudolf Bultmann that Jesus' life and activity were not messianic when measured by traditional standards.[45] Yet to conclude with him that Jesus did not portray any messianic claim would be to overstate the case. Indeed, Jesus did not conform to the political hopes usually connected with messianic expectations. Some of his followers may have thought the picture would change when he came to Jerusalem to celebrate the Last Supper. But Jesus did not take over the city and assume a public messiahship (cf. Luke 24:21). He probably even refused the title *Messiah* whenever it was attributed to him. Even Peter's confession that Jesus was the Christ, i.e., the Messiah, Jesus did not affirm (cf. Mark 8:29f.). Jesus showed no interest in the political and nationalistic aspirations which were associated with the coming of the Messiah and he did not want to be taken for a political liberator. We hear no word that he conspired against the Roman occupation army or that he wanted to revolt against it. Though the charges against him were finally of a political nature, he clearly denied them. "My kingship is not of this world," Jesus responded to Pilate's question (John 18:36). If his existence was not messianic in the usual sense, how, then, should we describe his life and destiny?

Perhaps we gain an understanding of his person when we remember that at Jesus' trial the high priest concluded from Jesus' answer to the question "Are you the Christ, the Son of the Blessed?" (Mark 14:61) that he had committed blasphemy. Why should Jesus' answer lead to such devastating conclusion? Jesus seemed to have recited only common Jewish eschatological expectations when he said: "I am; and you will see the Son of man seated at the right hand of Power, and coming with the clouds of heaven" (Mark 14:62). The matter becomes clear when we consider the Old Testament use of the phrase *ego eimi* (I am).

In the Septuagint we find the phrase *ego eimi* several times. It is especially prominent in Deutero-Isaiah where it renders into Greek the Hebrew *ani hu* (meaning I [am] he). In Deutero-Isaiah the phrase *ani hu* is used as a solemn statement or assertion that is always attributed to Yahweh (cf. Isa. 41:4; 43:10; 46:4). The phrase asserts polemically that Yahweh is the Lord of history, countering similar claims made by other gods. It also seems to be a concise abbreviation of longer forms of divine self-predication, especially "I am Yahweh." While the *ani hu* formula as the divine self-predication of Yahweh occurs outside Deutero-Isaiah only in Deut. 32:29, the self-predication "I am Yahweh" is rather widespread throughout the Old Testament. As Ethelbert Stauffer has pointed out, there is also some evidence that the *ani hu* was used liturgically in the worship at the Jerusalem temple, since the Levites presumably sang the Song of Moses, containing Deut. 32:29, on the Sabbath day of the Feast of Tabernacles.[46] The use of *ani hu* lived on in the worship of the temple and the synagogues and was known even to the Qumran community.[47]

At a few decisive places in the Gospels Jesus uses the term *ego eimi* in a way analogous to the Old Testament theophany formula *ani hu*. Jesus says, for instance, in Mark 13:6, "Many will come in my name, saying, 'I am he!' and they will lead many astray." In Matthew this theophanic self-predication is expanded into an explicitly eschatological formulation to read, "saying, 'I am the Christ' " (Matt. 24:5).

Thus, with regard to the answer that Jesus gave to the high priest in Mark 14:62, it is by no means self-evident that we encounter here the use of *ego eimi* in the absolute sense (i.e., with no predicate nominative) in analogy to the Old Testament revelational formula *ani hu* or one of its variations. If we just look at Jesus' answer we might assume with equal justification that it was simply a solemn way of saying "yes." The matter becomes clearer, however, if we look at the usage of *ego eimi* in other Markan passages.

The phrase *ego eimi* appears first in Mark 6:50 at the conclusion of the miracle of the walking on water, where Jesus tells his disciples, "Take heart, it is I; have no fear." Here the phrase functions both as a title and as a revelational formula. In Mark 13:6 Jesus warns his disciples: "Many will come in my name, saying, 'I am he!' and they will lead many astray." Again the phrase is used as a formula of revelation and its misappropriation will lead the believers astray. Considering this context we may also conclude that Jesus' use of the *ego eimi* in Mark 14:62 is more than a simple affirmation. It is indeed a revelational formula with which Jesus discloses himself and identifies himself with God. As the words following the *ego eimi* show, the secret is lifted and Jesus unashamedly admits to his messianic sonship. "In Mark 14:62 therefore Jesus is making an explicit Messianic claim, the Messianic Secret is being formally disclosed."[48]

Since the messianic secret was carefully preserved in Mark until that point, we may wonder whether Jesus' response does not reflect more the theology of the evangelist than it renders Jesus' own words. Indeed it would be overestimating the historical value of this passage if we fail to assume that it has been carefully edited to reflect the eschatological hopes of the nascent church. Yet there is also an indirect way of determining the historical veracity of Jesus' response.

Ernst Fuchs had pointed out that in his proclamation Jesus emphasized the will of God in such a way as only someone could do who stood in God's place.[49] In his parables, for example, Jesus does not simply tell us how God acts, but he tells us that God acts the way he himself acts. Let us illustrate this with the parable of the lost sheep (Luke 15:3-7). When the Pharisees and scribes murmured, "This man receives sinners and eats with them" (Luke 15:2), Jesus told them parables about the care for the lost and sinful, implying that God acts like Jesus. In this way Jesus' response at his trial would indicate that at the end of his earthly life Jesus not only acted as if he stood in God's place, but also he evidently affirmed his identity with God by using the revelational formula "I am." We conclude that most likely the *ego eimi* was Jesus' own response to the high priest. While Jesus did not conform to prevailing messianic expectations, this reply was at once understood as a messianic claim. Since this claim could not be reconciled with what they expected the Messiah to be, the high priest and many others concluded that Jesus had committed blasphemy. Small wonder that in conformity with the law they sought to put him to death and enlisted the help of the Roman authorities to execute their verdict.

2. The eschatological figure

If Jesus is God's self-disclosure in human form, then God has come to his people and the eschaton has commenced. The end-time has started and the kingdom is in the midst of the people. Since Jesus was cognizant of his role, his message and his actions conformed to it. As the eschatological figure he presented an eschatological message in an eschatological time.

Jesus did not give his listeners a timetable and inform them in detail about the things that were going to happen at some future point in history. He rather addressed his audience in a way that called for an immediate decision. He did not spell out certain esoteric eschatological doctrines but confronted the people with a radical decision for or against God. This demand for a decision was at the same time a decision for or against Jesus and his actions. His proclamation, his person, and his actions form a unity which provoked and called for a decision. "Follow me, and leave the dead to bury their own dead" (Matt. 8:22); "No one who puts his hand to the plow and looks back is fit for the kingdom of God" (Luke 9:62); "And blessed is he who takes no offense at me" (Matt. 11:6). These and many other passages paradigmatically show the urgency of an immediate decision here and now. The *now* is the decisive point of history—no longer the future, as in intertestamental apocalyptic or in the promissory history of the Old Testament. The decisiveness of the present which Jesus proclaimed is illumined by his own actions.

When John the Baptist sent two of his disciples to ask Jesus whether he was the promised one or whether they should wait for someone else, Jesus referred them to his actions and not to any titles which had been conferred upon him: "The blind receive their sight, the lame walk, lepers are cleansed, and the deaf hear, the dead are raised up, the poor have good news preached to them" (Luke 7:22). With this remark he applied to himself the Old Testament imagery which was connected with the time of salvation (Isa. 35:5f.). Similarly as Jesus at the wedding in Cana turned water into wine (John 2:11), this epiphanic miracle referred to the Old Testament understanding of wine as the symbol of the time of salvation. Jesus introduced himself as the one in whom salvation had become manifest. Jesus also talked about the new wine that should not be poured into old wineskins (Matt. 9:17). The old time is past; the time of salvation has been initiated. At one point Jesus stated it even more clearly, "But if it is by the finger of God that I cast out demons, then the kingdom of God has come upon you" (Luke 11:20). With Jesus of Nazareth the kingdom of God has started. What had been expected for centuries, what had been projected into the future or into the present for so long, has now begun. "The kingdom of God is in the midst of you," said Jesus (Luke 17:21). He did not call for an immediate decision because he himself was such an important preacher. Nor was it because his message contained important words of wisdom. The crucial point is that in Jesus' appearance the kingdom of God has commenced and thus it is time, decisive time. The today of Jesus is the goal of history.

The announcement of the kingdom of God (*basileia tou theou*) is at the center of Jesus' proclamation. A statistical comparison will show that in the Old Testament apocrypha, in the pseudepigrapha, in the targumic commentaries of the Hebrew Scriptures, and in Philo's writings, we find the *kingdom of God* very seldom mentioned. In the New Testament too it occurs only 22 times outside the synoptics, 10 of which are in the Pauline writings and 8 in Acts. When we look at the synoptics, however, we gain a different picture and are told that Jesus used this term 61 times. This frequent use of the term *kingdom of God* seems unusual at first. This is even more so when we consider that in Judaism the *kingdom of God* was understood in a twofold sense: (1) It denotes the enduring rule of God in the present world through which God reigns over Israel (cf. Dan. 4:31) and (2) it indicates the future reign of God through which God will sanctify his name and establish his rule over all nations (cf. Dan. 2:44).

When Jesus used the term *kingdom of God* he always meant it in the second, eschatological sense. For instance, we remember that in the Lord's Prayer he taught his disciples to pray: "Thy [God's] kingdom come. Thy will be done, on earth as it is in heaven" (Matt. 6:

10). It is not surprising that Jesus talked about the kingdom in an eschatological sense because if the present is decisive time, then the time of salvation is imminent. The disturbed communion between God and humanity is to be restored and salvation is already commencing. This becomes evident in Jesus' response to the disciples of John the Baptist (Luke 7:18-22). He tells them that in his coming, Old Testament expectations are now being fulfilled. But what are these expectations? We would shortchange Jesus' proclamation to see them only in the realization of the future eschatological age, when we will live with God and with each other without fear and anxiety. As the Beatitudes show, the acceptance of those who are despised and rejected is essential for Jesus and for his proclamation of the kingdom (Matt. 5:3-12).

When Jesus calls the poor "blessed" (Luke 6:20), this is revolutionary. Salvation is not announced to those who could be expected to enter the kingdom, the religiously faithful and the morally upright, but to those who were despised and who according to the prevailing opinion never had a chance to enter the kingdom. When Jesus ate with despicable people such as tax collectors and other public sinners of his time, it was a gesture of communion which also implied that he extended peace, trust, and forgiveness to them. He accepted them into the coming kingdom. Such action was not an idiosyncrasy of Jesus. Since he represented God, he announced that God himself loves those who are despised and lost. He conveyed the identification of God with those who are of low esteem (cf. Luke 1:52).

Jesus did not just pardon the sinner. He also announced that whoever belongs to the rule of God is governed by a different standard of living. The love toward neighbor which ensues from God's love toward us becomes the prime rule for people of the kingdom (Mark 12:28-34). Reminding his audience of this rule of conduct, Jesus did not necessarily say anything new in relation to what could already have been known from the Scriptures. Love as the guiding rule should have been known to every pious Jew (cf. Lev. 19:18 and Deut. 6:4). But with Jesus the commandment of love became an active force and remained no longer an abstract principle. It was demonstrated in Jesus' own actions and not directed only to the socio-economically and ethnically privileged. It was universalized and extended, even in a preferential way, to the poor (Luke 14:12ff.), who—in most eyes—were socially unacceptable. As the parable of the Good Samaritan shows, love knows no limits (Luke 10:30-37). It is more than pious duty. It is the giving of self in response to God's self-giving in Jesus and to God's calling humanity back to union with him.

Although Jesus emphasized the decisiveness of his own person and of the present time, he did not point to an impending disaster or to the imminent end of the world, except to reinforce the urgency of an immediate decision for or against God. As far as we know, the oral tradition of the sayings of Jesus, sometimes called "Q," contained no indication that Jesus was a "doomsday prophet" of the immediately approaching end of the world. If there are any authentic words of Jesus about such matters they should be found in the Q material; but no such evidence is there. This coincides with another finding: neither by his Jewish contemporaries nor in Jewish polemics after the resurrection of Jesus was he accused of announcing an immediate end of the world which did not come. We cannot imagine that they would not have made use of such false prophecy had it been possible. Evidently Jesus was not interested in such prophecies. The Gospels tell us that Jesus differed on this point from John the Baptist, who fervently proclaimed the immediate coming of the end. Why was Jesus interested neither in the immediate future nor in prophecies of the immediate end of the world? Perhaps we may get a better understanding of this phenomenon if we return once again to Jesus' self-understanding.

While Jesus did not make himself the focus of his teachings, it would be unrealistic to assume that he never said a word about himself. But is it really possible to clearly distinguish between the way in which people experienced him and reflected upon him after his resurrection and the way he actually talked about himself? The dilemma is most evident when we consider the titles of Jesus.

Most Christians would state without hesitation that Jesus was the Christ and that he called himself the Messiah. However, a careful analysis of the New Testament shows us that the title *Messiah*, or *Christos* in Greek, is used only 53 times in the Gospels, but 280 times outside the Gospels. It is entirely missing in the oldest source, Q, and so are the titles *Son of David*, *King of Israel*, and *King of the Jews*. Even Mark, the oldest gospel, does not give us clear evidence that Jesus used the term *Messiah*. The Gospel of John, which uses the term rather frequently, never does so in such a way as to indicate that Jesus himself had used it. This shows that the term *Messiah* could not have played an important role in the life of Jesus. He did not want to be mistaken for a Judas Maccabaeus or a Bar Kochba or any of the other numerous political and religious Messiahs who emerged in Israel before or after him.

There was, however, another less political and less nationalistic title which Jesus apparently did use, the title *Son of man*. This title occurs about 80 times in the Gospels and only four times outside of them. It occurs in all four Gospels, including the Q material, almost exclusively in sayings of Jesus and hardly ever by people addressing Jesus. As an indirect support for the thesis that Jesus could have used the title, we may note that it was rarely used in Jewish apocalyptic literature after the time of Christ. Only 4 Ezra and 1 Enoch use the term, while Rabbi Abbahu (ca. A.D. 300) says in the Jerusalem Talmud, "If a man says to you, 'I am God,' then he lies; if 'I am the son of man,' he will finally regret it" (y. Taan 2:1).[50]

Jesus and the first Christian community did not invent the term *Son of man*. It already had a definite connotation in later apocalyptic Judaism. There the main eschatological function of the Son of man was one of judging. Jesus, however, expanded and modified this picture of the Son of man who is coming to judge all nations. For him this title is not just one of exaltation but of humiliation and he connects it with the title of the suffering servant. Thus he who judges the world in the name of the Lord also suffers vicariously for it and reconciles it with God. This is expressed in an almost classic way in Mark 10:45 where Jesus says, "For the Son of man also came not to be served but to serve, and to give his life as a ransom for many."

With this reference we have already touched the first group of Son of man sayings, those that speak about the Son of man who is going to die and then be resurrected. The second group deals with the Son of man who has to come to judge and to save. The third deals with the earthly activity of the Son of man. All three have eminent eschatological significance but are not colored by popular nationalistic overtones. Jesus is the Son of man who lives unknown among the people. But in the end of time he will appear openly to judge and to redeem. Though he does not live as the Son of man in glory, his actions already show who he is. He is the master of the law; he can judge and forgive sins (Mark 2:10,28); he can condemn and provide salvation. According to the Gospel of John he even permits someone to fall down before him and adore him (John 9: 35ff.). This kind of adoration was strictly reserved for God, but Jesus as the Son of man, the representative of God, is eligible for such cultic devotion. One's attitude toward him decides the future of the individual. Thus the present is decisive; it is the time of the Son of man.

The deepest self-understanding of Jesus, however, cannot be condensed into a title. It is a strictly singular phenomenon, namely, that Jesus is the final self-disclosure of God. In Jesus there occurred the final self-disclosure of God and thus the end of all history is anticipated. Jesus' confession that he was the direct and final self-disclosure of God led to his being convicted as a heretic. This is not surprising.

John tells us of an instance in which Jesus attempted to show who he was, but to no avail. Here the crucial term *ego eimi* is again used in a way which parallels the synoptics. This easily misunderstood theophanic self-predication occurs in Jesus' reply to the Samaritan woman. When she responded to him in the traditional messianic expectation, "I know that Messiah is coming; when he comes, he will show us all things," Jesus corrected her by saying, "I who speak to you am he [*ego eimi*]" (John 4:25f.). Here Jesus revealed himself as the full self-disclosure of God. But the woman did not understand him. She was too much entangled in the traditional pattern of messianic thinking.

We can summarize the general impression which Jesus of Nazareth left: He emphasized his presence as the decisive hour, he emphasized himself as the full self-disclosure of God, and he emphasized that with him the kingdom of God had come. Nobody—not even his disciples—really believed him until after Easter. They were all caught up in the traditional thinking that the Messiah and the eschaton were close at hand but still outstanding. They shut their eyes to the present and expected everything in the near future. But this emphasis of Jesus raised yet new questions. Just what does Jesus' emphasis on the present mean? Is there nothing to come? Did everything already happen in the life and death of Jesus of Nazareth?

Jesus rejected any predictions of when the end of the world would occur. About that day nobody knows except God himself (Mark 13:32). Since God has entered this world in Jesus, we cannot postpone preparing for our encounter with God. We cannot wait until we assume the time has come that this world will soon come to an end. We must always be ready. Jesus is the decisive event in history. He did not comfort the criminal on the cross with some future expectation, but assured him that today he would be with him in paradise (Luke 23:43). Jesus' person, his proclamation, and his action demanded an immediate decision, and this decision implied an immediate reward. This does not mean that the future will be insignificant. Quite the opposite! Only because of Jesus' presence will our future make any sense.

Jesus and his destiny are, symbolically speaking, the lens through which the rays of all history since the creation of the world are focused and projected into the future. The future has now become predictable because it receives its future-directedness from Jesus Christ. In this way Jesus determined the future. He told his followers not to be worried about the future because in him and in their attitude toward him the future had been already irreversibly decided. Of course, this assertion ran counter to most of the popular messianic hopes and expectations. Most of the people expected the total fulfillment of history in the present, just as many still do today. They wanted in Jesus the political messianic leader who should once and for all redeem Israel from all its enemies. Even some of the disciples confessed after Jesus' death with bitter resignation, "But we had hoped that he was the one to redeem Israel" (Luke 24:21). Not until Jesus was recognized as the resurrected Christ did the mood change.

Perhaps Schweitzer was right when he claimed that Jesus remained an enigma. Even the resurrection did not provide a foolproof answer to his life and destiny. Now the question had to be decided whether his resurrection should be interpreted in a strictly apocalyptic way as the first act of the final eschatological drama, or whether it was the ultimate event of the proleptic anticipatory history of Jesus. Many contemporaries of Jesus seem to have interpreted it as the first act of the eschatological drama after which the other events of the final days were to follow in rapid succession. This hope, that the end should come soon, is traceable in many places in the New Testament. Most books of the New Testament were written in awareness of this expectation. But the answer they gave did not promote an intensification of the hopes for an immediate end. Instead they emphasized that something new had dawned with Jesus, especially with his resurrection as the Christ. History, as we know it, had in Jesus already come to an end.

9

JESUS THE CHRIST

Jesus of Nazareth was a historical figure who walked on this earth. *Jesus the Christ* did not live on our earth nor was he a historical figure—judged by the usual historical criteria. He cannot be confined to history, but he was and still is a creator of history. Jesus of Nazareth *had* a definite proclamation. Jesus the Christ *is* the essence of the Christian proclamation. Though Jesus of Nazareth must be carefully distinguished from Jesus the Christ, it is the Christian conviction that both together form a unity of person. The decisive question is, as Rudolf Bultmann recognized, how and in which way the proclaimer became the proclaimed, how and in which way Jesus of Nazareth became Jesus the Christ. The answer to this question is essentially identical with the answer to the question, Who is Christ?

The history of the life-of-Jesus research has shown that a strictly literal interpretation of the Jesus event does not suffice. The New Testament writers certainly shaped the picture of Christ as it is painted in the New Testament. Each one introduced his own perspective and emphasis. Yet the impetus for painting a picture of Christ rather than presenting a biography of Jesus must have come from the outside, from something that happened to Jesus of Nazareth at Easter. This Easter event not only allowed the disciples to see Jesus in a new light, but in a new and amazingly bold spirit they understood him to be totally different from what they had previously thought. Correspondingly, they also saw themselves in a new light.

We might take Peter as an example. Before Easter he was the leader of the Twelve; after Easter he was the leader of the Christian community. Moreover, not only had his role changed but he had also become a different person. Before Easter he proudly declared that he would never fall away even if everybody else would desert Jesus (Matt. 26:33). A few hours later the same Peter in order to save his own skin denied that he ever had anything to do with Jesus (Matt. 26: 69-75). After Easter, however, the boasting coward had vanished. Peter preached everywhere about Jesus the Christ and, when reprimanded by the Jewish authorities to desist from this subversive activity, replied, "We must obey God rather than men" (Acts 5:29) and even gave them a lesson on Christ and his significance.

Before Easter we encounter a group of people who had joined the Jesus movement for various personal or ideological reasons. These followers even let their leader die alone, with the exception of some women (one of them being his own mother who was present beneath the cross) and perhaps John. After Easter we encounter the same followers as bold evangelists who are remarkably unanimous in their understanding of Jesus the Christ and who are ready to die for him if necessary. To treat the Easter events as mere psychological phenomena could never sufficiently explain this turn of events which led to the rapid expansion of the Christian faith.

A. The turning point of the resurrection

The origin of the New Testament and its witness to faith in Jesus as the Christ cannot be explained without the "happening" which the Christian community called the resurrection. The first Christians were not interested in ancestor worship or gathering together to remember something unique which had happened with Jesus in the past. For them the resurrection of Christ became both the basis for the present and the provision of the future. This is especially expressed with the title *kyrios* (Lord) which was conferred upon Jesus Christ by the post-Easter Christian community. The term *kyrios* was used, for example, in talking about the Emperor in the official

Roman state cult or in talking about pagan gods. It also served in the Septuagint to render the Hebrew name *Yahweh* into Greek. In the hymn in Phil. 2:5-11, which describes the whole salvific mission of Jesus, the term *kyrios* indicates the end of Jesus' earthly career and implies equality with God: Every knee shall bow and Jesus shall be proclaimed *kyrios*. This new status does not threaten God's sovereignty but rather increases God's glory

1. The newness of Christ's resurrection

The new status which Jesus attained is unthinkable without Jesus' resurrection. In one of the oldest creedal statements in the New Testament (Rom. 10:9) the confession "Jesus is Lord" runs parallel to faith in his resurrection from the dead; both affirmations together have salvific character. Such equality with God signifies cosmic lordship as well as lordship over individual Christians. For instance, it was decisive for Paul's call and for his missionary activity that Jesus Christ was Lord; this means designated Son of God *in power* through his resurrection (Rom. 1:4). Jesus did not just become a kind of superhuman mediator between God and us through his resurrection. In fact Paul at times does not even strictly distinguish between Jesus Christ and God. The term *kyrios* signifies the way in which God deals with the world; it expresses his rule over the world. All other powers and "lords" are derived and secondary while Jesus Christ's lordship is unconditioned and all-pervasive.

The fact that Jesus became Lord through his resurrection means also that the one who was the hidden Messiah became the revealed Messiah. In other words, the term "Christ the Lord" expresses that Jesus of Nazareth was not just a human being but God himself. Thus he is not a fact of the past but, as Christ the Lord, he is the decisive factor who provides both present and future.

Through Jesus' resurrection something entirely new had dawned. The newness of the resurrection is indicated both in the affirmation that Jesus became Christ and Lord and that he was the hidden Messiah who was now disclosed as the revealed Messiah. But the character of newness becomes even more evident when we consider the resurrection of Christ in the context of God's creative activity. The Bible suggests in many places that God's salvific activity must be seen as parallel to God's creative activity in the beginning. For instance, Deutero-Isaiah, the book that proclaims salvation through the sacrifice of the servant of Yahweh, intimately connects the creation in the beginning with salvation as the goal of history (cf. Isa. 42:5; 45:8). Similarly the Gospel of John in its opening verses sees the coming of Christ in the perspective of the creation in the beginning. Also Paul points out a clear correspondence between the appearance of the first Adam and the appearance of Christ as the last Adam (Romans 5).

It would be erroneous to interpret this emphasis on creation as if the resurrection were to open for us an opportunity to return to an ideal state of the past. Such an interpretation would force us to employ the cyclic view of history represented by most religions and philosophies. But in fact the very opposite is indicated by Paul when he says: "For in him all things were created, in heaven and on earth, visible and invisible, whether thrones or dominions or principalities or authorities—all things were created through him and for him" (Col. 1:16). This means that everything is created in and moves toward Christ. When Paul calls him the firstborn of creation (Col. 1:15) he wants to emphasize that Christ, being equal to God, does not stand only at the beginning of creation. Through his resurrection Christ is also the goal toward which creation moves. Clearly, such an understanding cannot accommodate a static view of creation. Creation is instead dynamic: the world was once created, then came the Fall and the distortion of this good and perfect creation, then came Christ who enabled its restoration, and finally the parousia will come when the creation will be restored to its originally intended beauty.

The "very good" which God pronounced over his creation (Gen. 1:31) does not mean unsurpassable. Here lies the fallacy of understanding our world as the best possible one. Even our present day world is still good, but it could be better. To deny this is to belittle the facts of evil and death. To understand Christ as the goal toward which creation moves requires a radical reorientation in our conception of the Fall of humanity and of our sinful state. The Fall can no longer be viewed as the descent from a God-provided origin to some kind of lower level, i.e., a state of constant sinfulness. The Fall is rather the initial denial of harmony with God, a denial which permeates creation up to the present day. Each of our sinful acts is a reaffirmation of this initial denial and thus a rejection of God's plan for us and a rejection of his redemptive act in Christ (cf. Heb. 1:1ff.).

God is continually with his creation even in its alienated or fallen state. Nothing is farther away from the biblical understanding than the notion of a deistic God who from far beyond watches in a detached manner the predetermined course of the universe. Even immediately following the Fall God does not in wrath withdraw from the first humans but instead, in an act of compassion, provides them with necessary clothing (Gen. 3:21). The church's desire to find a primal gospel even in the words of the curse (Gen. 3:15) and the endeavor of a gospel writer to trace the ancestry of Jesus back to Adam and finally to God himself (Luke 3:38) witness to the fact that God's acting in the beginning and his acting in Jesus Christ are seen as a unity. Paul also attests to this in pointing to Christ as the antitype of Adam. In an antithetical manner through Christ, the law is superseded by grace, sin by justification, and death by life (Rom. 5:12-21).

Death is not superseded by life in order to restore the original state. For the resurrected Christ death is no longer a possibility. In a similar way grace is not the opposite of law nor is justification just the reverse of sinfulness. Jesus Christ's resurrection does not indicate the fulfillment of a process of restoration that had already started with the Old Testament covenant community. His resurrection is the first point of a *new* creation, a creation in perfection. It is not just accidental that Paul in his Letter to the Romans progresses from declaring Christ as the new Adam (Chap. 5), to our participation in the new creation through Baptism (Chap. 6), to the tension which exists within us as citizens of a new world who still live in the old one (Chap. 7), to the implications for the whole creation of God's creative act in Christ's resurrection (Chap. 8). The occurrence of something radically new permeates Paul's vision.

God's creative act in Christ's resurrection goes beyond this present creation. It witnesses to a new creation which will replace this present one at some point. This is where the question of the empty tomb becomes important—not as a proof for the historicity of the resurrection of Jesus Christ but as an indication that this present creation is not permanent. This creation will be replaced by and transformed into something new. Not even the first Christian community used the story of the empty tomb as a proof of Christ's resurrection (cf. Matt. 27:62—28:15, esp. 28:13-15). Thus the inauguration of the new creation inspires in us the hope that we will be incorporated in it.

2. The existential quality of Christ's resurrection

It should now be evident that the Christian belief in the resurrection does not just result from a gradual development of the idea of resurrection in the Judeo-Christian faith. The idea of the resurrection from the dead was indeed a part of the worldview both of Jesus and of the first Christian community. But the resurrection of Jesus does not merely serve to verify the validity of the apocalyptic idea of resurrection. For instance, Paul in 1 Corinthians 15 does not suggest in the course of his argument that there already exists a common agreement on the idea of a resurrection. Rather he refers to and explains the specifically Christian tradition concerning Christ's resurrection. This means that Christ is not only the first one to be resurrected, as would have been expected according to apocalyptic thinking, but that he is the very presupposition of our own resurrection.

Paul drives this point home very eloquently: "If Christ has not been raised, then our preaching is in vain and your faith is in vain" (1 Cor. 15:14). The resurrection of Jesus Christ cannot be isolated from the rest of world history and refuted as irrelevant. It is both the presupposition of the Christian existence through a community of people who participate proleptically in a newness of life and also it is the foundation of the Christian hope for the final realization of this new life.

We become aware of the full implications of Christ's resurrection, however, only when we consider it in the context of apocalyptic hopes. Only in relation to the apocalyptic view of history, with its conviction of a resurrection at the end of time, can the resurrection of Jesus Christ be understood as an anticipation of this end. The fact that the disciples could recognize their once-familiar leader in the post-Easter experiences, in something entirely different from the possibilities of this life, and that they would call the reality behind these experiences "resurrection," can only satisfactorily be explained from an understanding of the apocalyptic hopes. Otherwise it could easily have been interpreted as an encounter with a spirit or phantom (cf. Luke 24:37).

Within the horizon of apocalyptic hopes and expectations the disciples realized that God had verified the authority that Jesus had already claimed in his earthly life. They also realized that in the destiny of Jesus the end of history had occurred in proleptic anticipation and that God had disclosed himself in fullness in Jesus as the Lord. Through the particularity of the resurrection of Jesus Christ the apocalyptic idea of a common resurrection was transformed into the Christian hope in the resurrection. Thus the New Testament proclaims Jesus not only as "the first to rise from the dead" (Acts 26:23) and as "the beginning, the first-born from the dead" (Col. 1:18), but also as the one in whom we shall be united "in a resurrection like his" that "we too might walk in newness of life" (Rom. 6:4f.). Likewise we trust in God who "raised the Lord and will also raise us up by his power" (1 Cor. 6:14). Although apocalyptic ideas provide the background material for a full understanding of the implications of Christ's resurrection, our own hope for resurrection is not founded on these ideas but depends solely on Christ's resurrection.

The resurrection of Jesus as the Christ does not lend itself to strictly empirical verification as does the historical fact of the crucifixion of Jesus of Nazareth. Since the resurrection implies a claim which transcends earthly reality (that Jesus is the Messiah), an empirical proof is as little possible as was the case with proofs for the existence of God. The New Testament sources must have known this. Otherwise they would have omitted or at least been more defensive in relating the rumors of the Jews that "his disciples came by night and stole him [Jesus' corpse] away" (Matt. 28:13). Similarly we hear that when the resurrected Christ appeared for the first time among his disciples "they were startled and frightened, and supposed that they saw a spirit" (Luke 24:37). Such reaction on a part of the disciples also does not easily lend itself to "proof" of the facticity of the resurrection.

When we caution that there is no empirical proof possible of the resurrection, we do not imply that the New Testament understanding of this event is merely one of two options (the other being to explain the Easter event in a "natural" way). On the contrary, the change which took place from before to after Easter becomes most plausible if we assume that something happened which transcends a this-worldly reference system, i.e., a new creation of God. Such a claim does not imply that we can therefore prove, in the modern scientific sense of the word, the actuality of these events. The God-component of any event is not accessible to rational, scientific verification. In order to remain intellectually honest, however, an interpretation of this event should allow for the possibility of a God-component. That is exactly the line of argument to be derived from the biblical writers. There is no requirement that we follow their understanding. But any other kind of interpretation (e. g., stolen corpse, seeing a vision, etc.) is intellectually less satisfactory than what they provide. It is not without meaning that the event of the resurrection as portrayed in the biblical narratives is not self-evident. To recognize the true identity of the resurrected one or to grasp the significance of the empty tomb one needs the reality of God as the key to interpretation. This means that the language of facts remains confined to a reference system of this world. The recognition that there is something else above and beyond, however, depends completely on God's revealing action. God has to disclose to us what he has done so that we are able to grasp its true significance. Thereby God discloses himself as the one who he said he was, the provider of a new future.

B. Stations of Christological reflection

Of the main stations on the long journey of Christological reflection, the first one, mirrored in the New Testament, asked above all how the Christ event, i.e., the resurrection, affected both the future of the Christian community and the history of the whole world.

1. God's decisive action (New Testament)

The New Testament writers convincingly showed that Jesus Christ was God's divine act. In him had occurred the final self-disclosure of God. But they varied considerably on how they related this event to the situation in which they found themselves.

Mark, as the oldest gospel, stood closer than the other gospel writers to the bewilderment caused by Jesus' death and resurrection. In his concern to combat all utopian dreams of the impending end, he asserted that Jesus wanted no outsider to understand fully the secret of the kingdom of God. Only his disciples, in an encounter with the Easter event, have the privilege of understanding completely the life, destiny, and proclamation of Jesus (Mark 4:11f.). Before Easter even the disciples could not really understand him (Mark 6:52; 9:32). Through the Easter experience the interim period between Easter and parousia became no longer a time of frustrated waiting but one of intense activity. The period between the resurrection of Jesus Christ and his final coming is the time of world mission. However, unlike Matthew and Luke, Mark did not elaborate on the activities of the exalted Christ during this time and he mentioned the emerging church only implicitly in connection with the task of world mission.

The *Gospel of Matthew* presents a much more elaborate and clear understanding of the present. This gospel wanted to show that the promises of the Old Testament had found their fulfillment in Jesus. He did not come to abolish the law and the prophets, but to fulfill them (Matt. 5:17f.). He fulfilled the Immanuel promise (Isa. 7:14; Matt. 1:22f.), the Galilee promise (Isa. 9:1f.; Matt. 4:12-15), the Bethlehem promise (Mic. 5:2; Matt. 2:5f.), the servant of the Lord promise (Isa. 53:4; Matt. 8:17), and many others. Consequently a multitude of Old Testament eschatological titles is bestowed upon him. He is the Messiah, the Son of David, the King of Israel, the Son of God, and the Son of man—to name just a few. This was intended not so much to show that Jesus was the bringer of the eschaton but that he stood in true continuity with the Old Testament.

Such continuity was considered crucial in order to show that the church that Jesus founded was, through his authority, the true Israel (Matt. 16:18). The historical nation of Israel had neglected and thus lost its commission to be the light of the nations. The church was called upon to replace it and to step into continuity with the Israel of promise. Though according to Matthew there are specific orders and structures in the church (Matt. 18:15ff.), it is not here to stay. It is only a transitory community. The church is also far from being a pure community composed only of true believers. Not until the final judgment will the just be separated from the unjust (Matt. 13:30). Yet the church is already on its way towards this final judgment when Christ will appear and select the chosen ones. The theme of the coming judgment is consistent throughout the gospel. The Sermon on the Mount (Matt. 5–7), the sending out of the Twelve (Matthew 10), and the Apocalypse (Matthew 24) all indicate the judgment as *the* coming event.

Luke finally moved beyond the notion of the present time as a strict interim period by introducing an understanding of history as salvation history. From the opening chapters of his gospel he placed Jesus in the context of world history (Luke 2:1-4 and 1:5f.). By so doing the evangelist did not simply want to convey the idea that the life and destiny of Jesus are subject to the course of history. Jesus is rather the focal point through whom all history receives its significance and proper valuation. Luke distinguishes three main epochs of history:

(1) the time of Israel;

(2) the time of Jesus as the center of history; and

(3) the time of the church.

It is only natural in this scheme that John the Baptist is thus depicted as the last prophet and not as the forerunner of Jesus (Luke 16:16), since Jesus is without forerunner and without precedent. The whole epoch of the law and the prophets leads up to this moment and then, suddenly, Jesus appears as the center of time.

For Luke the decisive event had occurred. Jesus had come and some day will come again to usher in the final end of all history and to judge the living and the dead. But the end will bring nothing essentially new concerning salvation. The same Christ who ascended will return as the exalted Lord. This view of history is by no means one of resignation or pessimism. God has provided the present period as the time of the church. In viewing the life and destiny of Jesus through Luke's eyes we realize that he has announced the coming of his kingdom. The truth of what Jesus stood for and the truth of his proclamation are guaranteed through his miracles, his resurrection, and his ascension. Moreover, Christians are not alone in the world. The exalted Christ in heaven is active in his word as it is proclaimed in history. His people work in "his name" and in "his Spirit." The Christians live in this world in a state of hope without fear and without utopian expectations. To incorporate Christian existence into the world and at the same time to keep it open for the final end of all history were the main concerns of Luke, both in his gospel and in the Acts of the Apostles.

The *Gospel of John*, written at a later date, replaced the eschatological terms of the synoptics with its own terminology. For example, the standard synoptic term "the kingdom of God" is used only twice in John. Likewise the term "this aeon" is replaced by "this cosmos," "future aeon" by "eternal life," and "the end of the aeon" by "in the last day"—to begin to mention just a few characteristic changes. It is also the only gospel that refers to the "ruler of this cosmos," and, in contrast to the synoptic Gospels, has no specific apocalyptic passages (cf. Mark 13; Matthew 24; Luke 17; 21).

In the Gospel of John, Jesus talks about his "Father's house" instead of about "heaven" (John 14:2), and he says he "will come again" (John 14:3), a phrase not used in the synoptic Gospels. On the other hand, he assures those who believe in the one who sent him that they already have eternal life (John 5:24). They will not even come into judgment, but have already passed from death to life. When Martha tells Jesus about her dead brother, "I know that he will rise again in the resurrection at the last day," Jesus replies in a similar way, "I am the resurrection and the life; he who believes in me though he die, yet shall he live, and whoever lives and believes in me shall never die" (John 11:24ff.). Does this mean that through the Christ event we already have eternal life now and that there is nothing else to come?

It would be a serious misunderstanding to assume that John concentrated strictly on the present as the time of salvation. It is true that according to John salvation is a present reality for the believer. But that does not mean the future is eliminated; instead it is actualized. John wanted to demonstrate that in Jesus Christ the exclusive opposition between God and the world is overcome. Jesus is the *incarnate* word of God (John 1:14). One can see from the authority claimed by Jesus and in the actions which he performs that God himself speaks and acts in and through him (John 15:9ff.). In Jesus the opposition between the present life and the life beyond is overcome. Therefore, the opposition between life and death, between time and eternity, and between present, past, and future is only a relative one. Even the law of gravity can be suspended when confronted with Jesus Christ (John 6:19). Through the entrance of God into the sphere of the created, the boundaries of this world have only relative, though not irrelevant, character. The main task has been accomplished; the ruler of this world has already been judged (John 16:11).

While in Jesus Christ the opposition between this life and the future life is overcome, for the believer a new dichotomy emerges. Jesus was not the kind of Messiah that was expected. He came to his own, but his people received him not (John 1:11). The Gospel of John is the gospel of great misunderstandings. In fascinating style the gospel writer pointed out that the unbelievers are confronted with Jesus like a color-blind person with traffic lights. One may have all the necessary knowledge but in the decisive moment not be able to grasp the exact meaning. The unbelievers constantly miss the meaning of Jesus. They exclude themselves from participation in the real future because only believers can discern that it is Jesus who opens the real future. The believers have the promise of the comforter or the Holy Spirit (John 14:15ff., 25f.; 16:4b-11, 12-15) whom Jesus Christ will send to guide them into all truth. The comforter bridges the gulf between the historical Jesus who is no longer among them and the proclamation of the gospel. He legitimizes the existence of the believers as a waiting existence, an existence of participation in the salvation which has been brought about through Jesus but which is not yet commonly accessible.

When we now turn to *Paul* we must remember that although his writings are the earliest in the New Testament, he was not a disciple or follower of Jesus during Jesus' life on earth. Once a persecutor of the early Christian community, he became one of its most fervent advocates. Though it is safe to assume that he had some knowledge of Jesus and the Christian faith before he was converted, such knowledge was not extensive. Soon after his conversion, however, he became one of the most influential Christians. He understood in a profound way how to incorporate the life, death, and resurrection of Jesus Christ into his message. His proclamation of Christ is deeply shaped by his eschatological outlook.

The key to understanding Paul's message is his call. When Paul introduces himself to the Roman congregation he says:

> Paul, a servant of Jesus Christ, called to be an apostle, set apart for the gospel of God which he promised beforehand through his prophets in the holy scriptures, the gospel concerning his Son, who was descended from David according to the flesh and designated Son of God in power according to the Spirit of holiness by his resurrection from the dead, Jesus Christ our Lord, through whom we have received grace and apostleship to bring about the obedience of faith for the sake of his name among all the nations, including yourselves who are called to belong to Jesus Christ (Rom. 1:1-6).

Paul introduces himself as one called to serve as apostle. "He is a man who has been appointed to a proper place and a peculiar task in the series of events to be accomplished in the final days of this world."[1] Those events have the Messiah as their central figure, the Christ Jesus, crucified, risen, and returning for judgment and salvation. It is important for Paul that Jesus Christ, who lived here on earth as a descendant of David, is the fulfillment of Old Testament prophecies. This establishes continuity between Paul's proclamation and the Old Testament faith. On the other hand, it is also important that through his resurrection Jesus of Nazareth was exalted as the Lord Jesus Christ and designated Son of God. This establishes and emphasizes the continuity between the Old Testament promises and the resurrection of Jesus Christ. According to Old Testament expectations and promises, the series of events which are to accompany the end had started with Jesus' coming and his death and resurrection.

Through his death and resurrection as the Messiah, Jesus had taken his place at the right hand of his father in heaven. "What remained was his *parousia* and the coming of the kingdom of heaven in power and glory."[2] The ethnic particularity of salvation became obsolete when Jesus, formerly the Messiah of the Jews, was enthroned as Lord and Savior of the whole world. Our Savior is at the same time the Lord of the universe and all of humanity, all cosmic powers: the whole universe belongs to him (Phil. 2:9ff.). Through his enthronement all people by means of faith have access to his kingdom and to salvation. This fact constitutes the gospel for the non-Jewish people. Paul was chosen to proclaim this gospel in the interval between the resurrection of Jesus Christ and his coming power.

Paul was convinced that we live in the final era. The old aeon has passed away and the Messiah has come. But the new aeon is not fully here because the Messiah has not yet returned in power. For Paul, however, this "not yet" offers no reason for bewilderment. The events of the final era will occur successively according to the preordained plan of God and will culminate in the final goal, the destruction of the old world and the creation of a new and eternal aeon. The decisive events in this apocalyptic picture are the resurrection of the dead which was made possible and initiated by

Christ's resurrection (1 Corinthians 15) and the future surprising coming of the day of the Lord (1 Thess. 5:2).

Christ is the end of the law (Rom. 10:4) and the end of history. The old covenant no longer applies to us since a new covenant has been established (2 Cor. 3:6). But we still live in a transitional period, a time of faith (2 Cor. 5:7) and of waiting (Rom. 8:23ff.). This does not mean that the coming eschaton is totally outstanding. Our interim existence is determined by the future because salvation is active in us. We participate in the gifts of grace, in faith, love, and hope (1 Corinthians 13). We have died with Christ in our Baptism; we live in Christ and Christ lives in us (Gal. 2:20). This means that the Christian existence is a dialectical existence. It is lived in the world but not from this world. The power of existence is given us from beyond, the beyond which will come to us in the eschaton.

Though Paul actualized the future eschaton by saying that we already live with Christ, he continued to look forward to being resurrected with him and living with him in a manifest way (2 Cor. 4:14; 1 Thess. 4:14). While Jesus emphasized the present as the time of decision, Paul emphasized it as the time of faithful and active waiting to enter into the fulfillment of the new creation. Paul included the Christ event in his kerygma and proclaimed it as a part of "Christian" time. For him the decisive turning point of history was already past.

Especially in his discussion with a Gnostic group in Corinth, who claimed already to be living in the fullness of the Spirit, Paul emphasized the proleptic and preliminary eschatological character of Christian existence. The interim is not yet the time of fulfillment. The eschaton is still to come and faithful existence is the only way to be prepared for it. The interim is the time of the proclamation of the gospel and the time when we can and should realize the (ethical) teaching of Christ. In our new allegiance to Christ we enjoy an existence of freedom from law, yet without libertinism. On the other hand, Paul emphasizes, for those who are disappointed because the eschaton has not yet arrived, that the eschatological fulfillment will not tarry. It is a future event affecting us, our earth, and the whole creation. Christ's resurrection was the first part of it and, since we know that the resurrection of the dead is an integral part of the eschatological events, the end cannot be postponed indefinitely.

Jesus' resurrection has validated for us the apocalyptic idea of the resurrection of the dead. By anticipating it through his own resurrection as the Christ, he has provided us with a foundation for hope. On account of his person, his actions, and his proclamation Jesus emphasized the present as the time of decision. Paul, and with him the other New Testament writers, interpreted Jesus in the light of his resurrection as the Christ. They emphasized that in this "Christ" time we are called to faithful and active waiting to enter into the fulfillment of the new creation foreshadowed in Christ's resurrection. This means that for the New Testament writers the event of Jesus Christ marked the decisive turning point in history.

2. Equality with God (trinitarian controversy)

Once it was clear to the Christian community that God had acted decisively in Jesus Christ for the future of the world and of humanity, the question emerged as to how this Jesus Christ was related to God. In other words, how is the bringer of salvation related to the sender of salvation? A solution to this question was even more urgent since, in the Greek environment into which the Christian faith rapidly spread, the New Testament terms for the exalted Jesus, such as Christ, Son of David, or Son of man, hardly carried any meaning apart from the original Hebrew context. Even *Christ*, meaning the anointed one, was a translation of the Hebrew term *Messiah*.

The Apologists of the second century attempted to translate the term *Christ* as *logos*. Of course, the precedent for doing so was the prolog of the Gospel of John with its statement that "in the beginning was the word [*logos*] and the word was with God, and the word was God . . . . And the word became flesh and dwelt among us" (John 1:1, 14).

The equating of Jesus Christ with *logos* was picked up by the Apostolic Fathers. Ignatius, for instance, affirms "that there is one God, who has manifested himself by Jesus Christ, his son, who is his eternal Word [*logos*] proceding forth from silence" (*Letter to the Magnesians* 8:2). He is "our only teacher" (*Magn.* 9:2), "by which the father has truly spoken" (*Rom.* 8:2). Ignatius wants to tell his readers that Jesus Christ is God's personal self-disclosure to humanity, in whom God broke through his silence. Analogies to this are also found in Gnostic literature in which the *logos* is the heavenly revealer who leads his people to new insight and redemption.

With the Apologists the welding of Hebrew history and Greek spirit becomes evident. In his *Dialogue with Trypho* Justin Martyr conceives of God as the unmoved mover for whom Jesus Christ presents the link for his involvement in the world. He speaks of the "unbegotten God . . . the ineffable Father and Lord of all . . . . He is not moved or confined to a spot in the whole world, for he existed before the world was made."[3] We cannot see God but only Christ, "who was according to his will his Son, being God, and the Angel because he ministered to his will."[4] Jesus Christ conversed with Moses from the burning bush and spoke with Abraham, Isaac, and Jacob. Justin continues by demonstrating that God's promises in the Old Testament were all executed through Jesus Christ; he then summarizes: "And that Christ, being Lord, and God, the Son of God, and appearing formerly in power as Man, and Angel, and in the glory of fire as at the bush, so also was manifested at the judgment executed on Sodom, has been demonstrated fully by what has been said."[5] Then he continues showing the intimate connection between God and Christ (the *logos*). "They call him the word [*logos*], because he carries tidings from the Father to men: but maintain that this power is indivisible and inseparable from the Father . . . . This power [Christ] was begotten from the Father, by his power and will, but not by abscission, as if the essence of the Father were divided."[6] Justin points here to the eternal procreation of the Son from the Father.

Even in his understanding of Christ as *logos* his frame of reference is Greek. This becomes evident when we turn to his *First Apology*. There he declares, "When we say also that the word [*logos*] who is the firstborn of God, was produced without sexual union, and that he, Jesus Christ, our teacher, was crucified and died, and rose again, and ascended into heaven, we propound nothing different from what you believe regarding those whom you esteem sons of Jupiter."[7] Concepts like the virgin birth, ascension, the interpreting word, and leader of all, etc., are all images which were already present in the Hellenistic world. Justin Martyr also connects Christ's activity with the Greek world when he states: "We have been taught that Christ is the firstborn of God, and we have declared above that he is the word of whom every race of men were partakers; and those who lived reasonably [*meta logou*] are Christians, even though they have been thought atheists; as, among the Greeks, Socrates and Heraclitus, and men like them."[8]

The *logos* is now understood not only as *the* Word. In analogy to Stoic thought the Word now becomes the world reason and is an expression of the cosmic order of things. Whoever is in accordance with that order, Justin declares, cannot be thought of as an atheist. Implicitly he knows about God and his precepts and obeys them. Against Hellenistic polytheism the Apologists could now maintain Judeo-Christian monotheism. They did not introduce another God but affirmed the one God who through his *logos spermatikos* (seminal *logos*) was present in that which was compatible to Christianity in pagan religions. Whatever was contrary to the Christian faith in these religions, however, must have been the product of human sinfulness or the work of demons. Of course, when Christ was merely understood as the *logos*, the mighty arm of God, so to speak, he could easily be classified as secondary.

Origen, the most influential theologian of the early church paved the way for defining Christ's status in relation to God. In the first systematic theology ever written, *On First Principles*, Origen declared that God alone is unbegotten, while the Son is only-begotten, eternally proceding from the Father, "because his generation is as eternal and ever-lasting as the brilliancy which is produced from the sun . . . . This Son, accordingly, is also the truth and the life of all things which exist."[9] Implied here is the divine preexistence of Christ and his mediation in the creation of the world. Through him all things were created (cf. the prolog of the Gospel of John). To accomplish this task of mediation Christ must be in such intimate contact with God as the rays of the sun are in contact with the sun itself.

Christ is without beginning in time[10] and he existed before we became aware of his incarnation as Jesus of Nazareth. Christ is from the same substance with the Father or, what is synonymous for Origen, of the same hypostasis. Through his incarnation, however, Christ came to be "another figure of that person besides the person of God himself."[11] Thus he is another or even a second person next to the Father. Thus we have two moments in Origen's Christology: (1) the eternal procreation which could lead to a merging of God and Christ, if overly emphasized, and (2) the subordination of Christ to God which could lead to a loss of the divinity of Christ if absolutized. Origen held both in tension and thus escaped both the danger of losing the person of Christ through his merging into the divine unity and the danger of losing Christ's divinity through asserting his independence.

It was not long until the Alexandrian presbyter Arius picked up Origen's Christology and declared his dissatisfaction with the notion of eternal procreation. He feared that this would move Christ too closely to the level of God and endanger Christian monotheism. Consequently he claimed that Christ was created before everything else but yet was created in time so that there was a time when he was not. While Arius maintained that Christ was the mediator between God and the world, he still regarded him as a creature, though of the most prominent kind. Christ was perceived to be dissimilar in everything [*kata panta*] according to the being of the Father.[12] Small wonder that Arius soon got in trouble with his bishop, Alexander, who convened a council and excommunicated Arius for heresy, i.e., for denying the true divinity of Christ. Alexander refers especially to the Gospel of John, which for him clearly shows that Christ cannot have an origin in time. Christ must be eternal and one with God. Alexander was also afraid that Arius's position would render Christ's accomplishment worthless, since Christ was not really God. In the view of Arius the unity of the Godhead was dissolved at the expense of regarding Christ as a semidivine messenger of God in analogy to sons of God in Greek mythology. Alexander knew too well that such figures could not provide salvation.

Athanasius, Alexander's successor in A.D. 328 and a strong defender of orthodoxy, pointed out the danger of Arianism when he charged that it either leads to polytheism or to atheism.[13] Since the Arians considered the Word (*logos*) to be a creature, a work out of nothingness, Athanasius claimed they believe in two gods, "in the true God and . . . in one who is made and fashioned by themselves and called God."[14] To consider the *logos* as merely one among many other things is actually atheism. Athanasius asserted by way of contrast that "there is One God, and not many, and One is his Word, and not many; for the Word is God, and he alone has the form [*eidos*] of the Father."[15]

Emperor Constantine, under whom the Christian faith had become the favored religion of the Roman empire, felt responsible for the unity of the Christian faith. Initially, he did not quite understand the significance of the issue at stake in the fight between Arius and the defenders of orthodoxy. Thus Constantine sent Hosios of Cordoba with an imperial letter to Alexandria in which both Alexander and Arius were reprimanded, the first because of the farfetched questions he had asked and the other because of the mindless answer he had given and the tenacity with which he defended it.[16] He advised both to settle the issue because it was of little importance and asked them to forgive each other and so to restore to the emperor his "quiet days and untroubled nights."[17] But Eusebius, who relates to us this letter, concludes the episode with the telling words, "The evil, however, was greater than could be remedied by a single letter, insomuch as the acrimony of the contending parties continually increased, and the effects of the mischief extended to all the Eastern provinces."[18]

When Hosios of Cordoba in A.D. 324 returned to the emperor from his trip to Alexandria, he brought with him the conviction that the unity of the faith and of the church was at stake. In the Latin West the distinction between *substance* and *person* had been established for a long time. For instance, Tertullian (ca. A.D. 200) had declared that several persons can own the same property ("substance"). When Hosios affirmed the unity of substance (*ousia*), then Alexander was satisfied, since this term assured him of the unity of the Godhead. When Hosios then pointed to the twofoldness of the persons, Arius was content, since this indicated for him that the distinction between Father and Son was maintained in the Godhead. Only Alexander, however, could agree to the *homoousios* (one being) of Father with the Son, following the precedent set by Dionysius of Alexandria a generation before. Bishop Dionysius of Alexandria had at that time agreed to the *homoousios,* proposed by the Roman bishop Dionysius to alleviate any doubts of his unorthodoxy.

Since no actual agreement was in sight, the emperor felt he should convene an ecumenical council so that the matter could be officially decided and peace restored. In the summer of A.D. 325 approximately 300 bishops gathered at Nicea, a town not far from Constantinople. Included were bishops from every part of the empire, though the Eastern representatives dominated in number. Constantine himself felt it was his duty to remove error and propagate the true religion. He feared that a divided church would offend the Christian God and bring vengeance upon the Roman Empire and its emperor. Constantine opened the council and instructed the bishops to reach unanimous agreements, not motivated by hate or partiality, but by a desire to seek out the true teaching of the church and the apostles. The Arians were first asked to put forth a statement of faith which, as one would expect, was quickly rejected.

A mediating statement was drawn up by Eusebius of Caesarea which stated that we believe "in one Lord Jesus Christ, the Word of God, God of God, Light of Light, Life of Life, Only-begotten Son, First-born of every creature, begotten of the Father before all worlds."[19] This statement was vague enough so that the Arians could agree with it, though they did not like to concede that Christ was born before all creation. Next the orthodox responded and, with the decided approval of the emperor, gladly agreed to the statement, provided that it would also contain the term *homoousios*. This would assure that the unity of the divine being would be exactly the same for the Son as for the Father. In the following deliberations several other changes were made: (1) the phrase "Word of God" was replaced by "Son of God," so that one could not interpret this as referring only to the *incarnate logos*; (2) "God of God" was specified as "true God of true God" to alleviate any inferiority of the Son; (3) "only-begotten" was clarified as "begotten of the Father, only-begotten, that is, from the being of the Father"; and (4) it was finally added "begotten, not made, of one being [*homoousios*] with the Father," to reject any possibility of regarding Christ as God's creature. It is clear that these amendments were serious changes which did not find the automatic majority of the council fathers.

Since the council fathers knew that the emperor favored the term *homoousios*, the discussion had to be carried out carefully in order to escape the imperial wrath. Origenists, fearing the loss of the dialectic between equality and subordination, recognized that the formulations did not deny that the Son was part of the Father. Also the change from "made" to "born" attempted to preserve the insight that Christ was not a creature of God. Though few were totally satisfied, eventually most of the fathers signed the creed of Nicea which read:

We believe in one God, the Father almighty, maker of all things visible and invisible; and in one Lord Jesus Christ, the Son of God, the only-begotten of the Father, that is, of the substance of the Father; God of God, light of light, true God of true God; begotten not made, consubstantial with the Father; by whom all things were made both which are in heaven and on earth; who for the sake of us men, and on account of our salvation, descended, became incarnate, was made man, suffered and rose again on the third day; he ascended into the heavens and will come to judge the living and the dead. [We believe] also in the Holy Spirit. But those who say "that there was a time he was not," or "he did not exist before he was begotten," or "he was made of nothing," or assert that "he is of other substance or essence than the Father," or that the Son of God is created, or mutable, or susceptible of change, the Catholic and apostolic Church of God anathematizes.[20]

Most agreed to sign the anathemas, because some of the condemned phrases were later inventions not contained in Scripture and others did not seem credible in any case. Only Arius and a few of his ardent followers refused to sign and as a result were promptly exiled.

The symbol of the 318, as it was called at that time—referring to the number of council fathers present, or the Nicene Creed, as it is familiar to us today, affirmed two items: the unity of the Godhead and the divinity of Christ. The first point was also affirmed by Arius. Yet he could only maintain God's unity by excluding Christ from the Godhead and making him subordinate to the Father. The Alexandrians, however, also affirmed the divinity of Christ. In maintaining both points they preserved the Christian tradition. But it is a tradition which always contained a logical contradiction in itself since both unity of the Godhead and divinity of Christ could not be equally maintained without either considering Christ to be inferior—he was also human—or by splitting the Godhead in two. Even Origen's proposal, to bridge the contradiction by affirming Christ's eternal procession from the Father, did not really solve the issue because it suggested Christ's inferiority.

The actual dilemma was that of Greek thought itself. If we start our deliberations with the unity of being, as the Greeks did, we are unable to differentiate between God and Christ and still maintain their essential oneness and equality, because a plurality of being is impossible in Greek thought. The crucial term *homoousia*, though sounding genuinely Greek, had its origin in the Latin environment. The Latin influence becomes evident when we hear that at the decisive session the emperor addressed the bishops in Latin "and the interpretation was supplied by one at his side."[21] Sozomen then tells us that the Emperor "was not wholly unpractised in the Greek tongue,"[22] showing again that Constantine's frame of reference was Latin. The term *substance*, the Latin translation of *ousia*, is always an attribute of God while the distinguishing factor then becomes the different personhood. In this way we can talk both about the person of God and about the person of Christ who yet have or share the same substance. In the Latin language it was easy to assume that two persons owned the same substance or property (i.e., the divinity) while these persons remained distinct.

We are not surprised to learn that later bishop Athanasius, who accompanied as deacon his bishop Alexander to the council at Nicea, did not at that time employ the term *homoousios*. Only after extensive journeys to the West, including his exile in Trier, did he begin to employ the once-dreaded term. Athanasius fought most of his life to get the decisions of Nicea accepted in the East. Yet as an unfortunate product of his efforts a large portion of Christianity became alienated from the one church. Though the term *homoousia* is Greek, its meaning was simply foreign to the Greek mind.

We should also mention in this context the controversy concerning the Holy Spirit. At Nicea further elaborations were not made on the being or function of the Holy Spirit. It was not until A.D. 381 at the Council of Constantinople that a creed was issued which was more extensive in its discussion of the Third Article. Now we hear, "[We believe] . . . in the Holy Spirit, the Lord and the giver of life, who proceeds from the Father, with the Father and the Son is worshipped and glorified, he has spoken through the prophets."[23] Though the Spirit is elevated to the same level as the Father and the Son the council is careful to avoid attributing to the Holy Spirit *homoousia* with the Father and the Son. The phrase, familiar to us, that the Holy Spirit "proceeds from the Father *and the Son*" is not contained in the Constantinopolitan Creed. It is of Western origin and was initially intended to underscore that Christ was of the same being with the Father. It does this by saying that the Spirit proceeds equally from the Father "and the Son" (*filioque*). Eastern theologians by contrast usually affirmed that the Spirit proceeds from the Father through the Son and is shared by all creation.

This controversial issue between East and West was not just one of theological method, whether to start with the unity of the Trinity, as the East preferred, or to start with the Father and the Son with the Spirit understood as the unifying factor, as Western theologians stipulated. Underlying the controversy which contributed to the split between the church in the East and in the West was even more the fundamental question whether one group of churches could unilaterally change a creed when the creed had been formulated by an ecumencial council. It was in the Nicene Creed that the Eastern theologians first discovered the insertion of the *filioque* by Western authorities. The East insisted that only a general council of the combined Eastern and Western church could alter a creed decided upon by an ecumenical council. But such a council was never summoned, neither by the pope, who was at first reluctant to change the Nicene Creed, nor by the emperor, who advocated such an amendment to squelch the Spanish adoptionist heresies. Thus the East continued steadfastly to refuse the "heresy" of the *filioque* which was gradually accepted in the West. Only recently has the Roman Catholic church in the West given indication that it might be willing to drop this change in the creed in order to heal the break between the Eastern and the Western churches.

3. Truly human and truly divine (Christological controversy)

Once the church had officially decided on the essential equality of God and Christ, the next question was to interpret how the divinity and the humanity of Christ are related to each other. At stake here was not only the unity of the person but once again the soteriological concern as to whether Christ could provide salvation for us. Already Origen had posed the issue when he said, "Man as a whole would not have been saved if the Lord would not have assumed the whole man."[24] Gregory of Nazianzus picked up the same concern and stated:

> For that which he [Christ] has not assumed he has not healed; but that which is united to his Godhead is also saved. If only half Adam fell, then that which Christ assumes and saves may be half also; but if

the whole of his nature fell it must be united to the whole nature of him that was begotten, and so be saved as a whole.[25]

Since the whole human being is contaminated by sin, the whole human being must be cleansed through the indwelling of the deity. Gregory advances still another argument in this same letter in which the soteriological concern does not immediately become evident. Since God is incomprehensible, he can be comprehended only if he converses with us through the flesh as through a veil. In other words, God must become human so that we can understand him. There were several proposals which gradually evolved to address these concerns raised by Origen and Gregory.

(a) The first proposal is that of Apollinaris of Laodicea (ca. A.D. 310-390) who later became bishop of his hometown which is located near Antioch (Syria). Apollinaris intended to continue the Christological tradition of Athanasius. Christ is not to be differentiated according to his divine and his human being, but he is composed of God with a human body. Since God is present in the human body, the role of the *sarx* (flesh) is totally passive. Thus Apollinaris confessed that the one Son does not consist of "two natures, one worthy of adoration and one not worthy of adoration," but one nature of the God-logos as it has become flesh and is together with its flesh adored in one adoration.[26] While this notion leads to a deification of the human *sarx*, we also note that the integrity of the human person is here lost. To render the human being completely docile to the divine power, Apollinaris assumed that human reason (*nous*) in Christ is replaced through the divine *logos*. Apollinaris even argued that if the *logos* would have united himself with the full human being, the human being would merely be an inspired human being in analogy to the semidivine beings of pagan mythology, but not the incarnate *logos*. The church, however, did not accept his line of reasoning. At the Council of Constantinople (381) the proposal of Apollinaris was rejected with the remark that it violated the integrity of the human person of Jesus Christ. Thus the danger of docetism, that Jesus was not really a human being, had been rightly avoided.

(b) The Antiochian school, represented through theologians like Diodore of Tarsus (before A.D. 394) and his student Theodore of Mopsuestia (ca. A.D. 352-428), took a stand opposite that of Apol-

linaris. They did not want to fuse the divine with the human but insisted on a clear distinction between God and humanity and also between the divine and human in Christ. The dictum, "what God has not assumed he has not redeemed" was interpreted to mean that the human soul or mind (*nous*) must also be assumed so that the divine *logos* can be present with the the whole human being Jesus. Christ must not only assume a body (*sarx*), as Apollinaris claimed, but also the human mind or reason (*nous*). The *logos* dwelt in this human being in such a way as to allow the human being still to undergo a normal ethical development. Only in the resurrection has the human become a perfect tool of the Godhead.

The unity of knowledge and honor which the Antiochians asserted to exist between the divine *logos* and the human Jesus did not, however, lead to a unity of the person. Although Theodore rejected the idea that there were two sons, the divine and the human, a notion which many theologians attributed to him, he continued to strictly distinguish between the two natures. In this proposal there is not physical salvation taking place by which God assumes our humanity so that we participate in his divinity. It is rather an ethical or spiritual salvation provided by the example of the divine and by the congruence of the will. The Antiochian intention is clear: God is so high above us that he cannot really come down to us and contaminate himself with our worldly affairs. There is thus not genuine interaction between God and humanity.

(c) Especially Cyril of Alexandria (c. 400–444), as the representative of the Alexandrian school, protested vehemently against this proposal, declaring, "We do not distribute the sayings of our Lord in the Gospels to two hypostases or persons, . . . since Christ is not double but only one . . . . All the sayings in the Gospels must be attributed to one single person, one single incarnate hypostasis of the logos. For our Lord Jesus Christ is one according to Scripture."[27] According to Cyril the unity of the person of Christ must be maintained. This means that, once united, the hypostasis or nature cannot be separated. Moreover, one cannot divide or distribute the divine and human properties or peculiarities between the two persons or hypostases. They must all be attributed to one single person, the incarnate hypostasis of the divine *logos*. There exists a hypostatic union between the *logos* and the flesh (*sarx*) which the *logos* assumed.

Though occasionally Cyril talked about two natures, the most important thing for him was the single, unique nature, the paradoxical unity of God and humanity in the one Jesus Christ. While the body (*sarx*) of Jesus has its own life and human soul, "the *logos* had become human by forming with the flesh ensouled with a reasonable soul in an inexpressible and unfathomable way a hypostatic union."[28] It is important that Cyril recognized the limits of conceptuality by mentioning the "inexpressible." It is also important that he no longer assumed, as had been done before, that the *logos* entered a human being but that he *became* a human being without ceasing to be God.[29] We encounter here the insistence on Jesus Christ being *vere deus et vere homo*, truly God and truly human. On the negative side, one must also mention Cyril's love for power through which he finally managed to have Nestorius, who was educated in Antioch and who later became patriarch of Constantinople, and his followers condemned (A.D. 431) by depicting them as Arian and Antiochian heretics.

We are inclined to think that the conceptual framework of the Council of Chalcedon (A.D. 451), at which the main doctrinal decisions concerning the person of Christ were finally made, was contributed by the West. This would not be surprising, in light of the Council of Nicea and its definitions of the trinitarian controversy. Indeed, the true Godhead and its paradoxical involvement in human destiny were already well expressed by Tertullian when he said, "And the Son of God died; it is by all means to be believed, because it is absurd. And he was buried, and rose again; the fact is certain, because it is impossible."[30] Similarly, Tertullian insisted on the two natures of Christ saying, "We see plainly the twofold state, which is not confounded, but conjoined in One Person—Jesus, God and Man."[31] Indeed when Pope Leo wrote his tome for the forthcoming Council of Chalcedon, he declared that "the same who, remaining in the form of God, made man, was made man in the form of a servant. For each of the natures retains its proper character without defect; and as the form of God does not take away the form of a servant, so the form of a servant does not impair the form of God."[32] This means that there are two natures preserved after the incarnation with neither of them being in any way diminished.

When we read the creed of Chalcedon we notice, however, that only the affirmation of "the peculiar property of each nature being preserved and being united in One Person"[33] is taken over from Leo's tome, while most of the other affirmations are more akin to Cyril's position. We hear that our Lord Jesus Christ

> is perfect in Godhead and perfect in manhood, very God and very man, of a reasonable soul and body consisting, consubstantial with the Father as touching his Godhead, and consubstantial with us as touching his manhood .... He must be confessed to be in two natures, unconfusedly [*asynchytos*] immutably [*atreptos*], indivisibly [*adihairetos*], inseparably [*achoristos*].[34]

In many ways this decision of Chalcedon was a landmark of theological reflection. After centuries of sometimes explosive debates the church admitted that it could not solve the issue at hand. It had to admit that it did not know how the divine was related to the human in Jesus Christ. While affirming that both full humanity and full divinity are present in Jesus Christ, it could only delineate the limits of Christological reflection. The two natures are neither fused nor mixed, neither divided nor separated.

Endowed with imperial sanction, the Christological "solution" of Chalcedon with its affirmation of the two natures of Christ eventually prevailed as official theology. But most common people, especially in Asia Minor, Syria, Palestine, and Egypt preferred a single nature of Christ, the divine. Contrary to the church's official theology, they were interested only in Christ's divinity, not in his humanity. Since Chalcedon, as we have seen, decided differently, this council also facilitated the first lasting split in official Christendom, between the monophysite church which became dominant in Armenia and affirmed the one nature of Christ along the lines of the Alexandrian school; the Nestorian churches, prevailing in Persia; and the rest of the East and the West, who affirmed Chalcedon. Since a decision against Chalcedon was also a decision against the emperor, the "heretical" region within 200 years took refuge in the rise of Islam under which they felt they had more religious freedom than among their "orthodox" Christian brothers and sisters.

Though Christological reflection did not end in A.D. 451, the main issue was settled: even after his incarnation Jesus was still fully divine without thereby being forced to deny his full humanity.

From this point on the affirmation of Jesus as *vere deus et vere homo* (truly divine and truly human) was the starting point of Christological deliberation.

4. Our Savior (Middle Ages and Reformation)

Christological reflection did not lie dormant in the centuries between Chalcedon and the Reformation. Whether we take the affirmations of the Fifth Ecumenical Council of Constantinople (A.D. 553) that Christ has only an impersonal humanity (i.e., that his humanity does not function independently of his Godhead) or the rejection of the Spanish adoptionistic heresy of the 8th century (i.e., that Jesus was the adopted Son of God), these decisions brought nothing new. They only conformed to the earlier decisions of the great councils. We should also note that soon, especially in the West, interest in the person of Christ waned in favor of concern for his salvific benefits. A consensus seemed to prevail regarding *who* Christ was. Now the decisive question was *how he could provide our salvation*. This question had been posed before, in connection with Christ's divine and human "natures." Yet the Western church was no longer interested in the being of Christ but rather in his activity.

The most influential theory of Christ's salvific activity came from Anselm of Canterbury, a monk residing in a monastery of Bec in upper Italy and later archbishop in England. In the summer of 1098 he finished a book which was so appealing that earlier drafts of portions of the opus were secretly copied and distributed without his knowledge. The slim work was named *Cur Deus Homo?* (Why God Became Human). In it Anselm proposed a theory of satisfaction which eventually, especially since the Council of Trent, became the normative doctrine of the Roman Catholic church. Even Protestants have been impressed by it. Anselm's proposal replaced the earlier theory of deception or ransom advanced by Origen, Augustine, Gregory the Great, and many others. According to the earlier theory the devil had gained possession of the whole human race through the Fall. Salvation for humanity was made possible when Satan sought to take possession of the sinless Christ. It was asserted that because Satan took Christ, who was both sinless and human, he lost his right over humanity in general. According to this model, our salvation was accomplished by Satan's being deceived about the true nature of Christ. For instance, Origen stated that Christ offered himself to the devil as a sacrifice for us. The devil accepted the sacrifice, intending to nail Christ to the cross and triumph over him. Yet he could not lay hold of the pure soul of Christ and the devil's seeming victory was turned to defeat when the Savior rose from the grave. Since the devil, however, was bound by an agreement, he had to forfeit humanity.

Anselm rejected the theory of deception, stating that it does not present a convincing reason why God could not have simply freed humanity by his own volition.[35] Anselm contends human sinfulness is of such a magnitude that it can be removed only by God himself. If we assume we could contribute something to its removal or that someone else could do so, we "have not as yet estimated the great burden of sin."[36] When we understand that even the minutest sin is an attempt to depose God, we too will pose the question as to how we can ever get right with God. Anselm answers that to accomplish this, God became a human being and lived a fully obedient life. Since he lived his whole earthly life in conformity with God there was no need for him to die. But when he voluntarily died he had done more than was expected of him. Such excessive merit earns compensation. Since, however, he does not need anything for himself and since, because of his divine status, such merit has unlimited significance, he lets those who follow him participate in his benefits. With this theory Anselm felt that God's honor was maintained. God only gives compensation for that which was above and beyond the necessary, and attributes this to us because of Christ's human-divine status.

We should not assume, however, that the classical Alexandrian Christology was forgotten. Thomas Aquinas, for instance, returned to it when he asserted in his *Summa Theologica* that through his most complete union the God-man took our humanity into himself: "As to the full sharing in divinity, which is true happiness and the purpose of human life."[37] At the same time Thomas picked up Anselm's theory of satisfaction when he declared that through the hypostatic union there occurs a manifoldness of activity in which salvation is brought to us, such as in Christ's free suffering[38] or in his exemplary display of virtues.

We are not surprised that even in the *Augsburg Confession* (1530), the first authoritative document of the Reformation, we find the reaffirmation of the ancient trinitarian and Christological dogma. In Article 1 we read: "We unanimously hold and teach, in accordance with the decree of the Council of Nicaea, that there is one divine essence . . . and that there are three persons . . . . The word 'person' is to be understood as the Fathers employed the term in this connection, not as a part or a property of another but as that which exists of itself."[39] Similarly, in Article 3 the two natures of Christ are affirmed when we read that "the Word—that is, the Son of God—took on man's nature in the womb of the blessed virgin Mary."[40] Jesus Christ is both truly God and truly human but there is just one person.

Martin Luther followed the reaffirmation of the ancient dogma when he emphasized the unity of God. Luther's use of the word *triune* seems to have originated through his remarks against the term *Dreifaltigkeit*, i.e., threefoldness. He claimed: "Threefoldness is very bad German. In the Godhead is utmost unity."[41] Still today there are many Lutheran churches in Germany named "Church of the Triune God," while many Roman Catholic churches are called "Church of the Threefold God." This shows that this conceptual emphasis on the unity of God (God as triune), which the Roman Catholic tradition refused to accept, became a denominational shibboleth. Luther knew that it is impossible to explain rationally why and how God is three and yet one. He accepts from tradition the eternal procession of the Son from the Father[42] and he is aware that the term *trinity* is not used in Scripture. Thus there is no pregiven vocabulary in which to express this subject matter. Even so "the matter we must maintain, though we talk with terms as we choose."[43] Luther even admits, "I hear that there is one essence and three persons. I do not know how it happens. But I want to believe it."[44] We might be inclined to call this an attitude of fideism or even charge Luther with sacrifice of the intellect. But, as we will see, such a verdict misses Luther's intentions.

Luther mentioned once in a sermon:

> Augustine and other ancient teachers have said: the external work of the Trinity is undivided [*Opera trinitatis ab extra sunt indivisa*]. Father, Son, and Holy Spirit is one creator, not three . . . . This is how

far the Turks and the Jews and the pagans get. But we shall not only look at God from outside in his works, but God wants that we also recognize him from inside. But how is he inside? There is Father, Son, and Holy Spirit. That is not to adore three Gods. Inside he is one united being and three persons.[45]

When we encounter God as Father, Son, and Holy Spirit, we not only have an outside view of God as do other religions, but we have access to God's inner being, access to his heart, so to speak. With this statement Luther does not attempt to explain the Trinity. He was mindful of Philip Melanchthon's statement in the opening of his *Loci Communes* (1521), the first Lutheran dogmatic, "The mysteries of divinity we have the more rightly adored than investigated."[46] A rejection of the triune God would only leave room for a natural knowledge of God, a knowledge from the outside. The acceptance of the triune God, however, leads us to an intimate understanding of God's identity as God has chosen to reveal it.

It is Christ who serves as the mirror of God's heart. Luther already advanced this very early in his career in the *Heidelberg Disputation* (1518) where he claimed, "True theology is practical theology, and its foundation is Christ whose death is apprehended in faith."[47] This thesis contains three major points: (1) The foundation of theology is Christology and we cannot adequately talk about God without talking about Christ. (2) True theology is soteriology (practical theology), i.e., theology is not primarily concerned about God's or Christ's being but about their benefits for us. (3) The work of Christ (his death) can be apprehended only through faith and not through rational investigation.

With this approach Luther rejected all theological and Christological speculations unless they were beneficial for understanding our salvation. Luther also stated in his work on the Psalms, "The cross alone is our theology."[48] This meant a rejection of mystical or speculative theology and taking seriously the incarnation of Christ. It also meant that all theology has its center in God's revelation in Jesus Christ. God has shown himself to us in Jesus Christ and consequently Christ is our only avenue to God. Yet God in Christ is not empirically verifiable. Since God became human in Jesus Christ, we can grasp him only in his humanity; this means for Luther the crucified Christ. "For this reason true theology and recognition of God are in the crucified Christ."[49]

There are several important aspects of Luther's emphasis on the cross:

(a) The cross makes impossible any attempt on our side to approach God. "The works of God, though they look like they are always deformed and bad, are nevertheless immortal merits."[50] God acts differently from the way we would expect. If we rely on our own idea of how God should act, we would always miss him. Thus Luther juxtaposes the theologian of the cross and the theologian of glory, saying, "a theologian of glory calls evil good and the good evil. A theologian of the cross calls the thing what it actually is."[51] The reason for this reversal lies in a differing perspective. If we attempt to approach God through the created order, we will always miss him and adore a figure instead of God. If, however, we approach God through the suffering and the cross of Christ, we obtain sure knowledge based on God's own revelation.

(b) The cross of Christ and the suffering of God are so amazing that they cannot be the result of our own imagination. Either they are total nonsense or they really are what they are claimed to be. A theology of the cross is therefore contrary to speculation. The cross is good not because it is something we would logically associate with God, but it is good because it is God's chosen way of dealing with us.

(c) The cross is so surprising and unusual that God himself must interpret it in order to show us its significance. This means that the cross assures God's sovereignty and gracious activity in the God-disclosive process. Without God pointing out the significance of the cross, we would simply miss its meaning and reject it as a sign of defeat. Yet God tells us that the cross is the decisive victory over the powers of sin and death.

(d) For Luther, therefore, the cross is indicative of the way God acts. The primary way God works is under the appearance of the opposite or, what is closely related to it, God works out of nothing. According to Luther God completes when he destroys, he makes alive when he brings to death, he saves when he judges, and he reveals himself when he disguises himself. The working of God under the appearance of the opposite and creation out of nothing should not, however, be used as a heuristic principle. Although God always works in such a way that he causes surprise, God is not automati-

cally associated with negativity. God cannot be limited to being on the side of the downtrodden or at the site of a disaster.

Luther tells us in his *Lectures on Romans* that God acts like a dentist. At first his actions really hurt and there is a lot of pain and blood involved. But just when we think that everything has taken a turn for the worse, God does his actual work and we realize afterwards that our condition is even better than it was before. God must open our eyes so we can understand his miracle, the cross. It is futile to look for him in heaven or in the sublime things where our wisdom would assume him to be. Luther took with extreme seriousness the notion that Christ is God incarnate. Thus he reminds us that the lap of the mother, the cradle, and the cross are the steps on which we ascend to God. In this way we must actually descend in order to ascend to God.

Luther emphasized the incarnational aspect of Christ by maintaining the strict unity of both natures, the human and the divine. This was his point of contention against other groups of the Reformation, against the Reformed and the Spiritualists. In his *Confession concerning Christ's Supper* (1528) Luther declared, "The humanity is more closely united with God than our skin with our flesh—yes, more closely than body and soul."[52] Since Christ is truly human and truly divine there is no God apart from the man Jesus Christ. The unity of God and Christ leads to the assertion of Christ's omnipresence. While Zwingli asserted God's omnipresence, he wanted to restrict Christ's presence to his "local" abode in heaven. Yet Luther insisted that since Christ participates in the being of God, he is just as omnipresent as God. The question then arises whether such omnipresence can only be asserted of Christ's divine nature or also of his human nature. Luther argues for the unity of the person and asserts the *communicatio idiomatum*, the mutual participation in the respective properties. "What is man's can be rightly asserted of God and what is God's can be asserted of man."[53] Like Zwingli, the spiritualists thought differently and did not admit a mutual exchange of the human and divine attributes. Luther insisted, however, that God is not present in Christ as he is present in other creatures. In Christ he is present in the very unity of the person. Thus it was easy for Luther to agree with tradition and call Mary the one who gave birth to God. This one person, Jesus Christ, has the characteristics of both natures. God is not in Christ but God is Christ and vice versa.

Luther showed in his Christological reflections the same concern as that of the early church. If Christ suffered and died only as a human being, we are not saved. Only God's own involvement can change our lot. Luther therefore asserted, "there is a *communicatio idiomatum*, because what Christ suffered is also attributed to God, since both are one."[54] Even Melanchthon thought this assertion, allowing that the (impassible) deity was involved in suffering, was too extreme and stated: "this *entire* Jesus Christ is our Redeemer; in his human nature he died for us, and although he still possessed his divine nature, he did not use its might, but manifested his humility to the Father."[55] Luther himself did not confuse both natures of Christ. But much more strongly than did Melanchthon he asserted the unity of the person and the total involvement of deity in our worldly affairs.

The final consequence of the *communicatio idiomatum* was Luther's assertion of the ubiquity of the body of Christ. Once God and Christ were equated and the *communicatio* of the respective properties of the two natures was affirmed, the ubiquity of the whole person of Christ was a logical consequence. Merely demonstrating a logical consequence, however, was not important to Luther. Decisive for him was a soteriological concern. There is an essential difference between the omnipresence of God the Father, on the one hand, and the presence of God in the elements of the altar, on the other.[56] In the first, we can never lay our hands on God. God is present but elusive. In the second, however, God invites us to touch him in bread and wine. It is different, Luther states, whether God is simply here or whether he is here *for us*. If he is here for us, he gives us his word, binds himself to it and says, "Here you shall find me."

The previous discussion raises the question as to why is it so important for Luther that he really encounter Christ in bodily form in the elements. Why is it not sufficient for Luther that the exalted Christ would be spiritually present, as Zwingli had conceded? One concern is certainly Scripture. Christ's real presence is not contrary to Scripture but according to it. Another concern is the soteriological emphasis, which Luther shares with the early church. Christ's presence in the sacrament, pointed out to us by God's Word, allows us to encounter God in bodily form and shows us that God wants to have communion with us. God in Christ comes to us in such a way that everything anti-Godly must yield. God became human so that we can become Godlike, as Irenaeus had claimed centuries earlier.

Since we have mentioned so often Luther's soteriological concern in his Christology, it is no surprise to us that for Luther Christology always leads to soteriology. This is expressed in the famous "article by which the church stands or falls" (*articulus stantis et cadentis ecclesiae*). We read in the *Smalcald Articles* (1536) that "Jesus Christ, our God and Lord, 'was put to death for our trespasses and raised again for our justification' . . . . Nothing in this article can be given up or compromised even if heaven and earth and things temporal should be destroyed."[57] Similarly, in the explanation of the Second Article of the Apostles' Creed in Luther's *Small Catechism* we are immediately told that Jesus is truly human and truly divine. Then the emphasis shifts quickly to the salvific activity through which he has redeemed us. Clearly decisive is the *pro me*, the *for me* character of Christology. Luther goes so far as to say that even Satan knows that Christ was resurrected. Yet Satan does not believe that this happened for him too. If he would believe that—which he does not—even he could be saved. This means that purely historical knowledge does not save.

In 1535 in his first disputation on Rom. 3:28 ("For we hold that a man is justified by faith apart from works of the law"), Luther declared, "If Paul is understood to be speaking of acquired or historic faith, he is laboring entirely in vain."[58] Important alone is the relevance of history for me. Yet this relevance cannot be obtained apart from historical inquiry. Unlike some existentialists, Luther does not dispense with history. But he reminds us that the best historical knowledge does not amount to anything apart from the all-decisive awareness that this history touches my existence.

Since Christ is God's gift for us and since Christ must primarily be considered under the soteriological aspect, it is evident for Luther that salvation is God's doing alone. In picturesque language Luther puts it this way: "It is accordingly as blasphemous to say a man is his own god, creator or producer, as it is blasphemous to say that he is justified by his own works."[59] God provides the basis for our salvation by coming down to our human level. Through a miraculous exchange God enters our sphere of sinfulness so that we can enter his divine realm. This does not mean that we are made new in a physical or biological sense. Christ's justice is rather accounted to us for our justification. Righteousness cannot be acquired by us through our good deeds but it must be imputed to us. Luther does not want to curb our own efforts. Yet he declared, "It does not depend on our wanting and running, but on God's compassion."[60] Again Luther says, "Just as good fruits do not make the tree good, so good works do not justify the person."[61] This means we can be justified only through God's gracious declaration. Because we are not physically new beings, even when we are justified we are under temptation and will again succumb to sin. Therefore Luther admonishes us in his *Small Catechism* that the old Adam should be drowned daily through repentance so that a new human being can emerge.

If God does everything and we are unable to contribute anything to our salvation, the question emerges concerning the value of our human activities. Luther gives high praise to our works and activities. But the decisive question for him is one of sequence. Which comes first, our works or God's action? Luther states, "It is impossible that faith is without strong, many, and great works . . . . [But] faith and justification do not ensue from the works but works ensue from faith and justification."[62] "We confess," Luther says, "that good works must follow faith, yes, not only must, but follow voluntarily just as a good tree not only must produce good fruits, but does so freely."[63]

This means that human activity is a necessary response to God's activity in Christ. Whenever our human activity does not follow, God's activity is not understood in its existential implications. Luther here follows the apostolic precept that "we cannot but speak of what we have seen and heard" (Acts 4:20).

C. The two aspects of Christ

When we now consider the significance of Christ for us today we need to follow the basic decision of the ancient church, reiterated through the centuries, to regard Christ as truly human and truly divine. Also for us, however, this twofold aspect dare not end in speculation. It must rather be seen in light of the existential question of Christ's significance for us today.

1. The human face of God

When we talk about Jesus Christ as truly human we are first of all confronted with the incarnational aspect of Jesus Christ. Jesus Christ, the human face of God, came down and lived among us. In this way, to speak of Jesus Christ implies a history. In the past the very historicity of Jesus of Nazareth has occasionally been disputed. Such exteme skepticism is rare today. What is questioned today is the dogmatic relevance of Christ. The verdict of many is that Jesus certainly lived and he even had some good thoughts. But that he was more than a gifted person is to be doubted. The dogmatic relevance, however, cannot either be affirmed or denied apart from the history of Jesus of Nazareth. The interconnectedness between history and dogma makes it impossible to retreat from history into a purely kerygmatic Christology. Only through the *vere homo* (truly human) does the *vere deus* (truly God) speak to us.

Apart from Jesus of Nazareth, Christ is in danger of being turned into a philosophical idea. When that occurs we have what Luther opposed, a speculative or docetic Christology. While Jesus is accessible only through the New Testament kerygma, the kerygma itself is tied to history; it interprets events which happened in our world. Thus the kerygma presupposes the underlying historical events and without them it would be without content. If we do not scrutinize these events, the kerygma is in danger of becoming distorted, since we are threatened with the loss of its presupposition. If we inquire about the history underlying the kerygma, we do not mean either to devalue the kerygma or to end up with a purely historical faith. We must, however, pose questions of an historical nature in order to understand the content of the kerygma as far as that content pertains to our world. While, as we have seen in the last chapter, we cannot and do not mean to arrive at a biography of Jesus, we can obtain a fair picture of Jesus' intention, certain features of his proclamation, and some points of his life through historical investigation. He does not remain a stranger to us or a lifeless abstraction.

When we examine the historical evidence, we even get the impression that Jesus' life and destiny imply certain conclusions which transcend empirical verification and observation. Rudolf Bultmann expressed this by saying that "Jesus' call to decision implies a Christology."[64] This means that Jesus confronted his audience in such a way that it raised the question of his Messiahship. But such a question cannot be decided on empirical grounds. Similarly, Ernst Fuchs claimed that Jesus' conduct implied a Christology. He noted that Jesus emphasized the will of God in such a way that he claimed to stand in God's place. Thus Jesus' conduct provided the context for his proclamation. Both examples show that Christological conclusions can legitimately be drawn from Jesus of Nazareth. Their truth value, however, cannot be decided on purely historical grounds.

Jesus of Nazareth leaves us with a profound sense of ambiguity. On the one hand, everything he said and did must be subjected to rational scrutiny. The criteria for historicity laid down by Ernst Troeltsch at the turn of the century are also valid for Jesus. Everything must be subjected to and explained by the principles of analogy, correlation, and causal nexus. As a historical figure Jesus of Nazareth is not exempt from this approach. Moreover, the very fact that Jesus can be subjected to these principles demonstrates his historicity. But, contrary to a common suspicion, such principles imply no value judgment. For instance, when the Gospel of John shows in a comparison with Gnosticism that it employs Gnostic vocabulary, then this does not say anything about the authenticity of the Jesus material contained in this gospel. It only tells us something about its relation to Gnosticism. The this-worldly methods of historical scrutiny can make no assertions about otherworldly claims to truth.

When Jesus is subjected to historical scrutiny, his character as Christ remains hidden. Everything in the life of Jesus which is beyond the usual life of a human being is by definition ambiguous. This means that the extraordinary need not be explained by reference to some divine quality. They can be interpreted within a strictly this-worldly reference system. For instance, the virgin birth can be explained as a narrative patterned after virgin birth stories in other religions. Jesus' death can be interpreted as intentional suicide after a failed mission; the empty tomb as resulting from the theft of Jesus' corpse (Matt. 28:13); the appearances of the resurrected as a vision of a ghost (Luke 24:37); and the prior announcements of his death and resurrection as later editorial interpolations.

This means that in and of itself the human side of Jesus necessitates no salvational consequences. Whatever transcends the usual destiny of a human being can be explained in such a way that it stays within a this-worldly reference system. This can also be illustrated through the many misunderstandings of Jesus found in John. Whenever Jesus makes a claim which goes beyond the historical (e.g., "you must be born anew," John 3:3), it is misunderstood by his audience and interpreted in a this-worldly reference system (e.g., "How can a man be born when he is old?" John 3:4). The Christ is not accessible through historical investigation or rational deduction. The New Testament itself recognized this when we hear that Jesus responded to the confession of Peter ("You are the Christ, the Son of the living God") by saying, "flesh and blood has not revealed this to you" (Matt. 16:16f.).

Though no logical rectilinear continuation is possible between the Jesus of history and the Christ of faith, we dare not abandon the human face of God. The Christ can be approached only through Jesus. Any other foundation would end in speculation or wishful thinking. But how can we make the transition from Jesus to Christ? We remember that Jesus confronted his audience with a decision either to accept him as the one he claimed to be or to reject him. Some followed him and others rejected him. When confronted with the New Testament kerygma, our situation is different from that of Jesus' contemporaries—because of the Easter event. This event demonstrated in the eyes of his original followers and of all subsequent followers after Easter that he was not an imposter; it vindicated his messianic claim. Thus our decision for Christ both originates in Jesus of Nazareth and conforms to the decision of those who followed him since Easter. Because of his identity as the Christ, Jesus transcends our humanity. This means that we cannot have the perfect faith of Jesus. But through Jesus Christ, the present Lord, and in conformity with the Christian community everywhere we can have faith in Jesus.

Occasionally, the emphasis on the incarnation has also gone to the other extreme that forever limits Jesus to a this-worldly reference system. This can occur in two ways, as a continuation of the liberal tradition or in an excessively Christomonistic approach to theology. In the first, Jesus is often reduced to a political Messiah and is interpreted as a liberator or a revolutionary. The new world to come is collapsed into this-worldly goals and the transformation of the world takes place in and through the physical instead of with the physical under the stimulus of the metaphysical. Dorothee Soelle, for example, writes, "Imitation has been practised always and primarily in suffering. Today more is demanded, changing the world. By opening myself to Jesus' way I am changed."[65] The goal of discipleship is to change the world. The incentive for revolutionary engagement is received from God's own history which is at the same time our history. "The metamorphosis of God," she writes, "pre-existence, incarnation and exaltation—represent the history of humanity—identity, estrangement and identification."[66] The history of Jesus becomes our history and provides the power to propel it forward. Yet any concern for the presence of Christ beyond Jesus' earthly career becomes irrelevant.

We encounter another, similarly structured approach which does not go beyond Jesus of Nazareth in the Christomonistic concentration on the divine in Jesus Christ. Although Luther presented a radically Christocentric approach to the Christian faith and affirmed that only God's human face, Jesus of Nazareth, gives us access to the true knowledge of God, for Luther God could still be experienced everywhere. Karl Barth, on the other hand, the most prominent representative of neo-Reformation theology, while admitting that world religions allow for a knowledge of God, labeled this approach unbelief and an attempt to reach out for God instead of letting God reach down to us. In other words, God's self-disclosure outside of Christ, even in a very limited form, was still rejected.

For Dietrich Bonhoeffer, in some ways a student of Barth, even the religious sphere began to disintegrate. Especially in his *Letters and Papers from Prison* he claimed that the religious premise for our discourse about God has been steadily waning. We are now mature, mature enough to make it on our own without reference to God. Therefore the religious dimension, which Bonhoeffer largely equated with immaturity and with the need for a *deus ex machina*, a God of the gaps, is rapidly vanishing. Only Christ remains to disclose God to us. Since God is edged out of the world, even in Christ we do not find a God of power and might. The incarnated God is weak and helpless. Bonhoeffer asserts that "the Bible directs man to God's powerlessness and suffering; only the suffering God can help."[67] Of course, we could turn to the resurrected one. But "even as the Risen One, he does not break through his incognito."[68] Bonhoeffer clearly places his emphasis on the incarnate Christ, though he admits that when Christ returns, we will encounter him in his glory.

When we turn to the so-called death-of-God theologians we are told by them that they follow the course set by Barth and Bonhoeffer. For instance, William Hamilton continues the emphasis on incarnation when he states, "To speak about God and to know him means therefore, to shape everything that we say and pray into the pattern of Jesus the humilated Lord."[69] However, Hamilton remains so centered upon the incarnated Christ that he arrives at the conclusion that God has somehow withdrawn from the world and is somehow dead. Hamilton does not reject the notions of ascension, exaltation, and the kingly office of Christ. Yet they have no precise meaning for him anymore, because for us today it remains Good Friday. Hamilton has given up the dialectic tension between the truly human and truly divine in favor of a nondialectic emphasis on the truly human. This means that the paradoxical revelation of God's weakness is neglected and that Hamilton ends up only with weakness (i.e., of humanity) but without God.

This consequence is drawn out even more drastically by Thomas J. J. Altizer when he declares that the death of God in Jesus of Nazareth is a historical event, signifying not only the death of the God of religion but of the God of Jesus Christ. The death of God in Jesus of Nazareth means an actual death. Significantly, however, Altizer does not end on that note but still looks for the renewal of God beyond Christianity, a renewal which may occur in the depths of every person or in the mysticism of the East. Altizer's Hegelian approach leads him to accept David Friedrich Strauss' idea that God incarnated himself in humanity as a whole. But Altizer also adds to this a new religious awareness attained through mysticism.

We can see from this brief discussion that an exclusive emphasis on the incarnation endangers both the divinity of Christ in particular and the Godhead of God in general. We must always be careful to maintain the paradoxical character of the incarnation and also be aware of the offense which this paradox implies. This offensiveness shows itself in two ways: (1) by the coincidence of opposites which is without analogy in human history, and (2) by the antirational mode of God's presence.

The coincidence of opposites is perhaps expressed best in Luther's Christmas hymn "From Heaven Above to Earth I Come," where we read:

> *The blessing which the Father planned*
> *The Son holds in his infant hand.*

or

> *In manger-bed, in swaddling clothes*
> *The child who all the earth upholds.*[70]

The finite is enabled to hold the infinite or, as the Gospel of John says, "the word [*logos*] became flesh" (John 1:14). This does not mean that the divine and the human merged so that we encounter a partly divine and partly human being. We are confronted here, as Paul Tillich said, with the essence under the conditions of existence.

The biblical witnesses tell us that this coincidence of opposites occurred in such a way that not even Jesus' family was aware of his divine being. He lived on this earth as one of us. When Jesus started his ministry his friends were highly concerned about the dire consequences which his "presumptuous" behavior might have. We even read that "they went out to seize him, for people were saying, 'He is besides himself' " (Mark 3:21), which means to say that he cannot be held responsible for his behavior. Similarly, his mother and his brothers called him to return home (Mark 3:31). It is not by accident that apart from Mary none of his immediate relatives played an important role among his disciples. At his crucifixion too, from among his relatives only his mother was present. Not even Easter changed the situation radically. In the early church we no longer hear anything about Jesus' mother. We only hear that James, his brother, assumed a leading position among the Christians in Jerusalem. When the disciples encountered the resurrected one, they first reacted in disbelief. At Pentecost when they proclaimed the resurrected one to their fellow citizens, the disciples were declared to be drunk. Others, less inclined to vindictiveness, stood by in amazement (Acts 2:12f.).

There have always been claims, especially among the followers of Calvin, that the divine and the human did not really coincide. The divine somehow shines through Jesus like a light shining through the cover of a lamp. Here it is especially possible to point to Jesus' miracles. But the miracles in themselves are not automatically convincing. The *extra-Calvinisticum,* the assertion by Calvinistic and Pietistic groups that the divinity does not really coincide with Jesus' humanity and that it can be traced in this-worldly events, does not do justice to the biblical narrative.

We must also remember that God is present in Jesus Christ in a way that reason would not expect. If God's presence in Jesus of Nazareth were reasonable, we would assume that the so-called proofs of the existence of God would make use of this argument. But all of these proofs circumvent Christ and deal exclusively with the created order. The nonreasonable character of God's presence in Jesus was in Paul's mind when he told the "reasonable" and "enlightened" Christians in Corinth, "For Jews demand signs and Greeks seek wisdom, but we preach Christ crucified, a stumbling block to the Jews and folly to the Gentiles" (1 Cor. 1:22). We must be careful not to assume, as has often been done, that Paul here equates the theology of the cross with every kind of nonsense, claiming that the more obstruse things get the more they are God's doing. We have already heard from Luther that God does not act in foolish and stupid ways but rather in a way in which we do not expect, a way which causes surprise. This becomes clear when Paul mentions in the same letter, "None of the rulers of this age understood this; for if they had, they would not have crucified the Lord of glory" (1 Cor. 2:8). Paul admits that Jesus' crucifixion occurred with good intentions and not out of evil motives. The "rulers of this age" did not realize who Jesus was, considered him to be a usurper of power and a blasphemer, and acted accordingly.

How can we then understand God's action in Jesus if it does not conform to our reason? Paul addresses this question when he states: "So also no one comprehends the thoughts of God except the Spirit of God. Now we have received not the spirit of the world, but the Spirit which is from God, that we might understand the gifts bestowed on us by God" (1 Cor. 2:11f.). God himself must open our eyes through his Spirit of discernment if we are to realize that Jesus is not just a human being but also God's human face. This safeguards the priority of God's activity in the salvific process and assures us that we are not led astray by our own ideas.

2. The avenue to a new dimension

When we contemplate the divine aspect of Jesus, we encounter a new dimension which would otherwise not be accessible to us. This new dimension makes us aware that Jesus both is and implies God, an event which also indicates our salvation and even a change in the cosmos. In the Letter to the Colossians we read that "in him the whole fulness of deity dwells bodily" (Col. 2:9), which means that Jesus Christ is and implies God. Yet Jesus' full divinity is not just another historical fact, such as the Civil War or the Great Depression. The true divinity is in history and at the same time beyond it. It is as impossible to prove the divinity of Jesus in particular as to prove the existence of God in general. God's presence in Christ cannot be established in a historical, exegetical, or dogmatic manner. The life-of-Jesus research has shown that the divinity of Christ is not a historical and exegetical matter, just as the Christological controversies have shown that the divinity of Christ is not a dogmatically ascertainable fact.

If we assert, however, that Christ's divinity is somehow to be seen apart from his historicity, we negate the incarnation and advance a docetic Christ. When we acknowledge that Christ's true divinity is both in and at the same time beyond history, we say that it is not at our disposal and that it cannot be manipulated by us. But we also affirm that we can recognize it, once it is pointed out to us. The true divinity is thus not just part of the human being Jesus in such a manner that it lies dormant, awaiting its activation as a way of filling in the gaps. It is one with him and also beyond him.

When Paul asserted that "man believes with his heart [that Jesus is Lord] and so is justified and he confesses with his lips and so is saved " (Rom. 10:10), he implied that acknowledgment of the divinity of Christ can come only through faith and not from rational investigation. While the humanity of Jesus is the presupposition for the acknowledgment of the divinity of Christ, the latter is not a mere consequence of the former. It involves, moreover, the trust that the human being Jesus really was who he said he was. Thus we trust the human being Jesus as God. Jesus is the ground and the source of faith, out of which faith in Jesus as the Christ occurs. Jesus as such does not become the object of faith. Christians do not believe in Jesus but in Jesus as the Christ. The Jesus of history is open to a faith that incorporates Jesus as the Christ into itself. Even more, if Jesus is truly divine he is equal to God. This is shown in a very interesting way in the biblical documents.

In the Old Testament the proper name for God is Yahweh, which is translated in the Septuagint as "Lord" (*kyrios*). Yet in the New Testament the Christians assert that Jesus is *kyrios*, meaning that Jesus is God. This is again shown by Paul when he cites the confessional formula, "If you confess with your lips that Jesus is Lord and believe in your heart that God raised him from the dead, you will be saved" (Rom. 10:9). The fact that Jesus is Lord (i.e., God) assures a strict monotheism. It implies that God incarnated himself as Jesus of Nazareth. Jesus was God not just after his baptism or his resurrection but from the very instant he took on human form in Mary's womb. For that reason Mary is rightly called Mother of God (*theotokos*). Yet Mary herself did not incarnate Jesus. She rather accepted his incarnation in her. Thus it would be totally unwarranted to call her co-redeemer or to adore her because of her special relation to Jesus Christ. Adoration is reserved for God alone.

Since Jesus was truly divine we must conclude that this divinity belonged to him throughout his life on earth. This means that in considering Jesus we must also talk about God's suffering and even God's death. In the perspective of philosophy God is usually considered impassible and consequently unable to suffer. According to the Judeo-Christian tradition, however, God is involved in history. He is part of history and of all the agonies connected with it. Since Christ's divinity was exposed to all the conditions of his humanity, at his death the incarnate God—human and divine—ceased to be. This does not, however, mean that God ceased to be. The world was not without God until Christ was resurrected. Here we must distinguish between God in himself and the God for us. (If we do not make this distinction also the dialog of Jesus with God the Father would not make sense; strictly speaking it would only be monolog.) So when we talk about the weakness of God and of his suffering, we are talking about God incarnate, the God who reveals himself to us. Yet we do not talk about God in himself. When we overemphasize the incarnation, the distinction between Christ as God incarnate and God in himself is not maintained. We then hold them to be identical instead of asserting their dynamic relationship within the Godhead.

Since the human being, Jesus of Nazareth, is in personal union with God we must conclude that we also encounter in him the goal of humanity. True divinity was incarnated throughout a lifetime in the truly human being Jesus. The human being Jesus lived throughout his life in conformity to the divinity. Since this was a personal union and not a complementarity of human and divine, the divinity did not assist the humanity during the earthly life. Jesus' life took place under the conditions of human existence. Yet his life was conducted in such a way that there was a unity of will and of action between the human and the divine. Jesus did not live as a God upon the earth but as God wants humanity to live, in unity with him. Thus Jesus is the exemplary human being, the pioneer and perfecter of our faith. Jesus demonstrated in his own life what humanity is for, not estrangement from God but harmony and closeness to God. For Jesus the distant God became so close that he could even address him as his Father. Jesus, although tempted by sinfulness like all people, did not succumb to it. Thus we are encouraged to imitate him, not in his singular status as truly human and truly divine, but in his life-style of conformity to God's will.

Since Jesus showed in his life that the unity of God and humanity is once again possible, he is the end and goal of humanity. He points the way to the new humanity which he represented. He laid open the road for our unity with God and became the pioneer and perfecter of our life (Heb. 12:2). He marks the end of sinful humanity and the beginning of a new creation. Thus we encounter in him our salvation.

There are basically two ways in which Christ's salvific activity can be described. (1) The first can be called the monistic approach, and was most persuasively advocated by Anselm of Canterbury. Anselm argues that we cannot give satisfaction to God since we already are indebted to him through our sinful behavior. But God becomes human and fulfills the satisfaction which God requires from us. His merits are then attributed to us. This means that salvation is worked out between God and God incarnate and is applied to us. Paul also referred to this approach when he stated: "All this is from God, who through Christ reconciled us to himself and gave us the ministry of reconciliation" (2 Cor. 5:18). God's wrath, caused by our sinfulness, is changed into love. Again, we read in the Letter to the Colossians, "And you, who were dead in trespasses and the uncircumcision of your flesh, God made alive together with him, having forgiven us all our trespasses, having canceled the bond which stood against us with its legal demands; this he set aside, nailing it to the cross" (Col. 2:13f.). Satisfaction for our sins took place on the cross when Jesus died for our sins, fulfilling God's demands for justice and therefore setting us free from the condemnation due us through our sinful behavior.

(2) The other approach, which we want to call the dramatic dualistic one, was best portrayed by Origen with his theory of the betrayal of the devil. Luther alluded to this when he wrote in his hymn, "A Mighty Fortress Is Our God":

> *Though hordes of devils fill the land*
> *All threat'ning to devour us,*
> *We tremble not, unmoved we stand;*
> *They cannot overpow'r us.*
> *Let this world's tyrant rage;*
> *In battle we'll engage!*
> *His might is doomed to fail;*
> *God's judgment must prevail!*
> *One little word subdues him.*[71]

This "little word" which overcomes the powers of darkness is Jesus Christ. So we hear Jesus say, according to Luke, "But if it is by the finger of God that I cast out demons, then the kingdom of God has come upon you" (Luke 11:20). We remember that the Gospels depicted Jesus' whole ministry as a fight against seductive, anti-Godly powers. We recall the temptation story in the beginning and Jesus' struggle in Gethsemane at the end. But Jesus did not succumb to these powers. He was victorious and liberated us from them. God then gave the final validation to this victory. Paul reminds us of this victory when he exclaims, "O death, where is thy victory? O death, where is thy sting? The sting of death is sin, and the power of sin is the law. But thanks be to God, who gives us the victory through our Lord Jesus Christ" (1 Cor. 15:55f.).

While the monistic approach focuses primarily on the God who provided redemption, the dramatic dualistic approach shows us that from which we have been redeemed, the seductive and destructive anti-Godly powers. If we would emphasize only the monistic approach, the question of the object of salvation, humanity, and of that which separates us from God, the adverse powers, would hardly come into focus. Moreover, God could easily be misunderstood as an insulted tyrant who will not give way until he sees blood. Exclusive emphasis on the dramatic dualistic approach would impede the sovereignty of God and his decisive action. Moreover, it might be misunderstood as a mythological battle between an evil and a good principle. All this means that there is no single foolproof conceptuality which can convey the salvific meaning of God's action in Jesus Christ. Only the use of complementary approaches will give us an adequate view of God's activity.

A complementary view is also necessary when we encounter the cross and resurrection. Often the idea is advanced that the resurrection is the objective proof of the significance of the cross. But the resurrection does not belong to the realm of history, because the resurrected Christ is not a historical figure subject to the limitations of space and time. Yet it is also not possible to consider the resurrection simply as the other side of the cross. Resurrection and cross are not one, but form a unity in interdependence. The cross alone is a mystery and an offense, even for the believer. Strictly and logically speaking, it does not make sense that God incarnate suffers and dies. But for the believer the resurrection explains the significance of the cross by pointing beyond it. Thus the cross provides the basis for the resurrection and the resurrection provides the interpretive context for the cross.

3. The cosmic Christ

So far we have primarily considered the individual aspect of salvation. Yet this notion needs expansion in two ways: it must be expanded to include all of humanity and the whole creation. While Christians are occasionally charged with egotism in regard to salvation, they confess every Sunday the words of the Apostles' Creed, which extends salvation at least to those who lived before Jesus walked on this earth.

Relevant in this context is the phrase "he descended into hell" or, as it is now more adequately translated, "he went to the dead," one of the last statements which was incorporated into the Apostles' Creed. Though the descent into the realm of the dead is nowhere explicitly stated in the New Testament, it is presupposed or at least implied at several places. For instance, Matt. 12:40 indicates a passive stay in that realm, whereas other passages point to Christ's activity in this realm. References such as Rev. 1:18 ("I died, and behold I am alive for evermore, and I have the keys of Death and of Hades") show Jesus Christ has won the victory over the powers of the realm of the dead. At other places, in the context of Christ's death and resurrection, the redemption of some or all of the dead is mentioned (Matt. 27:51-53). Finally, there are some references, such as 1 Peter 3:19, where this descent is understood as the proclamation to some or all who are in the realm of the dead ("he went and preached to the spirits in prison").

A passive sojourn in the realm of the dead proved not very interesting for theological development. Christ's victorious entry into the realm of the dead, on the other hand, is vividly expressed by Luther. Following tradition, Luther connected this entry with the liberation of the Old Testament patriarchs from the limbo of the fathers and their transition to heaven.[72] That Jesus must have been active in the realm of the dead following his death on Good Friday is concluded from the idea that the divinity of Christ cannot just rest and inactively lie in the tomb.

The church acted wisely when it never decided dogmatically that only some people, i.e., the Old Testament patriarchs, could have benefited from Christ's descent. Some theologians (e.g., Melito, Marcion, and Ephraem) even thought that Jesus Christ redeemed all the dead, except perhaps for some very bad persons, and others (e.g., the Alexandrian theologians and Origen) thought that those who had died before the great flood were also saved. It is interesting to note that the presbyter Rufinus of Aquileia in northern Italy, who lived for a long time in the East and who translated the works of Origen, mentions a creed being used in his hometown around A.D. 370 which already contained the phrase of Christ's descent and which was subsequently introduced into the Apostles' Creed.[73]

But what does this mean? Is Christ's descent into hell illegitimate speculation based on unclear New Testament passages which we should confine to their literal meaning, i.e., that on Good Friday Christ went to the dead as everyone else does at death? Theologians, whether in the early church or in more recent times, who have reflected on this phrase and on the biblical passages which it interprets, did not merely speculate on the whereabouts of Christ's divinity after his death. They were much more concerned that those who were geographically or temporally distanced and therefore unable to live their life in conformity with Christ during their earthly lifetimes might be in some way confronted with his offer of salvation. They found the possibility for such an offer beyond death in Christ's descent to the dead.

The church confessed then and still confesses today that one can be saved only by the compassion shown to us in Jesus Christ. While the church maintained that one's response to the existential encounter with Christ has ultimate significance, the church did not feel that it could assert that all persons who did not have the chance for such an encounter during their life on earth would have to suffer eternal consequences, the loss of eternal bliss. On the contrary, the church, without circumventing the salvific power of Christ, affirmed its hope that there was a possibility that those could also be saved who had not encountered Christ during their lifetime on earth. Yet the church never went so far as to declare that everyone will therefore eventually be saved, nor did it feel it was its task to define how someone could be saved through Christ's descent.

Our reflections today must show a similar restraint. While we fervently hope and pray that all of humanity will be saved, we cannot take for granted that it will indeed be so or outline a way in which God will reach this goal. We do know that we will be saved only for Christ's sake. Contemplating the destiny of millions of people who have died since Christ's sojourn on earth without ever having known about him, or those who have known about him in such a distorted way that no appropriate response to him was possible, it is not unscriptural to conclude that these people might be given a similar opportunity.

Finally we must venture beyond the human level to consider all of creation. The phrase in the Apostles' Creed, "He ascended into heaven and is seated at the right hand of the Father," gave rise to the celebration of Ascension Day. But it is as little understood as the festival itself, which has been celebrated at least since the fourth century. Some exegetes claim that in the earliest tradition the resurrection of Christ was understood as his exaltation to God (cf. Rom. 8:34), while Luke introduced an interim between resurrection and ascension during which Christ returned to this earth. For most people today the problem is not whether there is actually a distinct ascension of Christ after his resurrection. The problem is rather the spatial imagery involved in the exaltation, an act which seems untenable in today's worldview. In our uneasiness we are actually in good company. Already Luther objected to Zwingli's literal interpretation of Christ sitting at the right hand of the Father. Since the heavens are continuously moving, this would mean that Christ could not sit still for one moment. "They speak childishly and foolishly of heaven, assigning to Christ a particular spot in heaven like a stork with its nest in a tree."[74]

We should not understand Christ's sitting at the right hand of the Father in a spatial way. Just as we might say that someone is our right hand, it means that Christ is God's right hand. He has been inaugurated into power and is as omnipresent and omnipotent as God the Father. This guarantees for us that his salvific work on earth actually has significance before God. Consequently we hear the exalted Christ say, "All authority in heaven and on earth has been given to me" (Matt. 28:18). His participation in God's power appropriately marks the conclusion of Christ's salvific involvement with this world as we await his final parousia. We know him to be present where the decisions are made concerning the course of the world and are sure that the promises connected with his coming will one day be fully redeemed. This leads us to the final point in our investigation of Jesus Christ.

Jesus Christ is and implies a cosmic change. Already we notice that his resurrection appearances point to someone with abilities which are beyond those of a human and earthly being. His resurrected state is and implies a new and unprecedented change in our world. The human Jesus was transformed into the resurrected Christ. When we read in Col. 1:18, "He is the beginning, the firstborn from the dead, that in everything he might be preeminent," two points are implied: (1) In the resurrected Christ something new has commenced and (2) this something will also be applied to us. Paul mentions the implications for us when he says, "If any one is in Christ, he is a new creation; the old has passed away, behold, the new has come" (2 Cor. 5:17). This means the new creation is something in which we participate already now. Yet this new creation is omnipresent in Christ (cf. Gal. 6:14f.).

If we deviate from Christ, our participation in the new creation ceases and we return to our former state of being. Thus we, together with the whole creation, wait for the final redemption when deviation will no longer be possible (cf. Rom.8:23). The whole creation, says Paul, "waits with eager longing for the revealing of the sons of God" (Rom. 8:19). That which has started in Jesus Christ and that in which we now participate proleptically is still to be completed. Although we participate in the new creation, we are not yet transformed and perfected. The public disclosure of our new state is still pending. Since we are still prone to deviate from our new status, Paul exhorts us through imperatives to realize that which we are. But he also confesses about himself, "Not that I have already obtained this or am already perfect; but I press on to make it my own, because Jesus Christ has made me his own" (Phil. 3:12). Both the interim status of our existence and the fragmentary fulfillment of the final destiny of the world calls for completion. One day, but not indefinitely, Jesus Christ will bring about the universal and public victory of God. Then, Paul says, "when all things are subjected to him, then the Son himself will also be subjected to him who put all things under him, that God may be everything to every one" (1 Cor. 15:28).

Surprising as it may sound, the goal of everything does not lie in Christ. God alone is the goal of everything, with Christ as its mediator and fulfiller. Jesus Christ, in his own death and resurrection, realizes the goal and gives us access to it through redemption and final judgment. The one God alone, however, is the final goal. This means that Christology necessarily leads to theology. But does it also mean that the differentiation between Father, Son, and Holy Spirit is only a temporary one? If we were to affirm this would we also have to affirm Arius's dictum that there was a time when Christ was not? The categories of time simply do not apply to the triune God. Though the triune differentiation is intrinsic to the way God discloses himself to us, this does not imply that Christ and the Holy Spirit will some time cease to be. Since the redeemed will enjoy the fullness of the Spirit, the Holy Spirit will provide the eternal link with and basis for communion with the Father. The Son, however, having completed his purpose of action to subject all things to God, "will also be subjected to him who put all things under him, that God may be everything to every one" (1 Cor. 15:28).

PART 4

THE SPIRIT WHO EMPOWERS

The Holy Spirit has never received prominent attention in dogmatic reflection, usually being the corollary to something else. Nevertheless, the Spirit has always provided the impetus for the activities of Christians. Already the first Christians felt that they were empowered by the Spirit. This assertion has been continued through the centuries. Before we contemplate how the Spirit works through the church, which is the corporate structure of the Christian life, we should devote some attention to the general features of the Spirit and to its functioning.

10

THE HOLY SPIRIT

The Spirit is not confined to the church but is present throughout God's creation. This becomes immediately evident when we consider the biblical usages of the term *Spirit*.

A. The biblical documents

1. Ruah *as God's empowering Spirit (Old Testament)*

In the Old Testament *spirit* denotes the natural phenomena of wind, breath, and, more generally, that which gives life to the body (Gen. 6:17). It can also be used to describe the seat of emotions and of intellectual functions (Gen. 41:8; Job 32:8). Yet in Job 32:8 we already note a very interesting remark, "But it is the spirit [*ruah*] in a man, the breath [*neshamah*] of the Almighty, that makes him understand." It is God's Spirit and not our self-acquired education which leads to wisdom. Even the insights we gain through experience are not unrelated to God's Spirit. The faculties that relate to life and its mastery are not perceived as inherent but as given by God. *Ruah* is the "wind" which proceeds from Yahweh and which will eventually return to him, constituting the breath of life. "If he should take back his spirit [*ruah*] to himself, and gather to himself his breath [*neshamah*], all flesh would perish together, and man would return to dust" (Job 34:14f.). Often *ruah*, the breath of human beings, cannot be separated from the *ruah* of Yahweh.

But the *ruah* of Yahweh is not just the enlivening wind that becomes the breath of human beings. When the Psalmist says that "by the word of the Lord the heavens were made, and all their host by the breath of his mouth" (Ps. 33:6), we notice that *ruah* is used here synonymously with "word" (*dabar*). It is this same word which is used in the Genesis story to describe God's creation of the world. Yahweh's breath is the creative power of life that determines our life span (Gen. 6:3) and tames the natural forces (Exod. 15:8). When it is imparted to individuals it can indicate exceptional qualities. Pharaoh, for instance, looks for a man "in whom is the Spirit of God" (Gen. 41:38) so that he may tackle the problems connected with the threatening famine. To be filled with the Spirit of God can also mean to be endowed "with ability and intelligence, with knowledge and all craftmanship, to devise artistic designs, to work in gold, silver, and bronze" (Exod. 31:3f.).

While now only isolated individuals are endowed with the Spirit of God, at the end-time Yahweh will pour out his Spirit "on all flesh." Then he promises to Israel that "your sons and your daughters shall prophesy, your old men shall dream dreams, and your young men shall see visions" (Joel 2:28). Similarly, we hear in Ezek. 36:26f., "A new heart I will give you, and a new spirit I will put within you; and I will take out of your flesh the heart of stone and give you a heart of flesh. And I will put my spirit within you, and cause you to walk in my statutes and be careful to observe my ordinances."

Though humanity is not without spirit, only the Spirit of God leads to right living and the fulfillment of the will of God. The Psalmist attests to this when he prays, "Create in me a clean heart, O God, and put a new and right spirit within me. Cast me not away from thy presence, and take not thy holy Spirit from me. Restore to me the joy of thy salvation, and uphold me with a willing spirit" (Ps. 51:10ff.). Life, power, and freedom are not taken for granted but are seen as related to God. He gives his Spirit and we are vigorous, wise, and renewed. He takes his Spirit away and we become confused, sick, and like those in the pit. Our *ruah* (spirit) can be properly understood only in light of God's communion with us. Most Old Testament texts which mention the Spirit of God show God and humanity in a dynamic relationship. Our full humanity can be developed only in relationship with God. While we will find our fulfillment on a universal scale in the eschaton, it has been and is anticipated to various degrees already, whether within the Israelite covenant community or outside of it, since God's activity has created and sustains his whole creation.

2. Increasing independence of ruah (intertestamental writings)

In contrast to the Old Testament, in intertestamental Judaism the distinction evolved between spirit and body so that body was considered to be of earthly derivation, while the spirit connected humanity with the heavenly dimension. Consequently, there developed the notions of the immortality of the soul and of preexistence. Rabbi Simai (c. 210), for instance, taught:

> All creatures that have been created from heaven (i.e., from heavenly substances), their soul and body is from heaven; and all creatures that have been created from the earth (from earthly substances) their body and soul is from the earth. Therefore, when a man keeps the Torah and the will of the Father in heaven, see, he is like the creatures from above.[1]

Interesting for us is not so much the notion of a dual origin of body and soul which is expressed by Rabbi Simai, but the fact that humanity is seen in a twofold relationship, on the one hand connected with and rooted in this world, and at the same time related to God. If humanity lives in conformity with God's will, it evidently must live according to its heavenly destiny.

The writers of the Old Testament apocrypha and pseudepigrapha understood even more clearly that the human spirit is molded by outside forces, most prominently by the Spirit of God. Though the Spirit of God is especially the spirit of prophecy through which one prophesies and sees hidden things (Sir. 48:12f.), we also hear about the spirit of understanding (Sir. 39:6; T. Levi 2:3), and of wisdom (Wis. 9:17). The Spirit of God therefore enables one to be discerning and to live in accordance with the will of God. But the Spirit also has a cosmic function. It is the instrument of divine creation when God sent forth his Spirit and built the world (Jud. 16:14).

Judaic thought attributes to the Spirit a growing measure of autonomy. Strack-Billerbeck remarked that often the Holy Spirit which speaks through Scripture is personified by saying that he speaks, calls, or proclaims.[2] This is done especially in cases when one scripture passage is employed to explain another passage. The Holy Spirit also seems to become God's partner by performing the same functions that had formerly been attributed to God's justice and compassion. Yet the Spirit does not become an independent actor but rather a divine reality that meets humanity and elicits their response.

3. *The life-giving power of the* pneuma *(New Testament)*

Regarding the New Testament, we want to emphasize those lines which have bearing on our present understanding of the work of the Spirit in the world. But before doing so, we should at least allude to Gnostic literature, since there the spirit is a dominant category. The most important feature for us in Gnosticism is the break in the unity between God and the world. Since power is now thought of as a substance, the life-giving power of God eventually became understood as being held captive in the body. Thus humanity no longer had a twofold relationship but rather a dual nature. God, being spiritual, bound his spiritual nature to matter in creation and it is from matter that this spiritual nature seeks once again to be redeemed. Since God is Spirit, he is not the actual creator of matter but its life-empowering force. Therefore, matter itself is not redeemable. We are redeemed from our bodies by returning to our spiritual existence with God.

When we hear Jesus saying in Matt. 12:28, "But if it is by the Spirit of God that I cast out demons, then the kingdom of God has come upon you," we notice that the Old Testament notion has been retained and that the Spirit of God has the power to perform unusual deeds. The filling of the people with the Spirit as the eschatological sign is also mentioned in the Gospels (Mark 1:8). The prime example of this, of course, is Jesus himself in his baptism (Mark 1:10ff.). Just as God in the beginning created the world through his Spirit, now God creates the first form of the new creation through his *pneuma* (Matt. 1:18; Luke 1:35).

While Matthew and Mark mentioned the Spirit of God relatively seldom, the story is different with Luke. The presence of the Spirit characterizes the time of the church. At Pentecost the disciples were filled with the Holy Spirit (Acts 2:4) and everyone who is baptized into the Christian community likewise receives the Holy Spirit.

For John, the Spirit assumes a more cosmological function; the Spirit is seen as a sphere which stands in antithesis to the flesh. So John talks on the one hand about the Spirit which comes from above and, on the other hand, about the flesh, the devil, and the present cosmos which comes from below. "God is Spirit, and those who worship him must worship in spirit and truth" (John 4:24), as we hear Jesus say. The Spirit that is identified with God and with Christ is the life-empowering force, since "it is the spirit that gives life, the flesh is of no avail; the words that I have spoken to you are spirit and life" (John 6:63). Of course, the spirit is not a natural human option, since "that which is born of the flesh is flesh, and that which is born of the Spirit is spirit" (John 3:6). True life can be found only in the sphere of the Spirit and this means with God. As the paraclete sayings indicate, the Counselor will be "the Spirit of truth, whom the world cannot receive" (John 14:17). Though John does not compromise the insight that we cannot obtain true knowledge on our own, he also indicates that God has brought truth to us when the "word became flesh" (John 1:14). Thus those in the world do not live in a godless vacuum. Through Christ's coming everyone has the possibility of a rebirth (John 3:7) and of living according to the Spirit. Unlike the Old Testament, which spans many centuries, John does not reflect upon how this enlivening Spirit may also be active in places where he is not explicitly recognized. The case is similar with Paul.

As in John we notice that Paul identifies the Lord (Jesus Christ) with the Spirit when he writes: "Now the Lord is the Spirit, and where the Spirit of the Lord is, there is freedom" (2 Cor. 3:17). Unlike Gnostic thought, the spiritual and the physical are not opposites. Paul confesses that "it is sown a physical body, it is raised a spiritual body" (1 Cor. 15:44). The reason for this confident confession that the physical will be transformed into the spiritual lies in the fact that whereas the first Adam became a living being, "the last Adam became a life-giving spirit" (1 Cor. 15:45). The physical therefore obtains its direction from the spiritual because of Christ and his resurrection.

The transformation into the Spirit or into being in Christ is not just a future event. Already now God has given us the Spirit as a guarantee, or down payment, of the future (2 Cor. 5:5). Christians are reminded to "walk not according to the flesh but according to the Spirit" (Rom. 8:4); the Spirit is the norm of life and expresses the will of God. Since Christians too must be reminded of the new life in Christ, we are not surprised that non-Christians perceive their relationship to God even less. But Paul does not simply excuse them. On the contrary, he states: "Ever since the creation of the world his invisible nature, namely, his eternal power and deity, has been clearly perceived in the things that have been made. So they are without excuse ; . . . they became futile in their thinking and their senseless minds were darkened" (Rom. 1:20f.). The presence of God and of his Spirit in the world is not to be disputed. But this does not imply that everyone perceived him as being active in the world. God can be grasped only where through his Spirit he makes himself graspable, in his historic manifestation in Jesus Christ. From this reference point the Spirit's life-sustaining activity in the world needs to be affirmed and clarified. This seems to be the line of reasoning that the early church pursued.

B. The early church

In the Old Testament the "Holy Spirit" is not conceived of as an independent entity but as the Spirit of God. The same is true for the New Testament. In the latter, however, the relationship is complicated by the emergence of Jesus Christ. Since Jesus is also not conceived of as an entity independent of God, but is referred to as the Son of God (the Father) the question emerges how Jesus Christ and the Spirit are related to one other.

1. An intimate relationship

Clarifying the relationship between God, Spirit, and Jesus Christ, the church noticed that God through his Spirit incarnated his Son and that he also resurrected him through the power of the Spirit. Yet the relationship goes further. In 2 Clem. 9:5, for instance, we hear that "Christ, the Lord who saved us, though he was originally spirit, became flesh and so called us." This means that Jesus was spirit before he became flesh. Another very interesting passage indicating a similar line of reflection is found in the Shepherd of Hermas:

> The Holy Spirit which pre-exists, which created all creation, did God make to dwell in the flesh which he willed. Therefore this flesh, in which the Holy Spirit dwelled, served the Spirit well, walking in holiness and purity, and did not in any way defile the spirit. When, therefore, it had lived nobly and purely, and had laboured with the Spirit, and worked with it in every deed, behaving with power and bravery, he chose it as companion with the Holy Spirit; for the conduct of this flesh pleased him, because it was not defiled while it was bearing the Holy Spirit on earth (*Hermas, Sim.* 5.6.5f.).

We note in this passage the emphasis on the intimate unity of the Spirit and the Son. It even refers to them as they were in the preexistent state with the same term, Holy Spirit, and states that through the Holy Spirit all divine power was made. Before Jesus was incarnate, he was in a state of divine power in glory; he was Holy Spirit and then assumed flesh.

Bishop Theophilus of Antioch (c. 169) in his three books to Autolycus picks up this trend of thought and develops it further when he says:

> He [God] and this Logos as his servant in the things created by him, and through him made all things (cf. John 1:3). He is called Beginning because he leads and dominates everything fashioned through Him. It was he, *Spirit of God* (Gen. 1:2) and *Beginning* (Gen. 1:1) and *Sophia* (Prov. 8:22) and *Power of the Most High* (Lk. 1:35), who came down into the prophets and spoke through them about the creation of the world and all the rest . . . . In order for the real God to be known through his works, and to show that by this Logos God made heaven and earth and what is in them, he said: "In the Beginning, God made heaven and earth."[3]

Two items are here noteworthy: (1) God is present in the *logos* as the God who discloses himself. (2) As the connection between Prov. 8:22 and John 1:2 shows, the essence of the *logos* is the *pneuma* or Spirit. On another occasion Theophilus connects the *logos* with *sophia* and relates it to the *pneuma* when he says:

> He is God who heals and gives life through Logos and Sophia. God made everything through Logos and Sophia for by his Logos the heavens were made firm and by his Spirit all their power (Psalm 32:6). His Sophia is most powerful: God by Sophia founded the earth;

he prepared the heavens by intelligence; by knowledge the abysses were broken up and the clouds poured forth dews (Prov. 3:19f.).[4]

In God *pneuma* and *logos* are seen as an inseparable unity. We also notice that *pneuma* and *sophia* are interchangeable. With these descriptions nothing is said, however, about the internal relationship of the deity. Primary emphasis is given to God's self-disclosure or his external work. While the creaturely character of the *pneuma* is not denied, Theophilus endeavors to show that in the *pneuma* God himself is active. Thus the *pneuma*, the life-creating power of creation, was enfleshed in the historical reality of Jesus.

Irenaeus of Lyons advanced the idea of the intimate relationship between God, Son, and Spirit even further, and, what is most interesting for us, in explicit contradistinction to Gnostic thought. In opposition to Gnostic speculations of numbers and systems, Irenaeus claims that God does not "derive His being from things made, but things made from God. For all things originate from one and the same God."[5] God is personal and at the same time the supreme, almighty, and powerful creator of all things by his word, whether visible or invisible, heavenly or earthly, in our control or beyond it. Against Gnostic attempts to divide the deity into *logos*, the principle of thought, and mind, the active intention, Irenaeus affirms the indivisible unity of God. He is "all mind, all reason, all active spirit, all light, and always exists one and the same," Irenaeus gathers from the Scriptures.[6] "But God being all Mind, and all Logos, both speaks exactly what He thinks and thinks exactly what He speaks."[7] Thus God is not a compound being, but a being in unity of Father, Son, and Spirit. Irenaeus agrees with the Scriptures that God "by His Word and Spirit, makes and disposes and governs all things, and commands all things into existence."[8] Affirming that God needs no intermediaries to create the world, Irenaeus says that God's "*offspring* and His *similitude* do minister to Him in every respect; that is, the Son and the Holy Spirit, the Word and Wisdom; whom all the angels serve, and to whom they are subject."[9] Son and Spirit are seen as a unity, though they are not undistinguished.

The Spirit is even called the similitude of God, evidently in reference to his spiritual being. In the same section Irenaeus also remarks that, contrary to Jewish thought, the Father cannot be known without the Word, i.e., without the Son. This would mean that the working of the Spirit outside the church cannot be discerned without reference to God's self-disclosure in his Son. Irenaeus makes it further clear that those things which are of corruptible, earthly, transitory, and compound nature cannot be images of those things that are spiritual, "unless these very things themselves be allowed to be compounded, limited in space, and of a definite shape."[10] In other words, there is no natural knowledge of God possible, unless God takes the initiative and makes himself known within space and time. "For in no other way could we have learned the things of God, unless our Master, existing as the Word, had become man."[11] Yet the communion of God with humanity and the imparting of God to humanity are not simply achieved through the incarnational process but essentially though the pouring out of "the Spirit of the Father."[12] We notice again that *logos* and *pneuma* work hand in hand.

2. Near homoousia *of the Spirit (Nicea and Constantinople)*

Athanasius intensifies the notion of the intimate interrelatedness of Father, Son, and Spirit when he writes, "As the Son is in the Spirit as in his own image, so also the Father is in the Son."[13] He then relates the salvational process to all three by noting, "There is one sanctification which is derived from the Father, through the Son, in the Holy Spirit."[14] Yet there is a clear procession, since the Son as Son is sent forth from the Father, and the Son in turn sends the Spirit. Since the Son pertains to the essence of the Father, and the Spirit to the essence of the Son, there is not gradation in perfection. All three are one.

Athanasius also claims that the Spirit is involved in the incarnational process: "When the Word visited the Holy Virgin Mary, the Spirit came to her with him, and the Word in the Spirit moulded the body and conformed it to himself; desiring to join and present all creation to the Father through himself."[15] It is significant that creation is related to incarnation. As the Spirit has been involved in salvation, he has also been active in creation. Athanasius assures us that "The Father creates all things through the Word in the Spirit; for where the Word is, there is the Spirit also, and the things which are created have their vital strength out of the Spirit from the Word."[16] In analogy to Old Testament thought, creation is not seen as self-subsistent but as deriving its vital strength from God's Spirit. The Spirit also seems to be continually with the creation, since "the Father, through the Word, in the Holy Spirit, creates and renews all things."[17]

That the Spirit creates and renews is echoed in many other writers, such as Basil, Didymus, and Cyril of Alexandria.[18] But Athanasius goes one step further when he says that in the Spirit through the Word the Father perfects and renews all things.[19] Athanasius thinks of creation and sanctification as a single work. The creative action of the Spirit is thus seen in the context of God's sanctifying operation. As Shapland says in his introduction to Athanasius' letter to Bishop Serapion of Thmuis, according to Athanasius, "God cannot create without imparting to His creatures something of His own character; and the continuance of His works is only secured by His presence within them."[20] Creation leads to God's preservation and finally to redemption. As Gregory of Nyssa so well remarked, "We should be justified in calling all that Nature which came into existence by creation a movement of Will, an impulse of Design, a transmission of Power, beginning from the Father, advancing through the Son, and completed in the Holy Spirit."[21]

The culmination of these reflections came in A.D. 381, at the Council of Constantinople, when the Creed of Nicea was modified especially to reemphasize the function of the Spirit. Now it is affirmed that the Spirit was involved in the incarnational process by saying that Jesus Christ "was incarnate from the Holy Spirit and the Virgin Mary." Also the Holy Spirit is referred to as "the Lord and life-giver, who proceeds from the Father, who with the Father and the Son is together worshiped and together glorified, who spoke through the prophets." Most of these insertions reflect scriptural precedents: "incarnate from the Holy Spirit" in Luke 1:25, the Holy Spirit as "Lord" in 2 Cor. 3:17, as life-giver in John 6:63, and as "proceeding from the Father" in John 15:26. The phrase "who with the Father and the Son is together worshiped and together glorified," however, is not expressly mentioned in Scripture. We find a resemblance of this phrase when Athanasius says that the Spirit is glorified with the Father and the Son."[22] Also, a letter of Basil states that "the Son is confessed to be of one substance with the Father, and the Holy Ghost is ranked and worshiped as of equal honor."[23] Though the Nicene-Constantinopolitan Creed essentially claims the *homoousia* of the Spirit, it scrupulously avoids the terms so as not to alienate those who did not want to elevate the Spirit to the status of God.[24]

C. The Reformers and contemporary theologians

We have noticed that the Spirit is primarily involved at three points: (1) in God's life-giving power of creation, (2) in God's incarnation in Jesus Christ, and (3) in God's vivifying and sanctifying work in the church. While the last two can be related to the work of the Spirit in the church, the first one seems to be more inclusive. These are also the lines of thought portrayed in the Reformation period.

1. The Spirit in history and salvation history (the Reformers)

According to the Reformers the dominant work of the Spirit was carried out in the salvation process. But especially for Luther it was clear that God was also active in history. And how else would he be active in history than through his Spirit? Luther, for instance, writes, "God has done many good things, through Balaam and the impious prophets and tyrants, and still does them, because whatever the ministry has is not of itself but of God. For that reason it is effective through the power of the Holy Spirit, although in ungodly persons."[25] On another occasion he states, "If a prince governs well, it is not innate nor is it learned only through books, but it is learned through the inspiration of the Holy Spirit with experience."[26] This means that everything which occurs in conformity with God's rule is done through the discerning and guiding power of the Holy Spirit. Luther learned from the Old Testament that God is not confined in his activities to Israel. His conviction that God also works outside the realm of salvation is especially well expressed in his notion of the *Wundermänner* who are sent by God at critical points to change the course of world history and avert evil.[27] The Holy Spirit is at work in salvation history as well as in political history, in the church as well as in the profane godless world.[28]

Luther observes that the Spirit does not just affect the course of history. The Spirit is also active in the common life of people and in natural (biological) functions. Thus Luther states:

Spirit is whatever is done in us through the Spirit; the flesh is whatever is done in us in accordance with the flesh and apart from the Spirit. Therefore all the duties of Christians—such as loving one's wife, rearing one's children, governing one's family, honoring one's parents, obeying the magistrate, etc., which they regard as secular and fleshly — are fruits of the Spirit. These blind men do not distinguish between vices and the things that are good creatures of God.[29]

Luther shows here that the Spirit is the force in all of life that urges us to live in a way that insures harmony, peace, and the preservation of humanity. What we often take for granted and assume to result from our own ingenuity, the natural law, human reason, or even enlightened self-interest, Luther understands as the work of the Holy Spirit.

If it is true, as Scriptures and the early church attest, that the Spirit is God's creative and enlivening Spirit, we need not be surprised by Luther's conclusions. He recognized that without the Spirit our world is threatened by chaos and destruction. But he did not assume that everyone is automatically aware of the working of the Spirit. Neither did he reflect on how one could become aware, except to say that some are blind to the Spirit's workings. We may conclude that the Spirit is active in our world, an activity which can be acknowledged and reinforced through our own actions—unless we blind ourselves to its works (cf. Rom. 1:20).

With reference to Gen. 1:2, Calvin holds views similar to those of Luther:

> The beauty of the universe (which we now perceive) owes it strength and preservation to the power of the Spirit .... For it is the Spirit, who, everywhere diffused, sustains all things, causes them to grow, and quickens them in heaven and in earth .... In transfusing into all things his energy, and breathing into them the essence, life, and movement, he is indeed plainly divine.[30]

Calvin recognizes the Spirit as God's life-giving and life-preserving power. It is significant that Calvin does not see this function of the Spirit as independent from the soteriological activity of the Spirit. In the paragraph following this quote, Calvin also asserts that the Spirit is the author of generation and preservation as well as of regeneration towards future immortality. Creation and new creation are rightly seen as evolving from each other through the power of God's Spirit.

There is in the Lutheran confessional documents a remarkable silence concerning the work of the Holy Spirit in and through creation. If we remember what Luther had said, we can, of course, understand that the assertion in the *Augsburg Confession* that "lawful civil ordinances are good works of God" (Art. 16) implies that this is "through the power of the Spirit." But this is not stated there explicitly. In Article 18, "On Free Will," we could again expect a discussion of the work of the Spirit. But on the contrary, we only find there the assertion that we do not "have the power, without the Holy Spirit, to attain the righteousness of God—that is, spiritual righteousness." While this statement is certainly true, it becomes lopsided—if not wrong—when it is isolated and absolutized, as has happened quite often in Lutheranism. The Holy Spirit does not just work towards the new life of spiritual righteousness but also towards creation and preservation of life in a much more comprehensive sense.

This failure to mention the Spirit's creative activity outside the process of salvation is symptomatic of the Lutheran Confessions. It reflects their limited intention of attempting to reform certain abuses in the church—at that time primarily the idea that one could obtain salvation through one's own efforts. On account of this narrow scope they cannot serve fully to reground the church and were not intended for that purpose. This truncated conception of the work of the Spirit is still seen in Regin Prenter's noteworthy book *Spiritus Creator*. While he emphasizes the life-creating and life-saving work of the Spirit, Prenter falls prey to this tendency of limiting the work of the Spirit to the salvation process when he says, "Sanctification is simply another expression for the creative work of the Spirit."[31] Sanctification is certainly an important work of the Spirit. But it is not synonymous with the creative and preserving activity of the Spirit which is also conducted outside the church, i.e., where sanctification does not take place.

2. Rediscovering the Holy Spirit (contemporary theology)

Contemporary systematic theologians devote ample space in their writings to the Holy Spirit. In volume 3 of his *Systematic Theology* Paul Tillich offers an extensive treatment of the Holy Spirit.

He illuminates the function of the Spirit in reference to the ambiguities of life. The divine Spirit is manifested in the human spirit primarily through faith and love. The Spirit creates a spiritual community through the new being in Christ. The spiritual community has an impact on culture by opening an avenue to the spiritual presence. While the secular culture as such is not spiritual, Tillich affirms "that it is open to the impact of the Spirit even without the mediation of the church."[32] Yet Tillich also affirms the "convergence of the holy and the secular," since the secular also stands under the source of all life, i.e., the Spirit, and therefore the secular can transcend itself vertically. In other words, the world is not its own goal. It exists, whether it acknowledges it or not, toward God. The spiritual presence creates a theonomous culture and a theonomous reality, reestablishing the essential unity of morality, culture, and religion that was destroyed under the conditions of existence.[33]

Though Tillich recognizes the active presence of the Spirit in morality and culture, it is significant that, in contrast to Scripture, he does not acknowledge that the activity of the Spirit is operative beyond humanity. He only affirms that the impact of the spiritual presence on the human spirit implies an impact on the psyche, "the cells, and the physical elements which constitute man."[34] We might not be wrong to assume that a decisive impulse for seeing the work of the Spirit restricted to the human sphere was the preoccupation with salvation in the German Lutheranism out of which Tillich came.

Pierre Teilhard de Chardin in his evolutionary concept of life has overcome this anthropocentrism with regard to the activity of the Holy Spirit. In *The Divine Milieu* Teilhard states, "The same beam of light which Christian spirituality, rightly and fully understood, directs upon the Cross to humanise it (without veiling it) is reflected on matter so as to spiritualise it."[35] There is a general drift of matter toward Spirit and one day "the whole divinisable substance of matter will have passed into the souls of men; all the chosen dynamisms will have been recuperated; and then our world will be ready for Parousia."[36] The goal of the creative process, with the Spirit as its creative principle, is the spiritualization and divinization of matter and of humanity. Through divine action the world will one day be received into the christosphere. In his deliberations Teilhard arrives at a new definition of the Spirit: Spirit is no longer independent of matter, or in opposition to it but laboriously emerging from it under the attraction of God by the way of synthesis and centration.[37] The Spirit is the creative and life-giving power of God. It is the interior side of all life and of all being. The Spirit elevates matter and moves it towards God. It becomes clear that for Teilhard creation is only the starting point for the whole divinization process. While we must be impressed with his recognition of the all-encompassing work of the Spirit, we may also wonder about the facility with which everything and everyone participates in the evolutionary process. The resistance to the Spirit by the forces and powers of darkness that the New Testament sources intimate does not seem to be taken sufficiently into account.

Among other contemporary theologians it is especially Wolfhart Pannenberg who reflects on the function of the Spirit. In analogy to Old Testament insights, he regards the Spirit "as the marvelous depth of life out of which all life originates."[38] The breath of life that permeates all of life is at the same time the fount of truth and freedom. The Spirit enlivens us and thereby sets us free to show us the truth of life. Pannenberg sees the Spirit active in the self-transcendence of life. This self-transcendence is at the same time an activity of the living organism (our own spirit) and the activity of a power which lifts the living organism beyond its limits and through this activity grants it a deeper quality of life. Thus the work of the Spirit is not confined to the givenness of the human consciousness.[39]

Since we humans continuously assess our environment in order to adapt and live in it, we need a basis beyond ourselves from which to assess our approach to life. This point, Pannenberg concludes, can be found only in that which brings all reality together, i.e., in the Spirit. The Spirit is therefore also the basis for trust, hope, and love. Yet Pannenberg realizes that we are not continuously connected with the power of the Spirit. We need the Christian message to tell us about the new life in which we are no longer subjected to the ambiguities and limits of this life. In other words, we depend on a new life so that our striving can receive eternal validity. "But the Spirit of this new life, which fills the community of faith, is none other than the one who animates all life."[40]

From our brief review we arrive at the following conclusions:

(*a*) The church was right when, under the impression of the Christ event, it emphasized that the Spirit makes Christ present to faith. In other words, the sphere of the Spirit's operation is above all conterminous with the area of the specifically Christian faith.

(*b*) The church also realized that salvation history is the key to and the center of a much larger history, the history of humanity and of nature.

(*c*) In initially using the terms *logos* and *Spirit* both as parallel terms and interchangeably when speaking about God's relation to the world, the church asserted that God's creative and preserving power, active in all creation, is undivided. To emphasize that God is active through his same power in history in general and in salvation history, it is proper to speak of the creative and sustaining presence of the Spirit in all the world.

(*d*) Since the self-disclosive history of God culminates within salvation history in the Christ event, the church has never endowed the presence of the Spirit in the world (i.e., outside Christ) with revelatory significance. Moreover, only because our finite spirit is touched by the infinite are we capable of recognizing God's self-disclosure in Jesus Christ.

(*e*) Human reason, moral discernment between right and wrong, and culture as expressions of the human are not self-originated results of a natural human faculty. They stem from the work of the Spirit in the world (e.g., the kingdom on the left). Therefore, unreason, the pursuit of injustice instead of right, and a culture marked by human depravity are signs of the denial of the metaphysical basis of this world and are manifestations of the anti-Christ. Yet the very fact that the Spirit of God sustains even a fallen world and that God erects the victory sign of the cross within it shows that in his compassion God does not condone the world's depravity but opens it for the future of a new creation.

(*f*) If we perceive the Spirit as being active only in the church, we fall prey to a Manichean dualism which surrenders the world to anti-Godly powers. If we perceive the Spirit as being active without differentiation in the world and church, we rob the incarnation of God of its decisive significance. The Spirit of God has created and sustains this world and all it contains; the Spirit has renewed it through the incarnation, death, and resurrection of Jesus Christ; and the Spirit will bring it to its fulfillment in the new life to come, the anticipations of which Christians can already enjoy.

11

THE CHURCH

The Christian church has been intimately connected with the activity of the Holy Spirit ever since its birth on Pentecost and the outpouring of the Holy Spirit on the disciples. This same church, however, also dates back to Jesus Christ whose name it bears. Yet it seems strange that Jesus of Nazareth, who emphatically proclaimed the nearness, even the presence of the kingdom of God, could have established the church.

The term *church* (*ekklesia*) occurs only three times in the Gospels and only in Matthew. Of these, Matt. 18:17 contains the term *church* twice and very likely reflects later practice. Furthermore, it seems to speak of the church in a localized setting. The other passage, Matt. 16:13-20, contains the famous confession of Peter. When we read this passage we notice that it actually consists of two different stories. In the first Jesus asks his disciples who they they think he is and Peter answers with the famous messianic confession, "You are the Christ, the Son of the living God" (Matt. 16:16). In this instance Jesus himself neither confirms nor denies the validity of the answer. Instead we hear Jesus saying in the second story:

> You are Peter, and on this rock I will build my church, and the powers of death shall not prevail against it. I will give you the keys of the king-

dom of heaven, and whatever you bind on earth shall be bound in heaven, and whatever you loose on earth shall be loosed in heaven (Matt. 16:18f.).

Of course, the question must be raised as to the original source and meaning of this promise. Even if we would doubt that this saying originated with Jesus himself, there can be no doubt that it is of ancient character, since the Aramaic terms *cephas* [Peter] and *cepha* [rock], which underlie the present Greek, indicate an earlier form.

The assumption that Peter was here commissioned by Jesus to be the foundation of the church would make sense only if Jesus knew himself to be the Messiah, a notion which the evangelist seems to share (Matt. 16:20). If Jesus was the Messiah, then the circle of the disciples was not just a group of people who followed a leader. They actually formed the core of an eschatological community that responded to the presence of the Messiah. This eschatological community was not a religious splinter group or a holy remnant but the community of the new people of God. That these people prefigured the new Israel is attested by the fact that Jesus directed his activity to all of Israel and, unlike the separatist Qumran community, not only to a select few. Since Peter was the spokesman of the disciples, the task and promise given to him would publicly acknowledge his position as one whom Jesus recognized and affirmed. The Gospels, however, do not present an inherent reason as to why Peter should have risen to such a position. As far as we know, his selection is founded solely on Jesus' will.

It would be wrong, however, if we would on the basis of these texts simply identify the church with the kingdom of God. The early Christian community also recognized this problem when it preserved Jesus' proclamation of the kingdom of God not only as a present reality but also as an eschatological goal. The kingdom of God will be fully realized only in the eschaton, whereas the present time is already determined by the foreshadowing of the eschaton. The church, then, is an eschatological phenomenon, awaiting the full realization of the kingdom and living today in proleptic anticipation.

A. The formative period

During the few years which are spanned by the New Testament documents, we encounter an amazing growth of the church. At the beginning of his ministry, Jesus appointed twelve apostles in analogy to the twelve tribes of Israel, and sent them out to be his messengers (Mark 3:14). Barely 40 years later there were Christian congregations in Rome, Athens, Corinth, and in many places of Asia Minor and Palestine.

The mission of the Twelve had been clearly confined to Israel (Matt. 10:5). This is not surprising since Jesus himself usually did not go beyond the Israelite boundaries. The Twelve only did what was common among the Jewish people of their time, heeding the dictum that "he who is sent by a man is as he who sent him."[1] Similar to their master, Jesus' disciples had power over unclean spirits on their journeys. We hear too that they addressed their audience with an eschatological message of the impending coming of the kingdom and pronounced judgment over those who rejected them and their message (cf. Luke 10:1ff. and Matt. 10:5ff.; cf. also Mark 6: 6-13). When the Son of man will sit on his glorious throne the Twelve "will also sit on twelve thrones, judging the twelve tribes of Israel" (Matt. 19:28). They will also participate in the messianic wedding feast (Mark 2:19). Jesus even taught his disciples to pray with a special prayer (Matt. 6:9-13). The disciples did not only enjoy the blessings of the commencing eschatological reign. Like Jesus their life should be characterized by an attitude of servanthood (Mark 10:41-45) and they will be persecuted and put to death (Mark 13:9-13 and 10:38). Being the Messiah, Jesus instructed his disciples, giving them the new law (Sermon on the Mount) as the rule of life in the messianic community.

When he saw his earthly life coming to a close, Jesus assembled the Twelve to celebrate with them the Last Supper. Whether we accept the synoptic tradition that Jesus' Last Supper was a Passover meal celebrated on the day of the Passover feast (cf. Mark 14:14 and par.) or whether we follow the Gospel of John in which this meal was celebrated a day earlier (cf. John 18:28), this farewell meal did not yet make any lasting impression on the disciples. With the exception of Peter, who at least followed Jesus to the point of having to deny him, the rest of the disciples were remarkably absent during the trial and crucifixion. As indicated by the appearance of the resurrected one in Galilee (Mark 14:28; 16:7; Matt. 28:16), the disciples may even have fled from Jerusalem, fearing that they were next in line to be executed. Perhaps only some women among his followers stayed in Jerusalem (Mark 16:1 and par.; John 20:1). As the amazement with which they encountered the resurrected Christ indicates, however, not even these women expected anything significant to happen after Jesus' death. The center of discipleship was not so much a sacred tradition which the disciples continued to cherish after Jesus' death, but the personal and intimate bond which they once had with their leader. Otherwise the reaction of the two disciples going to Emmaus (Luke 24:19ff.) would be unexplainable. It reveals the deep sorrow and despair that surrrounded the disciples once their leader was no longer among them.

The striking change from the disciples of Jesus to the followers of Jesus Christ seems to have occurred through the Easter events. During the life of Jesus of Nazareth we can already distinguish three groups among his followers. The first one is the group of the disciples (*mathētēs*), out of which comes a second, more select group, the twelve disciples or the twelve apostles (Matt. 10:1-2), and finally there is a larger group of nonitinerant followers (Luke 10:38-42). The circle of the Twelve continued to be maintained when the disciples gathered after Easter. Because Judas Iscariot had forfeited his place, Matthias was chosen to replace him among the apostles. He met their criteria, having been a disciple who had accompanied Jesus of Nazareth and who had witnessed his resurrection (cf. Acts 1: 21-26). The Twelve provided continuity with the earthly Jesus and had also encountered the resurrected Christ (1 Cor. 15:5). They were the leaders of the new people of God and proclaimed the message of the resurrected one (Matt. 28:16ff). Representing the twelve tribes of Israel, they symbolized the claim of Jesus and of the Christian community upon the whole Jewish nation (cf. Matt. 19:28).

As the Christian community grew beyond the confines of Israel, it was no longer considered mandatory to maintain the circle of the Twelve. When James, the son of Zebedee, was killed, his place among the Twelve remained vacant. At this time those called apostles gained in importance, a group whose origin can also be traced to Jesus of Nazareth. Originally the apostles were virtually identical with the Twelve. While the usage of the term *disciple* is primarily confined to the Gospels and Acts, the term *apostle* is predominantly used in the Pauline letters and Luke-Acts. Prerequisite for being an apostle is that one is called and sent by Jesus. The apostles were the bearers of the New Testament proclamation and the first Christian missionaries. When we consider the passage describing the first sending out of the Twelve (Mark 6:7; Matt. 10:1-5 uses the terms *disciples, the Twelve,* and *apostles* synonymously), we notice that the apostles were sent out with the authority of the one who sent them. In other words, they were Jesus' emissaries.

We remember that Jesus' disciples abandoned their calling upon his imprisonment and death. Since the apostles could originally be recruited from among all of Jesus' disciples, there is no necessary continuity between the apostles whom Jesus called and sent and the apostles who through the resurrection event became the bearers of the Christian *kerygma* and the foundation of the Christian church. This is also true for Peter. Karl Heinrich Rengstorf is right when he asserts that "the Gospels and Acts make it quite clear that it was exclusively the act of the risen Lord that this scattered group became a community full of hope and ready for action. The act of the risen Lord, however, was the renewal of the commission of the disciples in their definite institution as *apostoloi* [apostles]."[2] In its Christian form the apostolate does not stand in unbroken continuity with the apostles whom Jesus of Nazareth called and sent. There stands in between the decisive turning point of the resurrection, which empowered the proclamation of the resurrected Christ and the gathering of his community.

While the apostles were witnesses to the resurrection, not all who saw the resurrected Christ became apostles. The resurrection encounters are not at the same time call experiences. As we see especially well in the concluding chapter of the Gospel of John, constitutive for the ministry of Peter is not merely his encounter with the resurrected Christ but his commissioning. Similarly, when Paul introduced himself to the Christian community in Rome, he emphasized that he had been called to be an apostle (Rom. 1:1).

There are two facets of the apostolic office which are worthy of note. (1) An apostle has an authoritative position within the Christian community. Together with his fellow apostles he represents the risen Lord. (2) Being an apostle means to be a missionary. The apostle has the task of proclaiming the one in whose authority he is sent. This task is not just a temporary one which after its completion allows him to turn to other business, but it is valid for the whole interim period between Christ's resurrection and his parousia (cf. Acts 1:6ff.). Being an apostle is therefore a lifelong task. Since the Lord is truly present through him, an apostle is also empowered by the Holy Spirit. Thus the beginning of missionary activity and the actual starting point of the church was Pentecost, the point at which the Spirit was made manifest among the apostles.

The Spirit did not transform the disciples into superhuman beings but took them as they were and used them as tools (cf. Acts 10:36). They did not become ecstatic tools void of their own will and responsibility but were empowered to carry out the will of their Lord without restraint and fear (cf. Acts 4:19f.). We do not know how many apostles there were in the nascent Christian community. Presumably they included the Twelve plus a few others, such as James and Paul. Thus they were recruited mostly, though not exclusively, from among the disciples of Jesus of Nazareth.

The change in terminology from *disciples* to *apostles* not only indicates the transition from the followers of Jesus to the followers of and believers in Jesus Christ, but also signifies the shift from an exclusive mission to Israel to the universal mission which included all nations. This shift is already pronounced by the resurrected Christ when he commanded his disciples to go to all nations (Matt. 28:19; Acts 1:8). Yet there was an intense struggle among the apostles until they realized the full implications of this new mission. First, the disciples and apostles were instructed that they should be missionaries only within the confines of Israel. From Pentecost onward, however, the apostles addressed people "from every nation" (Acts 2:5). But in this passage Luke also indicates that all of them were devout Jews.

When Peter addressed his listeners at Pentecost, it is evident that they were associated with Judaism. He called them to repentance because they had not followed the Messiah and because their indifference had even contributed to the crucifixion of the Messiah. Since this Messiah is now enthroned in power at the right hand of God, it is only proper to recognize him as such (and become Christian). Luke wants to demonstrate with Peter's remarks that the Christians are not a separatist community. They considered themselves standing in true continuity with the messianic expectations of the Jewish faith (now fulfilled). The people who followed the call of the apostles devoted themselves to the apostles' teaching and fellowship, the celebration of the Lord's Supper, and to prayers (Acts 2:42). Unlike the community in Qumran, the first Christian community did not conceive of itself as a remnant. They did not isolate themselves from the Jewish people and they did not demand a special initiation ritual. Even Christian Baptism can be seen in analogy to the Jewish baptism of repentance. Yet what was significant was that these people confessed Jesus as Lord (Rom. 10:9). Christ's resurrection and the pouring out of the Holy Spirit gave the disciples the assurance that Jesus was the Messiah and that they were the messianic community. The whole history of Jesus could now be appropriated as a history of the fulfillment of Old Testament promises (cf. the Gospel according to Matthew).

Contrary to a first impression, the frequent references to the Christians as the saints (e.g., Acts 9:13; Rom. 1:7) do not indicate that the nascent Christian community felt itself superior to the Jewish people. In analogy to the Old Testament community (Exod. 19:6) they called themselves "a chosen race, a royal priesthood, a holy nation" (1 Peter 2:9). But it would be an oversimplification to see them merely as a continuation of the Old Testament community. They are holy because of Jesus Christ (1 Cor. 1:2). It was important for them that they confront Israel with the message of Jesus as the Messiah (Acts 2:36). In a sense, however, they did continue Jesus' ministry to the lost sheep of Israel (Matt. 15:24). Even Paul, for whom the mission to the Gentiles had become crucial, was concerned about his own Jewish people (Rom. 11:1). What is more, he argued that the mission to the Gentiles was a means by which later all Israel would be saved (Rom. 11:14-26).

Similar to Jesus, the first Christian community, though recruiting only from among the Jews, did not exclude the Gentiles from salvation. At the Apostolic Council James declared, with explicit reference to the Old Testament, that Gentiles too are eligible to be incorporated into the Christian community (Acts 15:13ff.). This extension of mission as described in Luke-Acts, first to the Samaritans, then to those who were pious sympathizers with Judaism (e.g., Cornelius), and finally to non-Jewish people, as we shall see, need not be conceived as a radical innovation on the part of the Christian community. Of course, the rejection and outright persecution of the nascent Christian community by pious Jews may have speeded up the process of extending missionary endeavor beyond Judaism.

In the Jewish tradition a broader definition of the people of God was to be characteristic of the time of messianic fulfillment. Thus it can be affirmed that "many nations shall join themselves to the Lord in that day, and shall be my people; and I will dwell in the midst of you" (Zech. 2:11). The Christian community understood Jesus to be the Messiah. According to Luke-Acts it was then natural that James quote Old Testament passages describing the time of messianic fulfillment so that he could justify and even advocate the legitimacy of mission among the Gentiles. Thus it is strange that the Christian community in Jerusalem under the leadership of the apostles confined itself primarily to the Jewish nation.

A pressing problem, however, arose when the missionaries among the Gentiles posed the question whether one needed to become a Jew first and be circumcised before one could become a Christian. After much discussion it was decided that those who were missionaries among the Gentiles need not make new converts first conform to Judaism before they could become Christians. Needless to say, most Jewish Christians were much more conservative on this issue than those who were working in the Gentile mission fields. But when it became evident that Israel as a whole would not accept Jesus as the Messiah and when in A.D. 70 Jerusalem, the rallying point of Jewish Messianic hopes, was destroyed, the way was opened for an all-inclusive catholic church within a predominantly Hellenistic environment. Luke, writing from this perspective, divided God's history of salvation into three epochs. There is first the history of Israel which includes John the Baptist (Luke 16:16). Then comes the history of Jesus' activity on earth (Luke 4:16-19). Finally there is the epoch of the church and its exalted Lord.

In the beginning of Acts the church is introduced as having a mission to the end of the earth (Acts 1:8). The empowering with the Holy Spirit, constitutive for the Christian community, is seen in antithesis to the confusion of humanity at Babel when it attempted to reach God by building a mighty tower (Gen. 11:1-9). Now at the proper time God has reached down and poured out his Spirit, as foretold in Joel 2:28f. Thus the church exists not only in a messianic but also in an eschatological time. Although there remain tribulations and persecutions for the church and its members, Christians know that these tribulations will not continue forever (Acts 14:22). Christians are not to withdraw from the world or become pessimistic concerning its affairs. They know that they are to be a light for the Gentiles and to bring salvation to the uttermost parts of the world (Acts 13:47). While the church is the tool of the exalted Lord in this world, this is an interim arrangement, and it is not here to stay. Jesus has already fulfilled the first of his promises and most certainly his second advent will soon follow.

Now, however, nearly two millenia have gone by and the Lord has not yet returned. In many ways the church has been accepted in the world. Thus it has often forgotten that it is merely an interim institution and not a part of the established order. When we traverse its history we realize that the church has had many ups and downs, times of faithfulness and times of betrayal. Yet the church has always recovered, because its very structure—which in the Nicene Creed is confessed to be one, holy, catholic, and apostolic—contains in itself the remedy for reform.

B. The present structure

Empirically speaking, the four structural ingredients of the church—oneness, holiness, catholicity, and apostolicity—seem to be contradicted by its very appearance. In the United States alone there are more than 400 Protestant denominations. Even if we take all Protestant denominations as one, which they are not, there remains the rift between Protestants and Roman Catholics since the 16th century as well as the split between the Orthodox churches and the Western church already since 1054. Such a history indicates that oneness was never a strong point of the church. When we listen to Paul and other New Testament figures, however, we discover that the church was never conceived of as one monolithic structure but as the one church which manifests itself differently in a variety of local situations (cf. 1 Cor. 1:2).

1. *The rediscovery of unity*

The most important sign of unity has always been that of material unity, i.e., agreeing to the rule of faith. The common celebration of the 1600th anniversary of the Nicene-Constantinopolitan Creed (A.D. 381) showed that though the rifts are deep, the basic creeds are shared in common. Even the *filioque* clause, the phrase unilaterally inserted into the creeds by the Western church, asserting that the Spirit proceeds from the Father and the Son, is no longer considered a theological *conditio sine qua non*. The West now seems willing to regard this clause as optional. Moreover, an amazing thing is happening in our generation. The faithful of all denominations, Protestants, Catholics, and Orthodox alike, are growing more and more together. For instance, in many United States denominations perhaps one-third of the church members did not grow up in the denomination to which they now belong. While this can mean an increasing indifference to doctrinal matters, it certainly also witnesses to a growing feeling that the factors once thought to be indispensable for achieving unity are really not so decisive.

There is an ever stronger growing together of denominational structures in teaching, ecclesial rites, and structural cooperation. At the Second Vatican Council (1962-1965), for instance, Protestant and Orthodox believers, formerly considered heretics and schismatics, were officially invited as guests and observers. In the first constitution published by Vatican II, the "Constitution on the Sacred Liturgy," the opening sentence reads, "It is the goal of this most sacred Council . . . to nurture whatever can contribute to the unity of all who believe in Christ."[3] In its Decree on Ecumenism the council even declared: "Promoting the restoration of unity among all Christians is one of the chief concerns of the Second Ecumenical Synod of the Vatican."[4]

Today Roman Catholic scholars freely admit that historical circumstances forced the church at Trent to take a clear and strong position against Protestant doctrinal "innovations," thereby minimizing the issues which the Reformers emphasized. This occurred even in matters where the Reformers were in harmony with the Bible and the fathers. Even more, Trent emphasized the issues the Reformers attacked. By the time of Trent the Reformers had rejected the visible, external, juridicial, institutional, and hierarchical church and emphasized the invisible, internal, and charismatic church. In turn the Roman Catholic church decided to put almost exclusive emphasis on "the Church as a hierarchically organized society, directed from above by the bishop of Rome."[5] Now the tide has changed and many points of division are seen to be no longer of a doctrinal nature but largely stem from historically conditioned antagonistic entrenchment.

Recent years have not only brought about the rediscovery of the already existing unity between the Roman Catholic church and the Evangelical churches, but there has also been an amazing rediscovery of the unity that exists within the Protestant fold itself. At the Fifth Assembly of the World Council of Churches in Nairobi (1975), the Assembly recommended that the churches "provide opportunities for a careful study and evaluation of the concept of conciliar fellowship as a way of describing the unity of the Church."[6] Similarly, the so-called Lima document, *Baptism, Eucharist, and Ministry*, published in 1982 by the Commission on Faith and Order, witnesses to the amazing unity that exists within those churches represented in the Faith and Order Commission. To indicate at least in passing some of the main facets of this newly discovered unity we should look at both the documents of Vatican II and the results of the ecumenical dialog among a multitude of different denominations.

(a) The rejuvenation at Vatican II. Ecclesiology was one of the most important topics for Vatican II. The "Dogmatic Constitution on the Church," the "Constitution on the Sacred Liturgy," the "Pastoral Constitution on the Church in the Modern World," the decrees on Ecumenism, on Eastern Catholic churches, on the Bishop's Pastoral Office in the Church, on the Apostolate of the Laity, on the Church's Missionary Activity, and the "Declaration on the Relationship of the Church to Non-Christian Religions" are all in some way or another concerned about the structure and task of the church. Most other publications of the council also deal with issues which affect the basic understanding of the church. Yet Vatican II was neither a repetition of Trent nor a continuation of the centralization process of Vatican I, at which papal infallibility was proclaimed.

The eccesiology of Vatican II is ecumenical. To be sure, the Roman Catholic church did not suddenly reject its past. In fact Vatican II did not say anything different from Trent. Yet it was its great accomplishment that it placed the accents so differently. We hear now that the church has not only a hierarchical *but also* a charismatic dimension and that in both of these dimensions the Holy Spirit with various gifts "adorns her with the fruits of His grace."[7] Since the Christocentricity of the church gained renewed emphasis, the council refers to the distinction between the visible (structural) church and the invisible church and admits that "many elements of sanctification and of truth can be found outside of her visible structure."⁸ In following Christ as its example, the church emphasizes that it does not seek earthly glory but proclaims humility and self-sacrifice, even by her own example. Of course, the church includes those who "are fully incorporated into the society of the Church who, possessing the Spirit of Christ, accept her entire system and all the means of salvation given to her, and through union with her visible structure are joined to Christ, who rules her through the Supreme Pontiff and the bishops."⁹ But the church recognizes "that in many ways she is linked with those who, being baptized, are honored with the name of Christian, though they do not profess the faith in its entirety or do not preserve unity of communion with the successor of Peter."¹⁰

Vatican II reaffirms the decision of Vatican I to attribute to the Roman Pontiff, the "Vicar of Christ," infallible teaching authority. But the council recognizes "that by divine institution bishops have succeeded to the place of the apostles as shepherds of the Church, and that he who hears them, hears Christ, while he who rejects them, rejects Christ and Him who sent Christ."¹¹ While the Roman Pontiff stands in succession to Peter, the bishops are seen as the successors of the apostles. The college or body of bishops together with the Roman Pontiff—but not without him—exert supreme and full power over the universal church. Though the individual bishops do not enjoy the prerogative of infallibility, they can proclaim the doctrine of Christ infallibly. Infallibility is no longer exclusively reserved for the Roman Pontiff. The infallibility promised to the church resides also in the collective body of bishops when that body exercises supreme teaching authority together with the successor of Peter.

The laity are considerably upgraded as those who are "in their own way made sharers in the priestly, prophetic, and kingly functions of Christ. They carry out their own part in the mission of the whole Christian people with respect to the Church and the world."¹² Through Baptism and confirmation the laity are commissioned to the apostolate by the Lord himself. Through the lay apostolate the faithful participate in the saving mission of the church. While the functional and hierarchical differentiation between the Roman Pontiff, the bishops, and the laity is maintained, all three now enjoy equal participation in the work of the church.

How did the council arrive at its generally well balanced insights? As an answer we could point to the growing awareness that a divided Christendom is a scandal to both unbeliever and skeptic, or we could mention the increasing necessity of a common witness against the onslaught of materialism and secularism. Beyond these more external reasons, however, is an important internal one, namely the rediscovery of the Bible. While in the Roman Catholic tradition the Bible had enjoyed unparalleled reverence, it had never become the book of the laity. Now, however, the council "earnestly and specifically urges all the Christian faithful, too, especially religious, to learn by frequent reading of the divine Scriptures the 'excelling knowledge of Jesus Christ' (Phil 3:8). 'For ignorance of the Scriptures is ignorance of Christ.' "[13]

The church is concerned that suitable and correct translations are made from the original texts into the different languages and, contrary to Trent, the Latin Vulgate is no longer considered the normative text. Believers should be able to read the Bible in their own language, as Luther had demanded. Encouragement is given, upon proper approval, to produce these translations "in cooperation with the separated brethren as well" so that everyone can use them.[14] Careful exegesis of the Scriptures is encouraged so that one can determine the meaning which the sacred writers had intended and which God wanted to manifest through their words. Since the council also emphasized, however, the interpretation of Scripture within the living tradition of the church, we might wonder whether this does not put Scripture into the straitjacket of tradition. But, as we will now see, these concerns are alleviated to a large extent.

With Trent the gospel was affirmed as the source of all saving truth and moral teaching. Tradition was not seen as a human product but as coming from the apostles and developing in the church with the help of the Holy Spirit. Scripture and tradition exist in close connection and communication, "for both of them, flowing from the same divine wellspring, in a certain way merge into a unity and tend toward the same end."[15] The council does not want to treat Scripture and tradition independently or separately; instead, they must be taken together in a functional unity.

It is certainly true that the church always understands and interprets Scripture in the light of its ongoing tradition. This is also valid for the Protestant churches, as the bilateral talks between various denominations reveal. Exegetical studies have posed the question whether one can so easily determine the point at which Scripture ends and tradition begins as Lutherans have often thought. It is now commonly accepted among biblical scholars that there exists an oral tradition behind the written documents of Scripture. While the council was unable to assign an unqualified priority to Scripture, it did make significant progress in that direction. By insisting on the study of Scripture and by making Scripture available to everyone, the council insured that tradition would not grow into an independent authority.

Though the non-Roman Catholic observers of the council were consulted for opinion on the items discussed at the sessions, Protestants cannot really regard this council as an Ecumenical Council. It was a council of the Roman Catholic church, which gave definite witness to a movement of renewal. Through the prominent presence of observers, council fathers were directly confronted with the painful division among Christians. It brought them to realize that there are hundreds of millions of Christians, baptized and believers in Christ, who are separated from the Roman Catholic church. It is in this light that the Decree on Ecumenism advocated the restoration of unity among all Christians as one of the main concerns of Vatican II.

Since the council agreed that the current ecumenical movement came into existence by the action of the Holy Spirit, it acknowledged that Catholics have a duty to participate in it. At the same time it cautions that the ecumenical involvement of Roman Catholics must be fully and sincerely Catholic, i.e., loyal to the truth received from the apostles and the fathers and in harmony with the faith which the Catholic church has always professed. Such participation should not deny the truth of one's own heritage, while at the same time admitting that ecclesial elements do exist among non-Catholic Christians. The council exhorts that one should rejoice when such elements are discovered in other churches. To discover them, one must become better acquainted with the mentality of non-Catholic Christians. Such an attitude as promulgated by the council is very different from the triumphalist or introverted stance many Protestants have associated with the Roman Catholic church prior to Vatican II. Yet the wide variety among non-Catholic observers at the council made painfully clear that the problem of division is not simply one between the Roman Catholic church and the non-Roman community. The search for unity must also be pursued among the churches of the Reformation themselves.

(b) The ecumenical dialog. The most significant signs of the increasingly meaningful ecumenical dialog have been the Faith and Order movement, which held its first preliminary meeting at Geneva in 1920, and the World Council of Churches, organized in Amsterdam in 1948. Although the World Council has incorporated the Faith and Order movement, the Faith and Order Commission includes participants of the Protestant, Roman Catholic, and Orthodox churches, while the World Council as a whole has participants from the Orthodox and the Protestant churches and, on many occasions, observers from the Roman Catholic tradition as well. Another significant sign of a growing together has been the increasingly close cooperation within confessional families, such as the Anglican Lambeth Conference, first held in 1867, the World Alliance of Reformed Churches, founded in 1875, the World Methodist Council, which was organized in 1951 but traces back to the 19th century, and the Lutheran World Federation, the largest of the confessional families, founded in 1947 but with roots in the Lutheran World Convention that first met in 1923. National councils of churches, established in many nations, give added impetus to ecumenical dialog and cooperation. There are also many similar arrangements on state, regional, and metropolitan levels. There are, moreover, local clusters of churches that sponsor joint programs, hire joint staff, and occasionally engage in ecumenical exchanges involving both members and pastors.

These are all signs that amid diversity and plurality more and more points of unity are being discovered. This movement toward unity becomes most noticeable in the so-called bilateral dialog between representatives of different confessional families. For instance, in the United States the main Lutheran branches have engaged in dialog with the Reformed Church, resulting in a book with the intriguing title, *Marburg Revisited: A Reexamination of Lutheran and Reformed Traditions.* In their final session the participants came to the following significant agreement:

> During these four meetings we have examined carefully the major issues which have aroused theological controversy between our tradi-

tions for generations past. At some points we have discovered that our respective views of each other have been inherited caricatures initially caused by misunderstanding or polemical zeal. In other instances it has become apparent that efforts to guard against possible distortions of truth have resulted in varying emphases in related doctrines which are not in themselves contradictory and in fact are complementary, and which are viewed in a more proper balance in our contemporary theological formulations.[16]

Such a statement is an important witness to the gradual overcoming of denominational entrenchment in which proper insights of one's own tradition become absolutized and distorted. A similar tenor can be heard in the "Leuenberg Agreement" of 1973 between the churches of the Reformation (Lutheran and Reformed) in Europe.

Another very interesting series of dialogs has been taking place in the United States between the Roman Catholic and Lutheran churches. The dialog started with an issue upon which there was apt to be only minor differences, the status of the Nicene Creed as dogma of the church. The Lutheran-Catholic dialog then proceeded to investigate the significance of Baptism and the Eucharist, ventured on to such potentially divisive issues as the infallibility and primacy of the papacy, and finally came to a far-reaching consensus on justification.

An amazing degree of commonality has been shown, largely because of the kind of questions which have been asked. For instance, Lutherans always insist on the real presence of Christ in the Lord's Supper. But, confronted by Roman Catholics, they are challenged as to why, on the one hand, they strongly affirm the real presence of Christ and then, on the other hand, absolutely refuse "to discuss theologically the nature of that presence or the manner in which a change is effected in the elements."[17] The tacit assumption behind this question is that perhaps Lutherans are not as far away from the Reformed position as they themselves assume. The Roman Catholics were surprised to learn that Lutherans believe as firmly in the real presence as do Catholics, but that they address the issue from a different tradition and a different concern.

Another interesting development arose in the discussions on infallibility. At first the Lutherans regarded the issue of papal infallibility as a strictly Roman Catholic problem to which they had little to contribute. But soon they realized that the issues at stake in a general doctrine of infallibility are not solely a Roman Catholic concern. Rather, they involve the very nature and truth of the gospel and "the credibility of the Church's preaching and teaching Ministry."[18] There is no doubt that in some form or other many results of these dialogs filter down to the local level, whether in the form of educational materials or simply in the general knowledge that the churches are growing closer together.

One should remember also the numerous study documents released by interdenominational agencies. One of the most remarkable is the so-called Lima document, a small booklet with the title *Baptism, Eucharist, and Ministry*, issued in 1982 by the Faith and Order Commission of the World Council of Churches. This statement is the fruit of a 50-year process of study stretching back to the first Faith and Order Conference at Lausanne in 1927. Since Vatican II Roman Catholic theologians have also been included in the deliberations. This document was transmitted to the churches along with a request for an official response as a vital step in the process of ecumenical reception.

In this document the statement on Baptism is the briefest, perhaps because Baptism is the least controversial issue. Baptism is both "God's gift and our human response to that gift. It looks towards a growth into the measure of the stature of the fullness of Christ (Eph. 4:13)."[19] Both infant and adult ("believer's") Baptism are allowed for. Potentially divisive questions, such as whether there is a separate act of the laying on of hands through which the gift of the Spirit is given, are not evaded but dealt with in a conciliatory manner in full recognition of different traditions and emphases.

While for Baptism the term *sacrament* is used only once, in the very last sentence, we are told that the Eucharist includes both word and sacrament. The document states that "the eucharistic meal is the sacrament of the body and blood of Christ, the sacrament of his real presence"[20] and that "the presence of Christ is clearly at the centre of the eucharist."[21] Furthermore, "Christ himself with all that he has accomplished for us and for all creation (in his incarnation, servanthood, ministry, teaching, suffering, sacrifice, resurrection, ascension and sending of the Spirit) is present in this *anam-*

nesis, granting us communion with himself. The eucharist is also the foretaste of his *parousia* and of the final kingdom."[22] This treatment of the Eucharist also illustrates how rather diverse traditions are brought together in this statement. For instance, in one paragraph we hear, as is consistent with the Reformed tradition, that "the Spirit makes the crucified and risen Christ really present to us in the eucharistic meal," and then we hear also in analogy to Eastern usage that "the Church prays to the Father for the gift of the Holy Spirit in order that the eucharistic event may be a reality."[23]

The statement on the ministry acknowledges that the church has never been without persons holding specific authority and responsibility. Yet the ordained ministry has no existence apart from the church but is part of it since the church as a whole can be described as a priesthood. While "the New Testament does not describe a single pattern of ministry,"[24] according to biblical precedent the statement makes specific mention of the offices of bishop, presbyter, and deacon. Though there is an apostolic succession of the ordained clergy maintained in some churches, "the primary manifestation of apostolic succession is to be found in the apostolic tradition of the Church as a whole."[25] Though the apostolic succession of the ordained clergy can enhance an expression of continuity, the primary emphasis is on the succession in truth. It is affirmed that continuity in apostolic faith, worship, and mission is also preserved in those churches which have not retained the form of the historic episcopate.

When we come to ordination the issues become even more complex. Some communities resolutely refuse to ordain women, while others do so. Some insist on celibacy for the ordained while others allow for married pastors. Because ordination here "denotes an action by God and the community by which the ordained are strengthened by the Spirit for their task and are upheld by the acknowledgment and prayer of the congregation,"[26] this bipolar action allows for a diversity of criteria for those who are ordained within the different communities. Moreover, we hear that "God can use people both celibate and married for the ordained ministry."[27]

While we have not yet arrived at a mutual recognition of ministries, the booklet concludes by outlining various steps required of the different churches in order to achieve this mutual recognition. Not disregarding the many things we share in common, there is still a long way to go before we actually attain unity. The insight emerges that the way to unity is not one of victory but one of prayer, humility, and repentance, imploring the Lord of the church that he may bring about this unity. The arrogant and self-righteous attitude in which we rejoice when dialog conclusions seem to verify our own doctrinal assertions is recognized as an effective roadblock to unity.

Although we must become more aware than ever that "the message of reconciliation is scarcely believable to others when the people who bear the name of Christ are themselves at sharp odds with one another,"[28] proclamation also loses its force if we simply pretend that the still existing differences, painful as they are, are totally irrelevant. Our understanding of the church must necessarily be confessional, though it dare not become sectarian. It must focus on the common source that creates the church and the common goal that lifts and corrects our ecclesial vision. In talking this way about the church we are confronted with these aspects: the church as the whole people of God, their proclamation of God's word, and their administration of and participation in God's sacraments.

2. The whole people of God

(a) The circumference of the church. When we consider the church as the whole people of God we must avoid the twin dangers of exclusiveness and inclusiveness.

(1) The exclusivist error equates the institutional church with the whole people of God, asserting that only those who belong to the body of Christ, i.e., the visible church, can be reckoned among the people of God. Yet how do we define church membership? Is it sufficient merely to belong to a denomination or must one also participate in the ongoing life of the church? Membership in the German *Volkskirche*, for instance, is attributed to all those who have not officially renounced church membership and at least pay church tax. One can be a member "in good standing" without ever setting foot in a church sanctuary. In contrast, many American denominations attribute active church membership to those who commune at least once a year and/or financially support the church at least once during the same period. After a certain time of totally inactive membership, one is usually removed from the congregational roster un-

less the degree of participation improves. Such criteria hardly fit the description of the nascent church in Acts 2:42-46 where it states that day by day they attended the temple together and that they devoted themselves to the apostles' teaching and fellowship, the breaking of bread and prayer.

Regular attendance at worship and generous giving are not foolproof criteria by which we can determine who belongs to the whole people of God. Often these "positive attitudes" can result from simply following a certain tradition without much reflection, or from moralistic self-righteousness. Already Augustine equated the visible church with the institutional church, although he conceived of the invisible church as being in some contexts larger and in others narrower than the institutional church. Similarly, scenes of the last judgment, a favorite motif sculptured above church portals of European churches, often depict among the condemned those who bear distinctive signs of ecclesiastical office, such as the bishop's miter. This indicates that also for medieval Christendom, church membership did not necessarily coincide with belonging to the whole people of God.

(2) Since the perimeters of the invisible church can at times be more inclusive than those of the visible church, the suggestion has often been made to include in the invisible church either everyone regardless of religious affiliation, or at least the most loyal members of all religions or quasi-religious affiliations. Thus the distinction between Christians and non-Christians, or even between Christians and Christendom, is no longer expressed in terms of an absolute either-or but in a gradual "more or less." But is it not a confusion of terms and a potential act of Christian imperialism to count followers of non-Christian religions as anonymous Christians?

We must realize that the term *people of God* does not refer to anything of our own making, be it a church or a denomination or all of them taken together. It points first of all to the one who gathers, sanctifies, and enlightens people of all nations and of all ethnic and religious origins. At the beginning of any consideration of the whole people of God we must first reflect upon the nature of the church as it expresses itself in the will of its founder, namely, God in Christ through the power of the Spirit. This does not render irrelevant the institutional church. It remains the primary institution that treasures the Christian tradition and facilitates a Christian consciousness through its instructional media. Yet it must constantly be measured, criticized, and realigned according to the will of its founder.

(b) *The Christological foundation*. The Christian church is not a club which was founded to serve the interests of its members, nor is it merely a social institution through which a group of people attempts to reform society. The Apostles' Creed defines the church as being holy, catholic, and the communion of saints. Similarly, in the Nicene Creed, it is described as one, holy, catholic, and apostolic. The essential presupposition behind these statements is Christ. The church is not one because it lives undividedly. It is in fact greatly divided. It is one, rather, because it is founded by one person, Jesus Christ. The unity of the church is given through its source of origin and promised as part of its eschatological horizon. The eschaton will not be arranged according to confessional families or denominations. Similarly, the church is not holy because of the goodness of its members or because of its sacred buildings. The church knows of the sinfulness of its members, and it is commonplace to point out the profane influences on church architecture. But the church is nevertheless holy because it is sanctified through its founder, the source of all holiness.

Considering the church as the community of saints we arrive at similar conclusions. The members are not saints because of their conduct. In many ways their unsaintly behavior impedes the mission of the church. They are saints because their founder has called, accepted, and sanctified them. Similarly, the community aspect of the church is not established by the members themselves through a common concern or a common goal. The concerns and aspirations of its members are as diverse as the membership itself. Yet the founder of the church provides a common orientation and focal point.

All the central marks of the church are founded in Christ. There would not even be a Christian church without the Easter experience through which the followers of Jesus gathered together in his name after his death and resurrection. Moreover, we notice that the Eucharist is celebrated with reference to the express command of Christ, "Do this." Baptism finds its center as Christians are baptized into the death of Christ (Rom. 6:4; 1 Cor. 11:25). Similarly, the public proclamation of the apostles is done in the name of Jesus and centers around Jesus Christ who was delivered to death by his enemies and who has been raised from the dead and now serves as a point of hope and encouragement (cf. Acts 4, esp. vv. 2 and 18f.). Jesus Christ provides the source and the content of the Christian church. It is founded by him, proclaims redemption in his name, and celebrates the sacraments that he instituted.

(c) The work of the Spirit. Traditionally Pentecost is seen as the birthday of the church as the Holy Spirit was poured out on the followers of Christ. Since the "miracle of Pentecost" is also the occasion at which the language barrier separating different nationalities was overcome, this pouring out of the Spirit is often understood as an example of how the Spirit provides ecstasy. Yet, as we have seen, the Spirit of God is the foundation of life itself and does not have as its primary function the disclosing of otherwise inaccessible knowledge or experience. The Spirit is God's life-giving and sustaining power and will also bring about the eschatological fulfillment. For instance, we hear Yahweh promise to Israel, "I will give them one heart, and put a new spirit within them; I will take the stony heart out of their flesh and give them a heart of flesh, that they may walk in my statutes and keep my ordinances and obey them; and they shall be my people, and I will be their God" (Ezek. 11:19f.). Of course, the Spirit of God also provides ecstasy, excitement, and dynamic drive. Yet its main function is to be life-creating, life-preserving, and life-fulfilling.

The miracle of understanding at Pentecost stands in antithesis to the confusion and scattering of humanity at Babel (Gen. 11:7f.). The birth of the church and the outpouring of the Holy Spirit mark the rediscovery of a source of human unity that transcends ethnic and national diversity. The power of the Spirit enables humanity to rediscover its original unity. The outpouring of the Spirit and the birth of the church are therefore God's sign that he will once again bring together humanity in unity and community. Since human beings are unable to exist forever in individualistic isolation, the Spirit proleptically anticipates the intended communal structure in and with the church. The church foreshadows the eschatological phenomenon of human solidarity and seeks to practice it in the midst of today's life.

Although the creation of a new humanity as an inclusive community of people was initiated at Pentecost, almost immediately there were again dissensions. Human sinfulness has continued to assert the individual self at the expense of others and in disregard of our common ground and destiny. Only the power of the Spirit enables the church to be community. The church owes its unity to the power of the Spirit which unites us with Christ. This fact is illustrated many times in the New Testament when we are reminded that there is no unity apart from the unity in Christ. According to the Gospel of John, for example, Jesus reminds his disciples, "I am the vine, you are the branches. He who abides in me, and I in him, he it is that bears much fruit, for apart from me you can do nothing" (John 15:5). This means that the community is community only while in communion with its Lord.

(d) Images of the church. Another image for the church, that of a body, is often used by Paul. To free ourselves from the possible misunderstanding of the church as a corporation, we must first note that the term *body* is also an integral part of the Eucharistic vocabulary. Paul, for instance, asks rhetorically, "The bread which we break, is it not a participation in the body of Christ?" He then continues, "Because there is one bread, we who are many are one body, for we all partake of the one bread" (1 Cor. 10:16f.). The presence of the body of Christ is perceived in two ways: It is the blessing of liberation from our self-centered past which is made available in the Eucharist, and it is the power that unites the believers with Christ. It is important to recognize that the community does not simply participate in the body of Christ. Paul reminds us that we *are* the body of Christ and individually members of it (1 Cor. 12:27). We become part of Christ's body in Baptism (1 Cor. 12:13). The image of the body of Christ emphasizes our unity as individuals. In analogy to the members of a body we each have different functions but are all of equal status (cf. 1 Cor. 12: 14-26).

While the term "people of God" is used by Paul to connect the church with the whole history of salvation, the image of the body tends to be applied to specific historical situations. Some New Testament writers recognized the danger that could result from a narrow identification of the historical church with Christ or with his body. Therefore the church was also related to Christ's cosmic dominion. For instance, in Colossians, Christ is understood as the head of the whole world. Yet even here the church is his body and his power permeates it to assure its steadfastness and growth (Col. 2:19). The church, though not identical with Christ, is closely related to him. This gives the church a special place in history, as well as the obligation to be true to its source of power.

In the Letter to the Ephesians this cosmic aspect of the church receives special attention. Christ is designated the head of the church in which the fullness of Christ dwells (Eph. 1:23). As Christ's body, the church can even be the bearer of the Christian message to demonic powers (Eph. 3:10). We also notice that the writer draws an analogy comparing the relationship of husband and wife to that of Christ and the church (Eph. 5:22-33). Though this passage served primarily as a source of instruction to the married, indirectly we obtain an insight into the relationship between Christ and the church. We hear that the church is subject to Christ (Eph. 5:24) and is to be obedient to him. In comparing husband and wife with Christ and the church, the idea of sacrificial love as it was revealed in Christ's sacrificial death stands in the forefront (Eph. 5:25). This passage seems to refute the allegation that while Christ preached the coming of the kingdom of God, the church emerged in its place. It clearly indicates that the church is the new community created through Christ's redemptive act.

In talking about Christ as the head of the church, we must again define what we mean by *church*. In New Testament usage, the term *church* means first the local church, such as the church at Cenchreae (Rom. 16:1) or at Corinth (1 Cor. 1:2 and 2 Cor. 1:1). This might convey the impression that *church* simply means the local congregation. But in looking more closely at the Greek text we notice that "the church at" really means "the church as it is at."[29] The church is not the local church by itself nor is it produced by adding up all the local churches. Each Christian community, however small, represents the whole church. Whether there are problems of injustice (1 Cor. 6:4) or of adhering to certain traditions (1 Tim. 5:16), the issues and problems within the church are hardly ever a matter of only local concern. They usually affect the whole church.

(e) Representing Christ. The church exists wherever the Christian community is in union with its founder and head, Jesus Christ. This has been discovered more and more in the ecumenical dialog. Even the most vigorous ecumenical movement cannot produce the

unity of the church by implementing new plans or models for unity. But it can and does appeal to the source of unity which we share. It can and does call upon the local manifestations of the church, urging them to live up to the intentions which Jesus Christ has for his church. By discovering our common basis and goal in Christ, unity is furthered and strengthened. By returning to the Christocentric concern manifest in the very origins of the church, our sense of unity on the local level continues to be strengthened.

The church is founded by Christ and finds its unity in and with him. But it also represents Christ. The church is the visible expression of his lordship. This should not, however, lead to a triumphalistic attitude. It is because of Christ alone that the gates of Hades will not prevail against the church (Matt. 16:18). Only through the wisdom of God in Christ can the church withstand the evil powers and proclaim the good news (Eph. 3:10). Therefore Paul can exclaim in joy, "For I am sure that neither death, nor life, nor angels, nor principalities, nor things present, nor things to come, nor powers, nor height, nor depth, nor anything else in all creation, will be able to separate us from the love of God in Christ Jesus our Lord" (Rom. 8:38f.).

Christ has charged the church with the privilege of representing him. This means that the church is also endowed with saving power. It is the agency which treasures and administers Word and sacrament and it is under the great commission to go into all the world to baptize and to preach. But the great commission also reminds of the responsibility of "teaching them all that I have commanded you" (Matt. 28:20). This implies two things: (1) The church must be obedient to the same word which it proclaims to others and (2) the church does not proclaim its own word but that of its Lord. The church, therefore is the mediator of Christ and his gospel. Small wonder that already in the early church Cyprian declared that "there is no salvation out[side] of the Church."[30] That he meant here more than the church as an institution becomes obvious when he states on another occasion, "He can no longer have God for his Father who has not the Church for his mother."[31]

The Roman Catholic church has especially adhered to the notion of the church being Christ's representative. Yet, until Vatican II this representation was understood in strictly institutional terms. The church was equated with the Roman Catholic church and to be cut off from it through excommunication meant to be cut off from the gospel of Christ. While it is certainly true that the church is the body of Christ and that it manifests him in this world, this prerogative is not confined to just one or even several of its ecclesiastical manifestations.

Yet Christ can be known only through the body of Christ which treasures his memory, celebrates his presence, and instructs the people in this living tradition. Without the church the knowledge of Christ would diminish rapidly among humanity. Moreover, the Christian faith needs a living context in which to express itself. Even Count Zinzendorf, who established his own (separate) Christian community, claimed emphatically that apart from community he would not accept one as a Christian.[32]

The church is indeed Christ's representative, mediating his message, issuing the offer of salvation, and providing the context for Christian nurture. Yet it is presumptuous to confine the notion of church to one church, to a certain denomination, or even to the sum total of the established churches. The church is where the Christian community assembles to order its life according to the word of its founder and to spread the good news of Christ. Without such a church, in all its manifestations, we have at most a religious relationship to God which adheres to some general moral and religious principles. But there is missing what is decisive, God's living Word in Christ.

(f) The common priesthood. The common priesthood of all who form the people of God is one of the rediscoveries of the Reformation. Since the term *laity* is derived from the Greek *laos*, meaning "people," we are not surprised that the grass roots movement of the Reformation facilitated this rediscovery. Originally *laos* meant, as the Septuagint usage shows, the people of God, Israel. Of course, the term could also simply denote people in general or a crowd. This is also true for the New Testament. But soon it was used to mean the Christian community. For instance, Paul writes in quoting Hosea, "Those who were not my people I will call 'my people' and her who was not beloved I will call 'my beloved' " (Rom. 9:25). This usage is continued in the early church.

In the early church, however, *laos* came more and more to signify the Christian community in distinction from its leaders, especially those leading in worship. This was not an innovation, because we find this distinction already in the New Testament with reference to synagogue practice (Acts 13:15). The laity was no longer seen as comprising the whole people of God but only the people in distinction from its leaders.

Another significant shift occurs in the transition from Judaism to Christianity. The opposition between *laos*, meaning the Jewish people, and Gentiles is no longer seen as an exclusive one. Now we hear how "God first visited the Gentiles, to take out of them a people for his name" (Acts 15:14). In this way the new people of God is no longer confined to a particular ethnic or national group.

The term *laity* is nowadays seldom used to refer to the people of God. In everyday language the opposite of "lay" is not "leader" but "expert." Both within the church and in secular professions a layperson is considered inferior and ignorant. We could choose to defend this state of affairs and point out that in the church as well as in all other fields, the information to be mastered has increased to such an extent that it can only be handled by experts. But the dilemma of distinguishing between laity and experts in the church becomes evident when we remember that the people of God, i.e., the laity, are also called the community of saints. Is it really permissible, we must ask, to distinguish between a large body of saints, the laity, and a few especially equipped supersaints (the clergy)? The conclusion seems to be that if we want to preserve the unity of the people of God, we are not allowed to distinguish in rank (and this also means ontologically) between the laity and its leaders, but only with regard to their respective function. Contrary to the too frequent assumption, the laity dare not be relegated to passivity, with only leaders being experts and active. *Laity* does not denote inferiority in rank, expertise, or activity. It refers only to the fact that the means with which they carry out their tasks are different from those of the leadership.

The differentiation between clerics and laity—and also a secondary commonality—are well captured in Roman Catholic canon law: "There is by divine ordinance a distinction between the *clergy* and the *laity* . . . . On the other hand, both clerics and laymen can be religious [i.e., members of religious orders]."[33] We notice here an appeal to a divinely instituted distinction between lay and clergy. Admittedly, the people of God never existed without a special leadership. But the question must be asked as to the meaning of this divinely instituted distinction. Perhaps Vatican II shed some light on the issue when it declared, "Though they differ from one another in essence and not only in degree, the common priesthood of the faithful and the ministerial or hierarchical priesthood are nonetheless interrelated. Each of them in its own special way is a participation in the one priesthood of Christ."[34] The question is here left open as to the meaning of a difference "in essence and not only in degree." Should we conclude that the clergy are by nature different from the laity? Perhaps we can pursue this question further only when we investigate the Roman Catholic understanding of the ministerial office.

According to Roman Catholic understanding, the laity shares uniquely in the one priesthood of Christ. This means two things. (1) The priesthood of Christ is not divided into one priesthood for the clerics and an inferior priesthood for the laity. There is only one common priesthood in which all Christians participate. (2) Christ is the only source of the church's apostolate. The lay apostolate is founded in living union with Christ and not in the special gifts of an individual. The documents of Vatican II affirm that "the laity, too, share in the priestly, prophetic and royal office of Christ, and therefore have their own role to play in the mission of the whole People of God in the Church and the world."[35] The ministry of the laity is not a truncated or additional ministry of the church. Through their relation to Christ the laity in their own way share fully in the church's ministry.

The ordained ministry cannot be understood or carried out in isolation from the general ministry of the whole people of God. This caution is not only directed against an understanding of the pastoral ministry in which the pastor is so elevated that he does not seem to need the laity, but also against a totally world-oriented ministry. In this type of ministry certain individuals become oblivious to the Christian community, since they perceive their task as an immediate involvement in the problems of this world. The ordained ministry needs the laity as its support and as those in whose midst it ministers.

The Roman Catholic church has rediscovered the necessity of the laity for the mission and the work of the church. Since it clearly distinguishes between laity and clergy, it realizes that the laity occupy a unique position. The laity belong both to the world and to the church in a way that is true neither of the clergy nor of monks. In this dual position the laity are the proper and irreplaceable agents through whom the mission and work of the church in relation to the world can best be accomplished. If we obliterate the distinction between clergy and laity and assume that the clergy can fulfill the witnessing function just as well as the laity, we endanger the effectiveness of the Christian ministry to the world. The validity of this distinction is shown more and more by the effectiveness of laypersons as they witness to the community in which they live and work.

Laypersons carry out a full and responsible mission in serving others in the midst of an egocentric world; they enlighten the darkness of the world with the Word of God; they take a militant stand against all injustice and a conciliatory posture in the midst of strife and dissension. Their involvement paradigmatically shows that the church exists for the world and not for itself. The church should not bask in the glory of Christ but, moving outward in mission, should share this glory and permeate the world with it. Since the laity live in both dimensions, the church and the world, they remind the church of its essential world-relatedness and of its missionary task. Moreover, since the church is related to the world, it can give credible witness only if it aproaches the world in unity. Thus the rediscovery of the missionary dimension of the church, the awakening to ecumenical dialog, and the rediscovery of the laity go hand in hand.

Another factor which led to the rediscovery of the laity has been renewed emphasis on the Bible in the ecumenical movement. What should have always been clear became once again evident, namely, that before God in Christ all Christians are of equal status. Paul, for instance, emphasizes that "there is no distinction between Jew and Greek; the same Lord is Lord of all and bestows his riches upon all who call upon him" (Rom. 10:12). All former distinctions in rank have lost their separating power because of the immediacy to Christ which is part of the Christian faith. Before Christ all are equal and no one can intercede before him on someone else's behalf. No one enjoys a preferential status in the process of salvation.

Baptism is the sacrament which confers upon all of us an equal status with regard to Christ. For instance, Paul reminds us, "For as many of you as were baptized into Christ have put on Christ. There is neither Jew nor Greek, there is neither slave nor free, there is neither male nor female; for you all are one in Christ Jesus" (Gal. 3: 27f.). Baptism is incorporation in Christ and so also into the Christian community. We are initiated into fellowship both with Christ and with our fellow Christians. Baptism can be understood as the basic ordination of each Christian, commissioning him or her to be part of the church and of the witnessing commmunity. As sign and seal of this ordination the minister lays hands on each one baptized and the baptized receives the Holy Spirit. Incorporation into the church is to mean total devotion and service in and with the community of believers.

Ordination for the "ordained clergy" is not an additional or separate rite, but must be seen in analogy to the commissioning of certain individuals for the special tasks which arise within the Christian community. It is as dangerous to divide Christians into ordained and unordained as it is to assume that there are full-time Christians and part-time Christians, or trained and untrained ones. Through Baptism all Christians are ordained to full-time service and must be trained in one way or another. It is relatively unimportant whether this means special instruction prior to adult Baptism or in the process following infant Baptism which leads to confirmation. But one cannot be fully aware of what it means to be a Christian without the basic knowledge of what this privilege entails, both in general and also in specific situations.

Laity cannot be defined over against clergy or vice versa. Paul makes this abundantly clear with his imagery of the body. He states, "For just as the body is one and has many members, and all the members of the body, though many, are one body, so it is with Christ" (1 Cor. 12:12). On another occasion he affirms:

> For as in one body we have many members, and all the members do not have the same function, so we, though many, are one body in Christ, and individually members one of another. Having gifts that differ according to the grace given to us, let us use them: if prophecy, in proportion to our faith; if service, in our serving; he who teaches, in his teaching; he who exhorts, in his exhortation; he who contributes, in liberality; he who gives aid, with zeal; he who does acts of mercy, with cheerfulness (Rom. 12:4-8).

Several significant conclusions can be drawn from Paul's statement.

(1) Since all Christians are joined together, an individual Christian, a congregation, or even a denomination cannot act in whatever manner it pleases without considering the potentially destructive consequences. An individual member can easily bring discredit to the Christian faith, as can an individual congregation, or a denomination. Many people are only waiting for the chance to place the blame for all kinds of evil indiscriminately upon all Christians. When one Lutheran church body, for example, is torn by internal strife, this not only grieves all Lutherans but also allows others who do not differentiate to blame all Lutherans for this sign of disunity. This is also the case with other denominations, as recent history has testified.

(2) Only in mutual consultation and respect can one act in a way that is appropriate to representing Christ. Doing one's own thing is more often the sign of the sectarian than of the righteous.

(3) As the image of the body indicates, unity does not mean sameness or uniformity. Each one acts according to individual gifts and according to the requirements of the specific situation. Such coordinated action requires discipline and sensitivity but does not mean relinquishing one's individuality.

Just as clerics are commissioned to the exclusive service of furthering the kingdom, lay members are commissioned to fulfill individual tasks within their competency. The pursuit of a secular profession does not mitigate against this but instead will enhance their work by specifying and diversifying their range of competency. Confronted with the world, they share with their fellow Christians the general missionary and pastoral functions as the situation requires. They proclaim the gospel in word and deed to non-Christians, they teach as parents, they administer the sacraments when necessary (e.g., emergency Baptism), they listen to the confessions of their fellow workers, and they give exhortation and absolution. In their work within the church, moreover, the laity can contribute the skills they exhibit in the secular world, e.g., teachers as Sunday school teachers, banking personnel as financial secretaries, construction workers in building projects, etc. They at the same time continue their general Christian duties within the church as the need arises, e.g., evangelism and stewardship projects, adult education, preschool programs, etc. There are also other needs peculiar to every congregation, such as serving as ushers, acolytes, lectors, and perhaps as preachers.

The laity do not compete with the clergy nor do they serve as their backup system. Certainly laity and clergy cooperate with and support each other; but because the laity usually pursue secular professions and have not had an extended formal theological education, their time and theological expertise are limited. It is unrealistic and ill-advised to burden them with demands that in fact require full-time or even part-time personnel or extensive theological training. The laity are not lesser clerics; they are Christians charged with the reponsibility of witnessing in an alien world.

(g) The special leaders. Ministers and priests are neither persons who exist at the disposal of the congregation for tasks nobody else wants to tackle nor are they professional Christians who get paid for what they believe.

It is true that ministers are usually paid by the congregation in whose midst they serve. Yet it is questionable whether a full-time paid ministry should always be the norm. Especially in developing countries insistence on a full-time paid clergy sometimes creates severe difficulties. It can either impose an exorbitant financial strain on the local congregation or the salaries can be kept at such low levels that the pastor (and the pastor's family), though expected to exercise a full-time ministry, can hardly exist on the provided remuneration. Moreover, younger churches can quite often afford only a few theologically trained pastors, who in turn often supervise 15 to 30 Bible teachers or evangelists. This means, however, that the least theologically educated persons, the Bible teachers and evangelists, have the primary teaching responsibility, while the better-trained theologians spend most of their time performing ritual and administrative functions.

In most churches and denominations only ordained pastors are allowed to administer the sacraments, while anyone seems to be allowed to teach. This is especially prevalent in the American Sunday school system. The premise for this custom, however, is not well-founded. For instance, the *Augsburg Confession* states that without being properly called no one should publicly teach in the church (the public teaching is contrasted here against the teaching in the home which at the time of the Reformation was thought to be the prime duty of the father) or administer the sacraments.[36] To be properly called was thus not equated with the call to the ordained priesthood. This becomes clear when we hear how important his call to the doctorate (i.e., teaching office) was for Luther in the midst of his temptations. Luther argued that while those who are baptized are certainly entitled to be priests and bishops, nobody should execute the functions of these offices unless chosen and certified to do this by the Christian community. One cannot fulfill priestly functions indiscriminately wherever one chooses. This caution was especially emphasized against the enthusiasts who exercised their "priestly" functions wherever they felt the Spirit led them.

In this context it is also important that the "Constitution on the Church" of Vatican II declared, "Among the principal duties of the bishop, the preaching of the gospel occupies an eminent place. For bishops are preachers of the faith who lead new disciples to Christ. They are authentic teachers, that is, teachers endowed with the authority of Christ."[37] The Roman Catholic church here puts the teaching function first—and not the administrative or the ritual functions. The Protestant churches also usually claim to emphasize the Word, i.e., that they are teaching and preaching churches. One must wonder, however, why in reality they so devalue the teaching function that it can be exercised by virtually anyone. The priestly function, however, for which the words and motions are usually fairly well prescribed, they insist can be exercised only by those with the highest theological training.

In this context we should also remember that in the early church the deacons were allowed to administer Communion at least to the shut-ins. Perhaps where circumstances do not allow for an adequate number of well-trained and salaried pastors, but instead for a large number of deeply devoted and nearly unpaid evangelists, one might consider assigning to them those functions for which fairly well-prescribed liturgical texts exist. The actual teaching function can then be reserved for pastors who have sufficient theological training. This would alleviate the problem that, due to the lack of "qualified" pastors in many developing countries, congregations are unable to celebrate the sacraments on a frequent and regular basis.

In recognizing the differences between the teaching, administrative, and cultic roles, we can also notice that there is a certain gradation among the called leaders. This is true for any denominational organization regardless of how it views the role of the clergy. Whether one talks about the hierarchy of ministers, elders, and moderators, or whether one mentions the distinctions between congregations, societies, conventions, and general councils, or whether one moves in a more traditional fashion from deacons to priests, bishops, and archbishops, we notice a hierarchy of jurisdiction and often even one of ordination. In the Reformed and Roman Catholic traditions, the church structure and corresponding offices and clergy are understood to be derived from the divine law found in the biblical tradition. The free churches and the Lutherans, however, claim that hierarchies are designed for the sake of facilitating cooperation within and among churches.

While the existence of the leadership function in the Christian community can be rightly understood as divinely instituted, the New Testament does not present a clear order either for hierarchy or polity. The New Testament does not unambiguously spell out who should preside over the administration of the sacraments and who should proclaim the gospel. Nevertheless, Paul reminds us to do everything in orderly fashion and according to the tradition received from the Lord. This relatively unconstraining directive suggests that the called leaders should carry out with integrity whatever function for which they are called. Though usually only qualified persons are called to a certain office, their authority is not derived from their qualifications. A leadership position should never result in the glorification of the leader, but the leader's service instead should be carried out for the glory of Christ. The authority for any ecclesiastical office ultimately rests with Christ, in whose name the office is administered. An office thus never belongs to a person but to the Lord whom one serves in that capacity.

Since the officeholder serves and represents Christ, we can even speak of an identification of the called leader with Christ. According to Luke, Jesus told the disciples, "He who hears you hears me, and he who rejects you rejects me, and he who rejects me rejects him who sent me" (Luke 10:16). It would be wrong to infer from such a statement a special quality for the officebearer. Yet if someone wants to be true to one's calling, one necessarily identifies with that for which one stands. This does not, however, mean that one administers one's own church or issues one's own proclamation. The church and the proclamation belong to Christ alone. This also is the deeper meaning of liturgical vestments and of the habit worn by monks and nuns. They diminish as much as possible the emphasis on the individuals and seek to make transparent the Christ in whose service they live.

The called leaders administer Christ's gospel in his name and foster participation in and the spreading of the redemptive news. The material limits of this function are provided by the content of the gospel and not by one's own thoughts and desires or by the opinions of those people among whom one ministers. The formal limits are given by the specific location in which the ministry takes place. Since the call is always extended by a community of believers, one must be sensitive to their needs and desires. But they extend the call for Christ's sake and not on their own behalf. Their needs and desires must be judged by the demands of the gospel. The leader called to a certain Christian community can never let his or her calling be degraded to the point of becoming a mere employee of that community. Of course, a call can be revoked when a certain situation no longer requires a called leader. For example, one congregation can merge with another, resulting in a surplus of called leaders. A called person can also act contrary to the exemplary life-style demanded of those in leadership positions and the call can be revoked.

A call should never be revoked, however, because the Word of God preached by the leader is offensive to the church where he or she ministers. The question, nevertheless, remains as to whether it would be wise for a faithful servant to seek a call to a different location if the congregation now being served is no longer receptive to unbiased proclamation of the Word of God. Perhaps a different leader would encounter less bias in the given situation and could work more effectively. This cannot involve compromising the office but simply affirming an exchange of the bearers of the office to insure continued faithfulness. While the leaders are interchangeable, the functions of the office remain the same.

(h) The office of reconciliation. It should be self-evident that the office of the church should enhance and not detract from the es-

sence of the church. If the church is the body of Christ, or the community of saints, or the faithful who listen to the word of their Lord, then the office must be designed to enhance these basic characteristics. For instance, the *Augsburg Confession* asserts that in order to obtain faith in God's gracious acceptance of sinful humanity, God has instituted the office of the ministry, that is, provided the gospel and the sacraments.[38] In the Lutheran tradition this office of reconciliation is basically one and should not be divided into one office for preaching and teaching and another one for administering the sacraments. This one office has often been identified with the office and role of the pastor. In spite of the notion of the common priesthood of all believers, the laity have often felt that they did not participate in this office except as the receptors of ministry. That led to a deplorable inactivity on the part of the laity in the traditionally Lutheran countries of Scandinavia and in Germany.

The office finds its unity in Christ who is present in his church through Word and sacrament. Christ's presence cannot be divided by claiming that the teaching aspect should be more highly valued than the sacramental, or vice versa. Both are manifestations of Christ and of God's grace. But the function of the office, even when it is united in one pastor, does not exhaust itself with the narrowly conceived teaching and sacerdotal functions. One of the frequent observations of a conscientious pastor is that the multitude of demands on the office are greater than the time available to exercise them properly. The office, while in itself one, entails many different functions, since in a variety of ways it represents Christ to the Christian community and to all humanity. To facilitate the greatest possible effectiveness of the office, certain functions are often specialized and staffed with specially qualified people.

Increasingly popular are the so-called multiple staff ministries in which one pastor is mainly responsible for the teaching function, another for worship and preaching, while a third concentrates on the counseling aspect of the ministry. This does not mean that there are three different offices but that the one office is differentiated to maximize its proper functioning. Whether and how such specialization takes place depends upon local needs and should not be decided in advance. The idea that certain specializations are divinely decreed—for example, the distinction between the priestly office and the diaconate—does not always correlate with the needs in a given area. Thus, the diaconate in the Roman Catholic church often assumes more and more functions of the priestly office while remaining subservient. This issue is compounded by an increasing shortage of priests. Although people often are deprived of a priest, the church does not allow the deacon to administer in his place. Here it is important to assert that all Christians participate in the one office through which faith in God's love is acquired. On the other side, the Protestant emphasis on the full-time ordained minister often did away with all other options, such as deacons and deaconesses, subdeacons, etc. To be actively involved in the affairs of the church, one often has no other choice than to aspire to the ordained ministry.

According to the call to this particular office, the leader assumes the function of publicly witnessing through proclamation, action, and the administration of the sacraments. This is the reason why the administration of the sacraments, except for emergency cases, is reserved for called leaders. But it is not a "holy" function which can be performed only by "holy" people. Such a notion, however, is still sometimes advocated, for instance, when in some churches women are not ordained or are excluded from administering the Lord's Supper.

Baptism, the Lord's Supper and also those rites counted as sacraments by the Roman Catholic tradition have a public aspect. Witnessing to our neighbors or conducting family devotions is different from celebrating the Lord's Supper. Called leaders are the public representatives of the congregation beyond individual and internal matters. To emphasize the church's oneness, its corporate nature, and its joint witness to the world, the representation of the church through the teaching and sacerdotal office dare not be taken lightly. Wherever this priestly office has been downplayed, as in American denominationalism and in certain segments of the so-called Free Church movement, the unity of the church has suffered at the expense of sectarian individualism and self-serving idiosyncrasies have often emerged. On the other hand, the teaching and sacerdotal office dare not be divorced from the common priesthood of all believers. Where this has happened, as for instance in the Roman Catholic church or in segments of the so-called state churches, the church has become synonymous with its leaders and devoid of active and meaningful lay participation. In order to clarify the function and status of the church's leaders, we must now briefly investigate the call to the office.

The call to the office is always a mediated one, extended on behalf of the Lord of the church but actualized through representatives of the institutional church. The subjective call in which one feels called by God is secondary to the fact that one is objectively called by the church on behalf of Christ. Similarly, the laity is called to its apostolate through the visible sign of Baptism. Being called by the visible church gives the assurance that one stands in the context of the church and in its living tradition.

Since the leaders are called on behalf of Christ, the notion of an apostolic succession, prevalent in the Roman Catholic church and in the Anglican tradition, can be misleading. We have seen that the apostles exercised a unique and vital role in the first Christian communities. In an unrepeatable way they preserved the living memory of Jesus. Yet insofar as they had the responsibility of proclaiming the message of reconciliation, "establishing churches and building them up in the apostolic faith, their ministry had to be continued."[39] Our ministry must thus be seen in succession to the apostolic ministry, although not to the singular status of the apostles. It is therefore better to talk of a material or doctrinal succession in the sense of the truthfulness of the church, rather than of a formal or historical succession depending upon an unbroken line of tradition.

Though there is no specific Greek equivalent to the term *ordination*, there are a few instances of the laying on of hands in the New Testament that are analogous to Jewish ordination. (These are different from other instances describing the laying on of hands in the New Testament, for example to heal, to bless, or to hand on the spirit.) While the sending of Saul and Barnabas can still be understood in analogy to the Jewish custom of sending out apostles (Acts 13:1-13), we are fairly safe in assuming that the appointment of the seven deacons in Acts 6:1-6 resembles an ordination ceremony.

In contrast to Jewish practice, early Christian ordination is accompanied by prayers (Acts 6:6). It is significant that in Acts 6 the congregation chose the ones to be ordained while it is the apostles who ordained them and laid on them their hands. Another instance of ordination is presented in the pastoral Epistles with reference to Timothy (cf. 1 Tim. 1:18; 3:14). Though it is not clear whether he is ordained by presbyters or by apostles, we read that he is selected through prophetic voices. Before many witnesses he receives a brief summary of apostolic teaching and is instructed to serve faithfully under a solemn confession. Through the laying on of hands by the apostles or presbyters, or perhaps by both, he is ordained. He is also empowered by God with the gifts commensurate with his task. Timothy's work points in the direction of congregational leadership (1 Tim. 1:3), to ordain other leaders (1 Tim. 5:22), to guard the truth entrusted to him (2 Tim. 1:14), to lead the worship service (1 Tim. 4:13), and to enforce discipline in the congregation (1 Tim. 5:1f.).

The basic structure of ordination has not changed since New Testament times nor have the basic tasks of the called leadership. Ordination is done through the laying on of hands by ordained leaders. Scripture readings and prayers assume an important place in the rite. The service is always public, involving the participation of the assembled congregation. One is never ordained in general but for a specific call and service. Ordination is a liturgical act by which one is invested into a certain office and entitled to exercise the juridicial and spiritual authority over the rites and duties connected with that office. Often there are certain hierarchical levels of ordination, as in the Roman Catholic church where one is ordained subdeacon, deacon, or priest, to name just a few of its levels.

Ordination is closely connected with installation, i.e., the act in which one is designated to a certain task. In contrast to ordination, installation is repeated with each new task and is usually of a limited duration, occasionally even for a period specified in advance (especially for administrative offices). An installation recognizes the specific locale of service within the ministerial office. It presupposes an agreement on the specific function, place, range of duties, and remuneration, if any, that the particular call involves. It is performed publicly, with the participation of the congregation in whose midst the ministry will be performed. Installation, however, is not only for ordained ministers, but also for lay workers, such as Sunday school teachers, acolytes, ushers, altar guild members, choir members, and for many other offices. By including both laity and clergy under the rubric of installation we notice again that for the laity the service aspect of the Christian life is not fundamentally different from that of the professional leadership. The call to serve is different in scope and in authority but not in quality. This is not, however, equally recognized within the whole Christian church.

The Roman Catholic church, for instance, at the Council of Trent speaks of ordination as even conferring a spiritual and indelible character on the priest. The motivation behind the elevated status of the priest was the fear that the Reformers had obliterated the distinction between priesthood and laity. At Vatican II the Roman Catholic church rediscovered that the ordained priest, although set apart from the congregation, is not separated from those who still remain his brothers and sisters in Christ. Yet ordination is still considered a unique event and a priest is not ordained twice.

Today, also in the Roman Catholic church a certain openness toward a more functional and role-oriented emphasis of ordination has emerged. We are told that "there is nothing to prevent the Church freeing a priest temporarily or permanently from the obligations of his ordination to return him to the condition of life of the laity."[40] The indelible character seems to lie dormant or even cease completely when the priest no longer fulfills his priestly position. But the priestly character is indelible in the sense that a priest is a priest not only when he performs a certain ceremony but also when he is not "on duty." Once the priestly call is discontinued, however, as by resignation or dismissal from the priesthood, the character no longer adheres. The priest is not a priest once he is no longer a priest. Thus we cannot speak of a strictly ontological but rather of a functional understanding of ordination. This is reinforced through the understanding of the ordination to the priesthood as a sacrament. The sacramental grace conveyed in the sacrament of ordination is identical to the fundamental grace of justification. The grace conveyed through ordination is understood as a

> deepening and a re-orientation of baptismal grace in view of the specific mission and service of the priest. It thus allows for the development of a truly priestly spirituality, fundamentally identical with that of the rest of the faithful in the brotherhood of the same faith. This grace also unites the priest to the other members of his order in the brotherhood of their common mission.[41]

One cannot but notice the implicit tension contained in this statement. While it asserts the fundamental unity of all faithful, it also insists on a special "truly priestly spirituality."

We find the same tension in the Lutheran position. On the one hand, the emphasis is on the priesthood of all believers. On the other hand, we hear that in ordination a special blessing, the gift of the Holy Spirit, is imparted to the ordained.[42] By comparison, the Reformed tradition is much more informal, since it conceives of a plurality of offices which can be conferred on someone and can also be taken away. Therefore the Reformed do not regard ordination as the conferring of a status but simply as the designation of someone to a functional role. The Anglican communion meanwhile surpasses the Lutheran position on the other side. Importance is given to apostolic succession and one is ordained by a bishop standing in that succession. In recent years this formalistic transmission of the office by Anglicans has received positive attention by the Roman Catholic church. Most members of the Orthodox community and of the Old Catholic church accept the Anglican ordination and ministry as valid.

The most hopeful sign concerning the still-existing differences pertaining to the ministerial office is not found in comparing traditions, but in returning to the biblical documents which engender this ministry. Scriptural studies show us which of our emphases have biblical support and also reveal where we have gone astray, inventing a tradition of our own liking. We have noticed that the New Testament witness is far from unanimous when it comes to church order and organization. Also very little is said in the New Testament as to how leaders were appointed and what the requirements were for presiding over the Eucharist. The various lines of succession claimed by the early church were more the necessary constructs devised to combat heretics than a reflection of historical realities. Today there is a growing tendency to interpret episcopal succession as an effective means, but not a guarantee, of assuring the continuity of the church in apostolic faith and mission.

Continuity in faith, mission, and ministry is being recognized in churches which have not retained the historic episcopacy. Even Roman Catholics suggest today that "treatment of the apostolic succession of the whole community should be given precedence over treatment of hierarchical succession."[43] The formal matter of a strictly apostolic succession is more and more seen as secondary to the apostolicity of doctrine in a given church. Once apostolicity of doctrine is established, it also makes sense to look at the apostolicity of ministry. It is not uniformity in ministry but the apostolic rootedness of doctrine which provides the most promise for the future of the church. A united voice resulting from a reconciled diversity would confront the world with a message of peace, hope, and confidence amidst strife, uncertainty, and anxiety.

C. The three-pronged potential

When we attempt to outline the church's potential, we must look in three directions: to the past, to the present, and to the future. The church preserves the memory of that which gave rise to its existence, it plays a vital role in the present, and it provides hope for future.

1. *The guardian of the past*

The church cannot be separated from its foundation without losing itself. Especially in Europe many church buildings have become vast storehouses of art. But the church is not a museum. The church is conservative in the literal sense of the word, preserving that which is in harmony with the Lord who gave rise to the church. Yet it should continuously discern in a critical way what should still be preserved, and not hang on to things and traditions simply because they are old. Since, historically speaking, the source of the church lies in the past, the present direction of the church must be measured by the extent to which it remains true to its source. But the source of the church cannot be ascertained by referring in a literalistic way to the New Testament. There are different traditions already in the New Testament. Therefore, affirmation of the Reformation insight *Scripture alone* necessitates the discernment of tradition. What must be handed on is not a doctrinal statement in terms of a particular tradition, but "the very Person of Jesus himself as the incarnate Word of God, giving its authority to the Gospel and to the event of the authoritative Word of faith."[44] All other traditions must be judged by the gospel of Jesus Christ and the tradition that he engendered.

Since God's Word comes to us through the medium of tradition, tradition is necessary if we want to adhere to his Word. Scripture itself is the result of a traditioning process (cf. Luke 1:1-4 and John 20:30f.) and it is always interpreted within a particular tradition.

Even varying cultural traditions within the same confessional family influence the reading of the gospel tradition (e.g., the rise of liberation theology in predominantly Roman Catholic Latin America). A Roman Catholic will appeal to Scripture differently than will a Lutheran, and a Roman Catholic from Italy will read the Bible differently from one living in Argentina. These varying traditions remind us that God's Word is always spoken in and for a particular situation. But the very fact that different traditions exist contains within it the danger of provincialism and segregation if our historical peculiarity is absolutized. To avoid this danger we must remember that each particular tradition is part of the one tradition which goes back to our Lord and is embedded in the Judeo-Christian heritage.

The handing on of the gospel tradition so that it remains a living presence today is the precondition for the existence of the church and the Christian faith. In this respect Cyprian was certainly correct when he stated that there is no salvation outside the church. But the ecumenical dialog has made us aware that this tradition is not present in the same form and measure in each Christian group or individual. Initially, the canon of biblical writings, together with the creeds and the apostolic teaching office, evolved to safeguard the gospel tradition against false interpretations. But the Reformers discovered that in the course of time the official teaching office had tended to interpret tradition inadequately. Thus formal criteria, important as they are, are insufficient to insure the living presence of the gospel tradition. The Reformers, however, did not simply refer indiscriminately to Scripture in criticizing the teaching office. Martin Luther emphasized the Pauline insight of justification as a hermeneutical key in approaching the New Testament. Other Reformers proceeded in a similar way, using the perspective of the individual conscience under the guidance of the Holy Spirit (enthusiasts) or the glory of God and his kingdom (Calvin).

Often we do not realize that we approach the gospel tradition from a particular perspective. Dialog with others and ecumenical encounters have, however, made us more and more aware of our own hermeneutical key to the gospel tradition. We have also realized that the keys used in other traditions may open insights that are otherwise inaccessible from our own perspective. A careful analysis of different traditions will show that each of them, including our own, contains certain virtues and shortcomings. With traditions that are very close to our own, we usually have strong ecclesiastical ties, while we do not enjoy much fellowship with those who are dissimilar from our own. Since the life of the Christian church is lived in a continuous recalling, appropriation, and transmission of the gospel tradition, our listening to one another will enhance and enrich this process. Ecumenical isolation, on the other hand, leads to increasing one-sidedness and eventual distortion of the gospel.

Catholicity is not an attribute possessed by one particular tradition. Just as the wholeness of the body of Christ is God's gift, so too catholicity is a gift of God's grace and implies the task of its continuous appropriation."Catholic" therefore is not, as Vincent of Lérins claimed, that which has been believed always, everywhere, and by everyone. The living catholic tradition is instead a dynamic force operating throughout the church by the power of the Spirit and overcoming the idiosyncrasies of our own mind. Only the one gospel tradition which is attested to in a variety of ways can truly be called catholic. If one closes oneself off from that tradition, assuming in self-righteousness to have grasped it alone, solely, and completely, sectarianism or even heresy arises.

The church is always endangered by heresy. It is a threat coming from within the church when we refuse to listen to one another and, as the very terms *heresy* and *sectarianism* indicate, when we attack each other and cut our mutual ties. The emergence of sects and heretics is an assault on the unity of the Christian tradition. Since heretical or sectarian groups usually continue their existence within an isolated and absolutized strand of tradition, they always contain an element of truth. Since heresies are a deviation from the whole truth which the church cherishes, they usually concentrate on aspects of the tradition which have been neglected. The origin of heretical movements is a challenge for the church to reexamine its own understanding of tradition, to see whether it has neglected parts of the tradition, and to ask itself whether this was done out of necessity or by oversight.

The simple exclusion of heretics does not in itself lead the church to a deeper appropriation of the truth; it leads instead to impoverishment. As Augustine observed, heresies cannot "be produced through any little souls. None save great men have been the authors of heresy."[45] The attitude toward a heretic should be one of dialog and conversation in love; exclusion should be only a last and painful resort. Though the church cannot accept heretical views without abandoning its position as guardian of the tradition, heresy can also be a challenge to new unity and to a deeper understanding of truth.

The notion of the church as the guardian of the one tradition is especially important in face of the religious pluralism in the United States. At first one might regard American denominations primarily as sects. Following Ernst Troeltsch's distinction between church and sect, however, we soon realize that denominations are sectarian only in a very limited sense. Troeltsch's description of sects is fitting if we characterize denominations as relatively small groups that aspire to personal inward perfection and aim at direct personal fellowship among members of each group. Unlike Troeltsch's sects, they are not voluntary protest organizations that stand in pronounced opposition to the church, as do sects in Europe. Most denominations are well-institutionalized and those which did emerge in protest to religious oppression in Europe have long since forgotten the historical reasons for their existence. The splits still occurring on the American denominational scene indicate that denominations are not themselves sects but rather give rise to them as opposing or splinter groups who accuse them of having betrayed the gospel tradition.

The Bible seems to form the center of the common spiritual heritage in all denominations. But each defends its own way of interpretation, attempting to show that its own denominational teaching and polity most closely conform to the biblical pattern. That there is no joint appeal to a common tradition is underscored by the amazing competition which has been waged among the different denominations until very recently. Denominations emerged as voluntary organizations of like-hearted and like-minded individuals united on the basis of common beliefs for the purpose of accomplishing certain objectives. Thus for the immigrants, denominations kept alive deep emotions of kinship and belonging, becoming "the mouthpieces of the economic and sectional groups they represented."[46] While appealing to the common biblical tradition, the denominations represented and perpetuated the ethics of class and nations rather than the common ethics of the gospel. Only recently have denominations begun to learn that their common Christian heritage mandates that they join together in order to bear a unified witness to the world. They have begun to learn that one cannot naively reject all traditions save the biblical one without ending up in separatistic self-righteousness.

The church is a community of people which transcends the visible boundaries of its institutions. But the people do not transcend these boundaries simply because they share a common concern. Bonhoeffer aptly reminded us that "the church does not come into being through people coming together (genetic sociology). But it is in being through the Spirit which is effective in the community."[47] Therefore we do not merely "attend the church of our choice" but we are instead chosen and gathered as church. Belonging to the church means belonging to the Lord who has been active in the past, is active in the present, and will be active in the future.

If we remember that we belong to the communion of saints, we recognize that we are not the first Christians, but are part of that communion in, with, and through which Christ has worked in the past. A church unaware of the communion of saints is oblivious to God's activity in the past and deprives itself of a stimulus for the present. Even when the church does not recognize itself as communion of saints, it affirms this notion implicitly by using the Old Testament Psalter and other hymns which have come to us through the centuries. The acceptance of the Old Testament as part of our own tradition is an acknowledgment that the communion of saints transcends the confines of the Christian church. It is a witness to God's whole saving activity. The Old Testament is not just a negative backdrop against which the Christian faith shines in new light. Its people are part of God's people and in every respect our spiritual ancestors.

For the Christian church, however, the national limitations of Judaism are no longer valid. It does not hope for the national restitution of Israel and for the gathering of all nations at Mount Zion (cf. Isa. 2:3). The church stands in continuity to Israel and witnesses to the fulfillment of the promises given through Israel. Because Israel is the church's spiritual ancestor, the church cannot and dare not suppress Israel. The fact that Jewish people live among Christians should never have led to anti-Jewish actions but to loving witness. The presence of the Jewish people among us serves as a reminder that the gospel has not been preached and lived with the kind of love which would prompt the Jewish people to accept Jesus Christ as the Messiah. Their presence further reminds us of the still unresolved tension within God's saving history. Vatican II captured this sentiment well when it declared, "In company with the prophets... the Church awaits the day, known to God alone, on which all peoples will address the Lord in a single voice and 'serve him with one accord.' "[48] In the meantime the council wishes to "foster and recommend that mutual understanding and respect which is the fruit above all of biblical and theological studies, and of brotherly dialogues."[49]

Together with all the faithful, including the Jewish people, the Christian church waits for the coming of God and for the public establishment of the kingdom. By guarding the past the people of God also look forward to the eschatological future. From the hope that the past engenders, both as the reminder of God's past activity and the reminder that this activity is unfinished, we are sustained in our hope for the completion of God's saving work. The dynamic power of the church, extending from the past to the hoped-for future, does not leave the present untouched. The church is the heart of the present, anticipating the future proleptically.

2. The heart of the present

The church is an anticipating community, sharpening the conscience of society that it may conform ever more perfectly to the ultimate fulfillment for which all creation longs, providing a haven for the neglected in the midst of turmoil and injustice, and fervently anticipating the heavenly city.

(a) The conscience of society. In the Israelite theocracy the worshiping community was identical with the political community. It is different, however, in Christendom. Since the church first emerged, the question has been debated how the church should be related to society. As Eastern Orthodoxy, Western Catholicism, and the churches of the Reformation show, the issue was solved differently in different regions. The most serious challenge to the relationship of church and society, however, has been posed during the last 200 years, as a separation of church and state has occurred in almost all countries. Once the church no longer provides a transcendent halo for the state, the question emerges as to how one can understand the purpose and function of the church. One could assume, as has been done in Marxist countries, that the church is a private club which satisfies the religious needs of its members. While Christians agree on the voluntary nature of membership in the church, they realize that, unlike a club, the church is constituted by God and not by its members. Futhermore, the church does not first of all seek those who have a "religious antenna" but instead those who do not seem to care about the church—sinners and outcasts. One could also attempt to describe the church as a service institution: We participate in certain rituals, support the church financially, and receive eternal salvation as compensation. Yet even in its darkest moments the church has never completely forgotten that it could only be the institution of salvation because of God's promised grace and not because of our own efforts. While the church has many institutional features, it is an institution of a very special kind.

The church's reason for existence is the fact that Christ is risen from the dead and is both the head of the church and the redeemer of the world. Since the risen Lord is the head of the church, it is a mark of its truthfulness that it foreshadows the new creation and the glory of the risen Lord. The church cannot be silent in the face of a secular world. It is called upon to announce his ultimate victory over the world and to symbolize his presence within it.

H. Richard Niebuhr has perceptively pointed out that the relationship between Christ and culture, or between church and society, can assume basically five positions: The church can stand against society, it can affirm society, it can stand above society, church and society can hold each other in tension, and finally the church can transform society.[50] Though Niebuhr attempted to illustrate each of these types with examples from the history of the church, he admitted that none of the types appears in a pure form and all have both advantages and shortcomings. For this reason we do not want to separate these types and attribute them to distinct traditions. By learning from their particular shortcomings and advantages, however, and by carefully balancing them against each other, we attempt to arrive at a framework for the church's role in today's world.

(1) Opposition to society: If the church does not want to lose itself it must, first of all, stand in opposition to society. This does not mean that the church is against society. But to be relevant for the

world it cannot simply imitate the world. In a situation of unrest and instability the church provides a haven of rest and stability, the tranquil eye at the center of a stormy world. Over against the world's emphasis on transitoriness and change, it provides a strong sense of corporate identity. As a beacon of heavenly guidance, it cherishes the gospel tradition and the administration of the sacraments. The church has what the world cannot give, an ultimate reference point for life and the living presence of the resurrected one who protects it from ultimate destruction.

The church's otherness does not lead to isolation or withdrawal. Opposition to the world is always characterized by a momentum for mission. The acknowledgment that the world is corrupted by sin, that the world endangers our humanity and that earthly treasures are eaten up by rust and moths, leads to the realization that the world needs to be saved. The church's opposition to the world is opposition to human self-righteousness and to the belief in humanity's inherent natural goodness and moral perfectability.

By exposing the world as corrupt and under the dominion of seductive and anti-Godly powers, the church does not confine itself to redeeming individual souls. The church's opposition to society and its subsequent redemptive involvement must be directed to the whole of society, both to body and spirit, corporate structures and human beings. Yet a missionary approach to society would be futile if the church were not convinced that it also stands above society.

(2) The church as a necessary ingredient: Since the church addresses itself to the body and the spirit, society does not gain a full understanding of humanity without the church (or another religious organization) which keeps reminding the world that humanity is more than an extension of matter. When the church assumes the task of safeguarding the *humanum* in society, i.e., preserving and furthering the truly human element, the church does not rival the task of the state. It especially involves itself in areas neglected by society and examines and sharpens society's understanding of humanity. It makes society aware of its neglects and encourages it to accord justice to everyone.

In the process of bearing witness to the *humanum*, the church needs and demands a hearing in society. As the guardian of the temporal order, the state realizes that this order is not established once for all time, but must be continuously shaped and maintained. Moreover, in its functioning the state, in order to legitimize its authority and to promote virtue, must itself appeal to the ultimacy provided by the church. The only alternative is a state ideology, expressed in the frequent singing of the national anthem and the pledge of allegiance to the flag. But even the ideas of freedom, liberty, and concern for the well-being of the community—which are commonly associated with such state ideology—are by no means secular insights. They are historically grounded in deep religious commitments arising from the Judeo-Christian tradition. This is true for us in the West as well as in many developing countries. Even in Marxist ideology the similarity of many revolutionary insights to aspects of the early Christian tradition is not mere coincidence. The concern for the oppressed and outcast, the anticipation of the kingdom, and equality for all people, are in an intrinsic sense insights that stem directly from the gospel tradition. Yet in separating them from the liberating power of the gospel tradition, they become truncated and, in many instances, their application leads to new bondage and enslavement instead of new freedom and greater equality.

Society cannot disassociate or emancipate itself from the church, unless it eventually abrogates its task of maintaining temporal order and upholding virtue and patriotism. That most societies influenced by the West are still functioning relatively well is due to the fact that there is still so much Western, i.e., Judeo-Christian, tradition present in them which continues to form a bond of unity and to advance self-respect and mutual concern. The more this Judeo-Christian tradition is obliterated or attenuated, the more it becomes necessary for the church to act as the guardian of society and to function as a reminder of the eternal value and responsibility of each human being. However, this attempt by the church to rise above sinful society and to act as a beacon and reminder of a transcendent obligation arouses the suspicions of some. Therefore the tension between church and society becomes unavoidable.

(3) Church and society in tension: The church will always exist in tension with society. Even the United States, a country which prides itself on its clear separation of state and church, the state is

always in danger of becoming a church with its own faith or ideology, called "civil religion," and with the White House as a kind of sacred shrine. Is it really just accidental that in the United States most state capitols and the national capitol bear so much resemblance to St. Peter's Basilica in Rome, the heart of Roman Catholicism? Is it only by accident that some presidents have invited pastors to conduct worship services in the White House with invited guests as worshipers? On the other side, there is also a great temptation for the church to seek to become the state. More than once the church has attempted to legislate its own rules of conduct and impose them upon everyone.

To avoid the twin dangers of clerical domination of the state and of civil religion, some theologians have introduced the distinction between two kingdoms of God, the kingdom to the left (the world) and the kingdom to the right (the church). Picking up the biblical notion of a distinction between the world and the kingdom of God, Augustine outlined the progress of the city of God over the city of the world, intending to show the spiritual superiority of the former. While such a view left no doubt as to the abiding necessity of the church for society, it unfortunately also furthered a clerical domination over the world instead of holding it in check. It was not until Luther that a doctrine of the two kingdoms evolved which avoided the danger inherent in Augustine's system without abolishing the tension between church and state.

Unlike Augustine, Luther did not identify the kingdom of God with the kingdom to the right and the kingdom of the devil with the kingdom of the world. Though Luther distinguished between the kingdom of Christ and the kingdom of the world, the latter meant for him the totality of all orders of God, including the orders of nature as well as civil justice. The line of scrimmage between God and the anti-Godly powers runs through both kingdoms and Satan attempts to turn both into an anti-Godly chaos. Their common task as bulwarks of God against the destructive assaults of the devil testifies to their inner unity.

Luther's distinction between the two kingdoms does not provide a panacea for the problem of the relationship of church and society. But it does make one point unmistakably clear: No sphere of life can be excluded from Christ's lordship. The lordship of Christ over all of life takes place in different forms and with different methods.

If the distinction becomes blurred between the different forms and methods according to which the two kingdoms conduct their affairs, either clerical triumphalism or secular utopianism results. The church must remind society of the one under whose dominion it stands and under whose ultimate authority it conducts its business. Conversely, society serves as a reminder for the church that this world, though longing for wholeness and redemption, is still broken.

Christ is the Lord of the whole world and not only of the interior life of the Christian. This truth has been rediscovered by many who do not necessarily claim the name of Luther in their heritage. For instance, in the *Chicago Declaration of Evangelicals* we read that "we affirm that God lays total claim upon the lives of his people. We cannot, therefore, separate our lives in Christ from the situation in which God has placed us."[51] But there is still a frequent tendency within the church to shy away from specific corporate pronouncements on significant issues in society. The reason for this hesitancy is quite often that society is seen as the enemy of the church, instead of as an important way in which God is present in the world. To overcome this inadequacy the church must affirm society and dialog with it.

(4) The affirmation of society: Knowing about human sinfulness, the church cannot assume that God's presence in the world is self-evident to everyone. The church must therefore be the conscience of society, acting in solidarity with it and at the same time sharpening society's own conscience of the demands of God. In order to get a hearing in a secular society we must look for a common ethical sphere and establish common ethical goals for Christians and non-Christians. But where can we perceive such a common ground?

Today a metaphysically grounded natural law has fallen into disrepute. Luther's emphasis on a common knowledge of the natural law as he attempted to relate church and society may, however, contain more insight than we are willing to attribute to it. For instance, Emil Brunner cautioned that if there is nothing that is universally valid and no justice beyond ourselves that meets us as an undeniable demand, then there is no actual justice but only an organized power play. Even during the time of monarchy, kings and princes understood that they enjoyed their rule through the grace of God.

Today's dictators, however, rule in their own name and no longer feel themselves under the authority of higher powers. The individual human being has become the ultimate measure for right and wrong. The alarming frequency with which totalitarian systems have emerged during the last 100 years makes us wonder whether our humanity of itself is indeed a sufficient foundation to insure the *humanum*.

Ethological research, however, has adduced more and more evidence that there are some basic norms for human behavior. Thus Arnold W. Ravin claimed, "These universal or near-universal ethics . . . indicate some profound and fundamental needs in all men to behave within certain limits or ethical boundaries."[52] By nature human behavior is not as free and unspecified as we might initially assume. To be a human being means to act according to certain norms that enable us to live together and further our own species. The explicit forms which these norms assume, however, depend upon the environment in which the social behavior takes place.

This gives new significance to the traditional "theology of orders." In principle at least, the common moral norms are accessible to everyone and are intended to preserve the species rather than to constitute it. Because of this orientation it might be good to perceive them as orders of preservation instead of orders of creation. This is even more necessary since we know God's creation only in its fallen condition, i.e., under the aspect of preservation. The orders of preservation counteract the destructive tendencies of the anti-Godly powers. They are a sign that God does not want to destroy the world but to conserve it for Christ's sake and with Christ as its goal. The orders of preservation, therefore, ultimately have an eschatological character in that they function towards the eschatological fulfillment in the new creation.

Once we have explored our common ground and have affirmed God's preserving presence in society, we should also witness to God's presence in the midst of this fallen world. This means that we attempt to transform it so that it may bear more resemblance to the new creation which God intends to create.

(5) The transformation of society: The abiding presence of the anti-Godly destructive powers in this world makes the church's task of transforming society a continuous one. Any millennial or utopian ideas that advocate an evolutionary convergence of church

and society neglect the reality and radicality of evil in this world and forget the eschatological proviso limiting all human endeavors. Yet, short of establishing the kingdom of God, which by its very nature is an eschatological event, the church betrays its own reason for being if it does not press on to transform society.

The transformation process must go in two directions. (1) There is a need for a continuous transformation of that part of society which is the church so that it may become an example of the new community and a beacon of hope in the face of oppression and injustice. (2) There is also a continuous need for a transformation of that part of society which is outside the church. The truth that God is active in the world must come to ever clearer expression. Sinful humanity and the sinful structures it designs to perpetuate present inequalities that must be converted in order to become expressive of the will of the Lord. The process of such conversion foreshadows God's eschatological goal of salvation envisioned for all people. This pressing on for the emergence of the *humanum* includes on the social level: economic justice in the face of the exploitation of people by people, human dignity in the face of political oppression of human beings by other human beings, human solidarity in the face of alienation of person from person, and hope in the face of despair in personal life.

The respresentatives of liberation theology rightly remind us that we are ambassadors of God's redemptive news. We are accountable to the global human family and must become living witnesses to the coming of the kingdom. If we take seriously God's covenant extended to us in Christ, the eschatological vision of a renewed humanity is not just otherworldly. Paul's insight reinforces this when he claims, "And we all, with unveiled face, reflecting the glory of the Lord, are being changed into his likeness from one degree of glory to another (2 Cor. 3: 18). Pressing on in patient hope for signs of the new creation we take seriously our charge to be the conscience of society. We make people more sensitive to each other's needs and become living witnesses of the good news of God's new creation.

(b) The haven of the neglected. When the church acts as the conscience of society, it assumes a servant role, working on the fringes of society on behalf of those who are neglected and outcast. The

church must, however, be mindful that the speck in the neighbor's eye does not have priority over the log in one's own eye, lest our attitude become hypocritical (Matt. 7:3). The church's stand for the disinherited in a different societal context must not be placed above aiding the disinherited in one's own land. In acting on behalf of others, the church imitates Christ, who laid down his life for others.

In his *Letters and Papers from Prison* Dietrich Bonhoeffer vigorously advocated this servant role when he wrote, "The Church is the Church only when it exists for others .... The Church must share in the secular problems of ordinary human life, not dominating, but helping and serving. It must tell men of every calling what it means to live in Christ, to exist for others."[53] Other theologians have picked up this emphasis. Harvey Cox claims, for example, "The church's task in the secular city is to be the *diakonos* of the city, the servant who bends himself to struggle for its wholeness and health."[54] Similarly, Gibson Winter stated, "In the servant Church, ministry is servanthood within the world. Ministry is discerning the promise of the saving history in the historical decisions of public responsibility."[55]

While the servant role portrayed by Cox and Winter is a rather confident one, convinced that such involvement will lead to a brighter future, more recent writings have returned to Bonhoeffer who demonstrated the necessity for genuine suffering and self-giving. We have come more and more to realize the complexity of injustice, the depths of suffering, and the church's own limited resources. The greatest handicap for the church, however, is usually not its limited resources so much as its own posture. The power struggle within many church bureaucracies, the lack of thrift and exemplary life-style among both leaders and followers, and the dichotomy between word and deed are liabilities far greater than any lack of skill or of workers. When, however, the spirit of self-giving love prevails, the church can often be the leaven which makes change and renewal both possible and endurable.

The church has always seen its servant role as a characteristic ingredient of its being in the world. Following the example of the Lord, it is willing to serve even to the point of self-sacrifice (Mark 10:45). Aid for the neglected is service to the Lord. As he reminded his followers, "As you did it to one of the least of these my brethren, you did it to me" (Matt. 25:40). Assuming a servant role does not simply mean giving from one's surplus. It means standing up for the underprivileged and taking the risk of becoming one of them. It is solidarity with the suffering. Doing acts of charity is both an individual and a corporate task. As Gerhard Uhlhorn attested regarding the early church, such servant character does not go unnoticed:

> It was when misery became greater and greater in the perishing world, when the arm of the state was more and more paralyzed, when the authorities no longer offered assistance to the poor and the oppressed, nay, themselves took part in oppressing and exhausting them, that the Church became on a grand scale the refuge of all the oppressed and suffering.[56]

Even today the service of the church through Church World Service, Caritas, Miserior, Bread for the World, and many similar organizations are attempts to give a more human face to a technological world and to strengthen human solidarity and mutual care.

3. The reminder of the future

The church cannot remain silent in a world which assumes that the course of history is predictable and determined by humanity's own efforts and resources. In a secular and self-relying culture, the church is essentially countercultural. It witnesses to a future provided by God and not by humanity.

(a) Anticipation of the new world. The church is not self-sufficient. It gains its strength from its Lord, whom cross and tomb could not contain. The symbols of apparent defeat were turned into signs of triumph over the powers of destruction. When Christians live out their allegiance to the Lord, the cross of Christ takes on special meaning. It becomes the rallying point for the oppressed and powerless and the sign of inspiration that we will ultimately conquer all adversity and be able to participate in a new heavenly community. In the midst of a torn and divided community, the church already anticipates proleptically this new community on a local and even a global scale.

When we refer to proleptic anticipation, we must clarify three points:

(1) Anticipation of the heavenly city is not an attempt to accomplish now what is promised to us as an eschatological, i.e., heavenly, reality. The church is an interim institution between Pentecost and parousia, waiting and hoping for its fulfillment in the heavenly community of all the saints. Any utopian attempt which seeks to bring about in totality that which the church anticipates in hope, destroys the condition that makes its future-directed existence possible. For instance, it is one of the strange paradoxes of Marxism that it lives and strives for the creation of the heavenly community which it calls the classless society. But by refusing to admit that its attempts and programs are only provisional, Marxism destroys that which engendered and encouraged its hopes, i.e., the God-provided eschatological perfection. Moreover, since in a secular society perfection must be attained in this world, utopian systems are compelled to behave intolerantly and dictatorially in order to pursue their goals and thereby diminish the ideal vision they represent.

(2) Anticipation of the heavenly city is not a human accomplishment. It is a divine gift. We do not create community but discover it as something given. We do not ourselves attempt to fulfill a dream or an utopian vision but we live according to God's presence through his Spirit. The theocentric structure of the Christian community reminds us of God, our ultimate allegiance and authority. All utopian dreams and visions are destroyed by the cross of Christ, the vivid reminder that we still live under the realities of this world. Bonhoeffer rightly cautioned us that "God hates visionary dreaming; it makes the dreamer proud and pretentious."[57] Living under the new life means to live under the word of forgiveness, the source of new life, and under God's word which meets us through other Christians.

(3) Anticipation of the heavenly city is not just a spiritual reality, but something enfleshed in everyday life. Bonhoeffer rightly observed that "a purely spiritual relationship is not only dangerous but also an altogether abnormal thing."[58] The enfleshment of the anticipated heavenly city has perhaps been captured best in the monastic ideal. Monastic groups are usually formed to strengthen the spiritual life of their members. The monastic ideal, however, also informs their daily lives and transforms the surroundings in which they live and work through education, buildings, art, and community acts of charity. Similarly, Protestant counterparts, such

as the Oxford group of Frank Buchman or the Herrnhut brethren of Count Zinzendorf, had a profound impact both on their own members and on the communities in which they lived and worked.

The same kind of influence can emerge from the local worshiping community. The Christian faith is not merely a Sunday morning affair. It lays claim on the total lives of its members and has an impact on the community in which a congregation is located. As an anticipation of the heavenly city on the local level, the church cannot but become a visible sign, a beacon of hope and a bastion for a new humanity in a fallen and hurting world. The vision of the church is always larger than the local church. As J. Robert Nelson pointed out, "the primary task of the church in history is to be the bearer of that reconciling work in every generation."[59] To make such reconciling action credible, at least two criteria must be met.

(a) The church contradicts its task of being a beacon of hope if it is torn by strife and rivalry. Before it can be a witness to human unity, the church must show forth unity in its own life. Unity means realizing and making manifest our oneness as heirs of the kingdom and celebrating both the unity we seek and its fragments which we have already discovered. The ecumenical movement is a first serious step in this direction and shows us that our respective insights gain new clarity and correction when we come together to listen to the gospel tradition.

(b) Our credibility as bearers of the message of reconciliation can be maintained only if we extend this message beyond the local scene. Friedrich Nietzsche rightly reminded us that Christians should not just express love to those close to them but also to those who are most distant. As the bearers of the message of Christ we cannot stop at our own city walls but must go beyond them to the ends of the earth. This mission of the church goes hand in hand with the discovering our unity, since only a reunited Christian church can become the symbol and instrument of the unity of humanity. It is not by accident that these two concerns, the pursuit of Christian unity and the concern for human solidarity, surface most prominently among the different churches of the World Council of Churches.

Foreshadowing a new world which is torn neither by rivalry, strife, nor injustice, the church manifests these signs on a global scale. By erecting them in its own midst the church serves as a powerful stimulus for sensitizing the whole world. Without the presence of the church, the world would only grow colder and become more merciless. The reason why the church functions as the conscience of society, the haven of the neglected, and the anticipation of the new world cannot be derived solely from the dedication of its members, though that should not be underestimated. The church continues its task because it is inspired by a power which is stronger than all distortions, injustices, and self-centeredness, a power that has manifested that it can and will destroy the forces of darkness, nay, has even destroyed them already. This power is our Lord Jesus Christ, in whose name Paul admonishes us, "Be steadfast, immovable, always abounding in the work of the Lord, knowing that in the Lord your labor is not in vain" (1 Cor. 15:58). In having such a Lord, the church is not only the anticipation of the new world, but also the reminder of God's past actions and therefore a beacon of hope for a new world to come.

(b) The symbol of the future. The involvement of the church in the affairs of the world serves a dual purpose. On the one hand, the church actually serves those in need. On the other hand, the church, being aware that all of its efforts are at best patchwork, testifies with its actions to a world which will not be torn by strife and disease. Just as the miracles of our Lord functioned not only as help for people in need but also as signs of a new creation, the church is a symbol of the future. In all its activities and functions the church becomes visible as an eschatological symbol foreshadowing the new creation. Each absolution is a reminder of God's love which one day will manifest itself completely. Similarly, each celebration of the Eucharist points to the celestial banquet. The phrase in the Eucharistic liturgy, "this do in remembrance of me," does not just mean that we should remember Christ's sacrifice. It also is a reminder for God to recall the sacrifice of his Son and therefore speed the coming and completion of the kingdom.

That the Christian community is the symbol of the future also can be seen in the Lord's Prayer. As a constituent part of the communion liturgy of the early church, the Lord's Prayer belonged to that part of the service in which only baptized members were permitted to participate. Both "thou" petitions, "hallowed be thy name" and "thy kingdom come," are in content closely related to the expectant cry, "Come, Lord." They express a longing for that time when God's profaned and misused name will be forever glorified and the reign of his kingdom will be revealed. Other phrases of the Lord's Prayer also witness to a yearning for and expectation of the eschaton. For instance, in the petitions for bread and forgiveness, the church asks that God might already today and in this place grant the bread of life and the blotting out of sin which one day will be done completely. With these references the church becomes a beacon of hope in the darkness of this world.

Regarding Baptism, we quickly discern that the notion of dying and rising with Christ and of being incorporated into his body envisions more than membership in an institution. Baptism means conversion to Christ and becoming a confessing Christian. Paul's admonition that as baptized people we should walk in newness of life primarily implies two things:

(1) As baptized Christians we are in a state of transition from this aeon to the future one. This world, though unable to hold us completely, still ensnares us. Luther therefore rightly insisted in his Small Catechism on the "daily drowning of the old Adam" through daily repentance.

(2) Our Christian existence is a dynamic existence. Together with the whole creation we are yearning and longing for the revelation of the sons of God and the manifestation of God's kingdom.

Dying and rising with Christ makes sense only when it implies that we can break out of the natural cycle of birth and death from which this image is borrowed. It makes sense only if there is a time when death will no longer have the victory, when we can forever walk in newness of life. In other words, Baptism remains an empty shell unless it will be verified through the coming of the kingdom. As we wait for this kingdom, Baptism, as sign and symbol of that future verification, is administered in trust and hope.

In its actions, its liturgical celebrations, and its prayer life, the church is a symbol of the future. In part it foreshadows the things to come and in part it patiently but intensely hopes and waits for their ultimate realization. But the power and encouragement both for anticipation and expectation is derived from the experience of Christ. Through the presence of Christ and the power of the Spirit the church realizes that the life and destiny of Jesus Christ is the prime example of its own life and destiny. It knows beyond doubt that history ultimately will serve to make his kingdom triumph.

Intrinsic to the Christian faith is the hope in a common destiny for humanity. This hope is expressed in the vision of the unity of the whole church, of church and synagogue, and of all people under God's dominion. While the church cannot stand in judgment of others, it must remind all people that God wants them to be saved. The church would be overly optimistic, however, if it would claim with Friedrich Schleiermacher that "through the power of redemption there will one day be a universal restoration of all souls."[60] Indeed, the church's reason for being is to represent Christ to the world and to proclaim his gospel to the ends of the earth. But whether all will accept him, we do not know.

While we are hesitant to assume that everyone will eventually be saved, we should not too quickly give up our mission of bringing the world to Christ. It might be true that the church should not expect to score big victories on secular or religious fronts. However, if success were our criterion for engagement we would long ago have given up our efforts to make this world a better place to live. Strangely, those who have given up trying to convert the world in the traditional sense usually continue their efforts to achieve a more human world with ever-increasing vigor. If it wants to remain a symbol of hope, the church dare not leave humanity to its divisions, antagonisms, and potential self-destruction. The faithful proclamation of the gospel tradition must challenge every status quo, be it Muslim or Buddhist, Marxist or capitalist. Since Christ is present and active through his Spirit in non-Christian believers and in their religions, we can affirm whatever is good and wholesome in them. In turn we should challenge them to recognize the good and wholesome features in the gospel tradition. It borders on wishful thinking to expect that future dialog, amid all diversity and contradictions, will lead to the affirmation of one faith and one God. But such dialog could at least remove the barriers of misunderstanding and hatred and perhaps even foster understanding and reconciliation among people of different religions.

Though we do hope that God's word will make a difference in this world, creating increasing solidarity among all people, we dare not assume that all people will eventually listen to him. Even our most sincere proclamation of the gospel tradition through words of grace and acts of mercy can never take a universal homecoming of all people as a fait accompli. The realization of a common destiny for all as the whole people of God can only be a most daring eschatological hope and the content of fervent prayers. Nevertheless, sharing Christ in the most remote places of the earth is a reminder that in one way or another, with our approval or without, the Lord will one day be acknowledged as Lord of all creation, that God may be everything to everyone (1 Cor. 15:28).

As a symbol of hope the church must also be utterly disturbed about its own divided house. The division into different churches and denominations is never just the fault of others. It is also our own fault. The process of acculturation and the need of diversity on the local scene does not justify our present divisiveness. Immense progress towards representing the whole people of God has been made in the World Council of Churches, the various world federations of confessional families, the national councils, and the many bilateral dialogs. But institutional inertia seems to be the greatest obstacle to actual unity. Every day we increasingly discover how much we actually share in common and that the segregation into different denominations and churches is in many cases anachronistic and sinful.

The Fifth Assembly of the World Council of Churches in Nairobi (1975) again instructed its member churches to "provide opportunities for a careful study and evaluation of the concept of conciliar fellowship as a way of describing the unity of the church."[61] Conciliarity is not the same as the medieval concept of conciliarism, meaning the shift of power from a central authority (the pope) to the councils. Instead conciliarity recognizes the fact that the church always needs assemblies to represent its unity. Seen historically, councils are convened by churches which enjoy such a degree of unity that it can find expression in eucharistic fellowship. Yet also assemblies of churches which do not yet enjoy full eucharistic fellowship, while not councils in this strict historical sense, can decisively advance unity and have in fact done so. Conciliarity therefore does not make a prerequisite of organic union but aspires to it.

The goal of organic union does not mean the establishment of a centralized superstructure. Union rather is an expression of togetherness on all levels. We remember here the biblical notion that at each place where the church exists, the whole church comes to expression. Knowing how the local or regional church functions means knowing how the whole church functions. There is always an intrinsic connection between the local and the universal life of the church.

A divided church is an offense to the Lord and to his gospel as well as an impediment for mission. But a divided Christendom is not only a reminder of our sinfulness and of the task which lies ahead. It is also a reminder of the eschatological future, when our human divisiveness can no longer intrude on the manifestation of the whole people of God. Therefore, intermediate steps toward union are signs that the power of the Spirit is at work in his people and allow God's people to anticipate something of the great celestial banquet when all will share the same table and the same food. This vision of the whole people of God includes hope for the overcoming of the division between church and synagogue, between Jew and Gentile. The Jewish people are both an enigma to us and also a source of inspiration and hope. They are a vivid demonstration of the truth that God may lead his people through the valley of the shadow of death but will not abandon them. He continues to sustain, call, and nourish them. Yet the Jewish people are more than a symbol of survival. They are a symbol of insight.

Christians have at best tolerated the Jewish people. Nevertheless, the Jews did not turn their backs on us. Inspired by the Old Testament, they still perceive all of humanity "as the descendants of one father and the creatures of one Creator" and similarly cherish "a complementary vision of a reunited mankind under God at the end of time."[62] The Jewish people have even "recognized access to God and saving virtue outside of Judaism, since its own covenant with God bound the covenant-community only."[63]

The Christian community also knows that the ethnic restrictions of the covenant no longer hold, that the covenant ought to include all people. But in our missionary endeavors we should remind ourselves that Christ has already won the victory and that his love is greater than our accomplishments. The hope of the Jewish people can serve as a timely reminder that the wholeness of God's people, though it can be enhanced by our own actions, ultimately depends on God fulfilling his promises, promises which will not return empty.

If the church is the historical agency through which God is remaking the human world, if it is the living organism which connects the historical acts of God with the future establishment of the new Jerusalem, then it is wrong to focus solely on the world's pain and suffering. Even a servant needs moments of festivity and celebration to make his servanthood livable and meaningful. Festivity and celebration encourage us to look forward to the eternal Sabbath, the time of joy and rejoicing. Anticipation of the heavenly glory, as a reminder of God's past acts and of future eschatological perfection, is as important for the church as remembering that we still live in the valley of death and injustice.

Worship, proclamation, and the arts must be expressive of the glory of God. The church misunderstands its servant role when it opts only for multipurpose buildings and folding chairs. A world which is characterized by efficiency, by increasing the capital of its investors, and by a diminishing quality of life, needs to be reminded that we do not live by bread alone. A church which no longer uses art and architecture as forms of remembering and anticipating God's promises has a truncated understanding of the gospel tradition and of the people it addresses. Participation in the glory of God is more than verbal or literary assent. We must give glory to God with all senses and means of expression. While the Roman Catholic church is moving away from one-sided displays of splendor, rediscovering the necessity for proclamation, many Protestant denominations now realize that worship is more than listening to a sermon and singing a few hymns.

Liturgy dramatizes God's saving work in Christ and celebrates the future glory of all the saints. We use liturgical gown, processions, chanted liturgy, and perhaps occasionally even incense to celebrate God's past and future actions, employing our whole being and all our senses. Similarly, in proclamation we attempt to provide a balanced expression of the whole gospel tradition, giving adequate focus on Christ's death and resurrection without exclusively dwelling on the cross. As part of the gospel tradition, the Old Testament is also proclaimed in sermons. We remember with thanksgiving that God has acted in this world throughout all centuries, even before the incarnation of our Lord, and that God continues to do so until at last he dwells in the midst of his people.

Theology has recaptured in this century the significance of an eschatological vision. But the reappropriation of the so-called last things as an essential part of the church's faith still remains. Perhaps the church rightly feels that it is a threatening vision that the seer of the book of Revelation expressed when he said:

> I saw no temple in the city, for its temple is the Lord God the Almighty and the Lamb. And the city has no need of sun or moon to shine upon it, for the glory of God is its light, and its lamp is the Lamb. By its light shall the nations walk; and the kings of the earth shall bring their glory into it, and its gates shall never be shut by day—and there shall be no night there (Rev. 21:22-25).

Even some staunch church members and ecclesiastical administrators may feel uneasy over a vision in which God's presence will replace the churches and temples. How dearly we love the church structures and ecclesiastical empires which we erect and safeguard! But God's saving activity always threatens our security.

Confronted with the fleetingness of time and with our diminishing (natural) resources, the vision of eschatological perfection gains new credibility and urgency. The church betrays its own eschatological vision if in this time of trouble and turmoil it fails to remind us of the goal of all history, when God will be all in all and will dwell in the midst of his people. Such a message proclaimed with vigor and confident hope need not be used as a heavenly escape, as Karl Marx assumed. It can rather encourage us to take the parable of the faithful steward seriously because we know that our Lord, the Lord of all the world, is coming. When the church remains true to its calling, reminding us of this glad news, it can instill hope and courage and a sense of direction in the midst of a confused world. It can become a beacon and a rallying point for the future and a reminder that the powers of darkness shall not prevail.

12

THE MEANS OF GRACE

The means of grace which are administered by the church continually remind the church that it is not a club founded for the advancement of its member's interest nor a political power bloc nor a social service agency. The church treasures and dispenses the gifts of God to humanity, i.e., the means of grace, contained in and illustrated by the expression *Word and sacrament*. It is strange, however, that two of the three important terms just mentioned have no equivalent in biblical vocabulary. Though the term *word* (Hebrew *dabar*, Greek *logos* or *rhema*) is amply documented in the Bible, both *means of grace* and *sacrament* are missing there. Nevertheless, the content meant by these terms is well presented in the Bible.

A. God's Word

When we reflect on Judeo-Christian history we notice that God's Word is encountered there in a multitude of different ways. We hear, for instance, that Joseph is instructed in a dream to flee with the Holy Family to Egypt, we read Isaiah's vision in the temple, and we hear of the speaking of Balaam's ass. This multifaceted description of God's self-communication is analogous to that which we can gather from other religions. But there is one essential point at which we encounter a criterion with which we can distinguish all other religious talk from God's self-disclosive Word. We get a clue when we read in the Letter to the Hebrews, "In many and various ways God spoke of old to our fathers by the prophets; but in these last days he has spoken to us by a Son" (Heb. 1:1f.). God's self-disclosure in the humanity of Jesus Christ enables us to discern *the* Word in the midst of many words and to distinguish those elements in the Judeo-Christian tradition which are merely the incidentals of this history from that which is the Word of God spoken into a particular historical situation. The Word of God which is preserved in the Christian community and which encounters us today in the church's doctrine and proclamation assumes one of three basic functions. It (1) judges and condemns, or (2) it frees and affirms us, or (3) it guides us. The first of these three forms can easily be classified as law, the second as gospel, and the third can be associated with either law or gospel. We should note, however, that the term *law*, as used in the distinction between law and gospel, is not identical with the Law, meaning the Pentateuch, or with the Old Testament. In the same way the term *gospel* is not synonymous with the proclamation of Jesus or the New Testament kerygma. Law and gospel are instead two different functions of the one Word of God which both accuses and liberates. The respective function which they assume depends on our perception of God's word and our reaction to it.

1. *Relation between law and gospel*

The law has basically a twofold function within humanity, a civil and a theological one. According to the civil function, God preserves his creation and prevents its decay and the emergence of universal chaos. This means that the law is known to all people. This view has been held in the natural-law tradition and has received renewed attention today by ethologists who claim that the basic norms of moral behavior are common to all societies, human and nonhuman.

For the law to preserve public peace according to the civil use, it must be known by Christians, Jews, and pagans alike. Such common knowledge is suggested by the New Testament. For instance, Paul writes:

> When Gentiles who have not the law do by nature what the law requires, they are a law to themselves, even though they do not have the law. They show that what the law requires is written on their hearts, while their conscience also bears witness and their conflicting thoughts accuse or perhaps excuse them on that day when, according to my gospel, God judges the secrets of men by Christ Jesus (Rom. 2:14ff.).

Paul does not say here that the pagans know the law in the same way as the Jews to whom it was given directly by God at Mount Sinai. But he does insist that the pagans are aware of the law and must be just as responsive to and responsible for it as the Jews are to the Torah. The pagans do not know the divine will from the Torah but from that which is inscribed in their hearts.

On the basis of Rom. 2:14 Luther claimed that if God had never given the written law through Moses, our human spirit would still know by nature that we should worship God and love our neighbor. From the beginning of the world, Luther argues in his disputes with the Antinomians, the Decalog has been inscribed in the mind of humanity.

> Therefore there is one law which runs through all ages, is known to all men, is written in the hearts of all people, and leaves no one from beginning to end with an excuse, although for the Jews ceremonies were added and the other nations had their own laws, which were not binding upon the whole world, but only this one, which the Holy Spirit dictates unceasingly in the hearts of all.[1]

The natural law is largely congruent with the law of Moses and is to be distinguished from the positive law of a particular country and from the Jewish ceremonial law. Luther does not assert that the natural law is the same as the Mosaic law. Moses is not the originator of the natural law, but rather interprets and clarifies it. Luther therefore can say of the natural law that "it is clearly and well summarized at Mount Sinai and in a better way than by the philosophers."[2]

According to Luther the law inscribed in the hearts of all people is not, however, synonymous with the first or civil use of the law. Since the law is expressive of God's will and since all people are to some extent religious beings, the presence of the law as attested by Rom. 2:15f. also fulfills a theological function. As the eternal expression of God's will, the law is present in the human conscience and continually reminds us of God's will. It tells us that we have alienated ourselves from God and that we have not lived as we ought. However, because of humanity's alienation from God, this second use of the law, the theological or convicting use, is seldom given clear expression outside the Judeo-Christian tradition. Yet, because everyone can know God's will at least in part, there is no excuse for failing to live up to God's law.

When Paul tells us that "law came in, to increase the trespass" (Rom. 5:20), such an assertion sounds strange to our ears. How could the law in this second (theological) sense evoke sin and even magnify its power? Certainly there was sin already before any explicit confrontation with the law. Yet there is truth to Paul's striking assertion. As Jesus shows in the Sermon on the Mount, quite often transgressions against the law are done unconsciously. Thus sin lies dormant. Yet God wants sin to be exposed through the law and to be perceived for what it really is, revolt against God. In this way sin is increased and sharpened through the presence of the law. The more conscientiously we attempt to fulfill God's will, the more the law points out our shortcomings and our immense sinfulness. That which should originally convey God's love and concern—his law—becomes a cause for our despair and an expression of God's wrath.

Paul continues the statement that law increased the trespass by saying, "But where sin increased, grace abounded all the more, so that, as sin reigned in death, grace also might reign through righteousness to eternal life through Jesus Christ our Lord" (Rom. 5:20f.). In his Letter to the Galatians, Paul even states that "Christ redeemed us from the curse of the law, having become a curse for us" (Gal. 3:13). The law thus leads and directs us to Christ. Paul also calls the law "our custodian until Christ came" (Gal. 3:24). As our tutor or governor, as the term *custodian* can also be translated, the law curtailed our freedom of movement until we were finally released into freedom through Christ. Through Christ we recognize that the law is not God's entire Word nor the whole content of the Christian proclamation. The gospel stands alongside the law.

Law and gospel differ in their respective functions. The law meets us as God's Word demanding that something be done and forbidding the doing of something else. It accuses and condemns us because we have failed to live up to God's will. The gospel, however, proclaims that God's will has been fulfilled in Christ. It shows us the God who meets us in Christ and it reveals that he is a gracious God who has forgiven us our sins. Paul expresses this eloquently when he says, "But now the righteousness of God has been manifested apart from law, although the law and the prophets bear witness to it" (Rom. 3:21). God's righteousness has been manifested through the historical appearance of Jesus Christ. Because of him we can now conclude that God desires the redemption of his people and not their destruction.

This gospel of redemption was not first announced in the Christ event, though it comes there to its clearest expression. Paul reminds us that already "the law and the prophets bear witness to it." This means that the Old Testament also testifies to the gracious love of God culminating in the life and destiny of Christ. Karl Barth expressed this insight in his famous 1935 paper, "Gospel and Law." Barth did not intend to reverse the traditional flow from law to gospel but, by changing the sequence, he hoped to demonstrate that "law is in the Gospel, comes from the Gospel and is directed to the Gospel."[3] If we are going to find out what the law is, he claims, we must first of all know about the gospel, and not vice versa.

According to Barth, God's Word contains both law and gospel. Since the law is God's manifest will, we can hear it only where it comes loudly and audibly to us, i.e., in Jesus Christ. "When we see here the will of God being done, when, that is, we see his grace in action, the law is manifested to us."[4] When we perceive God's grace, we realize what the law actually demands. "The law, then, is in the Gospel as the tables of Sinai were in the ark of the covenant."[5] Barth even states that "the law is nothing else than the necessary form of the Gospel, whose content is grace."[6] This reminds us somewhat of Augustine when he defined evil as both a deficiency of the good and a necessary ingredient that helps us to perceive the good ever more clearly. But Barth reverses the argument put forth by Augustine. Now the goodness of the gospel makes us realize our depravity and sinfulness so that we cling to the gospel. Barth even defines the law as the form of the gospel, since it bears witness to the gospel. He claims that the sequence of law first and then gospel is legitimate only if we first look at Christ, who reveals himself through the law as our Savior. When we know that Christ affirms God's valid but misused law, we perceive our shortcomings and flee to God's grace revealed in Christ, who fulfilled the demands of the law. Barth actually proposes the sequence of gospel-law-gospel instead of law-gospel.

Barth has recognized that we gain a clear vision of the law only if we preach the Word of God as law and gospel contained in both Old and New Testament. The sequence of law-gospel may indeed leave the wrong impression that it is synonymous with the sequence of Old and New Testament. But Barth's rearrangement into gospel-law-gospel is even more misleading. It obscures the fact that law and gospel are the same Word of God. One cannot divide God's Word between statements which contain law and others containing gospel. The law or gospel character of God's Word depends on how it meets us, as condemnation or confirmation. If we envelop God's demand in his grace, his Word loses its seriousness and we are in danger of offering cheap grace. We should in this context heed Luther's caution that the proclamation of the law is the indispensable and necessary presupposition for the gospel.[7] Without the law we do not recognize our own deficiency and remain secure and proud of our moral capacity. In this way the law is God's alien work which prepares us to appreciate the gospel as God's proper work. Though certainly opposite in their functions, law and gospel remain the same Word of God.

2. *Guidance for the Christian life*

At the time of Jesus many people understood God's Word as a set of human regulations that assured them that they were righteous before God. Jesus addressed this situation in the Sermon on the Mount and on many other occasions. The same attitude prevails today among many people who are only superficially aware of the Christian gospel. They lead ethically virtuous lives, assuming that this life-style, though short of perfection, will ultimately be met with divine approval. The German poet Johann Wolfgang von Goethe expressed this sentiment very well when he declared in his dramatic poem *Faust*, "Whoe'er aspiring, struggles on, for him there is salvation."[8] Such an understanding of God's guiding Word will ultimately enslave people, since they falsely assume that by obeying the letter of God's Word they can become righteous. People thus become enslaved to ethical principles, such as "the greatest good for the greatest number of people" or "freedom and equality for the underprivileged," instead of responding to the real intention of God's guiding Word. Often these self-righteous attempts establish new barriers of injustice and inequality in their one-sided endeavor to establish an earthly utopia. This means that the law divorced from the gospel easily turns into a self-serving and self-justifying philosophy.

If Christ is the end of the law, as Paul claims, then the law no longer makes demands on the justified nor does it accuse and condemn them. Christ vicariously obeyed God's will for us and he fulfilled the law. But this does not mean he abolished it. The law is still binding for us as God's guiding will. If the law were no longer present for us, we would have to do God's will as by instinct. But such automatic goodness would require perfect saints who are continuously in tune with God.

Out of these considerations Calvin claims that there is a third use of the law. "The third and principal use, which pertains more closely to the proper purpose of the law, finds its place among believers in whose hearts the Spirit of God already lives and reigns."[9] This was also the line of thinking taken by Melanchthon, the Lutheran *Book of Concord*, and the theologians of Lutheran Orthodoxy. As biblical support for this third use of the law (for the regenerate), Calvin adduces texts primarily from the Old Testament. For instance, he quotes the psalmist, "Thy word is a lamp to my feet and a light to my path" (Ps. 119:105) and, at another place, "The law of the Lord is perfect, reviving the soul" (Ps. 19:7).

Certainly, Christians need moral directions and guidelines for their lives. They need to be able to discern God's will so that they can order their lives. Yet, once we are confronted with the gospel, once we understand the full implications of God's gracious gift, our response does not come from pressure or coaxing but instead by being moved to conform freely to God's will. Christians live up to the law not because it is demanded but because they love God and appreciate his righteousness. This means that not even the Old Testament law can be labeled exclusively as law. For instance, the Ten Commandments are not introduced with the summons, "This is what God demands." They begin, rather, with the reminder of what God has done for Israel: "I am the Lord your God, who brought you out of the land of Egypt, out of the house of bondage" (Exod. 20:2). The commandment to love one's neighbor is introduced in a similar way when we hear, "You shall love your neighbor as yourself: I am the Lord" (Lev. 19:18). Because God is gracious, we respond by directing to our neighbor the love we have received. This shows that in the Old Testament God's Word was originally spoken as gospel. It illustrates what kind of a God we have and evokes our response, a response freely given.

Responding to God's grace, the justified seek to know and to do the will of God. They acknowledge the existence of commandments in the Bible and use them as guiding moral directives. It would be potentially misleading, however, to regard these directives as law in the sense earlier described. They do not depict a legal and accusing use of the law but rather an evangelical use of the divine command. They do not originate from the demand "you shall ... in order to ...," but from the offer "you may ... because ...." They are guidelines to help us discern the will of God and not a set of legal devices to assure a righteous life.

In contrast to the fully law-oriented existence of many people, the Christian life is an existence which continually oscillates between two poles. Christians do not suddenly find themselves in the blissful state of the redeemed who are beyond the possibility of sinning. Paul indicates this by his frequent use of imperatives which indicate that redeemed Christian existence remains marked by sin. This existence has often been described as one in which the Christian is sinner and justified at the same time. Being a Christian is not a matter of a single conversion experience at one point in time but necessitates continuous struggle. Justification before God does not induce an ontological change. It is, rather, indicative of God's relationship to us, a relationship we can time and time again endanger by our actions. This does not mean that Christians are sitting on the edge of a sword always in danger of falling off the thin edge. But Christians can and do lapse into sin. God's Word then functions as law once again to drive them back to the gospel. This is one of the reasons why even in the Christian community the proclamation of the gospel alone without the law does not suffice. Because they are justified, Christians live from the gospel, responding to it by following God's will. As sinners, however, they live under the law, oblivious to God's grace. The law then serves to drive the sinners back to the gracious God who once again forgives and encourages them.

The breaking of the relationship with God, however, is never a bilateral action. God is never the one who severs the ties to his people. It is rather the people who turn away from God. This does not mean that the promise of the gospel becomes void once we turn our back on him. God's gracious word always abides. As Christians, however, we do not live under God's thumb. We are called to freedom as sons and daughters of God. Our freedom, however, is a limited freedom. We live in a freedom which is based on a relationship with God's Word. This Word is for Christians no longer characterized by demands which cannot be fulfilled but rather by orders and guidelines which allow us to live in a "responsive responsibility."

All these reflections on law and gospel reveal how difficult and yet necessary a proper understanding of this dialectic is to the Christian message. The Roman Catholic theologian Walter Kaspar recaptured well Luther's insistence on the distinction between law and gospel when he said that the concept of law and gospel "is regarded as the distinctive feature of the Christian faith as contrasted not only with Judaism but also with all pagan religions, with philosophy, ethics, and the like."[10]

3. Confession and absolution

The pronouncement of law and gospel assumes a particular form in the Office of the Keys, also known as confession and absolution. The Roman Catholic tradition considers penance a sacrament which includes the Office of the Keys and the action of confession and absolution. Lutherans however, see it closely associated with the sacraments but do not actually consider it to be one. For instance, in the *Augsburg Confession*, the consideration of penitence is located after Baptism and Holy Communion. In Luther's Small Catechism penitence is placed after Baptism and before the Lord's Supper, indicating a close connection between it and the two sacraments without admitting that it is an actual sacrament. Melanchthon, by comparison, in his *Apology of the Augsburg Confession* states that absolution is one of three sacraments (12.41 and 13.4). In the Calvinist tradition confession and absolution are not considered a sacrament.

While we will not pursue at this point the question of what constitutes a sacrament, it is evident that confession and absolution are intimately connected with the proclamation of law and gospel as the one Word of God. The main passages in the New Testament which undergird the function and Office of the Keys are found in Matthew. For instance, in connection with the word spoken to Peter concerning the rock on which Jesus will build his church, Jesus says, "I will give you the keys of the kingdom of heaven, and whatever you bind on earth shall be bound in heaven, and whatever you loose on earth shall be loosed in heaven" (Matt. 16:19). Binding and loosing on earth means here the power to exclude from and accept into the Christian community. In the Gospel of John this function is no longer restricted to Peter. It is understood in a more theological way in regard to the remission of sins. So Jesus says to his disciples, "Receive the Holy Spirit. If you forgive the sins of any, they are forgiven; if you retain the sins of any, they are retained" (John 20:22f.). That the Christian community, or at least the Twelve, understood themselves to share with Peter in the Office of the Keys is obvious from Matt. 18:18 where the function of the office is extended to a wider circle. Here Jesus says to his disciples, "Truly, I say to you, whatever you bind on earth shall be bound in heaven, and whatever you loose on earth shall be loosed in heaven."

The Office of the Keys is intimately connected with the proclamation of God's Word. This is indicated by the parallel drawn between the consequences of not listening to God's Word and the failure to receive the forgiveness of sins. When Jesus sent out the disciples he admonished them, "And if any one will not receive you or listen to your words, shake off the dust from your feet as you leave that house or town. Truly, I say to you, it shall be more tolerable on the day of judgment for the land of Sodom and Gomorrah than for that town" (Matt. 10:14f.). Because the reception of this proclamation determines life and death, those who are charged with proclamation shall shake off the dust from their feet as as sign that they have separated themselves from those who reject God's Word. Those entrusted with the proclamation of God's Word should make known that this proclamation has eternal significance for their listeners. The Office of the Keys here exists in close connection to the pronouncement of the one Word of God as law and gospel. Those who administer the keys are empowered to make the consequences of God's Word known either by absolving the listeners or by leaving them in their sins. Consequently God's Word is experienced as either liberating or condemning.

Since penance is inextricably connected with the Word of God, those entrusted with the public proclamation of the Word should also be entrusted with the matter of penance. This logic is especially well followed in the Roman Catholic church. Just as there exists a hierarchical teaching order, we encounter here a hierarchical order for those who administer the varying degrees of penance. Yet the Office of the Keys should never be considered purely a juridicial matter but is instead exercised on behalf of the God who issues the Word which gives life or death. Contrary to past practices, the Office of the Keys should not be a convenient means of enforcing ecclesial decisions. Although it is handled representatively, it is done so in the exclusive authority of the Lord of the church and not in the name of the leaders he appointed.

Since proclamation leads to penitence, the church soon realized that the forgiving of sins in Baptism is not sufficient. It is necessary that sins be repeatedly forgiven. This is well expressed in Luther's explanation of Baptism in his Small Catechism: "The old Adam in us, together with all sins and evil lusts, should be drowned by daily sorrow and repentance and be put to death, and that the new man shall come forth daily and rise up, cleansed and righteous, to live forever in God's presence."[11] Confession and absolution must be a daily process and not confined to special occasions when one has committed especially grave sins. This emphasis is also apparent from the first of Luther's *95 Theses*: "When our Lord and Master Jesus Christ said 'Repent' (Matt. 4:17), he willed the entire life of believers to be one of repentance."[12]

Just as a basic question arose about a third use of the law, a similar question emerges here concerning penitence. Is it proper to distinguish between three parts in the confessional process, i.e., contrition, confession, and satisfaction, as the Roman Catholic tradition teaches, or shall we agree with the Lutheran tradition that sees contrition and confession as sufficient (*Augsburg Confession* 11 and 12)? It is significant that in his *95 Theses* Luther rejects only a clergy-imposed satisfaction while insisting that "inner repentance is worthless unless it produces various outward mortifications of the flesh."[13] There is no law which can cover all eventualities and can spell out in each case what kind of restitution must be made. Moreover, since we are unable to reverse history, a sinful act can never be completely undone. Only the God who set history into motion and has it under his control can effect restitution in the true sense. There is no doubt, however, that the one who receives forgiveness needs ethical guidance in order to learn how properly to respond to the grace which has been freely received. Satisfaction or restitution for wrongdoings should never become a new law or a demand, but should be an opportunity to restore that part of God's creation which we have willfully impaired by our sinful actions. Where this opportunity is not grasped, Luther is right when he says that even the most convincing inner repentance is "worthless."

Even as a freeing word, God's Word is not to be taken lightly. God's Word asks for our response as the new beings which we are, a response expressive of our newly restored relationship with God. That God's forgiving Word leads to acts of penitence underscores the utmost seriousness of the penitential process. It might even be necessary that so-called church sanctions be imposed on the unrepentant sinner. Yet sanctions, such as exclusion from certain offices or activities of the Christian community, should always be administered to the benefit of the one being disciplined. The movement of the sinner from law to grace should be the central motivation of such sanctions. Though they should never be administered too quickly, they dare not be considered mere relics of medieval authoritarianism. Ultimately, as an administration of the law, they are a means of preparing the sinner for the liberating gospel. God is a God of grace who does not let sinners run without warning into their self-determined punishment. Instead God disciplines sinners that they might amend their ways and be saved.

B. God's sign

Word and sign are intimately connected. Jesus, for instance, accompanied his teaching with certain signs (usually miracles) and in a similar way the Old Testament prophets often connected their proclamation with certain interpretive signs. While the signs of the prophets varied, depending upon the particular circumstances at that time, the sacramental signs are not options which vary from occasion to occasion. They are symbolic actions which are repeated over and over again and are claimed to be commanded or even instituted by the Lord of the church.

1. Nature of the sacraments

There is still considerable divergence and disagreement in the understanding of the sacraments between different churches and especially among individual believers. Virtually all agree, however, that the sacraments have a sign character. They symbolize something in sign language. Next to and together with the Word these continuously repeated signs are an intimate part of the churches' proclamation and even signs of identity. The *Augsburg Confession*, for instance, states that the church "is the assembly of all believers among whom the Gospel is preached in its purity and the holy sacraments are administered according to the Gospel."[14] But the sacraments are not only signs by which one can identify Christians. They are also expressive of God's will. Thus the *Augsburg Confession* declares that "the sacraments were instituted not only to be signs by which people might be identified outwardly as Christians, but that they are signs and testimonies of God's will toward us for the purpose of awakening and strengthening our faith."[15]

Apart from this common notion that sacraments are important and vital signs of the church, however, there seems to be wide disagreement on the actual essence of the sacraments and even on their correct number. The *Heidelberg Catechism*, for instance, states that sacraments "are visible, holy signs, and seals instituted by God in order that by their use he may the more fully disclose and seal to us the promise of the gospel" (Ques. 66). To the question of the number of sacraments, the commentary answers: "The Reformed Church recognizes only two sacraments: Baptism and the Lord's Supper, those which have been instituted by Jesus Christ" (Ques. 68). The decisive point from which to arrive at two sacraments is their institution by Jesus Christ. Luther too defends the idea of two sacraments by referring to them as "instituted by Christ."[16] When Melanchthon, however, defines sacraments as "rites which have the command of God and to which the promise of grace has been added," he arrives at three sacraments, Baptism, the Lord's Supper, and absolution.[17]

Vatican II does not provide a precise definition of what constitutes a sacrament, but points out their threefold purpose: "The purpose of the sacraments is to sanctify man, to build up the body of Christ, and finally, to give worship to God."[18] Here the sacrament as a tangible sign always relates to the individual. It has a specifying function. As God's gift, it conveys God's grace to the individual and purifies and sanctifies him or her. While in a Lutheran approach the gift character is especially pronounced, Vatican II only implicitly mentions it by talking about the sanctifying purpose. Next to the upbuilding of the individual the community character dare not be forgotten. While Baptism gives the individual access to the community, the whole community gathers to celebrate the Eucharist. Fellowship in the Eucharist usually means fellowship in every sense of the word. Hence there is a need to be attentive in order that the *communio* aspect, the upbuilding of the body of Christ, does not become divided through the erection of barriers which attempt to safeguard one's own community at the expense of excluding others.

Finally the God-directed aspect must be mentioned. The sacraments, especially Baptism and Eucharist, are also celebrated to honor God and to give him thanks for the blessings we receive through the sacraments. In Roman Catholic thought this has been developed through the notion of the Eucharistic sacrifice. This term is at least potentially misleading, since we are unable to give God anything which we have not first received from him. Contemporary Roman Catholic theology has also recognized the priority of God's doing. Yet the thanksgiving aspect of the sacraments should not be forgotten. The "giving praises" to God is a constituent aspect of any liturgical action.

As do the Eastern churches, the Roman Catholic church accepts seven sacraments (Baptism, chrism/confirmation, penance, Eucharist, priestly orders, marriage, and anointing of the sick). The number *seven*, a "holy number," has certainly not evolved merely by historical accident but expresses the completeness of these actions. In order to justify their existence they are defined in the theology of the church as "the seven vital actions of Church in its liturgy which are efficacious for salvation."[19] In this definition the sacraments are not seen as necessary for salvation but as helps towards it. Much more important, however, they are seen more as vital actions of the church than as actions on behalf of Christ.

Karl Rahner picked up this ecclesial interpretation of the sacraments when he declared that since "the Church is of itself the final, irrevocable, eschatologically permanent word of salvation to the world," it is also "the primary sacrament."[20] Since Christ instituted the church, reasoning goes that he thus also instituted those sacraments which are not expressly commanded by texts of Scripture. According to Rahner, Christ instituted the sacraments mentioned in Scripture as part of the establishment of the church. While this mediated origin of the sacraments (by Christ through the church) would relieve us from the task of ascertaining that all the sacraments were actually instituted by Jesus (Eucharist) or at least by the risen Christ (Baptism), it would also leave open the possibility for more or fewer than the seven sacraments specified at Trent. This means that the actual number of the sacraments becomes arbitrary.

2. Historical origin of the sacraments

We might get a more well-grounded approach to the sacraments if we investigate their historical origin. The term *sacrament* in Latin initially had two meanings which have nothing to do with what we today understand by a sacrament. The word could denote a sum of money which two parties in a legal suit deposit in escrow pending the decision of the court. The sum contributed by the losing party was then used for religious purposes. The word *sacrament* could also mean a military oath of allegiance. This latter use seems to have influenced the Western theological meaning of the term. The transition from the military to the theological use is most clearly seen in Tertullian. He refers to the baptismal vows of the Christians, and states: "We were called to the service in the army of the living God in the very moment when we gave response to the words of the sacramental oath."[21] There is no doubt for Tertullian that in performing these sacraments we follow the command of the Lord. It is God who calls us, asking for our response to the promise contained in the sacrament. Thus God binds himself in the sacrament and in turn induces an obligation and response from us.

The Eastern churches preserved for sacraments the New Testament term *mystery*. The administration of the sacraments by the Eastern churches was declared valid by Vatican II. These mysteries, of which Baptism and Eucharist have prime importance, have their source in Christ. In the New Testament, however, the term *mysteries* is not used to denote the sacraments, but primarily the secret (mystery) of the kingdom of God (Mark 4:11f.) and/or the mystery (secret) of Christ (1 Cor. 2:7f.), meaning Christ crucified.

The use of the term *mystery* facilitated perceiving the Christian sacraments in analogy to the ancient mystery cults. The sacraments could be seen as cultic rites in which the destiny of the deity is portrayed by sacred action before the devotees in such a way as to give them a part in the destiny of the deity. Similarly, mysteries promise salvation and allow their devotees participation in the suffering of the deity. The church fathers were not unaware of the danger of confusing or deliberately mixing the Christian sacraments with pagan mysteries. Justin Martyr, for instance, claims that "the wicked devils have imitated in the mysteries of Mithras" the celebration of the Eucharist, "commanding the same thing to be done."[22] Tertullian too, remarks that the devil "by the mystic rites of his idols, vies even with the essential portions of the sacraments of God."[23] It may be understandable that the church in the West attempted to avoid the dangerously loaded term *mystery* by using the term *sacrament*. In so doing, however, the West took over the freight of the military and juridicial connotations, a move which bore the danger of a rather one-sided ethical emphasis on the response to God's grace.

In the East the term *mystery* gave impetus to a perception of the ontological reality of the life into which the sacraments initiate. This may also be underscored by the so-called arcanum (secret) discipline, especially prevalent in the Eastern church between the end of the second and the end of the fifth century. Through this discipline the church attempted to keep secret the administration of Baptism and Eucharist as well as the related doctrines and rites from all except the baptized. For instance, John Chrysostom, referring to the Eucharist says, "Those who partake of the mysteries understand what I say."[24] This emphasis on initiation into the secret of God's action not only evoked a response to God's grace but meant for the initiated a different state of being. The West, less interested in divinization as the goal of salvation, preserved the ontological component of the sacraments only in the insistence upon Christ's real presence in the Lord's Supper and through the emphasis on the incorporation of the Christian into the redemptive drama through Baptism.

Because they point so clearly to the redemptive event encountered in Christ, Baptism and Eucharist have always occupied a central place as sacraments. The other five sacraments were only gradually added. Even today they are not equal to Baptism and

Eucharist. They can at most assume a peripheral position since they are certainly not all necessary for salvation (cf. priestly orders or matrimony). While we cannot concede the truly sacramental character of these additional five sacraments—even Rahner's thoughtful argument regarding the church as the central sacrament does not overcome this difficulty—the redemptive or preserving activity of God addressed in them should not be taken lightly. At the height of scholastic theology Hugo of St. Victor stated in his *De sacramentis christianae fidei* that some sacraments are necessary for salvation while others, although not necesssary for salvation, advance sanctification. Unaware of the future discussion, Hugo distinguished here between sacraments in the proper sense, Baptism and Eucharist, and what the Roman Catholic church now calls sacramentals, namely, rites or items that in analogy to the sacraments attempt to produce certain effects. Augustine's definition, for instance, that sacraments "contain the announcement that He [Christ] has been born, has suffered, has risen" could hardly be used to substantiate all seven sacraments.[25]

The church fathers used the term *sacrament* much more loosely than we do today. For instance, Augustine talked about the "sacrament of Christ's body, . . . the sacrament of Christ's blood" and the "sacrament of faith."[26] Augustine leaves no doubt, however, that a sacrament is intimately connected with the pronouncement of the gospel of Christ. He even called it the visible word: "The word is added to the element, and there results the Sacrament, as if itself also a kind of visible word."[27]

We recall that Luther declared in his *Small Catechism*, "It is not the water that produces these effects, but the Word of God connected with the water."[28] Augustine had anticipated this insight a thousand years earlier when he stated: "Take away the word, and the water is neither more nor less than water."[29] Sacraments are the visible signs of the pronouncement of God's redemptive word. This does not mean, however, that the sign itself that mediates the sacrament should be taken lightly. Augustine makes this point: "For if sacraments had not some points of real resemblance to the things of which they are sacraments, they would be no sacraments at all. In most cases, moreover, they do in virtue of this likeness bear the names of the realities which they resemble."[30] The sacraments are not only visible signs of an invisible grace announced in and with their administration, but they also themselves depict that grace which is announced in them, e.g., Jesus' cross and resurrection.

3. Efficacy of the sacraments

Since the sacraments are the visible side of God's redemptive Word, their efficacy is analogous to the word. The *Augsburg Confession* illustrates this very eloquently when it mentions Word and sacrament in one breath: "For through the Word and the sacraments, as through instruments, the Holy Spirit is given, and the Holy Spirit produces faith, where and when it pleases God, in those who hear the Gospel."[31] The sacraments are powerful instruments of God's grace and should not be administered casually but "according to the Gospel."[32]

Since they are God's means of grace, their efficacy does not depend on the righteousness of those who administer them. The effectiveness of the sacraments and the assurance that we receive God's gifts would always be in jeopardy if their efficacy were contingent on the worthiness of the ministers. To alleviate potential doubts, the *Augsburg Confession* rightly declares, "Both the sacraments and the Word are effectual by reason of the institution and commandment of Christ even if they are administered by evil men."[33] Even when sacraments are administered by heretics they retain their validity. For instance, rebaptisms are a rare exception rather than the norm even in cases where denominations do not recognize each other. As far as possible, however, the church should always see to it that their ministers are examples of faith and conduct. This is done not only to assure right proclamation and administration of the sacraments but to inspire the faithful through the example of their leadership.

Since the sacraments can be effective without being administered by worthy celebrants, the question must also be posed as to whether there is a precondition from the side of the recipient in order to assure efficacy. Two assertions made by the Council of Trent have caused much dissatisfaction in this regard among Protestants. The council declared that the sacraments confer grace "on those who do not place an obstacle in the way," implying the notion of cooperation toward salvation.[34] Yet the council then stated that in the sacraments grace is "conferred from the work which has been worked" (*ex opere operato*). This says in effect that it is not faith that grasps the gift offered in the sacraments but that the gift is automatically conferred through the very act of the sacrament. Catholic scholars encourage us not to interpret this in a crassly mechanistic way. For instance, we hear that "the *opus operatum* does not mean that the sacraments produce their proper effects in an automatic and mechanical way, or by some sort of magic."[35] By the phrase, "from the work which has been worked" we should rather be assured that grace is not mediated in the sacrament by virtue of the personal merits of the minister or the recipient. On the contrary, Rahner affirms, "The *opus operatum* is the eschatologically efficacious word of God."[36] God's Word will not return empty but deliver the promises contained in it.

The question still must be asked what Trent actually meant when it referred to "those who do not place an obstacle in the way." We are told that "the mediation of grace, both in its actual occurrence and in its 'measure' is essentially dependent on the disposition of the recipient (which is a condition, not a cause)."[37] Though one might question whether the primacy of God's grace is here maintained, the *Augsburg Confession* does not totally exclude reflection on the condition of the recipient when it says that the Holy Spirit produces faith "in those who hear the Gospel."[38] Luther even seems to go one step further when he states in his *Small Catechism* that "the Word of God connected with the water, and our faith which relies on the Word of God connected with the water" produces these great saving effects.[39] When we hear regarding the Roman Catholic position that the mediation of grace "depends on the faith of the recipient as he lays himself open and surrenders to the sacramental grace, as also on the intention of the recipient," we notice that the recipient plays a much greater role than in Lutheran thought.[40] Such reflection on the recipients and their disposition is certainly necessary to avoid the idea of a mechanistic and impersonal mediation of grace. A stronger emphasis on the primacy of grace would, however, help to assure the certainty of salvation.

With its strong emphasis upon the attitude of the recipient, the Roman Catholic church seems to come close to certain trends in the Reformed tradition. For instance, Karl Barth, by his forceful renunciation of infant Baptism emphasized human cooperation even more strongly than does the Roman Catholic church. Barth does admit that Baptism without the willingness and readiness of the baptized remains true, effectual, and effective. While infant Baptism must not and ought not to be repeated, it is, however, not correct usage. Barth sees the attempts of Luther and Calvin to justify infant Baptism as unconvincing arguments that cannot suffice without exegetical and practical "artifices and sophisms."[41] He wonders whether the real reason for infant Baptism operative in the Reformers and in the theologians of today is the fear that without infant Baptism the Constantinian majority church would collapse. Even Luther, he says, once confessed that "there would not be too many people baptized, if, instead of being brought to baptism, they had to come on their own accord."[42] Barth, however, does not want such politico-practical questions to decide the theological issue. Since Baptism always demands a response on the part of the baptized, he simply wants "instead of the present infant-baptism, a baptism which on the part of the baptized is a responsible act."[43]

The Reformers did indeed devise all kinds of theories to justify infant Baptism, as we can see in Luther's case. Yet none of these sufficed. In the end it is very clear that for Luther Baptism is totally God's gift. It summons us to faith and its reality and validity do not depend on our faith. According to Luther the same holds true for adult Baptism.

Nevertheless, Barth has touched on a significant point. Our response to the grace offered in Baptism is important. Without this response Baptism is incomplete, unless we grant a mechanistic view of infusion of grace through infant Baptism. Vatican II was therefore very thoughtful when it decreed, "The rite for the baptism of infants is to be revised, and should be adapted to the circumstances that those to be baptized are, in fact, infants. The roles of parents and godparents, and also their duties, should be brought out more sharply in the rite itself."[44] This means that no sacrament, not even infant Baptism, should be administered lightly. If there is no reasonable assurance of facilitating a response of faith (through Christian upbringing), it would be frivolous to administer infant Baptism. Similarly, adult Baptism should never become just a traditional act, but a reasonable assurance of an adequate response should be secured. Even in the case of the Eucharist, an adequate notion and acceptance of the grace offered are minimal expectations for admission to this sacrament.

In cases where these safeguards insuring proper administration cannot be given, as in the case of so-called emergency infant Baptism, we accept Barth's insight that "the power of Jesus Christ . . . is not dependent upon the carrying out of baptism" and do not insist on baptism.[45] Emergency Baptism is much more a pastoral issue, i.e., for the sake of the good conscience of the next of kin, than a theological issue, i.e., for the sake of salvation. From this argument, however, it would be ill-founded to conclude that (infant) Baptism is not necessary for salvation. Since Baptism means incorporation into the visible body of Christ, however, this incorporation would be of such short duration in the case of emergency Baptism, that it would lose its meaning.

In question 74, the *Heidelberg Catechism* deals explicitly with the issue "Are infants also to be baptized?" and affirms without reservation that infants should be included in the new covenant. Under the influence of Barth, however, the contemporary commentary comes to the conclusion that the danger of creating indifference to a confessional stand is greater with infant Baptism than with adult Baptism. There is, however, no clear theological preference for infant Baptism over adult Baptism or vice versa. If we go so far as to base adult Baptism exclusively on the immediate response to God's grace, then the danger is great that it is no longer God's Word which has primacy but our own action.

The proper place for adult Baptism has always been the mission field. In that context the confessional response to God's action can be immediately given. That infant Baptism does not always lead to an actual confession can be gathered from the situation existing in some socialist countries. There it is infant Baptism and consequent confirmation that describes the actual confessional situation, since through govenment repression it deprives the children of many educational and professional opportunities. Adult Baptism, by comparison, would not lead to such "confessional" consequences, since education and professional career are by that time too well advanced. In such a situation adult Baptism might be an even wiser decision to circumvent the desired oppression of believers by an officially atheistic government.

We should always be mindful that Baptism is a sign which God erects and through which he includes us in his salvific covenant. It is not a sign of our own doing. This is also the case with the Eucharist. The Eucharist is in danger of becoming a sign which we erect when we presume to declare altar fellowship with other Christians, i.e., admit them to our Eucharist and vice versa. It is not us, however, but God who has erected the sign of the Eucharist and who invites us to participate in it. He has already declared fellowship with us through his presence. How can we then dare to withdraw this fellowship from others? This leads us to the next point, the sacraments as God's visible presence.

C. God's presence

Baptism and Eucharist are the sacraments of God's visible presence. God addresses individuals and confers upon them the benefits of these sacraments.

1. Baptism

When we first assess Christian Baptism we must start with the initial practice of Baptism in the original context of mission and conversion. Baptism is something which happens to an individual and which that person desires to have performed. It is not done by force, against the will of a person, but voluntarily. The active and passive moods come together in Baptism. For the one who is being baptized, the rite of Baptism is the visible sign and seal of repentance and affirmation of faith. Baptism and oral confession of faith belong together. Christian Baptism has always been connected with the confession of sins, professing that Jesus Christ is Lord, and calling on his name (Acts 22:16). The one who wants to be baptized asks for Baptism and comes to it. The formula *ti kōluei* (what prevents me?), which occurs frequently in connection with conversion Baptisms (cf. Acts 8:36), has juridical connotations and presupposes some kind of examination regarding possible hindrances to Baptism. A later addition to the Western textual tradition within the story of the Baptism of the minister of Candace points in the same direction. After the minister asked, "What prevents me?" the text continues, "If you believe with all your heart, you may [be baptized]," followed by the response, "I believe that Jesus Christ is the Son of God" (cf. Acts 8:37, a verse not found in some ancient manuscripts of the New Testament). A creedal confession in Jesus as the Lord is a necessary part of Baptism (cf. Rom. 10:9).

Decisive for our contemporary understanding of Baptism is what happens to the candidates. Baptism is neither an act performed by the candidates nor by the one who administers it. Since the middle of the second century Baptism has been administered in the name of the triune God. Because of Christ's death and resurrection, Baptism is an act of God. Through Baptism the baptized are given over to the triune God who receives them in grace and calls them into communion (1 Cor. 1:9). This dedication to Christ and reception into fellowship with God is underscored through the outward ritual. That which occurs in Baptism must be seen in analogy to the Old Testament "prophetic symbolism where the action and the meaning are one."[46] Through the water the body is washed and cleansed from all impurities (sins). God forgives the baptized all sins and pronounces them justified and holy (1 Cor. 6:11).

In the original rite of immersion, the death of the Old Adam and resurrection to new life were depicted even more dramatically. Through Baptism the death penalty that has been pronounced over all people is actualized. At the same time, however, through Christ's death and resurrection, there is the demonstration of new life. In Baptism we receive God's grace and are made part of the new covenant. This means that salvation and grace in their totality are imparted to us in Baptism. We become full members of the body of Christ and not just initiates who have only passed the first of several exams. It opens for us communion with God. Thus it is understandable that questions have been raised as to whether Baptism should not immediately lead to the Eucharist and whether the proper place for Baptism is not the eucharistic service. While the second of these questions can easily be answered in the affirmative, the first question needs more detailed discussion, as we will see later.

The grace which God extends to us in Baptism is not contingent upon our faith. If it were contingent upon us, Baptism could be effective only if we agreed to it. Yet God accepts us before we accept him. If we reject God's offer and do not respond to his unconditional grace, Baptism simply lies dormant. There is no magic involved in Baptism that works regardless of what we might do. God's prevenient grace necessitates our response to allow Baptism to serve as an instrument of his saving grace. Since Baptism is constituted by God's gracious acceptance of us and not by our wavering spirit, there is no need to repeat Baptism if we return to him. We can deny God's grace but we cannot negate it. We always remain children of God, regardless of how we behave. Thus there is no need to repeat the baptismal covenant, but only to grasp it anew.

In Baptism God extends his hand to save us. The question put to us is whether we grasp it. While our affirmation of Baptism is important, it is always subsequent to God's initiative and not constitutive of it. The acceptance which God extends to us in Baptism is to be actualized throughout a lifetime. "The old Adam in us, together with all sins and evil lusts, should be drowned by daily sorrow and repentance and be put to death," as Luther reminds us in his *Small Catechism*.[47] The Christian life is nothing but a daily Baptism through which we continuously affirm what God has done for us, so that the new person "should come forth daily and rise up, cleansed and righteous, to live forever in God's presence."

This existential actualization of Baptism, emphasized by Martin Luther, remains an empty phrase without its underlying juridical and eschatological significance. Baptism denotes not only a change of allegiance, from an allegiance to the world to that of God, but a change in identity. A child of this world and of its sinfulness becomes a child of God and of his promises. The naming of the baptized in the baptismal rite indicates that they have become different persons. In the missionary context, for instance, the old pagan names are put aside and new Christian names are assumed. Similarly, in infant Baptism the nameless babies are now given Christian names. That the Christian name often reflects so little of our Christian faith may be indicative of how little we realize that listening to a different tune (i.e., name) serves to express a different sense of belonging. In Baptism we become fully and really children of God.

By becoming children of God, i.e., his sons and daughters, we become full members of his kingdom. The occasional idea held that there is a Baptism by the Holy Spirit which is separate from the Baptism by water would imply that water Baptism is only a symbolic act—though this opinion usually leaves us in the dark as to what it might symbolize—while a later Baptism by the Holy Spirit is God's "real" activity. In this later act the gifts of the Spirit, of which speaking in tongues is often thought to be primary, are understood to be bestowed upon the baptized one. Three points should be remembered in the context of this issue:

(1) Through Baptism we become full members of God's kingdom, i.e., his property. There is no associate membership possible. Our membership either is full or is not at all.

(2) "The external rite of water-purification cannot be separated or divorced from the inner rite of soul-purification."[48] Action and meaning are one and interpret one another.

(3) Baptism in the name of the triune God, Father, Son and Holy Spirit, makes it clear that Christ and the Spirit cannot be separated or divorced. "Any one who does not have the Spirit of Christ does not belong to him," says Paul (Rom. 8:9). Paul also tells the Christians in Corinth, "Now the Lord is the Spirit" (2 Cor. 3:17). Through Baptism Christians become a new creation. They obtain all the gifts which the Spirit will pour out on us, including the promise of new life (cf. also Acts 2:38 and Titus 3:5).

Being endowed with the Holy Spirit reminds us, however, that the Spirit is an eschatological gift. Essentially, it is a witness to and a downpayment on something to come, i.e., the disclosure of the fullness of the kingdom. Thus the eschatological dimension, including its provisional character, its proleptic anticipation, and its expectant longing, dare not be forgotten. Otherwise, Baptism remains a sacrament of this world and a symbol limited to that which one sees. Instead, Baptism opens for us the larger dimension of the kingdom: we become heirs in hope of eternal life. Baptism joins us with all the company of heaven, with Christians past, present, and future. The body of Christ in which we are implanted through Baptism is larger than any one denomination or even all denominations taken together.

Baptism also means incorporation into the visible church. Baptism and local membership in a congregation go together. In contrast to a marriage ceremony, Baptism is always a rite which takes place within the context of a particular congregation. Thus the baptismal certificate is issued by the pastor of a local congregation or a representative. Within the local congregation, but not confined to it, is the arena in which the baptized ones bear witness to their new gifts as children of God. That some gifts are emphasized more than others and that some may even lie dormant for a while, may reflect the needs of the community as much as the special tasks and opportunities of the individual.

Finally, we must reflect on the relationship between faith and Baptism. "He who believes and is baptized will be saved," we read in an appendix to Mark's gospel (16:16). Yet faith is not something that we bring to Baptism as a precondition. The passive mode in which we are offered the good news as a gift always precedes the active mode of acceptance. Even our acceptance, as Luther reminds us, is ultimately not self-wrought. It too is a gift of God. So Luther comments in his explanation of the Third Article of the Apostles' Creed, "I believe that by my own reason or strength I cannot believe in Jesus Christ, my Lord, or come to him. But the Holy Spirit has called me through the Gospel, enlightened me with his gifts . . . in the one true faith."[49] Faith belongs to Baptism in an antecedent, concomitant, and subsequent way. In the confession of faith it precedes Baptism. In the act of faith it relies on the promise of God connected with water Baptism. In a leap of faith it participates in the hope founded on Baptism.

2. Eucharist

The Eucharist is in many ways the central sacrament of the Christian community. The significance which this sacrament has enjoyed from the very beginning can be seen from the fact that the words of its institution are recorded four times in the New Testament. The oldest document which contains the words of the institution is Paul's 1 Corinthians, perhaps dating back to the spring of A.D. 55. When Paul there says, "I received from the Lord what I also delivered to you" (1 Cor. 11:23-25), we notice the claim that these words date back to Jesus of Nazareth and also that Paul himself stands in a line of tradition which predates this letter. The second oldest literary source is Mark 14:22-25 which recurs with minor modifications in Matt. 26:26-29. Finally, there is a fourth source in Luke 22:15-20 which is extant in both a shorter and a longer version. In addition, John 6:51b-59 has often been interpreted as referring to the Eucharist without mentioning it explicitly.

While it is difficult to assign to any one of these references a clear historical priority, it is quite certain that their roots predate the present New Testament sources. Though it is of historical interest to ask whether the words of institution actually date back to the Last Supper which Jesus celebrated with his disciples, the significance of the Eucharist cannot be established by understanding it merely as a continuation of the Last Supper. To obtain a full understanding of the Lord's Supper we must also consider the meals which Jesus shared daily with his disciples and the meals he had with the sinners and outcasts of society. Furthermore, we must consider that we are separated from Jesus' own meals through his death and resurrection. Faith in the resurrected and exalted one, the expectation of his parousia and of the completion of salvation decidedly shaped the celebration of the Christian Eucharist.

Since the Eucharist is the prime sacrament of Christ's presence, the decisive and often divisive question is how this presence should be interpreted. The two poles here are the extreme symbolism of Zwingli and the idea of transubstantiation in the Roman Catholic teaching, with the Lutheran real presence holding a middle position. As the Leuenberg Agreement of the European Churches of the Reformation of 1973 recognized, many of the old stereotypes no longer hold as one reconsiders and reinterprets one's own history and the history of other denominations, and as biblical exegesis leads to new and deeper insight.

The Reformed tradition emphasizes that "although he [Christ] is in heaven and we are on earth, we are nevertheless flesh of his flesh and bone of his bone, always living and being governed by one Spirit, as the members of our bodies are governed by one soul."[50] Though this statement allows for a kind of "sacramental realism," we should not forget that, according to Reformed thought, Christ remains in heaven. Communion with him is brought about only through the Holy Spirit. This does not mean that Christ is present only symbolically in and with the elements. Reformed theologians do assert that we "eat the crucified body of Christ" and we drink "his shed blood."[51]

Lutheran theologians have, by comparison, traditionally emphasized Christ's real presence. For instance, we read in the *Augsburg Confession* that "the true body and blood of Christ are really present in the Supper of our Lord under the form of bread and wine and are there distributed and received."[52] Similarly, Luther says in the *Small Catechism* that the Lord's Supper "is the true body and blood of our Lord Jesus Christ, under the bread and wine, given to us

Christians to eat and to drink."[53] Unlike the Reformed tradition, the Lutheran emphasis on the real presence is not coupled with an equal emphasis on the circumstances of his presence. There is no reflection on the Holy Spirit as the mediator of the real presence or on the difference between Christ's presence in heaven and in the Lord's Supper. Lutherans insist on the ubiquity and ubivolipresence of Christ. This means that similar to God, Christ can be present wherever he wants and he can even be present everywhere at the same time. Lutheran doctrinal documents, however, show a remarkable restraint in pointing out the mode of the Lord's presence.

Over the centuries the Roman Catholic church became more and more specific about the mode of this real presence. At Trent it officially sanctioned the notion of transubstantiation, first declared at the Fourth Lateran Council (1215), and stated:

> By the consecration of the bread and wine a conversion takes place of the whole substance of bread into the substance of the body of Christ our Lord, and of the whole substance of wine into the substance of His blood. This conversion is appropriately and properly called transubstantiation by the Catholic Church.[54]

Christ's presence is here somehow "produced" through the words of institution. Especially in the ecumenical dialogs the question has been repeatedly raised as to what transubstantiation actually means. It is evident that it is opposed to a strictly symbolic understanding of the Lord's presence. It is, however, undecided whether it refers either to a substance in contrast to outward appearance or to a being which underlies all other factors. Thus one could conclude that "a symbolism and transignification" which maintains the realism of Christ's presence is within the limits that the doctrine of transubstantiation describes.

Each of these varying interpretations shows that the doctrine of transubstantiation emphasizes that it is God who acts in the Eucharist by effecting a change in the elements. But it is not a rationalistic attempt to explain the mystery of Christ's presence in the elements. As is the case with the Reformed and the Lutheran assertions concerning the real presence, the problems connected with the term *transubstantiation* show the limits of our theological efforts to explore the mystery of Christ's presence. The same is true for the Orthodox tradition. There too the terms *change, transubstantiation,* and *re-creation* indicate that the elements of bread and wine are inseparably united with the body and blood of Christ.[55]

It becomes clear that with different conceptual tools each of these views attempts to assert the actual presence of Christ in the sacrament. The discovery that we all seek to make the same point about Christ's presence in the Eucharist is exciting and significant. Yet it can also be depressing to realize that the main battle fought through the centuries concerned a word which was not even used in the original Hebrew, or rather Aramaic, namely, the word *is*. We must ever more remember that the Lord's Supper is primarily Christ's own doing. It is his supper, through which he mediates himself to us. As Jesus once shared the daily meal with his disciples and as he had dinner with the sinners and the outcasts of society, so also today he invites us (sinners) as his disciples to gather around his table and enjoy fellowship with him. Yet it is no longer the earthly Jesus who invites us but the resurrected and exalted Christ. Any memorial aspect must clearly remain secondary to the presence of the resurrected and exalted Lord.

Since Christ offers himself and his meal to us, he manifestly demonstrates that God in Christ is not a distant and alienated God, but rather he is present in and with us. Estrangement from God is overcome in the Lord's Supper and forgiveness of our sins and communion with God become visible. The Eucharist, however, is not just a sacrament of individual piety which enables communion between me and my Lord. Certainly Christians are recognized as unique individuals when they have communion with their Lord. But communion always takes place in the presence of other people gathered around the Lord's table. Here the practice of continuous communion mitigates against the *communio* aspect.

The Eucharist, however, is first of all *an ecclesial sacrament*. It is a sacrament of the ecclesial community through which its members are drawn together and celebrate communion with their crucified and resurrected Lord and with each other. Because of their union with the Lord, the individual members should radiate this union to all the faithful, creating and strengthening their bond of unity. Even beyond the individual community, the Eucharist unites all the faithful as the body of Christ and expresses the unity existing among the individual members and communions. Though common communion is often seen as signifying the ultimate union between two churches, we should note that the Eucharist is not our doing, but Christ's. We should not degrade the Eucharist with the triumphalistic notion which makes it a confirmation of *our* unity in Christ. Christ is the main agent and the gift we receive. He invites us to his altar and we cannot claim to invite others to his altar without turning it into an event of our own doing. Since the Eucharist is Christ's we should also expect that our participation in the sacrament joins us closer together as the body of Christ. Wolfhart Pannenberg picked up this notion very perceptively when he stated that the Eucharist is

> the source and root from which the unity of the Christian lives and is continuously renewed. This corresponds with the idea that fellowship in the Lord's Supper need not stand at the end of the process of church union, but it can also be already the present power of Christ on the way towards this goal.[56]

It is as wrong to expect that eucharistic fellowship would magically or automatically create church union as to assume that this fellowship is permissible only when this union has already been achieved. The Eucharist is both expressive of the union already existing and, since Christ is active in it, has unifying character and can properly be celebrated together on the way towards union.

We dare not be more discriminating than Jesus himself. He not only shared his meal with "saints" but he deliberately invited those who were on the outside and the fringes. The frequent notion in ecclesiastical circles that first there should be union, including mutual recognition of the ministerial office, before there can be the sharing in Christ's meal runs contrary to what Christ has instituted. He is the giver and we are the receivers. If we want to safeguard admission to the Eucharist by excluding all "unworthy" people we leave the false impression that only worthy ones can receive him. Jesus himself came not to the righteous, but to sinners and to those who had gone astray. If we exclude each other from the Eucharist, we resemble these "righteous" ones and actually exclude Christ from this meal by turning it into our own supper. Christ's presence should humble us and make us aware that we are all unworthy and in need of his presence to attain the full measure of his grace.

Next to the ecclesial aspect of the Eucharist and, theologically speaking, its actual presupposition, is the *Christological aspect*. The decisive gift of the Eucharist is Christ himself, with all he has wrought for us. This is the main reason why the church has tenaciously insisted that Christ is really present in this meal. Merely symbolizing his actions or remembering his achievements does not suffice. While the sacrament of the body and blood of Christ does remind us and God of Christ's sacrifice on the cross on Good Friday, his presence in the elements is decisive. Through his presence he sanctifies those who partake of the sacrament. If Christ were not really present in the elements, nothing would happen from Christ's side. The Eucharist would then be merely our own meal at which Christ presides only as he does at other meals when we ask his blessing. We would obtain only that which we bring to it. Yet if Christ is present, his sacrifice on the cross is appropriated to us in our consuming of the elements. We receive something which we are unable to obtain on our own, a renewed relationship with God, forgiveness of sins, and the prospect of eternal life.

Christ is not present in the Eucharist as the dead Jesus on the cross but as the living and resurrected Christ who has overcome death. His past sacrifice on the cross is visibly represented in the elements in the symbolic realism portrayed by the words of institution. This sacrifice is appropriated to us in the present, effecting forgiveness and renewal. As the living Christ he also beckons us to look to the future, when this sacrifice will find its completion in a new life.

Since God in Christ accepts the elements of his own creation, bread and wine, he reminds us of the close connection between the salvation provided through his body and blood and the elements of the earth. The earth is God's and is part of his redemptive plan. Christ takes and uses these elements and identifies himself with them. The earth is the Lord's and all that is within it. Salvation has a cosmic referent and is not just an interior, psychological process within the individual.

Christ's presence under bread and wine represents or, rather, reenacts three things: (1) The singular sacrifice on the cross, (2) the singular Last Supper which he celebrated with his disciples, and (3) the meals he shared with sinners and outcasts. Christ's sacrifice on the cross should stimulate us to sacrifice ourselves to God—to rededicate our lives totally to him, including our time, our possessions, and our priorities. The Eucharist is not only a celebration of

Christ's past and present deeds but of our rededication to him. Similarly, as a representation of the Last Supper and of Jesus' meals with sinners the Eucharist should stimulate us to gather in like manner *all* of God's children. We should form a community that shares with each other that which is vital for our lives. The community of the meal should become a community of mutual concern and of looking after one another. This has immense practical and pastoral implications since sharing in the Eucharist can no longer remain a closed rite. It urges us to open our doors in order to proclaim Christ to the ends of the world, to gather those on the highways and byways, and to share this food with those who, together with us, must be fed with the bread of eternal life.

Since Christ's Spirit is called upon (*epiklesis*) in the Eucharist, we are sanctified and renewed through his Spirit. The efficacy of the sacrament is not limited to psychological, group dynamic, or biological results. It is truly metaphysical, opening new life and making us new. As Christ shares himself with us, so we will want to share this new life with others in obedient stewardship and by daily living out his will.

A third aspect of the Eucharist is the *eschatological dimension*. This emphasis has been most sorely neglected since the patristic age. Theologians of the early church called the Eucharist "a medicine of immortality." This meant both increase in personal sanctification and, through Christ's presence, a stepping-stone toward the final goal of his sacrifice, i.e., undiminished union with God. The biblical image of a celestial banquet as a picture of the end-time is foreshadowed in the Eucharist. It is a meal of praise and hope, of victory in principle but not yet in completion. This can be seen in the early church's "Maranatha!" which can be translated either as an expectant shout, "Our Lord, come!" or as a triumphant claim, "Our Lord has come" (1 Cor. 16:22 and Rev. 22: 20) and which is still today part of the communion liturgy. The Eucharist properly bears a festive note of celebration. We look back to Jesus' death and resurrection and celebrate his victory over death, and we rejoice in his living presence when we gather with him around his table. Since neither cross nor tomb could hold him, we can be certain that Christ's final victory is already won.

While we treasure the *vision* of the fulfillment of God's reign in the eschaton, we dare not become enthusiasts who identify his kingdom with a particular ecclesial structure or with a certain restructuring of society. Christ's veiled presence in this meal still needs to be changed one day to the unveiled presence of the returning Lord. As we celebrate Christ's sacrifice we remind God that this sacrifice should not be in vain and that the parousia should not be outstanding indefinitely. On this earth the celestial banquet is celebrated only in anticipation and not yet in fullness. The eschatological dimension cautions against turning the Lord's Supper into a memorial meal. As was the case in the early Christian community, so also today the Eucharist is a reminder that the future fulfillment is still to come. The Eucharist is a down payment insuring that the fulfillment will not remain outstanding. One day God will redeem his promises.

The vision of the eschatological fulfillment can help us to overcome two dangers: resignation over the apparent lack of progress toward the approaching kingdom and resignation over the futility of our own efforts to bring it about. (1) The prospect of the final completion of God's reign in the parousia of Christ relieves us of the awesome burden of having to make ourselves into the body of Christ without spot or wrinkle. We can admit brokenness, disunity and failure, knowing that Christ will fulfill all our half-hearted and awkward efforts in his new creation. (2) The prospect that God will one day dwell among his people, a hope which we celebrate in the Eucharist, will not render us useless or even complacent. The eschatological goal inspires us ecclesiastically to show forth the unity which we share as Christ's body. It incites us ecologically to demonstrate that God is the Lord of all creation who will one day redeem it. And it prods us socially to find ways to extend the solidarity around the table to include every home and nation.

The Eucharist with all its facets (liturgy, actions, symbols, etc.) is the visible presence of divine grace and the lifeblood of the Christian faith. It has individual and cosmic dimensions, ecclesial and social implications, and touches the life of the individual and the life of the church as a whole.

In many denominations the Eucharist is no longer celebrated only twice a year or once a month but it has become the regular center of Sunday worship. This change not only recovers early Christian piety but also reminds us that worship means more than listening to a sermon, singing some hymns, and saying prayers (cf. Acts 2:

42, 46). Yet with this renewed emphasis on the Eucharist the question has been posed as to whether infants should also commune. Infant Communion is a regular practice in Orthodox churches. If Communion is really so important why should one wait until adulthood to participate in it? Richard John Neuhaus put the issue in the proper light when he wrote, "I believe the communing of infants is permissible (to deny that would be to hereticize the Eastern Churches). I am persuaded it is not mandatory and I am not persuaded it is desirable—for reasons theological, pastoral, liturgical, ecumenical, and psychological."[57] The argument for infant Communion is usually advocated in the following way: "If Baptism is the full initiation into the Church, then Communion could follow immediately."[58] Logically, the same argument could be applied to other "sacraments," such as ordination, marriage, extreme unction, etc. Luther, for instance, insisted that through Baptism one is already a priest, a bishop, and a pope. Nevertheless he demanded proper education and call as qualifications for exercising the priestly office. Full initiation does not imply that one should also immediately assume all the privileges of full citizenship in the institutional church. For instance, one does not allow infants to vote at congregational meetings, though theologically we could hardly bar them from exercising this right.

One might be tempted to argue against infant Communion on the basis that this practice was not mentioned until about A.D. 251 when Cyprian wrote of it in *De lapsis*.[59] Such an argument on the basis of a fairly late date could, however, also be used against infant Baptism, since this was not explicitly mentioned either until about A.D. 180, when Irenaeus referred to it. The rejection of infant Communion as a later innovation could then also lead to the rejection of infant Baptism, a move that not many who argue against infant Communion are willing to make. Also the rejection of infant Communion with the argument that it arose with the emergence of infant Baptism as the prevalent practice is unconvincing, since the Western church finally abandoned the former while it maintained the latter.

One might not be wrong in assuming that the reason infant Communion is practiced now almost exclusively in Eastern Orthodox churches is that in those churches participation in Communion is understood as a means toward divinization, the desired goal of salvation in Eastern piety. Thus one should not wait for Communion until adulthood, but start as soon as possible. As the juridical understanding of justification gained more and more importance in the West, there was less and less need felt for infant Communion. It was finally dropped completely in the late Middle Ages. In some ways that may seem regrettable. But even the Eastern churches are not very consistent in their practice. If it is indeed so vital that there be a natural move from the baptismal font to the altar, why is there not more urgency for infants to commune just as often as adults? Perhaps divinization for infants is considered to be more symbolic than real.

Though a recovery of the Eastern notion of divinization would be good for the West in order to balance its exaggerated juridical interpretation of justification, infant Communion might be the wrong move in this direction. As Christians progress in maturity and age, certain rites of passage, such as the sacraments, are helpful aids toward the goal of sanctification. If not on theological grounds, then on pedagogical ones we need to exclude Christian children from certain rites in which they are not yet fit to participate. The introduction of a flexible communion age seems a step in the right direction, removing a barrier and establishing guidelines for Christian life and growth.

It is certainly important that infants participate in the Eucharist as soon as possible. Yet in contrast to Baptism, the Eucharist is not only something which happens to the person (cf. Baptism as incorporation into the community of believers), but there is also a cognitive aspect. Even with Baptism the church insists on confirmation as the public affirmation of what happened to the person in Baptism. Since such a rite is not envisioned or even desirable with the Eucharist, Communion should take place when a rudimentary awareness of the basics of the Eucharist is present. With this awareness, the visible presence of the Lord can be experienced and the sanctification process be inaugurated.

13

THE CHRISTIAN HOPE

The Christian hope is at once the most elusive and, at the same time, the most essential ingredient of the Christian faith. Hope is as necessary for human life as oxygen; if there is no hope one might as well die. Yet an articulation of this hope is most difficult. On the one hand, the Christian hope from which and towards which we live dare not become a dreamboat which has lost touch with the promised reality. On the other hand, the eschatological hope can be expressed with such caution that its lose its convincing power and becomes anemic. Thus the eschatological hope must steer the difficult course between a travelog eschatology which pretends to know more "than the angels of heaven" (Matt. 24:36) and an anemic hope marked by an undue restraint which has lost its saltness (Matt. 5:13).

Since Albert Schweitzer's work at the turn of the century, theology has been dominated by eschatology. This is true not only for theology proper but also for the secular realm of the 20th century, entrenched as it is with eschatological hopes and expectations. The Bolshevik revolution of October 1917 attempted to bring about a classless society in worldwide human solidarity, features of which resemble Old Testament eschatological hopes. Similarly, German National Socialism set out to erect a Thousand Years' Reich and greeted its leader with *Heil!* (meaning salvation), again exhibiting millennial hopes. Yet both of these attempts to bring about the condition of the new world, both the classless society of communism and the Aryan master race of nazism, were not only doomed to failure but stained by the blood of millions of victims who stood in the path of "progress." Similarly, the new person whom Mao Tse-tung wanted to produce in mainland China, heralded by some churches as the dawn of a new humanity, barely survived the policies of its own proponents. The present-day pragmatic socialism in China seems to progress much faster than the highly rhetorical approach of Mao. Even philosophy has not been exempt from eschatological fever. Ernst Bloch's three-volume *Das Prinzip Hoffnung* (The Principle of Hope) resonates with messianic terminology.

There have always been eschatological hopes connected with the Christian faith which in turn became increasingly secularized. We know of the feverish hopes for an early return of the Lord by a large segment of early Christianity. We remember the progress of the heavenly city over the earthly city which Augustine outlined in his *City of God*. We can recall the claim of Joachim of Fiore that we live in the approaching final age, in which he mapped out the successive realms of the Father, the Son, and the Spirit. There have also been intermittent hopes for the end of the world, especially intense at the end of the first Christian millennium, but active also at the time of Martin Luther.

There is an eschatology in every religion, ranging from the hope of attaining Nirvana in Buddhism, to the hope of union with the world soul in Platonic thought, and the entering of the Valhalla in Germanic religion. Even today, when in many countries the power of religious thought is waning, very few people would admit that death is the final end. There is a desire to live on, either in some kind of immortal state, or in one's children, or in literary or scientific achievements. Even philanthropy can be a powerful expression of the fact that we are unwilling simply to fade away. We want to know that we will have a lasting influence beyond death in our will and legacies. Yet there is a big difference between refusing to admit one's mortality and actually being able to overcome it. It is not a matter of how high we can jump, but of whether we will ever be able to escape our earthly limitations. Even a collective feeling that humanity ought not die, a view to which many religious cults in their preoccupation with death and the dead certainly testify, does not endow such feeling with reality. Yet how can we obtain proof that there is a future for which to live and hope? The so-called near-death experiences, which have aroused the attention of many, do not in reality provide new hope. They are deliberately named "near-death" experiences and do not claim to be the experiences of persons who have returned from the confines of death.

In our age, when not only the future of the individual can be snuffed out without warning through a fatal heart attack or an accident, but when the future of the whole human race is at stake through the threat of nuclear holocaust, the idea of survival takes on a new dimension. If there is no future to hope for, either for us or for forthcoming generations, perhaps the attitude Paul quoted from Hellenistic paganism is on target: "Let us eat and drink, for tomorrow we die" (1 Cor. 15:32). It might very well be that the prevalent desire for instant gratification in our society is connected with the haunting feeling that we do not know if we still have a future or for how long. But how are we able to secure a future for ourselves? Is not the greatest liability for the hope proclaimed by the Christian faith that it has proclaimed this message now for nearly 2000 years without coming any closer to its realization? Is not the Christian faith, especially at the end of its second millennium, in danger of becoming a fringe phenomenon both in the traditionally Christian lands of Europe and North America and also among the vast populations of Asia and Africa?

We cannot deny that the direct influence of the Christian faith is on the decline. We should not overlook, however, the indirect influence which it continues to bear as it is plagiarized by secular and semireligious movements. The progressive drive of modern secularity cannot be explained without reference to the linear understanding of history in the Judeo-Christian religion. Similarly, the expansion of communism and its ideals is a secular derivative of the messianic hopes embedded in the Judeo-Christian faith. Moreover, although the old theory asserting Calvinism as the root of capitalism is overly simplistic, there is an intimate connection between the Calvinist spirit of election and the capitalist spirit of the expansion of amassed capital. While the direct influence of the Judeo-Christian hope may be on the decline, its illegitimate offspring may today have a better grip on humanity than any religion or ideology ever had in the past.

Though "new" religions from the East have made some inroads into the traditionally "Christian" West, one should not expect that they will fare any better than the Judeo-Christian tradition. Though they may attract many Westerners due to their novelty, they have no means by which to incorporate a progressive, world-affirming approach into their own worldview. They are in fact helpless in their confrontation with the onslaught of modern secularity, because the progressive spirit, intrinsic to the Judeo-Christian religion, is so foreign to them. If modern humanity wants to accept any guidance at all, that direction must come from the West, in whose midst these messianic ideas first developed. This means that the Judeo-Christian tradition which involuntarily provided the seeds of modern secularity can also provide guidance to the secular spirit which is now void of direction and of deeper meaning and has nothing remaining of its origins except its forward drive. How can the Judeo-Christian tradition, however, provide such guidance if it continues to cling to a hope which for nearly 2000 years has not come any closer to realization?

We should note first of all that the Christian faith is not just a verbal or literary event but rather seeks enactment in the daily lives both of its adherents and of others who come under its influence in a less explicit manner. Friedrich Engels, Karl Marx's collaborator, rightly recognized that in the name of the Judeo-Christian tradition actual societal change takes place.[1] As already mentioned, the Judeo-Christian tradition has deeply shaped the life of the "Christian" West and of many other parts of the world. The concern for the oppressed and the outcasts, the anticipation of the kingdom, the equality of all people—in an intrinsic sense these *are* insights which stem directly from the gospel tradition. Through the transforming power of the Judeo-Christian tradition there takes place a proleptic anticipation of the promised heavenly reality. Yet we must admit that this anticipation is one which is broken and tarnished through human pride and sinfulness; the parousia is still outstanding after nearly 2000 years.

At this point it is necessary to turn our attention to Christ and his resurrection. As Paul emphasized, Christ's resurrection stands as the first sign of the eschatological fulfillment. Since we know that the resurrection of the dead is one of the eschatological events, we know on the basis of Christ's resurrection that the end cannot wait indefinitely. Jesus' resurrection has validated for us the apocalyptic idea of the resurrection of the dead. By anticipating the final fulfillment through his own resurrection, he has provided us the foundation of hope.

A. Resurrection

While we must reject a totally materialistic picture of humanity, it is also unacceptable to search for eternal or divine qualities in us which could serve as the basis for the hope for a gradual purification of an immortal soul. It is certainly proper to distinguish between the material side of human existence and the more spiritual side described by Jesus with words such as mind, spirit, or soul. But this does not mean that the spiritual side is merely an epiphenomenon of the material or that the body is the mere accident of the spiritual. Any divine or eternal qualities which we might have are not connected with the body alone or the spirit alone but with our whole being. These qualities, constituent for our being, are not of our own achievement but are the result of God's life-endowing and life-furthering gift. If anything of us survives after death, it is by the grace of God and not by our own possibilities.

A mere survival, however, as depicted by the Old Testament concept of existence in Sheol, is not a desirable state. Such a concept does not resemble life and it is not an image which allows for personal identity. Other possible images, such as a collective future through union with the world soul or with the All-one, are also not especially enticing because they too devalue the identity of the individual. While we could wonder why the individual needs so much attention, we should not forget that it is exactly the personal relationship with God which is central to the Judeo-Christian tradition. Human beings are relational beings and the forsaking of our relationship with God or with our fellow creatures demotes us to something less than human. The issue is not one of personal fulfillment in an individualistic sense, as perhaps the notion of immortality would imply, but of overcoming our primordial alienation from God and of being able to enjoy forever a perfected relationship with God. Such hope, while it can be proleptically anticipated in this life, can find its ultimate fulfillment only in a new life, in a state of being which is no longer bounded by the restrictions we face in this life on earth. We hope for a fulfillment beyond death in the resurrection of the dead. The hope for our own resurrection from the dead is fundamentally based on the certitude of Jesus Christ's own resurrection.

1. *The resurrection of Jesus Christ*

The first Christian community was certain that Jesus was resurrected from the dead. All of contemporary theology from its conservative wing to the positions of the extreme liberal agrees on this. But as soon as we attempt to explain this observation and ask what it means that "Jesus Christ was resurrected from the dead," many diverse opinions emerge.

The resurrection of Jesus Christ provided the focal point of the first Christian community and has kept the Christian faith alive until today. In making this assertion, however, we cannot point to the resurrection of Christ in an attempt to remove the ambiguity of the cross. Rudolf Bultmann has made it unmistakably clear that the resurrection of Christ cannot be empirically proven as can the historical fact of the crucifixion. The resurrection is an inference drawn from a reading of the facts surrounding this event which can always be arranged to allow for other interpretations as well. Albert Schweitzer, for instance, attempted to explain the resurrection as a psychological phenomenon which occurred within the disciples. While such an immanent explanation has trouble explaining sufficiently how the Christian faith spread as rapidly and durably as it did, we notice that even Paul in his best attempt "to prove the fact" of the resurrection could at most make reference to the faith of others and to the Scriptures (documents of faith). Even if Bultmann overstated his case when he claimed that "cross and resurrection form a single, indivisible cosmic event,"[2] we agree with him that we cannot resort to the one event (resurrection) in order to prove the importance of the other (crucifixion). There remains, however, a decisive difference between the events of Good Friday and those of Easter Sunday. God in Christ acted very differently on these two occasions.

It is also questionable whether the resurrection of Jesus Christ serves only as a means of interpreting the historical Jesus. Admittedly, it was only in the light of the resurrection that the Christian community arrived at the interpretation of Jesus contained in the New Testament. The origin of the New Testament cannot be explained without the "event" which the Christian community called the resurrection of Jesus Christ. But the first Christians did not merely gather to remember that something unique had happened to Jesus. For them the resurrection was both the basis for the present and the promise of the future. This is especially expressed in the title *kyrios* (Lord) which was conferred on Jesus Christ by the post-Easter Christian community. The term *kyrios* was used, for example, in talking about the emperor in the official Roman state cult. It was also used in talking about pagan gods and in the Septuagint it rendered the Hebrew name Yahweh into Greek. In the hymn in Phil. 2:5-11 which describes the salvific mission of Jesus, the term *kyrios* is conferred upon Jesus at the conclusion of his earthly career and implies equality with God: Every knee shall bow and he shall be proclaimed *kyrios*.

This new status is unthinkable without Jesus' resurrection. In one of the oldest creedal statements in the New Testament (Rom 10:9) the confession of Jesus as the Lord runs parallel to faith in his resurrection from the dead; both have salvific character. This equality with God implies cosmic lordship as well as lordship over individual Christians. We remember, for instance, that it was decisive for Paul's call and for his missionary activity that Jesus Christ was Lord. Jesus Christ was designated Son of God *in power* through his resurrection (Rom 1:4). The term *kyrios* signifies the way in which God deals with the world; it expresses his rule over the world. All other powers and "lords" are derivative and secondary. Only Jesus Christ's lordship is unconditioned and all-pervasive.

The resurrection of Christ must also be seen in the context of God's ongoing creative activity. The Bible suggests in many places that God's salvific activity occurs in analogy to God's creative activity in the beginning. For instance, Second Isaiah, the book which proclaims salvation as offered through the sacrifice of the servant of Yahweh, connects the creation in the beginning with salvation as the goal of history (cf. Isa. 42:5; 44:6; 45:8). In its opening sentences the Gospel of John also sees the coming of Christ in the perspective of the creation in the beginning. Analogously, we discover also a clear correspondence between the appearance of the first Adam and the appearance of Christ as the last Adam (Romans 5).

This understanding of creation does not mean that the resurrection opens for us a way to return to some ideal past. Such a cyclic view of history, however, is basic in most religions and philosophies: after a new beginning the wheel of world history simply repeats the previous cycle. The very opposite, however, is indicated by Paul when he says, "For in him all things were created, in heaven and on earth, visible and invisible, whether thrones or dominions or principalities or authorities—all things were created through him and for him" (Col. 1:16). Everything is created toward Christ. When Paul calls him the first-born of creation (Col. 1:15), he wants to emphasize that Christ stands both at the beginning of creation and is also the goal toward which creation moves.

Christ as the goal toward which creation moves requires a reconsideration of the Fall of humanity and of our sinful state. The Fall of humanity is not a descent from a God-created goodness to some kind of lower-level sinfulness. The Fall is instead the initial denial of the Christ in a line which extends from the original creation to its final fulfillment. Each of our sinful acts is a reaffirmation of this initial denial and thus a rejection of God's plan for us and of his redemptive act in Christ (cf. Heb. 1:1ff.).

God is continually with his creation, even in its alienated or fallen state. He is not a deistic God who is far beyond watching in a detached manner the predetermined course of the universe. God remains fully involved in his creation. Immediately following the Fall, in an act of compassion, God provided the first humans with necessary clothing (Gen. 3:21). The church's attempt to find in the words of the curse a primal gospel (Gen. 3:15) and the endeavor of the gospel writer Luke to trace the ancestry of Jesus back to Adam and finally to God himself, show that God's acting in the beginning and his acting in Jesus Christ are perceived as a unity. Paul attests to this also in pointing to Christ as the antitype of Adam. Through Christ the law is superseded by grace, sin by justification, and death by life.

Death is not superseded by life in order to restore the original state. For the resurrected Christ death is no longer a possibility. Jesus Christ's resurrection does not mean the fulfillment of a restorative process that started with the Old Testament covenant community. His resurrection is the first point of a *new* creation, a creation in perfection. God's creative act in Christ's resurrection goes beyond this present creation. It witnesses to a new creation which will replace this present creation at some specific point. This is where the question of the empty tomb becomes important, not as a proof for the historicity of the resurrection of Jesus Christ, but as an indication that this present creation has no permanence, that it will be replaced by and transformed into something new. Not even the first Christian community used the story of the empty tomb as a proof of Christ's resurrection (cf. Matt. 27:62—28:15, esp. 28: 15). This inauguration of the new creation inspires in us the hope of being incorporated in it.

2. Christ's resurrection and our own resurrection

The Christian belief in the resurrection does not result from a gradual development of the idea of resurrection within the Judeo-Christian tradition. The Christian belief in the resurrection is basically Christ-centered. The idea of the resurrection from the dead was accepted by many Jews, by Jesus, and by the first Christian community. But the resurrection of Jesus does not simply verify the validity of this earlier apocalyptic idea. For instance, Paul in 1 Corinthians 15 does not refer to a common agreement regarding the idea of a resurrection; rather, he refers to and explains the Christian tradition concerning Christ's resurrection. This means that Christ is not only the first of the resurrected, as could be expected according to apocalyptic thought, but that he is also the presupposition of our own resurrection. Paul drives this point home very clearly: "If Christ has not been raised, then our preaching is in vain and your faith is in vain" (1 Cor. 15:14). Christ's resurrection is the presupposition of the existence of Christians as a community of people who participate proleptically in newness of life and is the foundation of Christian hope for the final realization of this new life.

The implications of Christ's resurrection go even further, however, when considered in the context of apocalyptic hope. In relation to the apocalyptic view of history with its conviction of a resurrection at the end of time, the resurrection of Jesus Christ must be understood as the anticipation of the end. That the disciples could recognize their familiar leader once again in their post-Easter experiences is something entirely beyond the possibilites of this life, and that they called the reality behind these experiences "resurrection" can be satisfactorily explained only in the context of apocalyptic hope. Otherwise they could have been interpreted as encounters with a spirit or a phantom (cf. Luke 24:37).

In the context of apocalyptic hopes and expectations the disciples affirmed that in the resurrection God had verified the authority which Jesus had claimed in his earthly life. They also realized that in the destiny of Jesus the end had occurred in proleptic anticipation, and that God had fully disclosed himself in Jesus, the Lord. In other words, through the resurrection of Jesus Christ the apocalyptic idea of a common resurrection is transformed into the Christian hope of resurrection. Thus the New Testament proclaims Jesus not only as "first-born from the dead" (Col. 1:18), but also as the one in whom we shall be united "in a resurrection like his" that we too "might walk in newness of life" (Rom. 6:4f.). We also trust in the God who "raised the Lord and will also raise us up by his power" (1 Cor. 6:14). Apocalyptic ideas do provide background material for a full understanding of the implications of Christ's resurrection. Yet our hope for the resurrection is not based on these ideas but depends solely on Christ's resurrection.

3. Resurrection of the body

The hope for our resurrection is expressed in the Apostles' Creed with the phrase that we believe "in the resurrection of the body." The question immediately arises as to what kind of body this might be. But the issue gets even more confusing when we notice that in the original Greek and Latin texts the word for body actually denotes "flesh" (*sarx* or *caro*). Moreover, if we try to claim in a literalistic manner that the creed contradicts the Bible where Paul states, "Flesh and blood cannot inherit the kingdom of God, nor does the perishable inherit the imperishable" (1 Cor. 15:50), we only add to the confusion.

Resurrection should not be considered in analogy to a strictly biological revivification, similar to what the biblical witnesses tell us about the young man in the village of Nain (Luke 7:15) or about Lazarus (John 11:44). If we attempt to think of resurrection along strictly biological lines, we encounter at once the problem of bodily identity, i.e., the question whether we would have to share elements of our bodies with others since through natural decay and the intake of food products we might easily incorporate elements into our own bodies which once belonged to other people. Second, the resurrection of a body similar to our present one would actually mean a continuation of the same limitations and tensions to which we now are subjected. Such a resurrection would stand in stark contrast to Christ's resurrection, for he was resurrected as a new creation with different possibilities than those he possessed before. When the early church included in the creed the belief in the resurrection of the "flesh," it did not intend to create these problems. It was instead trying to exclude the concept of a docetic, spiritualistic resurrection in Greek or Gnostic fashion. It is not the soul or some inner divine spark that lives on in eternity; we ourselves are resurrected. Such a resurrection is expressed in the idea of bodily resurrection.

In popular Greek the word *sarx* did not just mean flesh but also body. A bodily existence was thus conceived of as a real existence, in contrast to an existence encountered in a dream or in art. This is also what the resurrection of the body wants to affirm today. Resurrection is not a paranormal occurrence in analogy to occult phenomena or to hallucinations but a reality involving our whole being.

Death is not our final destiny. The resurrection which takes place at the parousia of the Lord includes everyone—with no exceptions. It is as wrong to say that those who are excluded from eternal joy will not be resurrected as to assume that the eternal judgment coincides with physical death. There is no escape from God since God, who is not confined to this life, is on both sides of death. Otherwise the last judgment loses its importance and simply becomes God's acceptance of those who are resurrected. Such a belief, of course, runs counter to the emphasis on the final separation of humanity (cf. the parables of the kingdom, especially Matthew 13). We must also affirm that this universal resurrection will be a resurrection in personal identity. If the one who is resurrected is not the same one who dies, redemption or damnation of that person becomes meaningless. Resurrection means, however, that for the one who is bound to die, God will provide that same one a future above and beyond death. Personal identity, like the ego, cannot be divided into parts; thus we cannot say that only part of me will be resurrected.

The question as to whether there will be different stages of resurrection seems almost speculative. The seriousness of our decision as we are confronted with the gospel and the seriousness of the final judgment suggest that the resurrected will enter at once into a never-ending immortal state. Apocalyptic ideas that first the dead will be resurrected in an unchanged way (i.e., so that they can be recognized), and that only then will they be condemned or accepted and enter into the state which they deserve (2 Baruch 50f.) seem to lie beyond the interest of the New Testament. When Paul, for instance, suggested that "the dead will be raised imperishable, and we shall be changed" (1 Cor. 15:52b), he expected that he himself would still be alive when Christ would return, and that he, together with other Christians, would be transformed as part of the new creation. Furthermore, even when Paul mentioned the dead, he seemed to talk only about deceased Christians and not about the dead in general (1 Thess. 4:13f.). The idea of a sequential progression—first a universal resurrection, then a final judgment, and then the respective transformation of those accepted and rejected—would introduce once again the concept of time, which is not applicable to anything in the hereafter.

We turn next to the content of our hope of the resurrection of the body. To conclude, from passages such as "in the resurrection they neither marry nor are given in marriage, but are like angels in heaven" (Matt. 22:30), that the state of the resurrection is an asexual state is a gross misconception; it indicates the desire for a travelog eschatology, which seeks to map out the beyond in minute detail. Paul emphasizes that the mortal cannot inherit the immortal, nor the perishable the imperishable. Resurrection is not a continuation of our present life, not even on a different level. Our present life, with its anti-Godly desires, must totally perish. It is the "otherness" of the resurrection which makes it so difficult to talk about it. Paul talks about the resurrection by contrasting it with our present conditions. Perishable/imperishable, dishonor/glory, physical/spiritual, and mortal/immortal are some of these antitheses he uses to show that nothing is exempt from this fundamental change (1 Cor. 15:42-54).

Yet if this change is so drastic, is not the "I" who will be resurrected so different from the "I" who died that we shall face a tremendous identity crisis? We underestimate the radicality of the resurrection if we hold the idea that the resurrection implies no radical change in identity and personality. After all, we are looking forward to a *new* creation. Even now our personality undergoes steady change as we advance from childhood to adolescense, maturity, old age, and senility. Though these changes can sometimes cause considerable identity crises, we remain nevertheless the same person.

4. "Between" death and resurrection

When death terminates our individual lives and resurrection is our destination beyond death we cannot but wonder what happens "between" these events. We observe that not everybody dies at the same time and that death does not coincide with the universal resurrection for which we hope. What is our destiny "between" our death and the common resurrection of which we will be part? Or do we perhaps face an individual resurrection?

Paul also encountered these kinds of questions when people asked him concerning those who had already died. Paul did not comfort these people by elaborating on the ideas of immortality, reincarnation, or purgatory, ideas which were certainly known to them. Instead he pointed out that there is no preferred state. Whether they are still alive at the return of the Lord or whether they have been dead a long time, their destiny lies in their confrontation with the returning Lord (1 Thess. 4:15). For us too it is neither necessary nor legitimate to speculate on an intermediate state between death and resurrection. This becomes especially evident when we consider that time is only a this-worldly category.

Augustine emphasized that time is an indication of transitoriness and is inextricably connected with this world. Time needs a basis of comparison because time is observable only through changes in objects. God created this temporal world, and through the transitoriness of this world we are able to observe time.

In considering God, however, one has to do away with time. Only for us is there time and hour, whereas for God everything occurs in the eternal now. God is co-temporal to all possible and actual time constellations. He who created the world and with it time and transitoriness is not subject to change but equipresent in each possible and actual change. In other words, past, present, and future are equally present before God. Time is part of God's ordering of creation (cf. Ps. 102:25-27 and Heb. 1:10-12). This means that time is an inadequate category to describe God and God's future beyond this material and space-bound world. When we seek to talk about that which is "between" death and resurrection and do not just mean the biological decay of the physical body, then the category of time as a measure of change is inadequate. Rather we must talk about the end or fulfillment of time or about eternity.

In talking about eternity we have to refrain from equating eternity with infinity, especially in its scientific sense. When used theologically, eternity denotes the dimension of God and in talking about it we encounter the same difficulties as we do in talking about God. Eternity belongs entirely to God and stands in contrast to the time of our world, which is limited by the creation in the beginning and by consummation in the end. In Greek philosophy, however, eternity is usually understood as timelessness, a state where there is no day, no month, no year. Especially Plato in his *Timaeus* thinks of eternity as the ideal state and of time as only a faint copy. Yet the Bible does not proclaim a distant eternal God faintly reflected in this world but a living God who gives time its direction. In the Christian understanding, time is on its way from creation via redemption to perfection.

When time has finally been completed and perfected through the redeeming power of God, its life-impairing characteristics will have been overcome. Of course, such completion and perfection of time is not due to the fact that there is eternity but that there is God. Eternity is an empty term apart from its reference to God. Only because there is a God—a God not of the dead but of the living, a God who does not want the death of the wicked but that the wicked be saved and live—only because there is such a God can we hope for the perfection of time and for eternity. Eternity as the sphere of God (and thus also of Christ) endows time with meaning and direction. In pointing to the fulfillment of time, eternity does not indicate a final monotony but an active, unrestrained, and unlimited participation in a new world which is in full harmony with the living God.

This leads us to the next question. When will this fulfillment be reached? At death or some "time" after? The Bible does not seem to give us a clear answer to the question of the point at which the individual attains the final state of fulfillment. At times death is depicted as leading to a final state and at other times as leading to a transitory state. In the New Testament the dead are often referred to as those who are asleep or as those who have fallen asleep (1 Cor. 15:20; Luke 8:52; 2 Peter 3:4). In this understanding they will sleep until judgment day and then they will be resurrected. This implies that at death they have not yet reached the final goal, heaven or hell, but are still waiting for it.

Other New Testament passages, however, indicate that with death some kind of finality is reached. For instance, when Jesus tells the parable of the rich man and Lazarus, he mentions that both entered their (preliminary) destinations, Abraham's bosom and Hades, immediately after they died (Luke 16:19-31). Jesus also promised the one criminal on the cross, "Today you will be with me in Paradise" (Luke 23:43).

In the Gospel of John we can notice an attempt to bridge the dichotomy between transition and finality. We hear Jesus say, "Truly, truly, I say to you, the hour is coming, and now is, when the dead will hear the voice of the Son of God, and those who hear will live." Then, almost in the same breath, the comment is made, "For the hour is coming when all who are in the tombs will hear his voice and come forth, those who have done good, to the resurrection of life, and those who have done evil, to the resurrection of judgment" (John 5:25, 28f.).

The New Testament writers realized that one's response to the confrontation with Jesus and his message determine the final outcome of life, either acceptance or rejection by God. But this did not mean that those who lived in accordance with the incarnate word of God would at one point leave this life and immediately enter into heaven. They knew that at the end of their earthly life all had to die. When they suggested that at death one fell into a sleep, this was not an attempt to compromise Jesus' decisive message of the immediacy of the eschaton. Rather they tried with this image to maintain both a sense of finality and of transition. They encountered in Jesus Christ God's final word and action which already allowed them to participate proleptically in the new creation; they observed in death an interruption of this proleptic participation which pointed to something beyond death. Whether finality or transition, one thing was clear to them: there is no vacuum after death.

Luther struggled with this same problem. He was convinced that the "between" following death would not be a neutral state but would already presuppose our being accepted or rejected by God. It would not be the final state itself but would still anticipate the final fulfillment and perfection of the resurrection. Often Luther "described" this state as a deep sleep without dreams and without any consciousness and feelings. He confessed that he often had tried to observe himself when he fell asleep. But he never succeeded. He noticed that one moment he was awake and then, suddenly, he woke up again. So it is with death: "As one does not know how it happens that one falls asleep, and suddenly morning approaches when one awakes, so we will suddenly be resurrected at the Last Day, not knowing how we have come into death and through death."[3] On another occasion he says, "We shall sleep until he comes and knocks at the tomb and says, 'Dr. Martin, get up!' Then in one moment, I will get up and I will rejoice with him in eternity."[4]

Actually Luther here confesses that we do not know much about the state between death and resurrection. Endowed with a sound and natural curiosity, Luther would have liked to find out where and how we exist between death and resurrection. But he realized that in staying as close as possible to God's self-disclosure as reflected by the biblical witnesses there is not much we can say about it.

In his restraint Luther differed decisively from the tradition out of which he came. The church, for instance, had rejected the notion, once adopted in some sermons by Pope John XXII, that the human soul sleeps after death and does not enjoy the beatific vision until judgment day. In an edict of 1336, Benedict XII, the successor to John XXII, declared that the soul of the just already enjoys the beatific vision.[5] This face-to-face vision of the divine essence and the resulting enjoyment exist continuously "and will continue even up to the last judgment and from then even unto eternity." The souls of those, however, "who depart in actual mortal sin immediately after death descend to hell where they are tortured by infernal punishments, . . . nevertheless on the day of judgment all men with their bodies will make themselves ready to render an account of their own deeds before the tribunal of Christ."

Although it would be one-sided to absolutize such a passage as Rev. 6:9 and conclude that the souls of the deceased who were faithful will remain under the altar of God until judgment day, is it not just as one-sided to assume that we can define our destiny between death and resurrection as beatific vision or infernal punishment? The final judgment then becomes merely a reaffirmation of what had already happened in death and loses its significance for our final destiny. The New Testament is much more reluctant definitively to assert what happens to us between death and resurrection. This tension within the New Testament reflects the difficulty we encounter when we attempt to "define" this intermediate state.

Contemporary Roman Catholic theologians no longer insist on an elaborate doctrine of purgatory. They understand that dogmatic definitions of the church want to safeguard the insight that although death is the final end of this life, it is not the end of human life altogether. Since the New Testament refrained from defining definitively how to talk about what takes place after death, various conceptualizations are available to theologians. Michael Schmaus, for instance, suggests two options: The first is the traditional concept of the immortality of a spiritual soul which will continue to exist. He concedes that this option tends to devaluate the significance of the resurrection. The other option, which he favors, holds that humanity enters at death into completion, and therefore the change to a new life occurs in death. Schmaus notes that this concept in turn faces the issue of reconciling many individual "resurrections" (at death) with the final universal resurrection.[6]

Is it, however, necessary to assume a distinction or even tension between an individual resurrection and the final universal resurrection? We do not hope for a "between" state but we hope and believe in "the resurrection of the body and the life everlasting." We also realize that death is not only the border of this life but the border of time itself. Beyond death there is no diminishing, aging, or increasing; there is only God's eternal presence. Of course, we see people encountering their own individual deaths at different points in time and we know that the last judgment, which provides the end of all possible and actual time, does not coincide with these different points in time. If it did, we would have to affirm an individualized last judgment, occurring at many different points, whenever someone departs from this life.

Since people cross the borderline of time at different points, we can use New Testament imagery and say that the dead "sleep" until judgment day. We also know that in God all time distinctions vanish. For God there is no sooner or later, not even a too late. In God's eternal presence there is no distinction between past, present, and future. This distinction exists only for us as time-bound creatures and not for the Creator. When we cross the borderline of time at death we encounter God's eternal presence. We are then coeternal not only with God but also with all other human beings. Regardless of when we cross this line we appear on the "other side" at the "same moment" as everyone else. Thus the passing from life into death will result in God's eternal judgment.

B. The end of history

The end of history and therewith the end of this world are intimately connected with the notion of a judgment day. For many, however, the thought of a final judgment smacks of medieval authoritarianism. Modern emancipated humanity revolts against the scene depicted above many medieval church portals—Jesus Christ sitting on his throne in judgment over humanity and separating the evil from the good.

To assess the credibility of such a notion it is good to remember that judgment is not totally foreign to our own experience. (1) Every year there is the draft of the professional sports teams and the decisions made by college athletic teams regarding those to be accepted or rejected, a decision which, although not deciding any ultimate future, clearly shapes the earthly future of those affected. Also in our own educational and professional experience judgment in terms of grades and performance evaluations is everywhere present. (2) We must also note that the final judgment is not just a matter of arbitration, since by our own efforts no one would be able to pass the narrow gate to acceptance. To be counted among the accepted is possible only through God's undeserved grace. The judgment reveals the immense difference between our world and the way we live in it and the new world to come. The last judgment must thus be seen in the larger context of the transformation of our present world.

1. Consummation of the world

The last judgment as a universal event demands the consummation—or at least transformation—of the categories of time, space, and matter, i.e., of the world as we know it. This is also the conviction of the New Testament:

> Immediately after the tribulation of those days the sun will be darkened, and the moon will not give its light, and the stars will fall from heaven, and the powers of the heavens will be shaken; then will appear the sign of the Son of man in heaven, and then all the tribes of the earth will mourn, and they will see the Son of man coming on the clouds of heaven with power and great glory (Matt. 24:29f.).

2 Peter has even greater detail: "But the day of the Lord will come like a thief, and then the heavens will pass away with a loud noise, and the elements will be dissolved with fire, and the earth and the works that are upon it will be burned up" (2 Peter 3:10).

Inquisitive spirits have always tried to investigate how such a consummation might be possible and modern scientific insights have paved the road for many speculations. For instance, the possible collision of our earth with other planets or planetoids would certainly darken the sun and the moon for us and might perhaps lead to the extinction of life on earth. A cosmic nuclear reaction could dissolve the elements with fire, and if militarists would employ all of the presently available nuclear "overkill" they could usher in the eschaton on their own. Also the all-too-real prospect of the global pollution of earth could lead to the end of earthly life. Teilhard de Chardin has observed, however, that such a cosmic disaster would affect only part of the universe and not the universe as a whole. In a parallel way a final heat death through an equilibrium of all energy levels would not lead to the consummation of this world but only to the end of life within it. At best, science can tell us that our universe does not possess eternal life. But it cannot show us that or how our universe will be consumed. By its very nature science works within the categories of space, time, and matter, and this means with the universe in which we live. The consummation of the world, however, does not just refer to existence *in* the universe; it refers to the very existence *of* the universe.

According to the New Testament, the consummation of the world is not primarily destructive. It is rather the incorporation of the universe into the creative and transforming act of Christ's resurrection. Paul has expressed this clearly in his Letter to the Romans: "The creation waits with eager longing for the revealing of the sons of God" and will be "set free from its bondage to decay," and we ourselves wait for adoption as God's children, "the redemption of our bodies." This is no vague or uncertain hope, because "he who raised Jesus Christ from the dead will give life to your mortal bodies also "(Rom. 8:19-23).

Salvation in the eschaton pertains to our whole being, to the whole cosmos, and to the whole creation. It is a salvation described as redemption from transitoriness. When the adoption we received in Baptism is made manifest, then, not merely in anticipation but in reality, we shall no longer be subjected to transitoriness. Consummation of the world means perfection and completion. It is the completion of time and the perfection of the limiting forms of space, time, and matter.

A preview of this new world can be gathered from the epiphanies of the resurrected Christ. The biblical witnesses tell us that the risen Lord was no longer limited in time, space, and matter. The material and spatial bounds of a closed room or of hunger could no longer confine him, although he could make use of them by appearing in a room or eating. In a similar way, he was no longer bound to the transitoriness of time; he could appear sooner, or later, or in the present. The perfection of the forms of this world also means the elimination of the anti-Godly distortions of this world, e.g., of sin, destruction, and death. Again this is shown in the resurrected Christ who is beyond the possibilities of sinning and of dying.

Whenever we talk about the new world to come we must point to Christ and his resurrection because "all things were created through him and for him" (Col. 1:16). There is no other goal of creation than Jesus who as the Messiah enabled the creation to move toward this goal. The consummation is thus the disclosure of the new world which has been enabled by and has already started in the resurrection of Jesus Christ. Martin Luther, in his picturesque language, expressed the point of the consummation very well when he said:

> This world serves for God only as a preparation and a scaffolding for the other world. As a rich lord must have a lot of scaffolding for his

house, but then tears the scaffolding down as soon as the house is finished, ... so God has made the whole world as a preparation for the other life, where finally everything will proceed according to the power and will of God.[7]

2. Final judgment

Everybody wants to be saved, but very few are willing to accept judgment as its prerequisite. H. Richard Niebuhr's famous phrase about 19th-century American liberalism that "a God without wrath brought men without sin into a kingdom without judgment through the ministrations of a Christ without a cross"[8] is a vivid description of humanity in general. We desire heaven but we do not want to accept that the only way to heaven is through judgment. The New Testament, however, in all its witnesses indicates that the only way to enter the new world is through judgment. The consummation of the world does not mean evolution or revolution but means the parousia of the Lord and the final judgment.

"For the Son of man is to come with his angels in the glory of his Father, and then he will repay every man for what he has done" (Matt. 16:27). "When the Son of man comes in his glory, and all the angels with him, then he will sit on his glorious throne. Before him will be gathered all the nations, and he will separate them one from another as a shepherd separates the sheep from the goats" (Matt. 25: 31f.). "For the Lord himself will descend from heaven with a cry of command, with the archangel's call, and with the sound of the trumpet of God" (1 Thess. 4:16). "We must all appear before the judgment seat of Christ, so that each one may receive good or evil, according to what he has done in the body" (2 Cor. 5:10). "And I saw the dead, great and small, standing before the throne, and books were opened. Also another book was opened, which is the book of life. And the dead were judged by what was written in the books, by what they had done" (Rev. 20:12). The imagery of these New Testament citations, which could easily be multiplied, certainly betrays Old Testament and Jewish apocalyptic influences. The language is that of a past age and need not necessarily be reiterated as such in our time. But the intention of these passages is nevertheless clear: there is a final judgment.

The final judgment has often been conceived of as the great awards day, especially by those adhering to the chiliastic hopes of a 1000-year rule over, and at the expense of, others. Yet the final judgment is not a judgment on the basis of our own merits but of our response to God's grace which he has extended to us in Jesus Christ. We are not awarded a certificate of loyalty because we just happened to be on the right side at the right time. Such cheap grace neglects our wrongdoings. Voltaire was wrong when he mocked that God would forgive because that is his job. Paul caught the seriousness of the final judgment when he cautioned, "For whatever a man sows, that he will also reap" (Gal. 6:7). Our Lord will surely take into consideration each of our individual situations and judge to what extent we have attempted to respond to his promise and to the exemplary life-style he has shown us through his earthly sojourn.

At judgment we will not all be measured by the same standards but rather according to our possibilities. "Everyone to whom much is given, of him will much be required; and of him to whom men commit much they will demand the more" (Luke 12:48). We are called to measure up to our own potential and not to any other ambiguous standard. Since this judgment will concur with the parousia of the Lord, it becomes clear that Christ will be the judge. In judging us in the name of God and as God, his judgment will be irrevocable, final, and binding. There is no higher court of appeal.

Since Christ the Savior is also the judge, even in all its seriousness this judgment has a comforting aspect. By confronting us with himself and his gospel, Christ has shown us the true direction of our life, and through his dying and resurrection has enabled us to pursue this direction of living in conformity with God. The first Christian community, who preserved for us all the dreadful apocalyptic imagery of the final judgment, was not terrified by this prospect. It recognized judgment as the necessary "entrance gate" to the new world to come. Thus *marana tha* ("our Lord, come!") was a familiar word in the first Christian community (cf. 1 Cor. 16:22), and the book of Revelation closes in a similar way with "Amen. Come, Lord Jesus!" (Rev. 22:20). Martin Luther recaptured this New Testament confidence in the face of the judgment when, contrary to the mood of the Middle Ages, he thought of this day not as one of wrath but of the glory of God, a day he looked forward to as he wrote in many of his letters: "Come, dear, last day."[9]

Is not, however, the very thought of such an ultimate, universal judgment day as obsolete as the apocalyptic imagery in which it is expressed? Our answer must be no, because human destiny is in fact moving toward participation in God's eternity. If we were to recognize this as our goal, we would seek to live each moment in accordance with the eternity of God. In truth, however, we are self-centered and live mainly in the light of ourselves and of transitoriness. When we die, we are unable to continue our self-centered lives; our temporal life ceases and only the eternity of God into which we are received abides. Death is the boundary which we cross as we enter into the eternity of God.

Death finalizes and completes our participation in the eternity of God. Our earthly life, which is known to us only partially as long as we live it, will then become known in its totality as it is confronted with the "blueprint" of God's eternal will. Then its irreversible fragmentariness will become visible and the discrepancy between the possibilities and the actualities of our earthly life will be what we experience as God's final judgment, a judgment which, in anticipation, we have already long ago pronounced upon ourselves in our earthly life. Only those who in this life have already made the connection with eternity in time, i.e., with Jesus Christ, have the assurance that the discrepancy between what was and what should have been will be overcome. They have this assurance because Jesus Christ, though human, never allowed this discrepancy to develop in his own life and death. Consequently, through alignment with him, their death will result in a resurrection not only to judgment but to eternal life.

3. Beyond mere justice

The question of a universal homecoming emerges at once when we are confronted with the final judgment and the assertion that not everyone will be saved. Jesus and the New Testament witnesses are convinced, however, of a twofold outcome. "The gate is wide and the way is easy, that leads to destruction, and those who enter by it are many. For the gate is narrow and the way is hard, that leads to life, and those who find it are few" (Matt. 7:13f.), we hear Jesus say. The Gospel of John makes a similar point, but actualized in the now: "He who believes in the Son has eternal life; he who does not obey the Son shall not see life, but the wrath of God rests upon him" (John 3:36). The book of Revelation also expresses this twofold outcome in typically apocalyptic fashion: "And the smoke of their torment goes up for ever and ever; and they have no rest, day or night" (Rev. 14:11).

It is important to recognize that the New Testament also contains many assertions that indicate God wants all people to be saved. Paul, for instance, in wrestling with the destiny of Israel, expresses the conviction that "God has consigned all men to disobedience, that he may have mercy upon all" (Rom. 11:32). Here the goal of the cosmos and of saving history is universal salvation which embraces the destiny of all individuals, Jews and pagans alike. Similarly we hear that God our Savior "desires all men to be saved and to come to the knowledge of the truth" (1 Tim. 2:4).

We are finally confronted here with a paradox that states both (1) that God's love wants all to be saved and (2) that God's justice requires all the disobedient to be punished. We could attempt to solve this paradox by asserting that God's justice and love are related to each other like law and gospel. God threatens with his justice in order that we might flee to his love. This anthropomorphic construct of a pedagogic God who punishes only in order to save (cf. Schleiermacher!) does not, however, consider that the judgment is the disclosure and finalization of our life attitude and not just a transition into the universal love of God. Such a view neglects the scriptural witness that if our life runs counter to the love God extended in Christ, the result is a dichotomy which cannot be bridged through evolution or amelioration.

Another attempt to overcome this tension between God's justice and love is the assertion that the condemned will be annihilated and thus all (who are left) will be saved. How can someone be annihilated, however, if there is no escape from God because God is everywhere—in death as well as beyond death? The solution of this paradox must rather be sought in considering what we mean by the terms *justice* and *love*. Do these terms actually describe the being of God or do they not rather disclose certain aspects of God for us? We must remember that we can express God's self-disclosure to us only in human language, and this means with necessarily anthropomorphic and inadequate conceptual tools. We wonder whether God is not just as much beyond our concepts of justice and love as he is beyond our understanding of a person when we call him a personal God.

We must also remember that God confronts us with his decision-demanding word when Jesus says, "Repent and follow me." As we ourselves accept God's offer to direct our lives according to his eternal purpose, the question of a universal homecoming loses its importance for us. Then the idea of a universal homecoming emerges only as a concerned speculation about the final destiny of others. In our sincere concern for others, however, we must acknowledge the ultimate hiddenness of the God who is beyond justice and love even as we pray that his never-ending grace will ultimately prevail.

C. The new world

When we now consider the new world to come, it is even more difficult to avoid meaningless generalities without once again indulging in a travelog eschatology. Yet we are not totally helpless, because Jesus and the New Testament writers affirm an ultimate future which to some extent can already be anticipated in our present life. We also remember that this ultimate future has become a present reality in the coming of Jesus, which intersects with our own world history. Since this ultimate future is so intimately connected with God and his coming to us, however, it can only be "described" in the analogous ways we also use to "describe" God himself, i.e., by using conceptualities borrowed from our world of experience and attempting to formulate them in such manner that they become expressive of a totally new and different reality.

The parables of the kingdom indicate that at one point it becomes evident who has entered the kingdom of God and who has not, at which point the good and evil will have been separated (cf. Matt. 13:30, 49ff.). Jesus even had to restrain enthusiastic disciples who demanded that, since the decision about one's entrance into the kingdom must be made now, the evidence of entrance or exclusion should also be disclosed. Jesus, however, rejected these attempts to build a pure "Christian community" here on earth by pointing to the future dimension of such a perfection: "Let both grow together until the harvest; and at harvest time I will tell the reapers, 'Gather the weeds first and bind them into bundles to be burned, but gather the wheat into my barn'" (Matt. 13:30). This future dimension will find its fulfillment with the final judgment. Then the distinctions which already exist invisibly will become visible and irreversible. The kingdom of God, or the new world to be disclosed, is described with the term *heaven* while the term *hell* denotes exclusion from the new world.

Heaven and hell as the final outcome of human destiny seem to indicate a world of fairy tales. In most religions heaven is understood as the location of the gods while hell is usually associated with the devil, demons, and other figments of human imagination. The New Testament, however, uses the term *heaven* at least as frequently as the term *kingdom of God*. At some places both terms are even merged into a "kingdom of heaven" (cf. Matt. 3:2; 5:3; and others).

It does not suffice, however, for us simply to resort to biblical literalism. Already Luther mocked the attempt to picture hell as built of wood or bricks so that it would have gates, windows, locks, and bars as does a house here on earth; and, of course, Christ did not destroy hell with a flag of cloth in his hand.[10] For Luther "hell means that death is accompanied by the feeling that the punishment is, at once, unchangeable and eternal. Here the soul is captured and surrounded so that it cannot think anything else except that it is to be eternally damned."[11] Thus Luther mocked at the *Schwärmer* (enthusiasts) who understood God's dwelling place in heaven in a local way. Because the visible heaven or sky is constantly moving, Luther concludes that this would mean that Christ too cannot sit still for one moment. It is, however, absurd to understand God's realm in a local way so that one thinks of the exalted Christ as sitting on high, perhaps like a stork in its nest. Luther was nevertheless certainly aware that the Bible in its pre-Copernican worldview often uses the terms *hell* and *heaven* in a local way.

Already in the Old Testament the term *heaven* is used both to describe the topography of the cosmos and to denote theologically the source of salvation, namely, God and his power. In rabbinic literature the word *heaven* can become a circumlocution for God. This distinction between a cosmological and the theological understanding of *heaven* is intensified in the New Testament. Theologically speaking, heaven can be the dimension of God, the source of salvation, and an integrating focal point for the present and future blessings of salvation in the new aeon. Such a theological understanding of heaven requires the transcending of the prevalent three-storied worldview of the Bible and is indicated in such passages as the confession of Solomon, "Behold, heaven and the highest heaven cannot contain thee; how much less this house which I have built!" (1 Kings 8:27), or the assertion of Paul, "He who descended is he who also ascended far above all the heavens, that he might fill all things" (Eph. 4:10).

In the earlier parts of the Old Testament Sheol or "hell" is understood indiscriminately as the shadowy existence of all who have died (cf. Ps. 89:48). At the same time it can refer to the dimension of alienation from God in death. In postexilic times, perhaps through the influence of Parsiism, Sheol is conceived of as only a temporary dwelling place and, moreover, different for the righteous than for the godless. Gehenna, the New Testament word for hell, presupposes resurrection and final judgment. The whole person with body and soul will be tormented in Gehenna, "where their worm does not die, and the fire is not quenched" (Mark 9:48). While hell does not originate in the eschaton (Matt. 25:41), it is only after the resurrection and judgment that it will be disclosed as the realm of eternal torment. In intertestamental apocalyptic thinking Gehenna was still associated with the Hinnom valley near Jerusalem, where King Ahaz and King Manasseh had once sacrificed to foreign gods. This kind of localization was abandoned in the New Testament. In contrast to apocalyptic literature, the New Testament usually did not paint the torments of hell in such drastic colors and, when it did, it did so to awaken the conscience of the listeners (cf. Matt. 10:28).

Hell and heaven receive their significance not as cosmological localities nor even as images representing such, but on the basis of what they affirm about God. Only in the world of fantasy is hell the domain of the devil. According to the biblical witnesses, however, even the anti-Godly powers are under God's control.

Hell is something we do not know. The allusions of the New Testament, such as "nether gloom of darkness" (2 Peter 2:17), "outer darkness," "weeping and gnashing of teeth" (Matt. 22:13), and "eternal fire" (Matt. 25:41), describe hell in terms of pain, despair, and loneliness. In so doing, words are taken from present negative experiences and used to point beyond them. These negative expressions attempt to describe the reaction of those who have experienced the disclosure and finalization of the discrepancy between their eternal destiny and their earthly realization. They express the anguish of knowing what one has missed without the possibility of ever reaching it. They witness to a state of extreme despair without the hope of reversing it. Such anguish and despair do not result only from a local separation from God. It will be rather a dimensional separation from God and from those God has accepted. Even so, God and the destiny of the accepted will somehow be made present as a curse.

Christians do not confess faith in hell but in "the resurrection of the body and life everlasting." Thus hell is of no ultimate concern to us. It serves only as an admonition that we reach our eternal destiny. In talking about life everlasting or heaven, we agree with Luther, "As little as children know in their mother's womb about their birth, so little do we know about life everlasting."[12] When we read about our habitation in the new Jerusalem, a city of gold, similar to pure glass, with walls of precious stones, and with 12 gates, each made of one pearl (Revelation 21), then this apocalyptic imagery resembles so much a world of fantasy that it looks more like an attraction in Disneyland than the eternal goal of our lives. Likewise, the promises that God will dwell with the elect "and they shall be his people, and God himself will be with them; he will wipe away every tear from their eyes, and death shall be no more, neither shall there be mourning nor crying nor pain any more, for the former things have passed away" (Rev. 21:3f.), and that God will be "everything to everyone" (1 Cor. 15:28) sound like wishful thinking. Even the much more restrained assertion that once we have reached our final goal we will see God "face to face" (1 Cor. 13:12) sounds unreal.

Union with God, abolition of anguish and sorrow, and permanent beauty and perfection are so discontinuous with this life of alienation, pain, suffering, transition, and change that we might want to discard these promises as utopian dreams. We would be right in doing so—if Jesus Christ had not shown us through his death and resurrection that such fulfillment is attainable. Because of Jesus Christ and because of the promise contained in the Christ event, the hope for a final realization of such promises is realistic. It shows us that our immanent and perpetual yearning for self-transcendence, for deification, for the elimination of death, and for progress toward perfection is not a utopian dream but will find its fulfillment in life everlasting. This Christian hope, however, also poses to us the all-decisive alternative: Do we understand as ends in themselves our own Marxist or Western materialistic attempts to fulfill our inborn desire for perfection through the pursuit of technological progress and peace for all people? If we do, we exclude ourselves from true fulfillment beyond this life. *Or* do we understand our endeavors here on earth as proleptic anticipations of that which "God has prepared for those who love him" (1 Cor. 2:9)? Only in this latter case can we hope for the true fulfillment which alone God can provide. "Only he who is certain of his future can relax and turn to today's business."[13] Thus it is necessary to check our life-attitude and once again put our trust in Jesus alone, the one who is "the pioneer and perfecter of our faith" (Heb. 12:2).

NOTES

Chapter 1: Theology

1. Eusebius, *The Church History* 4.3.1, NPNF (SS) 1:175.
2. Ibid. 4.3.3, 1:175.
3. Justin Martyr, *The First Apology* 46, ANFa 1:178.
4. Justin Martyr, *The Second Apology* 13, ANFa 1:193.
5. Origen, *Against Celsus* 1.32, ANFa 4:410.
6. Anselm of Canterbury, *Proslogion* IV, in *St. Anselm's Proslogion with a Reply on Behalf of the Fool by Gaunilo and the Author's Reply to Gaunilo*, trans., intr., and philosophical commentary M. J. Charlesworth (Oxford: Clarendon, 1965), p. 121.
7. Philip Melanchthon, *The Loci Communes*, critical intr. and trans. Charles Leander Hill (Boston: Meador, 1944), pp. 68f.
8. Karl Barth, *Church Dogmatics*, vol. 1.2: *The Doctrine of the Word of God,* trans. G. T. Thomson and H. Knight (Edinburgh: T. & T. Clark, 1956), pp. 299f.
9. Paul Tillich, *Systematic Theology*, vol. 1 (Chicago: University of Chicago, 1951), p. 12 (italicized in the original).
10. Anselm, *Proslogion* I, p. 115.

Chapter 3: Scripture

1. Papias, as quoted by Eusebius, *The Church History* 3.39.4, NPNF (SS) 1:171.
2. Justin Martyr, *The First Apology* 67, ANFa 1:186.
3. Vincent of Lérins, *The Commonitory* 2.6, NPNF (SS) 11:132.
4. Heinrich Denzinger, ed., *The Sources of Catholic Dogma* 783, trans. R. J. Deferrari (St. Louis: Herder, 1957), p. 244.
5. Ibid. 2331, p. 647.
6. "Dogmatic Constitution on Divine Revelation" 7, in Walter M. Abbott, gen. ed., *The Documents of Vatican II*, with notes and comments by Catholic, Protestant, and Orthodox authorities (New York: Guild, 1966), p. 115.
7. Ibid. 9, p. 117.
8. Ibid.
9. *Formula of Concord*, Solid Declaration 9, in *The Book of Concord: The Confessional Writings of the Evangelical Lutheran Church,* trans. and ed. Theodore G. Tappert (Philadelphia: Fortress, 1959), p. 505.

Chapter 4: God

1. Martin Luther, *Der Prophet Iona ausgelegt* (1526), WA 19:205f. (my trans.).
2. Anselm of Canterbury, *Proslogion* (preface), in *St. Anselm's Proslogion with a Reply on Behalf of the Fool by Gaunilo and the Author's Reply to Gaunilo*. trans., intr., and philosophical commentary M. J. Charlesworth (Oxford: Clarendon, 1965), p. 103.
3. Ibid. II, p. 117.
4. Immanuel Kant, *Critique of Pure Reason* A599, B627, abridged ed., trans. with an intr. N. K. Smith (New York: Random House, 1958), p. 282.
5. Anselm, *Proslogion* III, p. 119.
6. Ibid. IV, p. 121.
7. Ibid.
8. René Descartes, *Meditations on First Philosophy* in *Descartes: Philosophical Writings*, selected and trans. N. K. Smith (New York: Random House, 1958), p. 204.
9. Ibid., pp. 204f.
10. Ibid., p. 225.
11. Ibid., pp. 225f.
12. Aristotle, *Metaphysics* XII, 3; 1069b, 36f., in *The Basic Works of Aristotle*, ed. Richard McKeon (New York: Random House, 1941), p. 873.
13. Thomas Aquinas, *Summa Theologica* 1a.2.3a.r, Latin text and English trans., intr., notes, appendices, and glossaries (London: Blackfriars, 1964), 2:15.
14. Ibid. 1a.q2.a3.r, 2:15.
15. Ibid.
16. Ibid. 1a.q2.a3.r, 2:17.
17. Immanuel Kant, *Critique of Pure Reason* A604, B632, p. 285.
18. Charles Darwin in a letter to Asa Gray, November 26, 1860, published in *The Life and Letters of Charles Darwin Including an Autobiographical Chapter*, ed. Francis Darwin (New York: D. Appleton, 1898), 2:146.
19. Immanuel Kant, *Critique of Pure Reason* A623, B651, p. 293.
20. William Paley, *Natural Theology* I/8, reprinted in *The Cosmological Arguments: A Spectrum of Opinion*, ed. Donald R. Burrill (Garden City, N.Y.: Doubleday, Anchor Book, 1967), p. 170.
21. Immanuel Kant, *Critique of Practical Reason* V, 161, in *Critique of Practical Reason and Other Writings in Moral Philosophy*, trans. and ed. with an intr. Lewis White Beck (Chicago: University of Chicago, 1950), p. 258.

22. Ibid. V, 125, p. 228.
23. Ibid. V, 125f., pp. 228f.
24. Immanuel Kant, *Critique of Judgment* par. 86, trans. with an intr. J. H. Bernhard (New York: Hafner, 1951), p. 293.
25. Heinrich Denzinger, *The Sources of Catholic Dogma* 2305, trans. R. J. Deferrari (St. Louis: B. Herder, 1957), p. 635. It should be added here that with this statement no "naive" proof is advanced, because in the same breath the encyclical admits that "not a few obstacles prevent man's reason from efficaciously and fruitfully using this natural faculty which it possesses."
26. Ibid. 1785, p. 443, which is more affirmative than the statement quoted above.
27. Ibid.
28. Søren Kierkegaard, *Concluding Unscientific Postscript*, trans. D. F. Swenson and W. Lowrie (Princeton: Princeton University, 1941), p. 485; cf. also his penetrating criticism of the ontological argument, ibid., p. 298. For further treatment of the issue cf. Walter Lowrie, *Kierkegaard* (New York: Harper Torchbook, 1962), 2:335f.
29. Karl Barth, "The Word of God and the Task of the Ministry" (1922), in *The Word of God and the Word of Man*, trans. D. Horton (New York: Harper Torchbook, 1957), p. 186. The German original reads "theologians" instead of "ministers." Cf. *Anfänge der dialektischen Theologie*, ed. Jürgen Moltmann (Munich: Christian Kaiser, 1966), 1:199.
30. Dionysius the Areopagite, *The Divine Names* VII, 3, in *On the Divine Names and the Mystical Theology*, trans. C. E. Rolt (New York: Macmillan, 1951), pp. 151f.
31. Alfred North Whitehead, *Process and Reality: An Essay in Cosmology* (New York: Macmillan, 1960), p. 519.
32. Charles Hartshorne, *A Natural Theology for Our Time* (LaSalle, Ill.: Open Court, 1967), p. 137.
33. Cf. for this and the following Friedrich Schleiermacher, *The Christian Faith*, par. 50, ed. H. R. MacKintosh and J. S. Stewart (Edinburgh: T. & T. Clark, 1960), pp. 194f.
34. Martin Luther, *Lectures on Genesis*, LW 1:3, in his exegesis of Genesis 1:2; cf. also Paul Althaus, *The Theology of Martin Luther*, trans. R. C. Schultz (Philadelphia: Fortress, 1966), pp. 20-24, in his section on "God in Himself and God as He Reveals Himself."
35. Martin Luther, *Confession concerning Christ's Supper* (1528), LW 37: 228.

36. Dietrich Bonhoeffer, *Letters and Papers from Prison,* ed. Eberhard Bethge, trans. R. Fuller, rev. ed. (New York: Macmillan, 1967), p. 213.
37. Martin Buber, *I and Thou,* trans. R. G. Smith (New York: Scribner's, 1958), p. 135.

Chapter 5: Creation

1. Gerhard von Rad, "The Theological Problem of the Old Testament Doctrine of Creation" (1936), in *The Problem of the Hexateuch and Other Essays,* trans. E. W. T. Dicken, intr. Norman W. Porteous (Edinburgh: Oliver & Boyd, 1965), p. 138. Cf. also his *Old Testament Theology: The Theology of Israel's Historical Traditions,* trans. D. M. Stalker (Edinburgh: Oliver & Boyd, 1962), 1:139.
2. Giordano Bruno, *On the Infinite Universe and Worlds,* first dialog, in Dorothea Waley Singer, *Giordano Bruno: His Life and Thought,* with an annotated translation of his work *On the Infinite Universe and Worlds* (New York: Greenwood, 1968), pp. 261f.
3. Ibid., p. 257.
4. Benedict de Spinoza, *Short Treatise on God, Man, & His Well-Being,* Chap. 9, trans. and ed. with an introduction, commentary, and a Life of Spinoza by A. Wolf (New York: Russell & Russell, 1963), p. 57.
5. Georg Wilhelm Friedrich Hegel, *The Phenomenology of Mind,* trans. J. B. Baillie (London: George Allen & Unwin, 1961), p. 769.
6. Arthur Schopenhauer, *Panerga,* in *Sämtliche Werke,* ed. W. Freiherr von Löhneysen (Wiesbaden: Insel-Verlag, 1960), 4:143.
7. So Stanley Green in his instructive book, *Shaftesbury's Philosophy of Religion and Ethics: A Study in Enthusiasm* (Athens, Ohio: Ohio University, 1967), p. 51.
8. Immanuel Kant, *Critique of Pure Reason* A631ff., B659ff., trans. N. K. Smith (London: Macmillan, 1929), p. 526.
9. Voltaire, "God-Gods," in *A Philosophical Dictionary,* vol. 5, in *The Works of Voltaire: A Contemporary Version. Edition de la Pacification* (Paris: E. R. Du Mont, 1901), 9:242. Originally this article was not part of Voltaire's *Dictionary* but it was an article he contributed to the *Encyclopedia.*
10. Charles Hartshorne, *Man's Vision of God and the Logic of Theism* (Chicago: Willett, Clark & Co., 1941), p. 12. For a good introduction to both Hartshorne and Alfred North Whitehead which also shows their similarities and differences cf. *Two Process Philosophers: Hartshorne's Encounter with Whitehead,* ed. Lewis S. Ford, *AAR Studies in*

Religion, No. 5 (Tallahassee, Fla: American Academy of Religion, 1973).
11. Alfred North Whitehead, *Process and Reality: An Essay in Cosmology* (New York: Macmillan, 1960), p. 521.
12. Ibid., p. 523.
13. Ibid., p. 532. This statement does not imply that Whitehead understands God as a projection of a father image. God is rather for him the ground of all reality, including that of our finite being. This is substantiated when he says on another occasion that God can be conceived "as the supreme ground for limitations, it stands in His very nature to divide the Good from the Evil, and to establish Reason 'within her dominion supreme'" (*Science and the Modern World: Lowell Lectures 1925* [New York: Macmillan, 1960], p. 258).
14. Hartshorne, *Beyond Humanism: Essays in the New Philosophy of Nature* (Lincoln: University of Nebraska, Bison Book, 1968), pp. 315f.
15. Jürgen Moltmann, *Theology of Hope: On the Ground and the Implications of a Christian Eschatology*, trans. J. W. Leitch (New York: Harper & Row, 1967), pp. 137f. Moltmann has pointed out especially well the significance of this changed understanding of eschatology. Yet the emergence of a viewpoint comprising the whole universe is equally important for the relationship between salvation history and history.
16. Rudolf Bultmann, *Theology of the New Testament*, trans. K. Grobel (New York: Scribner's, 1951), 1:43f.
17. Rudolf Bultmann, *History and Eschatology: The Presence of Eternity* (New York: Harper, 1957), p. 37.
18. Rudolf Bultmann, "New Testament and Mythology," in *Kerygma and Myth: A Theological Debate*, ed. Hans Werner Bartsch, trans. R. H. Fuller (London: SPCK, 1953), 1:5.
19. Bultmann, *History and Eschatology*, p. 151.
20. Karl Barth, *Church Dogmatics*, vol. 3.1: *The Doctrine of Creation*, trans. J. W. Edwards et al. (Edinburgh: T. & T. Clark, 1958), p. 60.
21. Barth, *Church Dogmatics*, vol. 4.2: *The Doctrine of Reconciliation*, trans. G. W. Bromiley (Edinburgh: T. & T. Clark, 1958), p. 806.
22. Oscar Cullmann, *Salvation in History*, trans. S. G. Sowers (London: SCM, 1967), p. 156.
23. Ibid., p. 166.
24. Wolfhart Pannenberg, "Redemptive Event and History," in *Basic Questions in Theology: Collected Essays*, trans. G. H. Kehm (Philadelphia: Fortress 1970), 1:41.

25. Pannenberg, "Dogmatic Theses on the Doctrine of Revelation," thesis 3, in *Revelation as History*, ed. Wolfhart Pannenberg, trans. D. Granskou (New York: Macmillan, 1968), p. 135.
26. Pannenberg, "Insight and Faith," in *Basic Questions*, 2:36.
27. George G. Simpson, *The Meaning of Evolution: A Study of the History of Life and of Its Significance for Man* (New Haven: Yale University, 1950), p. 310. Of course, we do not want to leave the impression, and Simpson does not intend to do so either, that everything within the evolutionary process is totally unpredictable. There are always covariances within the evolutionary process and certain limits which are not exceeded or below which a certain species will not drop (cf. for instance, the minimum weight of mammals). Thus there evolves an internal balance within the evolutionary system tending toward optimal conditions of existence and survival. Cf. the excellent article by Paul Overhage, "Gebundene Mannigfaltigkeit," in *Gott in Welt: Festgabe für Karl Rahner*, vol. 2, ed. Herbert Vorgrimmler (Freiburg: Herder, 1964), esp. pp. 842ff.
28. Martin Luther, "Kaspar Crucigers Sommerpostille" (1544), WA 21: 521, 20-25, in a sermon on Rom. 11:33-36.
29. Cf. the excellent article by Arnold W. Ravin, "Science, Values, and Human Evolution," *Zygon* 11 (June 1976): 138-154, here p. 151.
30. Martin Luther, *Predigten des Jahres 1531*, WA 34/2 :237,3f., in a sermon on the festival of St. Michael.
31. Cf. Friedrich Schiller's poem "Resignation" (1786), *Gesammelte Werke in fünf Bänden*, ed. Reinhold Netolitzky (Gütersloh: C. Bertelsmann, 1959), 3:391.
32. G. F. W. Hegel, *The Philosophy of History*, preface by Charles Hegel, trans. J. Sibree, intr. C. J. Friedrich (New York: Dover, 1956), p. 15. Similarly it is difficult for us to agree with him (p. 36) when he says: "God governs the world; the actual working of his government—the carrying out of his plan—is the History of the World."
33. Friedrich Gogarten, *The Reality of Faith: The Problem of Subjectivism in Theology*, trans. C. Michalson et al. (Philadelphia: Westminster, 1959), pp. 55ff.
34. Albert C. Outler, *Who Trusts in God: Musings on the Meaning of Providence* (New York: Oxford University, 1968), p. 52.
35. Augustine, *Lectures or Tractates on the Gospel according to St. John* 24, NPNF (FS) 7:158.
36. Dietrich Bonhoeffer, *Letters and Papers from Prison*, ed. Eberhard Bethge, trans. R. Fuller, rev. ed. (New York: Macmillan, 1967), p. 213.

Chapter 6: Humanity

1. Gerhard von Rad, *Genesis: A Commentary*, trans. J. H. Marks (Philadelphia: Westminster, 1961), p. 75, in his exegesis of Gen. 2:7. Cf. also Josef Ploger, "*adhamah*," in TDOT 1:95f.
2. Martin Luther, *Psalm 147* (1532), LW 14:114, in his exegesis of Ps. 147:13 (my trans.).
3. Gerhard von Rad, ibid., p. 58, in his exegesis of Gen. 1:26-28.
4. Emil Brunner, *Man in Revolt: A Christian Anthropology*, trans. O. Wyon (Philadelphia: Westminster, 1967), p. 346.
5. Lynn White Jr., "The Historical Roots of Our Ecological Crisis" (1967), *in Ecology and Religion in History*, ed. David and Eileen Spring (New York: Harper Torchbook, 1974), p. 24.
6. Ibid., p. 23.
7. Martin Luther, *Sermons on the Gospel of St. John* (1537), LW 24:81, in his exposition of John 14:12.
8. Martin Luther, *Lectures on Genesis* (1535-1545), LW 3:117, in his exegesis of Gen. 17:7.
9. Georgia Harkness, *The Providence of God* (New York: Abingdon, 1960), p. 128.
10. *Lutheran Book of Worship* (Minneapolis: Augsburg, 1978), hymn 439.

Chapter 7: Sin

1. Georg Wilhelm Friedrich Hegel, *Vorlesungen über die Philosophie der Religion*, vol. 1, in *Sämtliche Werke*, ed. Hermann Glockner (Stuttgart: Fr. Frommann, 1928), 15:285.
2. G. W. F. Hegel, *Vorlesungen über die Geschichte*, in *Sämtliche Werke*, 11:413.
3. Friedrich Schiller, *Etwas über die erste Menschengesellschaft: Übergang des Menschen zur Freiheit und Humanität* (1789), in *Gesammelte Werke in fünf Bänden*, ed. Reinhold Netolitzky (Gütersloh: C. Bertelsmann, 1959), 4:103.
4. Erich Fromm, *The Heart of Man: Its Genius for Good and Evil* (New York: Harper & Row, 1964), p. 20.
5. Carl Gustav Jung, "The Phenomenology of the Spirit in Fairytales," 420, in *The Collected Works of C. G. Jung*, ed. William McGuire, 2nd ed. (Princeton: Princeton University, 1971), 9.1:230.
6. Cf. Pierre Teilhard de Chardin, *The Phenomenon of Man*, trans. B. Wall, intr. Sir Julian Huxley (New York: Harper & Row, 1959), pp. 301f.: "The involuting universe ... proceeds step by step by dint of

billion-fold trial and error. It is this process of groping, combined with the two-fold mechanism of reproduction and heredity . . . , which gives rise to the . . . tree of life." Cf. also p. 310, where he picks up the same terminology in talking about the "evil of disorder and failure" as a necessity in the evolutionary process.

7. For the following cf. Rivkah Schärf Kluger, *Satan in the Old Testament*, trans. H. Nagel (Evanston, Ill.: Northwestern University, 1967), pp. 87ff. and 133. Cf. also Georg Fohrer, *Das Buch Hiob*, in *Kommentar zum Alten Testament* (Gütersloh: Gerd Mohn, 1963), 16:44, for a brief description of the text. For a translation of the Babylonian Job cf. "I Will Praise the Lord of Wisdom" ("Poem of the Righteous Sufferer") trans. Robert H. Pfeiffer, in *Ancient Near Eastern Texts Relating to the Old Testament*, ed. James B. Pritchard (Princeton: Princeton University, 1950), pp. 434-437.
8. Kluger, ibid., p. 135.
9. Cf. for the following Werner Foerster, "*satanas*," in TDNT 7:156.
10. William Foxwell Albright, *From the Stone Age to Christianity: Monotheism and the Historical Process* (Baltimore: Johns Hopkins, 1957), p. 362.
11. Rudolf Bultmann, *Theology of the New Testament*, trans. K. Grobel (New York: Scribner's, 1951), 2:21. Raymond E. Brown, *The Gospel According to John (I-XII)* (Garden City, N.Y.: Doubleday, 1966), p. lvi, offers an interesting suggestion. While admitting that Bultmann's thesis that John is dependent on an early oriental Gnosticism cannot be disproved, he suggests that in many ways such a hypothesis is unnecessary. Brown in turn proposes that "OT speculation about personified Wisdom and the vocabulary and thought patterns of sectarian Judaism, like the Qumran community, go a long way toward filling in the background of Johannine theological vocabulary and expression." Such Jewish influence would then indicate that the Johannine understanding of the function and position of Satan is largely a consequent development of Old Testament and later Jewish thought.
12. Immanuel Kant, *Religion within the Limits of Reason Alone*, trans., intr., and notes Theodore M. Greene and Hoyt H. Hudson, with a new essay, "The Ethical Significance of Kant's Religion," by John R. Silber, 2nd ed. (LaSalle, Ill.: Open Court, 1960), p. 27.
13. Cf. for the following ibid., p. 30.
14. Emil Brunner, *Man in Revolt: A Christian Anthropology*, trans. O. Wyon (Philadelphia: Westminster, 1967), pp. 126f., rightly observed: "Kant's idea of radical evil remains the most serious attempt ever

made by any philosopher—who does not bring his system into conformity with the Christian revelation—about evil."
15. Reinhold Niebuhr, *The Nature and Destiny of Man: A Christian Interpretation* (New York: Scribner's, 1949), 1:180.
16. Gordon D. Kaufmann, *Systematic Theology: A Historicist Perspective* (New York: Scribner's, 1968), p. 310.
17. Martin Luther, *Heidelberg Disputation* (1518), LW 31:45 (expl. of thesis 6).
18. Martin Luther, *The Bondage of the Will* (1525), LW 33:180.
19. Ibid., pp. 65f.
20. Cf. Paul Althaus, in his excellent treatment of Luther's theology, *The Theology of Martin Luther*, trans. R. C. Schultz (Philadelphia: Fortress 1966), p. 168, who concludes that "Luther can regard Satan both as the instrument and as the enemy of God."
21. Karl Barth, *Church Dogmatics*, vol. 3.3: *The Doctrine of Creation*, trans. G. W. Bromiley et al. (Edinburgh: T. & T. Clark, 1961), p. 351. It is unfortunate that the German "das Nichtige" (the nothing) is simply rendered in English with "nothingness."
22. Ibid., p. 360; and Otto Weber, *Karl Barth's Church Dogmatics: An Introductory Report on Volumes 1.1 to 3.4*, trans. A. C. Cochrane (Philadelphia: Westminster, 1953), p. 194, who translates "das Nichtige" more appropriately with "the Nihil."
23. Barth, *Church Dogmatics*, vol. 3.3, p. 354.
24. Augustine, *Treatise on Rebuke and Grace* 33, NPNF (FS) 5:485.
25. So Pelagius according to Mari Mercator, "Commonitorium de Coelestio" 2.2ff., PL 48:85.
26. So Paul Althaus, *The Ethics of Martin Luther*, trans. with a foreword R. C. Schultz (Philadelphia: Fortress, 1972), p. 30.
27. Augustine, *The City of God* 19.25, trans. M. Dods, intr. Thomas Merton (New York: Random House, 1950), p. 707. The more popular wording, " The virtues of the pagans are splendid vices," however, is apocryphal and wrongly attributed to Augustine. Cf. Friedrich Loofs, *Leitfaden zur Dogmengeschichte*, ed. Kurt Aland, 6th ed. (Tübingen: Max Niemeyer, 1959), p. 333, n. 4.
28. Pelagius, according to Augustine, *On the Grace of Christ* 5.4, NPNF (FS) 5:219.
29. So R.A. Norris, *Manhood and Christ: A Study in the Christology of Theodore of Mopsuestia* (Oxford: Clarendon, 1963), p. 179. Cf. also H. B. Swete, *Theodori Episcopi Mopsuesteni*, in *Epistolas B. Pauli Commentarii: The Latin Version with Greek Fragments*, with intr., notes,

and indices, vol. 2: *I Thessalonians–Philemon* (Cambridge: University Press, 1882), pp. 332-337, where Theodore emphasizes emphatically that Adam was created in a state of mortality, and that therefore mortality was not our punishment for Adam's sin.
30. Augustine, *On the Grace of Christ* 18.17, NPNF (FS) 5:224.
31. Augustine, *Against Julian* 6.15.47, FaCH 35:356.
32. Augustine, *Against Two Letters of the Pelagians* 1.7.13, NPNF (FS) 5: 379; and Augustine, *Operis Imperfecti contra Julianum* 3.109, PL 45: 1294, where he says, "Ecce quare dixi, Neminem liberum ad agendum bonum sine adiutorio Dei."
33. Augustine, *On the Gift of Perseverance* 17, NPNF (FS) 5:531.
34. Konrad Lorenz, *Das sogenannte Böse: Zur Naturgeschichte der Aggression*, 33rd. ed. (Vienna: G. Borotha Schoeler, 1973), p. 333. The earlier English translation, *On Aggression*, trans. M. K. Wilson (New York: Harcourt, Brace & World, 1966), p. 251, has this quote misleadingly modified to: "The imagination of man's heart is not really evil from his youth up, as we read in Genesis."
35. Desiderius Erasmus, *On the Freedom of the Will*, in *Luther and Erasmus: Free Will and Salvation*, trans. and ed. E. Gordon Rupp and Philip S. Watson, vol. 17 of *The Library of Christian Classics* (Philadelphia: Westminster, 1969), p. 90. Cf. also the interesting study of Harry J. McSorley, *Luther: Right or Wrong? An Ecumenical-Theological Study of Luther's Major Work, The Bondage of the Will* (Minneapolis: Augsburg, 1969), who shows that Erasmus did not do justice to traditional Catholic doctrine, while Luther, apart from a necessitarian argument, shows in his biblical exegesis a truly Catholic stance (p. 369).
36. Erasmus, *On the Freedom of the Will*, p. 90.
37. Martin Luther, *On the Bondage of Will*, in *Luther and Erasmus*, p. 232.
38. Martin Luther, *Large Catechism* (1529), in *The Book of Concord: The Confessional Writings of the Evangelical Lutheran Church*, trans. and ed. Theodore G. Tappert (Philadelphia: Fortress, 1959), p. 419.
39. Cf. Irenaeus, *Against Heresies* 5.16, in ANFa 1:544.
40. Thomas Aquinas, *Summa Theologica* 1a.2ae.82.3, Latin text and English trans., intr., notes, appendices, and glossaries (London: Blackfriars, 1964), 26:38.
41. Ibid. 1a.2ae.82.2, p. 35.
42. Cf. *The Summa Theologica* 1a.2ae.110.3, literally trans. by Fathers of the English Dominican Province (London: Burns Oates & Washbourne, 1942), 8:352, where Thomas says that human virtues dispose

man fittingly "to the nature whereby he is a man; whereas infused virtues dispose man in a higher manner and towards a higher end, and consequently in relation to some higher nature, i.e., in relation to a participation of the Divine Nature."

43. "Decree on Justification" 5, in Heinrich Denzinger, ed., *The Sources of Catholic Dogma* 797, trans. R. J. Deferrari (St. Louis: Herder, 1957), p. 250.
44. Martin Luther, *Über das 1. Buch Mose, Predigten* (1527), WA 24:51, 12f., in his exegesis of Gen. 1:27.
45. Martin Luther, *On the Bondage of the Will*, in *Luther and Erasmus*, p. 140.
46. John Calvin, *Institutes of the Christian Religion* 2.2.1 and 2.2.17, trans. F. L. Battles, vol. 20 of *The Library of Christian Classics* (Philadelphia: Westminster, 1960), 1:255 and 277. Cf. also T. F. Torrance, *Calvin's Doctrine of Man* (Grand Rapids: Eerdmans, 1957), pp. 88ff., in his excellent analysis of this evident dichotomy. Torrance rightly claims that it is important to be aware of Calvin's distinction between the natural and the spiritual. While humanity is deprived of its spiritual gifts, it is only corrupted in its natural gifts. He also admits that "it is difficult to see how there can be any ultimate reconciliation between Calvin's doctrine of total perversity and his doctrine of a remnant of the *imago dei*, though the very fact that he can give them both in the same breath seems to indicate that he had no difficulty in reconciling them."
47. Johann Gerhard, *The Image of God*, in *The Doctrine of Man in Classical Lutheran Theology*, ed. Herman A. Preus and Edmund Smits (Minneapolis: Augsburg, 1962), p. 62.
48. Cf. for the following Michael Schmaus, *Der Glaube der Kirche: Handbuch katholischer Dogmatik*, 2 vols. (Munich: Max Hueber, 1969/70), 1:336.
49. Ibid., p. 650.
50. Augustine, *The City of God* 14.1, p. 441.
51. Ibid. 14.28, p. 477.
52. Ibid. 14.4, p. 445.
53. Albrecht Ritschl, *The Christian Doctrine of Justification and Reconciliation: A Positive Development of the Doctrine*, trans. and ed. H. R. MacKintosh and and A. B. Macaulay, 2nd ed. (Edinburgh: T. & T. Clark, 1902), pp. 383f.
54. Ibid., p. 335.
55. Ibid., p. 349.
56. Ibid., p. 337.

57. Ibid., p. 335.
58. Walter Rauschenbusch, *A Theology for the Social Gospel* (New York: Macmillan, 1917), pp. 77f. Cf. also *The Righteousness of the Kingdom*, ed. and intr. Max L. Stackhouse (Nashville: Abingdon, 1968), which contains an extensive and helpful introduction, plus a bibliography of Rauschenbusch's own writings and selected secondary literature.
59. Rauschenbusch, *A Theology for the Social Gospel*, p. 79.
60. Ibid., p. 81.

Chapter 8: Jesus of Nazareth

1. Rudolf Bultmann, *Theology of the New Testament*, trans. K. Grobel (New York: Scribner's, 1951), 1:33 (emphasis in the original).
2. Ibid., 1:3.
3. Philip Melanchthon, *The Loci Communes*, with a critical intr., trans. Charles Leander Hill (Boston: Meador, 1944), p. 68.
4. Hermann Samuel Reimarus, *The Goal of Jesus and His Disciples*, intr. and trans. G. W. Buchanan (Leiden: Brill, 1970), p. 80.
5. Friedrich Schleiermacher, *The Life of Jesus*, ed. and intr. Jack C. Verheyden, trans. S. Maclean Gilmore (Philadelphia: Fortress, 1975), p. 252.
6. Ibid., p. 265.
7. David Friedrich Strauss, *The Life of Jesus Critically Examined*, trans. George Eliot, ed. Peter C. Hodgson (Philadelphia: Fortress, 1972), p. 284.
8. Ibid., p. 736.
9. David Friedrich Strauss, *The Christ of Faith and the Jesus of History: A Critique of Schleiermacher's Life of Jesus*, trans. and ed. with an intr. Leander E. Keck (Philadelphia: Fortress, 1977 [Germ. orig., 1865]) p. 159.
10. Adolph von Harnack, *What is Christianity?* trans. Th. B. Saunders, intr. Rudolf Bultmann (New York: Harper, 1957), p. 31.
11. Ibid., p. 21.
12. Ibid., pp. 35f.
13. Ibid., p. 51.
14. Ibid., p. 54.
15. Ibid.
16. Ibid., p. 68.
17. Ibid., p. 144.
18. Ibid., p. 145.
19. Ibid., p. 128.

20. Ibid., p. 162.
21. Shailer Mathews, *The Social Teachings of Jesus: An Essay in Christian Sociology* (New York: Macmillan, 1917 [1897]), p. 134.
22. Ibid., p. 144.
23. Ibid., pp. 156f.
24. Ibid., p. 53.
25. Ibid., p. 54.
26. Ibid., pp. 228f.
27. Shailer Mathews, *Jesus on Social Institutions*, ed. with an intr. Kenneth Cauthen (Philadelphia: Fortress, 1971 [1928]), p. 40.
28. Ibid., p. 134.
29. Ibid., p. 39.
30. Ibid., p. 154.
31. Albert Schweitzer, *The Mystery of the Kingdom of God: The Secret of Jesus' Messiahship and Passion*, trans. with an intr. Walter Lowrie (New York: Macmillan, 1950), p. VIII.
32. Ibid., pp. 160f.
33. Ibid., p. 174.
34. Albert Schweitzer, *The Quest of the Historical Jesus: A Critical Study of Its Progress from Reimarus to Wrede*, preface F. C. Burkitt, intr. J. M. Robinson, trans. W. Montgomery (New York: Macmillan, 1968), p. 401.
35. Ibid., p. 337.
36. Ibid., pp. 370f.
37. Ibid., p. 399.
38. Rudolf Bultmann, "On the Question of Christology" (Germ. orig., 1927), in *Faith and Understanding* I, ed. with intr. Robert W. Funk, trans. Louise Pettibone Smith (New York: Harper & Row, 1969), p. 132.
39. Cf. James M. Robinson, *A New Quest of the Historical Jesus* (Naperville, Ill.: Alec R. Allenson, 1959), pp. 91f.
40. So Harald Riesenfeld, *The Gospel Tradition*, trans. E. M. Rowley and R. A. Kraft (Philadelphia: Fortress, 1970), p. 20.
41. Ibid., p. 24. Cf. also the excellent book by Asher Finkel, *The Pharisees and the Teacher of Nazareth: A Study of Their Background, Their Halachic and Midrashic Teachings, the Similarities and Differences* (Leiden: Brill, 1964), pp. 130ff., who shows how closely Jesus followed the rabbinic tradition. He also indicates that in his interpretation of the law Jesus followed more the rabbinic school of Hillel than that of

Shammai, since the former displayed more leniency in its decisions, while the Shammaites were for strict adherence to the law (pp. 135f.).
42. Cf. for the following Leonhard Goppelt, *Theology of the New Testament*, vol. 1: *The Ministry of Jesus in Its Theological Significance*, trans. John E. Alsup, ed. Jürgen Roloff (Grand Rapids: Eerdmans, 1981), pp. 23f.
43. Cf. for this and the following Abba Hillel Silver, *A History of the Messianic Speculation in Israel from the First through the Seventeenth Centuries* (Boston: Beacon, 1959 [1927]), pp. 6f.
44. Flavius Josephus, *Jewish War* 2.259, ed. with an English trans. H. St. J. Thackeray (London: Heinemann, 1956), 2:425.
45. Rudolf Bultmann, *Theology of the New Testament*, 1:27.
46. Ethelbert Stauffer, *Jesus and His Story,* trans. R. and C. Winston (New York: Knopf, 1960), p. 179.
47. Philip B. Harner, *The "I Am" of the Fourth Gospel: A Study in Johannine Usage and Thought* (Philadelphia: Fortress, 1970), p. 23.
48. So rightly Norman Perrin, "The High Priest's Question and Jesus' Answer (Mark 14:61-62)," in *The Passion in Mark: Studies on Mark 14–16,* ed. Werner H. Kelber (Philadelphia: Fortress, 1976), p. 82.
49. Ernst Fuchs, "The Quest of the Historical Jesus," in *Studies of the Historical Jesus*, trans. A. Scobie (Naperville, Ill.: Alec R. Allenson, 1964), pp. 20f. Cf. also Joachim Jeremias, *New Testament Theology*, vol. 1: *The Proclamation of Jesus*, trans. J. Bowden (New York: Scribner's, 1971), pp. 253ff., who makes the connection between the emphatic use of the word *ego* and Jesus' own conduct.
50. Hermann L. Strack und Paul Billerbeck, *Kommentar zum Neuen Testament aus Talmud und Midrasch*, vol. 1: *Das Evangelium nach Matthäus* (Munich: Beck, 1922), pp. 486f. Cf. also Stauffer, *Jesus and His Story*, pp. 163f.

Chapter 9: Jesus the Christ

1. Anton Fridrichsen, in his short but excellent study, *The Apostle and His Message*, Uppsala Universitets Årsskrift, 1947:3 (Uppsala: Lundequistska Bokhandeln, 1947), p. 3.
2. Ibid., p. 4.
3. Justin Martyr, *Dialogue with Trypho* 127, ANFa 1:263.
4. Ibid.
5. Ibid. 128, ANFa 1:264.
6. Ibid.
7. Justin Martyr, *First Apology* 21, ANFa 1:170.

8. Ibid. 46, 1:178.
9. Origen, *On First Principles* 1.2.4, ANFa 4:247
10. Cf. ibid. 1.2.2, ANFa 4:246.
11. Ibid. 1.2.8, ANFa 4:248.
12. Cf. Alexander's *Epistle,* in Socrates, *Church History* 1.6, NPNF (SS) 2: 4.
13. Cf. Athanasius, *Four Discourses against the Arians* 3.15f., NPNF (SS) 4:402.
14. Ibid. 3.16, NPNF (SS) 4:402.
15. Ibid. 3.16, NPNF (SS) 4:403.
16. According to Eusebius, *Life of Constantine* 2.69, NPNF (SS) 1:516.
17. Ibid. 2.72, NPNF (SS) 1:518.
18. Ibid. 2.73, NPNF (SS) 1:518.
19. Theodoret, *The Ecclesiastical History* 1.11, NPNF (SS) 3:49.
20. According to Socrates, *Church History* 1.8, NPNF (SS) 2:11.
21. Sozomen, *Church History* 1.19, NPNF (SS) 2:255.
22. Ibid. 1.20, NPNF (SS) 2:255.
23. Cf. "Creed of the 150 Holy Fathers," NPNF (SS) 14:163.
24. Origen, *Entretien avec Héraclide* 7, *Sources Chrétiennes,* 67:70.
25. Gregory of Nazianzus, *Epistle* 101.7, NPNF (SS) 7:440.
26. Apollinaris, *Epistola ad Dionysium* 1.6, in Hans Lietzmann, *Apollinaris von Laodicea und seine Schule* (Tübingen: J. C. B. Mohr, 1904), p. 258.
27. Cyril of Alexandria, *Epistola 17,* PG 77:115.
28. Cyril of Alexandria, *Epistola 4,* PG 77:46.
29. Cf. Cyril of Alexandria, *Dialogue on the Holy Trinity* 1, PG 75:682.
30. Tertullian, *On the Flesh of Christ* 5, ANFa 3:525.
31. Tertullian, *Against Praxeas* 27, ANFa 3:624.
32. Leo, *Tome,* NPNF (SS) 14:255.
33. Leo, *Tome,* NPNF (SS) 14:255 and *The Definition of the Faith of the Council of Chalcedon,* NPNF (SS) 14:265.
34. *The Definition of the Faith of the Council of Chalcedon,* NPNF (SS) 14: 264.
35. Anselm, *Cur Deus Homo?* 1.7, in *Basic Writings,* trans. S. W. Deane, intr. Charles Hartshorne (LaSalle, Ill.: Open Court, 1962), pp. 182ff.
36. Ibid. 1.21, p. 228.
37. Thomas Aquinas, *Summa Theologica* 3a. a1.a2.r, Latin text and English trans., intr., notes, appendixes, and glossaries (London: Blackfriars, 1964), 48:13.
38. Ibid. 3a.a4.a6.r, 48:133.

39. *Augsburg Confession* 1, in *The Book of Concord: The Confessional Writings of the Evangelical Lutheran Church*, trans. and ed. Theodore G. Tappert (Philadelphia: Fortress, 1959), pp. 27f.
40. Ibid. 3, p. 29.
41. Martin Luther, *Predigten des Jahres 1538*, WA 46:436, 7f., in a sermon on Trinity Sunday.
42. Martin Luther, *Die Promotionsdisputation on Georg Major und Johannes Faber* (1544), WA 39/2:293.
43. Ibid., WA 39/2:305, 23f.
44. Martin Luther, *Die Promotionsdisputation von Petrus Hegemon* (1545), WA 39/2:364, 8ff.
45. Martin Luther, *Predigten des Jahres 1541*, WA 49:238, 3-9, in a sermon on the day of the nativity of Christ.
46. Philip Melanchthon, *The Loci Communes*, with a critical intr. and trans. Charles Leander Hill (Boston: Meador, 1944), p. 67.
47. Martin Luther, WA.TR 1:72, 16f., according to Veit Dietrich (1531–1532).
48. Martin Luther, *Operationes in Psalmos* (1519–1521), WA 5:176, 32f.
49. Martin Luther, *Heidelberg Disputation* (1518), LW 31:53.
50. Martin Luther, ibid., LW 31:39 (my trans., cf. original Latin text in WA 1:353, 21f.).
51. Martin Luther, ibid., LW 31:40 (my trans., cf. original Latin text in WA 1:354, 21f.).
52. Martin Luther, *Confession concerning Christ's Supper* (1528), LW 37: 219.
53. Martin Luther, *Disputatio de divinitate et humanitate Christi* (1540), WA 39/2: 93, 6f.
54. Martin Luther, ibid., WA 39/2:121, 1f.
55. Philip Melanchthon, *Loci Communes* (1555), trans. and ed. Clyde L. Manschreck, intr. Hans Engelland (New York: Oxford University, 1965), p. 31.
56. Cf. for this and the following Martin Luther, *That These Words of Christ, "This is My Body" etc., Still Stand Firm against the Fanatics* (1527), LW 37:68.
57. Luther, *Smalcald Articles* 2.1, in *The Book of Concord*, p. 292.
58. Martin Luther, *Theses concerning Faith and Law* (1535), LW 34:109, in thesis 2.
59. Martin Luther, ibid., LW 34:114, in thesis 71.
60. Martin Luther, *Die Promotionsdisputation von Palladius und Tilemann* (1537), WA 39/1: 203, 5f.

61. Martin Luther, *Theses concerning Faith and Law* (1535), LW 34:111 (thesis 35).
62. Martin Luther, *Quaestio, utrum opera faciant ad iustificatione* (1520), WA 7:231, 9; 232, 11f.
63. Martin Luther, *Theses concerning Faith and Law* (1535), LW 34:111 (thesis 34).
64. Ruldolf Bultmann, *Theology of the New Testament*, trans. K. Grobel (New York: Scribner's, 1951), 1:43.
65. Dorothee Soelle, *Atheistisch an Gott glauben* (Freiburg: Walter, 1968), p. 49.
66. Ibid., p. 23.
67. Dietrich Bonhoeffer, *Letters and Papers from Prison,* ed. Eberhard Bethge, trans. R. Fuller, rev. ed. (New York: Macmillan, 1967), p. 188.
68. Dietrich Bonhoeffer, *Christ the Center*, intr. Edwin H. Robertson, trans. John Bowden (New York: Harper & Row, 1966), p. 117.
69. William Hamilton, *The New Essence of Christianity* (New York: Association, 1966), p. 94.
70. *Lutheran Book of Worship* (Minneapolis: Augsburg, 1978), hymn 51, stanzas 4 and 5.
71. Ibid., hymn 229, stanza 3.
72. Cf. Hans Schwarz, "Luther's Understanding of Heaven and Hell," in *Interpreting Luther's Legacy*, ed. Fred W. Meuser and Stanley D. Schneider (Minneapolis: Augsburg, 1969), pp. 92f.
73. Cf. Heinrich Denzinger, ed., *Enchiridium Symbolorum* 16, 34th ed. rev. by by Adolf Schönmetzer (Barcelona: Herder, 1967), p. 23; and cf. also J. N. D. Kelly, *Early Christian Creeds* (London: Longmans, Green, 1950), pp. 378f.
74. Cf. Martin Luther, *Confession concerning Christ's Supper* (1528), LW 37:347; the following quote ibid., p. 281.

Chapter 10: The Holy Spirit

1. According to Hermann L. Strack and Paul Billerbeck, *Kommentar zum Neuen Testament aus Talmud und Midrasch* (Munich: Beck, 1924), 2:430.
2. Ibid., p. 134.
3. Theophilus of Antioch, *Ad Autolycum* 2.10, text and trans. Robert M. Grant (Oxford: Clarendon, 1970), pp. 39ff.
4. Ibid. 1.7, p. 11.
5. Irenaeus, *Against Heresies* 2.25.1, ANFa 1:396.
6. Ibid. 2.28.4, 1:400.

7. Ibid. 2.28.5, 1:400.
8. Ibid. 1.22.1, 1:347.
9. Ibid. 4.7.4, 1:470.
10. Ibid. 2.7.6, 1:368.
11. Ibid. 5.1.1, 1:526.
12. Ibid. 5.1.1, 1:527.
13. Athanasius, *Ad Serapion* 1.20, in *The Letters by Athanasius concerning the Holy Spirit*, trans. with intr. and notes C. R. B. Shapland (New York: Philosophical Library, 1951), p. 115.
14. Ibid. 1.21, p. 120.
15. Ibid. 1.31, pp. 145f.
16. Ibid. 3.5, p. 174.
17. Ibid. 1.24, p. 127.
18. Ibid., p. 127, n. 8.
19. Ibid., p. 37, in Shapland's introductory remarks.
20. Ibid.
21. Gregory of Nyssa, *On the Holy Spirit: Against the Followers of Macedonius*, NPNF (SS) 1:320.
22. Athanasius, *Ad Serapion* 1.31, p. 142.
23. Basil the Great, *Letters* 90.2, NPNF (SS) 8:176.
24. Cf. the extensive comments by J. N. D. Kelly, *Early Christian Creeds*, 3rd ed. (London: Longman, 1972), pp. 342f.
25. Martin Luther, *The Licentiate Examination of Heinrich Schmedenstede* (1542), LW 34:315f., in his explanation of thesis 16.
26. Martin Luther, *In XV Psalmos graduum* (1532–1533), WA 40/3: 209,5f., in his comments on Ps. 127:1.
27. Gunnar Hillerdal, "Luthers Geschichtsauffassung," *Studia Theologica* vol. 7, fasc. 1 (1953), esp. pp. 42-53, where he says that Luther's doctrine of the *Wundermänner* is one of the most important parts of his understanding of history.
28. So rightly Paul Althaus, *The Theology of Martin Luther*, trans. R. C. Schultz (Philadelphia: Fortress, 1966), p. 440. It is noteworthy that in the index of the English translation of Althaus, references to the Holy Spirit are missing, while in the German original there are several significant references given that especially deal with Luther's understanding of the work of the Spirit in the political realm.
29. Martin Luther, *Lectures on Galatians* (1535), Chaps. 1–4, LW 26:217, in his comments on Gal. 3:3.

30. John Calvin, *Institutes of the Christian Religion* 1.13.14, ed. J. T. McNeill, trans. F. L. Battles, vol. 20 of *The Library of Christian Classics* (Philadelphia: Westminster, 1960), 1:138.
31. Cf. Regin Prenter, *Spiritus Creator*, trans. J. M. Jensen (Philadelphia: Muhlenberg, 1953), p. 192; quotation from p. 186.
32. Paul Tillich, *Systematic Theology*, vol. 3 (Chicago: University of Chicago, 1963), p. 247.
33. Ibid., p. 266.
34. Ibid., p. 276.
35. Pierre Teilhard de Chardin, *The Divine Milieu: An Essay on the Interior Life* (New York: Harper, 1960), p. 81.
36. Ibid., p. 86.
37. Pierre Teilhard de Chardin, *The Future of Man*, trans. N. Denny (New York: Harper, 1964), p. 93.
38. Wolfhart Pannenberg, *Gegenwart Gottes: Predigten* (Munich: Claudius, 1973), p. 106, in a sermon on John 4:19-24.
39. Cf. Wolfhart Pannenberg, "The Spirit of Life," in *Faith and Reality*, trans. J. Maxwell (Philadelphia: Westminster, 1977), p. 35. It is also interesting in this context that Helmut Thielicke, *The Evangelical Faith*, vol. 3: *Theology of the Spirit*, trans. and ed. Geoffrey W. Bromiley (Grand Rapids: Eerdmans, 1982), p. xxvii, rejects Pannenberg's attempt to emphasize the cosmological function of the Spirit and instead defines the Spirit "as the uncontrollable power of presentation or making present." Thielicke assumes that in so doing he retains a biblical approach to the Spirit.
40. Ibid., p. 38 (my translation).

Chapter 11: The Church

1. According to R. Newton Flew, *Jesus and His Church: A Study of the Idea of the Ecclesia in the New Testament* (London: Epworth, 1960 [1938]), p. 79.
2. Karl Heinrich Rengstorf, "*apostolos*," in TDNT 1:430.
3. "Constitution on the Sacred Liturgy" 1, in *The Documents of Vatican II*, Walter M. Abbott, gen. ed., with notes and comments by Catholic, Protestant, and Orthodox authorities (New York: Guild, 1966), p. 137.
4. "Decree on Ecumenism" 1, in *The Documents of Vatican II,* p. 341.
5. Bonaventure Kloppenburg, *The Ecclesiology of Vatican II*, trans. M. J. O'Connell (Chicago: Franciscan Herald Press, 1974), p. 3, gives an excellent description of the shift in emphasis and the rapprochement following Vatican II.

6. *Breaking Barriers, Nairobi 1975: The Official Report of the Fifth Assembly of the World Council of Churches, Nairobi, 23 November–10 December, 1975*, ed. David M. Paton (Grand Rapids: Eerdmans, 1976), p. 69.
7. "Dogmatic Constitution on the Church" 4, in *The Documents of Vatican II*, p. 17.
8. Ibid. 6, p. 18.
9. Ibid. 8, p. 23.
10. Ibid. 14, p. 33.
11. Ibid. 15, pp. 33f.
12. For this quote and the following see ibid. 31 and 33, pp. 57 and 59.
13. Ibid. 25, p. 127.
14. Ibid. 22, p. 126.
15. Ibid. 9, p. 117.
16. *Marburg Revisited: A Reexamination of Lutheran and Reformed Traditions*, ed. Paul C. Empie and James I. McCord (Minneapolis: Augsburg, 1966), Preface.
17. So Thomas E. Ambrogi, "Contemporary Roman Catholic Theology of the Eucharistic Sacrifice," in *Eucharist as Sacrifice*, Lutherans and Catholics in Dialogue, vol. 3 (New York: USA National Committee of the Lutheran World Federation, 1967), p. 162.
18. Paul C. Empie, T. Austin Murphy, and Joseph Burgess, eds., *Teaching Authority and Infallibility in the Church*, Lutherans and Catholics in Dialogue, vol. 6 (Minneapolis: Augsburg, 1980), p. 60, in the "Lutheran Reflections."
19. *Baptism, Eucharist and Ministry*, Faith and Order Paper No. 111 (Geneva: World Council of Churches, 1982), p. 3.
20. Ibid., p. 12.
21. Ibid., p. 13.
22. Ibid., p. 11.
23. Ibid., p. 13.
24. Ibid., p. 24.
25. Ibid., p. 28.
26. Ibid., p. 30.
27. Ibid., p. 31.
28. So, rightly, J. Robert Nelson, "Signs of Mankind's Solidarity," in J. Robert Nelson, ed., *No Man is Alien: Essays on the Unity of Mankind* (Leiden: Brill, 1971), p. 14.
29. Cf. for the following Karl Ludwig Schmidt, "*ekklesia*," TDNT 3:504f.
30. Cyprian, *Epistle 72* 21, ANFa 5:384.

31. Cyprian, *On the Unity of the Church* 6, ANFa 5:423.
32. According to A. J. Lewis, *Zinzendorf: The Ecumenical Pioneer; A Study in the Moravian Contribution to Christian Mission and Unity* (Philadelphia: Westminster, 1962), p. 67, Zinzendorf states in a conversation of 1736, "I acknowledge no Christianity without fellowship."
33. John A. Abbo and Jerome D. Hannan, *The Sacred Canons: A Concise Presentation of the Current Disciplinary Norms of the Church* (Canon 107) (St. Louis: Herder, 1952), 1:157.
34. "Dogmatic Constitution on the Church" 10, in *The Documents of Vatican II*, p. 27.
35. Ibid. 2, p. 491.
36. Cf. *The Augsburg Confession* 14, in *The Book of Concord: The Confessional Writings of the Evangelical Lutheran Church*, trans. and ed. Theodore G. Tappert (Philadelphia: Fortress, 1959), p. 36.
37. "Dogmatic Constitution on the Church" 25, in *The Documents of Vatican II*, p. 47.
38. Cf. *The Augsburg Confession* 5, in *The Book of Concord*, p. 31.
39. *One Baptism, One Eucharist, and a Mutually Recognized Ministry* 13, Faith and Order Paper No. 73 (Geneva: World Council of Churches, 1975), p. 33.
40. Piet Fransen, "Orders and Ordination," in *Sacramentum Mundi: An Encyclopedia of Theology* (New York: Herder, 1968–1970), 4:325.
41. Ibid.
42. Joachim Heubach, *Die Ordination zum Amte der Kirche* (Berlin: Lutherisches Verlagshaus, 1956), p. 101.
43. Johannes Remmers, "Apostolic Succession: An Attribute of the Whole Church," trans. J. Drury, in *Apostolic Succession: Rethinking a Barrier to Unity*, ed. Hans Küng, *Concilium: Theology in the Age of Renewal*, vol. 34 (New York: Paulist, 1968), p. 51.
44. Cf. for this and the following Gerhard Ebeling, *The Word of God and Tradition: Historical Studies Interpreting the Divisions of Christianity*, trans. S. H. Hooke (Philadelphia: Fortress, 1968), p. 146.
45. Augustine, *On the Psalms* 5, NPNF (FS) 8:601, in his comments on Psalm 125.
46. H. Richard Niebuhr, *The Social Sources of Denominationalism* (Hamden, Conn.: Shoe String Press, 1929), p. 24.
47. Dietrich Bonhoeffer, *The Communion of Saints: A Dogmatic Inquiry into the Sociology of the Church*, trans. R. G. Smith (New York: Harper, 1963), p. 116.

48. "Declaration on the Relationship of the Church to Non-Christian Religions" 4, in *The Documents of Vatican II*, pp. 664f.
49. Ibid. 4, p. 665.
50. H. Richard Niebuhr, *Christ and Culture* (New York: Harper and Row, 1956).
51. Ronald Sider, ed., *The Chicago Declaration of Evangelicals* (Carol Stream, Ill.: Creation House, 1974), from "A Declaration of Evangelical Social Concern" (front cover).
52. Arnold W. Ravin, "Science, Values, and Human Evolution, *Zygon* 11 (June 1976), p. 151. Cf. also Wolfgang Wickler, *The Biology of the Ten Commandments*, trans. D. Smith (New York: McGraw-Hill, 1972).
53. Dietrich Bonhoeffer, *Letters and Papers from Prison*, ed. Eberhard Bethge, trans. R. Fuller, rev. ed. (New York: Macmillan, 1967), p. 211.
54. Harvey Cox, *The Secular City: Secularization and Urbanization in Theological Perspective*, rev. ed. (New York: Macmillan, 1968 [1965]), p. 116.
55. Gibson Winter, *The New Creation as Metropolis* (New York: Macmillan, 1963), p. 59.
56. Gerhard Uhlhorn, *Christian Charity in the Ancient Church* (New York: Scribner's, 1883), p. 362.
57. Dietrich Bonhoeffer, *Life Together*, trans. with an intr. John W. Doberstein (New York: Harper, 1954), p. 27.
58. Ibid., p. 38.
59. J. Robert Nelson, "Signs of Mankind's Solidarity," in J. Robert Nelson, ed., *No Man Is Alien*, p. 14.
60. Friedrich Schleiermacher, *The Christian Faith,* par. 163, appendix, ed. H. R. MacKintosh and J. S. Stewart, trans. D. M. Baillie et al. (Edinburgh: T. & T. Clark, 1928), p. 722.
61. "Recommendations of Section 2: What Unity Requires," in *Breaking Barriers: Nairobi 1975*, p. 69.
62. Moshe Greenberg, "Mankind, Israel and the Nations in the Hebraic Heritage," in J. Robert Nelson, *No Man Is Alien*, p. 35.
63. Ibid., p. 37.

Chapter 12: The Means of Grace

1. Martin Luther, *Lectures on Galatians* (1519), LW 27:355, in his exegesis of Gal. 5:14.
2. Martin Luther, *Predigten des Jahres 1540*, WA 49:2, 1f., in a sermon on January 1, 1540.

3. Karl Barth, "Gospel and Law," in *God, Grace and Gospel*, Scottish Journal of Theology Occasional Papers 8, trans. J. S. McNab (Edinburgh: Oliver & Boyd, 1959), p. 3.
4. Ibid., p. 8.
5. Ibid., p. 10.
6. Ibid.
7. Cf. Martin Luther, *Against Latomus* (1521), LW 32:226f.; and Paul Althaus, *The Theology of Martin Luther*, trans. R. C. Schultz (Philadelphia: Fortress, 1966), p. 258.
8. Johann Wolfgang von Goethe, *Faust*, Parts 1 and 2 (11936f.), trans. G. M. Priest, vol. 47 of *Great Books of the Western World*, ed. Robert M. Hutchins (Chicago: Encyclopaedia Britannica, 1952), p. 290.
9. John Calvin, *Institutes of the Christian Religion* 2.7.12, ed. John T. McNeill, trans. F. L. Battles, vol. 20 of *The Library of Christian Classics* (Philadelphia: Westminster, 1960), 1:360.
10. Walter Kaspar, "Law and Gospel," in *Sacramentum Mundi: An Encyclopedia of Theology* (New York: Herder, 1968–1970), 3:297.
11. Martin Luther, *The Small Catechism*, "The Sacrament of Holy Baptism," in *The Book of Concord: The Confessional Writings of the Evangelical Lutheran Church*, trans. and ed. Theodore G. Tappert (Philadelphia: Fortress, 1959), p. 349.
12. Martin Luther, *The 95 Theses* (October 31, 1517), LW 31:25.
13. Ibid., thesis 3.
14. *The Augsburg Confession* 7, in *The Book of Concord*, p. 32.
15. Ibid. 13, p. 35.
16. Martin Luther, *The Large Catechism*, "Baptism," in *The Book of Concord*, p. 436.
17. *The Apology of the Augsburg Confession* 13 in *The Book of Concord*, p. 211.
18. "Constitution on the Sacred Liturgy" 59, in Walter M. Abbott, gen. ed. *The Documents of Vatican II*, with notes and comments by Catholic, Protestant, and Orthodox authorities (New York: Guild, 1966), p. 158.
19. Raphael Schulte, "Sacraments," in *Sacramentum Mundi*, 5:378.
20. For this and the following cf. Karl Rahner, "The Word and the Eucharist," in *Theological Investigations*, vol. 4: *More Recent Writings*, trans. K. Smyth (Baltimore: Helicon, 1966), p. 274.
21. Tertullian, *To the Martyrs* 3.1, FaCh 40:22.
22. Justin Martyr, *The First Apology* 66, ANFa 1:185.

23. Tertullian, *On Prescription against Heretics* 40, ANFa 3:262. It is not without significance that he too refers to the Mithras cult, perhaps implying the threatening nature of this cult for the Christian notion of the sacraments and the affinity of their rituals.
24. John Chrysostom, *Homily 15 on John 1:18*, FaCh 33:150.
25. Augustine, *Reply to Faustus the Manichaean* 19.16, NPNF (FS), 4:245.
26. Augustine, *Letters* 98.9, NPNF (FS) 1:410.
27. Augustine, *On the Gospel of St. John* 80.3, NPNF (FS) 7:344, in his exegesis of John 15:1-3.
28. Martin Luther, *The Small Catechism*, "The Sacrament of Holy Baptism," in *The Book of Concord*, p. 349.
29. Augustine, *On the Gospel of St. John* 80.3, NPNF (FS) 7:344, in his exegesis of John 15:1-3.
30. Augustine, *Letters* 98.9, NPNF (FS) 1:410.
31. *The Augsburg Confession* 5, in *The Book of Concord*, p. 31.
32. Ibid. 7, p. 32.
33. Ibid. 8, p. 33.
34. For this and the following quote see Heinrich Denzinger, ed., *The Sources of Catholic Dogma*, 849 and 851, trans. R. J. Deferrari (St. Louis: Herder, 1957), pp. 262f.
35. Raphael Schulte, "Sacraments," in *Sacramentum Mundi*, 5:380.
36. Karl Rahner, "The Word and the Eucharist," in *Theological Investigations*, 4:274.
37. Schulte, 5:380.
38. *The Augsburg Confession* 5, in *The Book of Concord*, p. 31.
39. Martin Luther, *The Small Catechism*, "The Sacrament of Holy Baptism," in *The Book of Concord*, p. 349.
40. Schulte, 5:380.
41. Karl Barth, *The Teaching of the Church regarding Baptism*, trans. E. A. Payne (London: SCM, 1948), p. 49.
42. Ibid., p. 53.
43. Ibid., p. 54.
44. "Constitution on the Sacred Liturgy" 67, in *The Documents of Vatican II*, p. 160.
45. Barth, *The Teaching of the Church regarding Baptism*, p. 23.
46. R. A. Barclay, "New Testament Baptism: An External or Internal Rite?" in *Initiation*, ed. C. J. Bleeker (Leiden: Brill, 1965), p. 183.
47. For this and the following quote see Martin Luther, *The Small Catechism*, "The Sacrament of Holy Baptism," in *The Book of Concord*, p. 349.

48. R. A. Barclay, "New Testament Baptism," p. 183.
49. Martin Luther, *The Small Catechism*, "The Creed," in *The Book of Concord*, p. 345.
50. *The Heidelberg Catechism*, with commentary, trans. A. O. Miller and M. E. Osterhaven (Philadelphia: United Church Press, 1962), p. 129, in the explanation of question 76; the term "sacramental realism" is used by the commentator on this question (cf. p. 130).
51. Ibid., p. 130.
52. *The Augsburg Confession* 10, in *The Book of Concord*, p. 34.
53. Martin Luther, *The Small Catechism*, "The Sacrament of the Altar," in *The Book of Concord*, p. 351.
54. Heinrich Denzinger, ed., *The Sources of Catholic Dogma* 877, pp. 267f.; cf. also p. 169 (430).
55. Cf. the theses in *Die Eucharistie: Das Sagorsker Gespräch über das hl. Abendmahl zwischen Vertretern der Evangelischen Kirche in Deutschland und der Russischen Orthodoxen Kirche* (Bielefeld: Luther-Verlag, 1974), pp. 23f. (esp. thesis 4).
56. Wolfhart Pannenberg, "Das Abendmahl—Sakrament der Einheit," in *Ethik und Ekklesiologie: Gesammelte Aufsätze* (Göttingen: Vandenhoeck & Ruprecht, 1977), p. 287.
57. Richard John Neuhaus, *Forum Letter* (March 21, 1980), p. 5.
58. So Eric Gritsch, "Infant Communion: Old Bone in New Contention," *Lutheran Forum* 13 (Lent 1979), p. 6.
59. Cyprian, *De Lapsis* and *De Ecclesiae Catholicae Unitate* 9 and 25, text and trans. M. Bévenot (Oxford: Clarendon, 1971), pp. 15 and 37f. For more historical information cf. also Roger T. Beckwith, "The Age of Admission to the Lord's Supper," *Westminster Theological Journal* 38 (Winter 1976), esp. pp. 125ff.; and Eugene L. Brand, "Baptism and Communion of Infants: A Lutheran View," *Worship* 50 (January 1976), pp. 36ff.

Chapter 13: The Christian Hope

1. Friedrich Engels, "On the History of Early Christianity" (1894–1895), in Karl Marx and Friedrich Engels, *On Religion*, intr. Reinhold Niebuhr (New York: Schocken, 1964), pp. 317f.
2. Rudolf Bultmann, "New Testament and Mythology," in *Kerygma and Myth: A Theological Debate,* ed. Hans Werner Bartsch and trans. R. H. Fuller (London: SPCK, 1953), 1:39. Even Bultmann admits that the resurrection of Jesus is often used as a miraculous proof in the New Testament.

3. Martin Luther, *Fastenpostille* (1525), WA 17/2:235, 17-20.
4. Luther, *Predigten* (1533), WA 37:151, 8ff.
5. For the following cf. "The Beatific Vision of God and the Last Days," in Heinrich Denzinger, ed., *The Sources of Catholic Dogma* 530–531, trans. R.J. Deferrari (St. Louis: Herder, 1957), pp. 197f.
6. Cf. Michael Schmaus, *Der Glaube der Kirche: Handbuch katholischer Dogmatik*, 2 vols. (Munich: Hueber, 1969–1970), 2:744ff. and 773ff.
7. Martin Luther, WA.TR 2:627, 29-628, 4.
8. H. Richard Niebuhr, *The Kingdom of God in America* (New York: Harper, 1959), p. 193.
9. Cf. Paul Althaus, *The Theology of Martin Luther*, trans. R. C. Schultz (Philadelphia: Fortress, 1966), pp. 420f., for an excellent treatment of Luther's eschatology.
10. Martin Luther, *Predigten* (1533), WA 37:65, 33. Cf. also Hans Schwarz, "Luther's Understanding of Heaven and Hell," in *Interpreting Luther's Legacy*, ed. Fred W. Meuser and Stanley D. Schneider (Minneapolis: Augsburg, 1969), pp. 83-94.
11. Luther, *Operationes in Psalmos* (1519–1521), WA 5:497, 16-19.
12. Luther, WA.TR 3:276, 26f.
13. Wolfhart Pannenberg, *What Is Man? Contemporary Anthropology in Theological Perspective*, trans. Duane A. Priebe (Philadelphia: Fortess, 1970), p. 44 (trans. alt.).

FOR FURTHER READING

Introduction

Aulén, Gustaf. *The Faith of the Christian Church.* Translated by Eric H. Wahlstrom. Philadelphia: Fortress, 1960.

Barrett, Charles D. *Understanding the Christian Faith.* Englewood Cliffs, N. J.: Prentice-Hall, 1980.

Ebeling, Gerhard. *The Study of Theology.* Translated by Duane A. Priebe. Philadelphia: Fortress, 1978.

Gilkey, Langdon. *Message and Existence: An Introduction to Christian Theology.* New York: Seabury, 1979.

Gonzalez, Justo. *History of Christian Thought.* 3 vols. Nashville: Abingdon, 1970–1975.

Hanson, A. T. and Hanson, R. P. C. *Reasonable Belief: A Survey of the Christian Faith.* Oxford: Oxford University, 1980.

Hodgson, Peter C. and King, Robert, editors. *Christian Theology: An Introduction to Its Traditions and Tasks.* Philadelphia: Fortress, 1982.

Jersild, Paul T. *Invitation to Faith: Christian Belief Today.* Minneapolis: Augsburg, 1978.

Kaufman, Gordon D. *Systematic Theology: A Historicist Perspective.* New York: Scribner's, 1968.

Lohse, Bernhard. *A Short History of Christian Doctrine.* Translated by F. Ernest Stoeffler. Philadelphia: Fortress, 1966.

Pannenberg, Wolfhart. *The Apostles' Creed in the Light of Today's Questions.* Translated by Margaret Kohl. Philadelphia: Westminster, 1972.

Pelikan, Jaroslav. *The Christian Tradition: A History of the Development of Doctrine.* 5 vols. Chicago: University of Chicago, 1971–.

Rahner, Karl. *Foundations of Christian Faith: An Introduction to the Idea of Christianity.* Translated by William V. Dych. New York: Seabury, 1978.

Chapter 1: Theology

Barth, Karl. *Church Dogmatics.* 13 vols. and index. Edited by G. W. Bromiley and T. F. Torrance, Edinburgh: T. & T. Clark, 1936–1977.

Brunner, Emil. *Dogmatics.* 3 vols. Translated by Olive Wyon. Philadelphia: Westminster, 1950–1963.

Calvin, John. *Institutes of the Christian Religion.* Edited by John T. McNeill. Translated by F. L. Battles. Vol. 20 of *The Library of Christian Classics.* Philadelphia: Westminster, 1960.

Macquarrie, John. *Principles of Christian Theology.* New York: Scribner's, 1966.

Prenter, Regin. *Creation and Redemption.* Translated by T. I. Jensen. Philadelphia: Fortress, 1967.

Ritschl, Albrecht. *The Christian Doctrine of Justification and Reconciliation: A Positive Development of the Doctrine.* Translated and edited by H. R. MacKintosh and A. B. Macaulay. Clifton, N. J.: Reference Book Publishers, Inc., 1966.

Schleiermacher, Friedrich. *The Christian Faith.* Edited by H. R. Mackintosh and J. S. Stewart. Translated by D. M. Baillie et al. Edinburgh: T. & T. Clark, 1928.

Segundo, Juan Luis. *A Theology for Artisans of a New Humanity.* 5 vols. Translated by John Drury. Maryknoll, N.Y.: Orbis, 1973–1974.

Thielicke, Helmut. *The Evangelical Faith.* 3 vols. Edited and translated by Geoffrey W. Bromiley. Grand Rapids: Eerdmans, 1974–1982.

Tillich, Paul. *Systematic Theology.* 3 vols. Chicago: University of Chicago, 1951–1963.

Chapter 2: Revelation

Baillie, John. *The Idea of Revelation in Recent Thought.* New York: Columbia University, 1956.

Barr, James. *Old and New in Interpretation: A Study of the Two Testaments.* London: SCM, 1966.

Cobb, John B. *A Christian Natural Theology Based on the Thought of Alfred North Whitehead.* Philadelphia: Westminster, 1965.

Cullmann, Oscar. *Salvation in History.* Translated by S. G. Sowers. London: SCM, 1967.

Dulles, Avery. *Revelation Theology: A History.* New York: Herder and Herder, 1969.

Gilkey, Langdon. *Reaping the Whirlwind: A Christian Interpretation of History.* New York: Seabury, 1977.

Kierkegaard, Søren. *Concluding Unscientific Postscript.* Translated by D. F. Swenson and W. Lowrie. Princeton: Princeton University, 1941.

Löwith, Karl. *Meaning in History.* Chicago: University of Chicago, 1949.

Niebuhr, H. Richard. *The Meaning of Revelation.* New York: Macmillan, 1941.

Pannenberg, Wolfhart, ed. *Revelation as History*. Translated by David Granskou. London: Macmillan, 1968.

Von Rad, Gerhard. *Old Testament Theology*. 2 vols. Translated by D. M. G. Stalker. New York: Harper & Row, 1962, 1965.

Chapter 3: Scripture

Barr, James. *The Bible in the Modern World*. London: SCM, 1973.

Childs, Brevard. *Biblical Theology in Crisis*. Philadelphia: Westminster, 1970.

Frei, Hans. *The Eclipse of Biblical Narrative*. New Haven: Yale University, 1974.

Frye, Northrop. *The Great Code: The Bible and Literature*. New York: Harcourt Brace Jovanovich, 1981.

Gadamer, Hans Georg. *Truth and Method*. Translation edited by Garrett Barden and John Cumming. New York: Seabury, 1975.

Kelsey, David. *The Uses of Scripture in Recent Theology*. Philadelphia: Fortress, 1975.

Kümmel, Werner Georg. *The New Testament: The History of the Investigation of Its Problems*. Translated by S. MacLean Gilmour and Howard Clark Kee. Nashville: Abingdon, 1972.

MacKnight, Edgar V. *Meaning in Texts: The Historical Shaping of a Narrative Hermeneutics*. Philadelphia: Fortress, 1978.

Ricoeur, Paul. *Essays on Biblical Interpretation*. Edited with an introduction by Lewis S. Mudge. Philadelphia: Fortress, 1980.

Robinson, James M. and Cobb, John B., eds. *The New Hermeneutic*. Vol. 2 of *New Frontiers in Theology*. New York: Harper & Row, 1964.

Stuhlmacher, Peter. *Historical Criticism and Theological Interpretation of Scripture*. Translated and with an introduction by Roy A. Harrisville. Philadelphia: Fortress, 1977.

Chapter 4: God

Cobb, John B. *God and the World*. Philadelphia: Fortress, 1969.

Ebeling, Gerhard. *God and Word*. Translated by James W. Leitch. Philadelphia: Fortress, 1967.

Gilkey, Langdon. *Naming the Whirlwind: The Renewal of God-Language*. Indianapolis: Bobbs-Merrill, 1969.

Kaufman, Gordon. *God the Problem*. Cambridge: Harvard University, 1971.

Küng, Hans. *Does God Exist? An Answer for Today.* Translated by Edward Quinn. Garden City, N.Y.: Doubleday, 1980.

Moltmann, Jürgen. *The Trinity and the Kingdom: The Doctrine of God.* Translated by Margaret Kohl. San Francisco: Harper & Row, 1981.

Niebuhr, H. Richard. *Radical Monotheism and Western Culture.* With Supplementary Essays. New York: Harper, 1960.

Ogden, Schubert. *The Reality of God and Other Essays.* New York: Harper & Row, 1966.

Pannenberg, Wolfhart. *The Idea of God and Human Freedom.* Translated by R. A. Wilson. Philadelphia: Westminster, 1973.

Schwarz, Hans. *The Search for God.* Minneapolis: Augsburg, 1975.

Zahrnt, Heinz. *The Question of God: Protestant Theology in the Twentieth Century.* Translated by R. A. Wilson. New York: Harcourt Brace Jovanovich, 1969.

Chapter 5: Creation

Gilkey, Langdon. *Maker of Heaven and Earth: A Study of the Christian Doctrine of Creation.* Garden City, N.Y.: Doubleday, 1959.

Heim, Karl. *The World: Its Creation and Consummation. The End of the Present Age and the Future of the World in Light of the Resurrection.* Translated by R. Smith. Philadelphia: Muhlenberg, 1962.

Overman, Richard H. *Evolution and the Christian Doctrine of Creation: A Whiteheadian Interpretation.* Philadelphia: Westminster, 1967.

Renckens, Henricus. *Israel's Concept of the Beginning: The Theology of Genesis 1–3.* New York: Herder, 1964.

Reumann, John. *Creation & New Creation: The Past, Present, and Future of God's Creative Activity.* Minneapolis: Augsburg, 1973.

Von Rad, Gerhard, *Genesis: A Commentary.* Translated by J. H. Marks. Philadelphia: Westminster, 1961.

Westermann, Claus. *Creation.* Translated by J. J. Scullion. Philadelphia: Fortress, 1974.

Wingren, Gustaf. *Creation and Law.* Translated by Ross MacKenzie. Philadelphia: Muhlenberg, 1961.

Chapter 6: Humanity

Brunner, Emil. *Man in Revolt: A Christian Anthropology.* Translated by Olive Wyon. Philadelphia: Westminster, 1947.

Moltmann, Jürgen. *Man: Christian Anthropology in the Conflicts of the Present.* Translated by J. Sturdy. Philadelphia: Fortress, 1974.

Niebuhr, Reinhold. *The Nature and Destiny of Man: A Christian Interpretation.* 2 vols. New York: Scribner's, 1949.

Pannenberg, Wolfhart. *What Is Man? Contemporary Anthropology in Theological Perspective.* Translated by Duane A. Priebe. Philadelphia: Fortress, 1970.

Pittenger, Norman W. *The Christian Understanding of Human Nature.* Philadelphia: Westminster, 1964.

Ruether, Rosemary Radford. *New Woman/New Earth.* New York: Seabury, 1975.

Schwarz, Hans. *Our Cosmic Journey: Christian Anthropology in the Light of Current Trends in the Sciences, Philosophy, and Theology.* Minneapolis: Augsburg, 1977.

Teilhard de Chardin, Pierre. *Man's Place in Nature: The Human Zoological Group.* Translated by R. Hague. New York: Harper, 1966.

Teilhard de Chardin, Pierre. *The Phenomenon of Man.* Introduction by Julian Huxley. Translated by B. Wall. New York: Harper, 1959.

Wolff, Hans Walter. *Anthropology of the Old Testament.* Translated by M. Kohl. Philadelphia: Fortress, 1974.

Chapter 7: Sin

Becker, Ernest. *The Denial of Death.* New York: Free Press, 1973.

Becker, Ernest. *Escape From Evil.* New York: Free Press, 1975.

Berkouwer, G. C. *Sin.* Translated by Philip C. Holtrap. Grand Rapids: Eerdmans, 1971.

Bonhoeffer, Dietrich. *Creation and Fall: A Theological Interpretation of Genesis 1–3.* Translated by John C. Fletcher and Kathleen Downham. New York: Macmillan, 1959.

Fromm, Erich. *The Heart of Man: Its Genius for Good and Evil.* New York: Harper & Row, 1964.

Griffin, David. *God, Power and Evil: A Process Theodicy.* Philadelphia: Westminster, 1976.

Hick, John. *Evil and the God of Love.* New York: Harper & Row, 1966.

Kierkegaard, Søren. *Fear and Trembling and The Sickness Unto Death.* Translated with introduction and notes by Walter Lowrie. Princeton: Princeton University, 1941.

Luther, Martin. *The Bondage of the Will,* LW 33.

Niebuhr, Reinhold. *Moral Man and Immoral Society: A Study in Ethics and Politics.* New York: Scribner's, 1932.

Schoonenberg, Piet. *Man and Sin: A Theological View.* Translated by Joseph Donceel. Notre Dame: University of Notre Dame, 1965.

Chapter 8: Jesus of Nazareth

Bornkamm, Günther. *Jesus of Nazareth*. Translated by Irene and Fraser McLuskey with James M. Robinson. New York: Harper & Row, 1960.

Bultmann, Rudolf. *Jesus and the Word*. Translated by Louise Pettibone Smith and Erminie Huntress Lantero. New York: Scribner's, 1958.

Fuchs, Ernst. *Studies of the Historical Jesus*. Translated by A. Scobie. Naperville, Ill.: Alec R. Allenson, 1964.

Gogarten, Friedrich. *Christ the Crisis*. Translated by R. A. Wilson. London: SCM, 1970.

Jeremias, Joachim. *New Testament Theology*, vol. 1: *The Proclamation of Jesus*. Translated by John Bowden. New York: Scribner's, 1971.

Perrin, Norman. *Rediscovering the Teachings of Jesus*. New York: Harper & Row, 1976.

Robinson, James M. *A New Quest for the Historical Jesus*. Naperville, Ill.: Alec R. Allenson, 1959.

Schillebeeckx, Edward. *Jesus: An Experiment in Christology*. Translated by Hubert Hoskins. New York: Seabury, 1979.

Schleiermacher, Friedrich. *The Life of Jesus*. Edited with an introduction by Jack C. Verheyden. Translated by S. Maclean Gilmour. Philadelphia: Fortress, 1975.

Schweitzer, Albert. *The Quest of the Historical Jesus: A Critical Study of Its Progress from Reimarus to Wrede*. Preface by F. C. Burkitt. Translated by W. Montgomery. New York: Macmillan, 1966.

Stauffer, Ethelbert. *Jesus and His Story*. Translated by Dorothea M. Barton. London: SCM, 1960.

Chapter 9: Jesus the Christ

Baillie, D. M. *God Was in Christ*. London: Faber & Faber, 1961.

Boff, Leonardo. *Jesus Christ Liberator: A Critical Christology for Our Time*. Translated by Patrick Hughes. Maryknoll, N.Y.: Orbis, 1978.

Bonhoeffer, Dietrich. *Christ the Center*. Introduction by Edwin H. Robertson. Translated by John Bowden. New York: Harper & Row, 1966.

Brunner, Emil. *The Mediator: A Study of the Central Doctrine of the Christian Faith*. Translated by Olive Wyon. Philadelphia: Westminster, 1947.

Cobb, John B. *Christ in a Pluralistic Age*. Philadelphia: Westminster, 1975.

Driver, Tom F. *Christ in a Changing World: Toward an Ethical Christology*. New York: Crossroad, 1981.

Moltmann, Jürgen. *The Crucified God: The Cross of Christ as the Foundation and Criticism of Christian Theology.* Translated by R. W. Wilson and John Bowden. New York: Harper & Row, 1974.

Pannenberg, Wolfhart. *Jesus—God and Man.* Translated by Lewis L. Wilkens and Duane A. Priebe. Philadelphia: Westminster, 1968.

Ruether, Rosemary Radford. *To Change the World: Christology and Cultural Criticism.* New York: Crossroad, 1983.

Schillebeeckx, Edward. *Christ: The Experience of Jesus as Lord.* Translated by John Bowden. New York: Crossroad, 1981.

Sobrino, Jon. *Christology at the Crossroads: A Latin American Approach.* Translated by John Drury. Maryknoll, N.Y.: Orbis, 1978.

Chapter 10: The Holy Spirit

Barrett, C. K. *The Holy Spirit and the Gospel Tradition.* London: SPCK, 1966.

Berkhof, Hendrikus. *The Doctrine of the Holy Spirit.* Atlanta: John Knox, 1976.

Bruner, Frederick D. *Theology of the Holy Spirit: The Pentecostal Experience and the New Testament Witness.* Grand Rapids: Eerdmans, 1970.

Dunn, J. D. G. *Jesus and the Spirit.* London: SCM, 1975.

Hendry, George S. *Holy Spirit in Christian Theology.* Philadelphia: Westminster, 1965.

Heron, Alasdair I. C. *The Holy Spirit: The Holy Spirit in the Bible, the History of Christian Thought, and Recent Theology.* Philadelphia: Westminster, 1983.

Jensen, Richard A. *Touched by the Spirit: One Man's Struggle to Understand His Experience of the Holy Spirit.* Minneapolis: Augsburg, 1975.

Lampe, G. W. H. *God as Spirit.* The Bampton Lectures, 1976. Oxford: Clarendon, 1977.

Moule, C. F. D. *The Holy Spirit.* Grand Rapids: Eerdmans, 1977.

Prenter, Regin. *Spiritus Creator.* Translated by J. M. Jensen. Philadelphia: Muhlenberg, 1953.

Ramsey, Michael. *The Holy Spirit.* London: SPCK, 1977.

Chapter 11: The Church

Barreiro, Alvaro. *Basic Ecclesial Communities: The Evangelization of the Poor.* Translated by Barbara Campbell. Maryknoll, N.Y.: Orbis, 1982.

Bonhoeffer, Dietrich. *Life Together.* Translated with an introduction by John W. Doberstein. New York: Harper & Row, 1954.

Dulles, Avery. *Models of the Church*. Garden City, N.Y.: Doubleday, 1974.
Jay, Eric G. *The Church: Its Changing Image through Twenty Centuries*. Atlanta: John Knox, 1980.
Küng, Hans. *The Church*. Translated by Ray and Rosaleen Ockenden. New York: Sheed and Word, 1967.
Minear, Paul. *Images of the Church in the New Testament*. Philadelphia: Westminster, 1960.
Moltmann, Jürgen. *The Church in the Power of the Spirit: A Contribution to Messianic Ecclesiology*. Translated by Margaret Kohl. New York: Harper & Row, 1977
Pittenger, Norman. *The Christian Church as Social Process*. London: Epworth, 1971.
Schwarz, Hans. *The Christian Church: Biblical Origin, Historical Transformation, and Potential for the Future*. Minneapolis: Augsburg, 1982.
Troeltsch, Ernst. *The Social Teaching of the Christian Churches*. 2 vols. Translated by Olive Wyon. New York: Harper & Row, 1960.
Wingren, Gustaf. *Gospel and Church*. Translated by Ross MacKenzie. Philadelphia: Fortress, 1964.

Chapter 12: The Means of Grace

Baptism, Eucharist and Ministry. Faith and Order Paper No. 111. Geneva: World Council of Churches, 1982.
Beasley-Murray, George R. *Baptism Today and Tomorrow*. New York: St. Martin's, 1966.
Brand, Eugene L. *Baptism: A Pastoral Perspective*. Minneapolis: Augsburg, 1975.
Brilioth, Yngve. *Eucharistic Faith and Practice, Evangelical and Catholic*. Translated by A. G. Herbert. London: SPCK, 1930.
Cooke, Bernard. *Ministry to Word and Sacraments: History and Theology*. Philadelphia: Fortress, 1980.
Cullmann, Oscar. *Baptism in the New Testament*. Translated by J. K. S. Reid. London: SCM, 1950.
Higgins, A. J. B. *The Lord's Supper in the New Testament*. London: SCM, 1952.
Jenson, Robert W. *Visible Words: The Interpretation and Practice of Christian Sacraments*. Philadelphia: Fortress, 1978.
Jeremias, Joachim. *The Eucharistic Words of Jesus*. Translated by Norman Perrin. Philadelphia: Fortress, 1977.
Schlink, Edmund. *The Doctrine of Baptism*. Translated by Herbert Bouman. St. Louis: Concordia, 1972.

Schwarz, Hans. *The Divine Communication: Word and Sacrament in Biblical, Historical, and Contemporary Perspective.* Philadelphia: Fortress, 1985.

Wainwright, Geoffrey. *Eucharist and Eschatology.* London: Epworth, 1971.

Chapter 13 : The Christian Hope

Brunner, Emil. *Eternal Hope.* Translated by H. Knight. Philadelphia: Westminster, 1954.

Bultmann, Rudolf. *History and Eschatology: The Presence of Eternity.* New York: Harper, 1957.

Gutierrez, Gustavo. *A Theology of Liberation: History, Politics and Salvation.* Translated and edited by Caridad Inda and John Eagleson. Maryknoll, N.Y.: Orbis, 1973.

Hick, John H. *Death and Eternal Life.* New York: Harper & Row, 1976.

Minear, Paul. *Christian Hope and the Second Coming.* Philadelphia: Fortress, 1974.

Moltmann, Jürgen. *Theology of Hope: On the Ground and the Implications of a Christian Eschatology.* Translated by James W. Leitch. New York: Harper & Row, 1967.

Niebuhr, H. Richard. *The Kingdom of God in America.* New York: Harper, 1937.

Pannenberg, Wolfhart. *Theology and the Kingdom of God.* Philadelphia: Westminster, 1969.

Rosenstock-Huessy, Eugen. *The Christian Future, Or the Modern Mind Outrun.* New York: Harper & Row, 1966.

Ruether, Rosemary Radford. *The Radical Kingdom: The Western Experience of Messianic Hope.* New York: Harper & Row, 1970.

Schwarz, Hans. *On the Way to the Future: A Christian View of Eschatology in Light of Current Trends in Religion, Philosophy, and Science.* Revised Edition. Minneapolis: Augsburg, 1979.

Teilhard de Chardin, Pierre. *The Future of Man.* Translated by N. Denny. New York: Harper & Row, 1964.

INDEX OF NAMES

Abbahu, 213
Abbo, J. A., 425
Alaric, 119, 169
Albright, W. F., 412
Alexander, 224f., 228, 419
Althaus, P., 41f., 407, 413, 422, 427, 430
Altizer, T. J. J., 181, 247
Ambrogi, T. E., 424
Amin, Idi, 31
Anaxagoras, 80
Anselm of Canterbury, 26f., 34, 37, 46, 73-75, 234f., 252, 405f., 419
Anthony, Third Earl of Shaftesbury, 106, 408
Apollinaris of Laodicea, 230f., 419
Aristides, 19f.
Aristotle, 18, 23, 27f., 61, 77, 406
Arius, 224-227, 258
Athanasius, 57, 224, 228, 230, 268f., 419, 422
Augustine, 24f., 26, 30, 57, 61, 119, 121, 160f., 162-166, 167, 169f., 234, 236, 295, 319, 326, 345, 357, 377, 388, 410, 413-415, 425, 428
Autolycus, 266

Bach, J.S., 185
Bar Kochba, 47, 203
Barclay, R. A., 428f.
Barth, K., 32, 42, 43, 71, 85, 111, 152f., 190, 246f., 345f., 359-361, 405, 407, 409, 413, 427f.
Basil, 24, 269, 422
Beckwith, R. T., 429
Benedict XII (Pope), 391
Berger, P. L., 43
Bethge, E., 408, 410, 421, 426
Billerbeck, P., 418, 421
Bloch, E., 377
Boccaccio, G., 66
Boehme, J., 103
Bonhoeffer, D., 65, 91, 123, 246f., 321, 330, 332, 408, 410, 421, 425f.
Brand, E. L., 429
Brown, R. E., 412

Brunner, E., 43, 130, 327, 411f.
Bruno, G., 102f., 408
Buber, M., 92, 408
Buchman, F., 333
Buddha, 71, 173, 193
Bultmann, R., 110f., 149, 174, 189f., 196, 207, 243, 381, 409, 412, 416-418, 421, 429

Calvin, J., 29f., 168, 248f., 271f., 318, 347, 360, 415, 423, 427
Celsus, 21f.
Chrysostom, John, 356, 428
Cicero, 41, 80
Clement, 59
Cobb, J. B., 33
Coelestius, 162
Constantine, 224-226, 228
Copernicus, N., 102
Cox, H., 330, 426
Cudworth, R., 105f.
Cullmann, O., 111f., 409
Cyprian, 300, 318, 374, 424f., 429
Cyril of Alexandria, 231-233, 269, 419

Darwin, C., 80, 406
Decius, 31
Descartes, R., 30, 75f., 105, 406
Didymus, 269
Dietrich, V., 420
Diodore of Iarsus, 230f.
Dionysius (Bishop of Rome), 225
Dionysius of Alexandria, 225
Dionysius the Areopagite, 24, 26, 86, 407
Driesch, H., 80

Ebeling, G., 425
Meister Eckhart, 92
Einstein, A., 108
Engels, F., 379, 429
Ephraem, 255
Epiphanius, 23
Erasmus, D., 165, 414
Eusebius of Caesarea (Bishop), 19, 225, 226, 405, 419

Feuerbach, L., 44, 71
Fichte, J. G., 83
Finkel, A., 417
Flew, R. N., 423
Foester, W., 412
Fohrer, G., 412
Ford, L. S., 408
Fransen, P., 425
Freud, S., 151
Fridrichsen, A., 418
Fromm, E., 142, 411
Fuchs, E., 191, 198, 244, 418

Gerhard, J., 168, 415
Gideon, 69
Gilkey, L., 43
Gladden, Washington, 183
Goethe, J. W. von, 103, 346, 427
Gogarten, F., 120, 410
Goppelt, L., 418
Gray, A., 406
Green, S., 408
Greenberg, M., 426
Gregory the Great, 234
Gregory of Nazianzus, 24, 229f., 419
Gregory of Nyssa, 269, 422
Gritsch, E., 429
Grünewald, M., 182

Hadrian, 19
Hamann, J. G., 84
Hamilton, Wm., 247, 421
Hannan, J. D., 425
Harkness, G., 138, 411
Harnack, A. von, 58, 181-183, 186, 188, 416f.
Harner, P. B., 418
Hartshorne, C., 33, 86f., 107, 108, 407-409
Hegel, G. W. F., 102, 104f., 119, 133, 141, 408, 410f.
Heraclitus, 21, 223
Herodotus, 134
Hesiod, 18
Heubach, J., 425
Hillel (Rabbi), 417
Hillerdal, G., 422
Homer, 18
Hosios of Cordoba, 225
Hugo of St. Victor, 357
Hume, D., 81

INDEX OF NAMES 441

Ignatius, 221
Innocent (Pope), 57
Irenaeus, 166f., 241, 267f., 374, 414, 421f.

Jaspers, K., 98
Jeremias, J., 418
Joachim of Fiore, 377
John XXII (Pope), 391
John of Damascus, 23f.
John Scotus Erigena, 25f.
Josephus, 19, 196, 418
Judas the Galilean, 47
Julian of Eclanum, 162
Jung, C. G., 142, 151, 411
Justin Martyr, 20f., 56, 222f., 356, 405, 418f., 427

Kant, I., 31, 45, 74, 79-86, 88, 104, 106, 150f., 170, 406-408, 412
Kaspar, W., 349, 427
Kaufmann, G. D., 151, 413
Kelber, W. H., 418
Kelly, J. N. D., 421f.
Kierkegaard, S., 85, 407
King, H. C., 183
Kloppenburg, Bonaventure, 423
Kluger, R. S., 412
Küng, H., 425

Leibnitz, G. W., 89f.
Leo (Pope), 232f., 419
Leontius, 24
Lessing, G. E., 42, 66, 103, 177, 189
Lewis, A. J., 425
Lietzmann, H., 419
Locke, J., 30, 117
Lombard, Peter, 28
Lonergan, B., 43
Loofs, F., 413
Lorenz, K., 150, 164, 414
Lowrie, W., 407
Luther, M., 28f., 30, 34, 41f., 61-63, 72f., 87f., 89, 106, 116, 118, 126, 137, 152-154, 159, 165f., 167f., 176, 236-242, 243, 246, 248, 249, 253, 255, 257, 270-272, 288, 308, 318, 326f., 335, 343, 346, 349, 351-353, 357, 359f., 364, 366, 367f., 374, 377, 391, 395, 397, 401, 403, 406f., 410f., 413-415, 420-422, 426-430

Maccabaeus, Judas, 203

McSorley, H. J., 414
Mao Tse-tung, 377
Marcion, 56, 58, 255
Mari Mercator, 413
Marx, K., 340, 379, 429
Mathews, S., 183-185, 417
Melanchthon, P., 29, 61, 176, 237, 240, 347, 349, 353, 405, 416, 420
Melito, 255
Mohammed, 66, 173, 193
Moltmann, J., 34, 109, 407, 409
Monod, J., 116
Moses, 66, 67, 68

Nelson, J. R., 333, 424, 426
Nero, 31
Nestorius, 232
Neuhaus, R. J., 374, 429
Newton, I., 76
Niebuhr, H. Richard, 323, 396, 425f., 430
Niebuhr, Reinhold, 171, 413, 429
Nietzsche, F., 333
Norris, R. A., 413

Origen, 21-23, 26, 223f., 227, 229, 230, 234f., 253, 255, 405, 419
Otto, R., 86
Outler, A. C., 410
Overhage, P., 410

Paley, W., 81, 406
Pannenberg, W., 34, 43, 112f., 274, 370, 409f., 423, 429f.
Papias, 56, 405
Paton, D. M., 424, 426
Peabody, F. G., 183
Pelagius, 162-165, 170, 413
Perrin, N., 418
Philo of Alexandria, 19
Pittenger, N., 33
Pius XII (Pope), 84
Plato, 18, 22, 77, 92, 389
Ploger, J., 411
Plotinus, 86
Prenter, R., 272, 423
Pritchard, J. B., 412
Psamtik II, 134

Quadratus, 19

Rad, G. von, 125, 130, 408, 411
Rahner, K., 354f., 357, 359, 427f.

Ranke, L. von, 88
Rauschenbusch, W., 171, 183, 416
Ravin, A. W., 117, 328, 410, 426
Raymond of Sebonde, 81f.
Reimarus, H. S., 176-178, 186, 187, 416
Remmers, J., 425
Rengstorf, K. H., 280, 423
Riesenfeld, H., 194, 417
Ritschl, A., 169-171, 415f.
Robinson, J. M., 190f., 417
Rufinus of Aquileia, 255

Salvianus of Marseilles, 119
Schammai (Rabbi), 418
Schiller, F., 83, 119, 141f., 410f.
Schleiermacher, F. D. E., 31f., 87, 103, 178-180, 336, 399, 407, 416, 426
Schmaus, M., 168, 392, 415, 430
Schmidt, K. L., 424
Schmidt, W., 71
Schopenhauer, A., 103, 105, 408
Schulte, R., 427f.
Schwarz, H., 421, 430
Schweitzer, A., 175, 181, 185-189, 205, 376, 381, 417
Semler, J. S., 176, 178
Serapion of Thmuis (Bishop), 269
Shapland, C. R. B., 269, 422
Shaftesbury, See Anthony, Third Earl of Shaftesbury
Sider, R., 426
Silver, A. H., 418
Simai (Rabbi), 418
Simpson, G. G., 116, 410
Singer, D. W., 408
Socrates (philosopher), 21, 223
Socrates (historian), 419
Soelle, D., 246, 421
Sozomen, 228, 419
Spinoza, Benedict (Baruch), 102, 103f., 408
Stackhouse, M. L., 416
Stalin, J., 31
Stauffer, E., 418
Strack, H. L., 418, 421
Strauss, D. F., 179-181, 185, 186, 247, 416
Swete, H. B., 413

Tatian, 56, 57

442 INDEX OF BIBLICAL REFERENCES

Teilhard de Chardin, P., 142, 273f., 394, 411, 423
Tertullian, 225, 232, 355, 356, 419, 427f.
Theodore of Mopsuestia, 163, 230f., 413f.
Theodoret, 23, 419
Theophilus of Antioch (Bishop), 266., 421
Theudas, 195
Thielicke, H., 423
Thomas Aquinas, 27f., 33, 77-79, 81, 167, 235, 406, 414, 419

Tillich, P., 32f., 248, 272f., 405, 423
Tindal, M., 42
Toland, J., 42, 103
Torrance, T. F., 415
Toynbee, A., 14
Troeltsch, E., 244, 320

Uhlhorn, G., 331, 426

Vincent of Lérins, 59, 319, 405
Voltaire, 106f., 397, 408

Weber, O., 413
White, L. Jr., 131f., 411
Whitehead, A. N., 33, 86, 107, 407-409
Wickler, W., 426
Winter, G., 330, 426
Wrede, W., 187

Xenophanes, 102

Zinzendorf, N. von, 301, 333, 425
Zoroaster, 145-147
Zwingli, U., 239f., 257, 367

INDEX OF BIBLICAL REFERENCES

Genesis
1–2 99
1:1—2:42 98
1 36f., 101
1:1 101, 266
1:2 266, 271, 407
1:4,5 100
1:6f. 116
1:10,12, 18, 21, 25 100
1:26-28 116, 124, 128, 129, 133, 166, 168, 411, 415
1:31 100, 210
2 36f.
2:4b-26 98
2:7 125, 144, 411
2:15-17 129, 143-144
2:18 127
2:19f. 129
2:24 127
3 141, 142, 154
3:10 155
3:12,13 142
3:15 144, 211, 383
3:19 125, 144
3:21 116, 144, 211, 383
4:1ff. 141
4:17ff. 141
4:26 67
6–9 141
6:1-4 141
6:3 261

6:5 158
6:17 260
8:21 157
8:22 115
11:1-9 141, 283, 297
17:1 67
17:7 411
18:14 91, 113, 119
18:20 155
21:33 68
28:10-22 68
32:25-32 68
41:8 260
41:38 261

Exodus
6:2f. 67
15:8 261
19:6 282
20:2 97, 108, 347
31:3f. 261

Leviticus
11:44 94
19:18 201, 347

Deuteronomy
5:6 97
6:4 201
6:20ff. 97, 108
7:9 93
18:9-14 70
26:5-11 68, 108
32:17 69
32:29 197

Judges
6–8 69
7:1 69

2 Samuel
6:6f. 94
12:13 155
12:24 93
24:1 95

1 Kings
8:27 93, 402
11:7f. 69

1 Chronicles
21:1,17 144, 145

Nehemiah
13:26 93

Job
1 128
1:6ff. 145
10:8-12 126
32:8 260
34:14f. 260f.
38–42 98

Psalms
8 98, 129
8:4,5 128, 129
11:7 94
14:1 26, 72
19 98
19:7 347
30:5,6 95, 266
33:10ff. 98
33:6 261
51:5 158

51:10ff. 115, 261
68:4 70
74 98
89:48 402
90:1-2 88, 139
102:25-27 88, 389
104 98
119:105 347
125 425
127:1 422
136 98
139:7-10 89
139:13f. 126
147:13 411
148 98

Proverbs
3:19f. 267
8:22 266

Isaiah
2:2f. 98, 109, 321
6 128
7:14 215
9:1f. 215
35:5f. 48, 193, 200
40:28 88
41:4 197
42:5 210, 382
43:10 197
43:25,27 157, 158
44:6 382
45:8 210, 382
46:4 197
49:6 98
53:4 215

INDEX OF BIBLICAL REFERENCES 443

54:1-5   158
55:3   94

Ezekiel
1   100
11:19f.   297
18:4   155
20:5   108
36:26f.   261

Daniel
2:44   200
3:1-6   129
4:31   200

Joel
2:28f.   261, 283

Amos
1:6-8   109
5:21-27   70

Micah
5:2   215
6:8   93

Zechariah
2:11   283
3:1ff.   145

Matthew
1:1   174
1:18   263
1:22f.   215
2:5f.   215
3:2   177, 401
3:8-11   193
4:1-11   154
4:12-15   215
4:17   351
5–7   215
5:3   401
5:3-12   201
5:13   376
5:17f.   54, 195, 215
5:19,20   195
5:21f.   54
6:8   89
6:9-13   200f., 278
7:3   330
7:13f.   398
7:19   193
8:17   215
8:22   199
9:17   48, 200
10   215
10:1-5   278-280
10:14f.   350
10:28   402
10:29f.   116

11:4f.   122, 193
11:6   199
11:11,13   193
12:28   263
12:31f.   157
12:34   193
12:40   255
13   386
13:30   215, 400
13:49ff.   400
14:12   192
15:24   282
16:13-20   276
16:16f.   245
16:18f.   215, 276, 300
16:19   350
16:20   277
16:27   396
18:15ff.   215
18:17   276
18:18   350
19:26   91
19:28   278, 279
22:13   402
22:30   387
23:15   194
24   215, 217
24:5   197
24:29f.   394
24:36   376
25:31f.   396
25:40   330
25:41   402
26:26-29   366
26:33   208
26:39   139
26:69-75   208
27:51-53   255
27:62—28:15   212, 384
28:13   213, 244
28:16ff.   278, 279
28:18   257
28:19   281
28:20   300

Mark
1:1ff.   174, 263
1:8   263
1:12f.   148
1:15   46, 193
1:21   193
1:22   194
2:9   194
2:10   204
2:15-16   157
2:19   278
2:28   204
3:7   193

3:14   278
3:21   248
3:22-27   148
3:31   248
4:11f.   215, 355
5:7   154
5:35   193
6:6-13   278, 280
6:30   193
6:50   198
6:52   215
7:24-30   194
8:27,28   194
8:29f.   196
8:31   193
9:32   215
9:48   402
10:38,41-45   278
10:45   203, 330
12:19   193
12:28-34   201
13   217
13:6   197, 198
13:9-13   278
13:32   205
14:14   278
14:22-25   366
14:24   57, 94
14:28   278
14:61-62   195, 197, 198, 408
16:1,7   278
16:16   366

Luke
1:1-4   174, 317
1:5f.   216
1:25   269
1:35   263, 266
1:37   91, 113, 119
1:52   138, 201
2:1-4   216
3:38   211
4:16-19   283
6:20   201
7:15   385
7:18-22   201
7:22   47, 199
8:52   390
9:62   199
10:1ff.   278
10:16   309
10:18,19   148
10:30-37   202
10:38-42   279
11:20   48, 193, 200, 253
12:48   397
13:1-5   120, 148
14:12ff.   201

15:2-7   198
16:16   195, 216, 283
16:19-31   390
17   217
17:21   200
19:7   193
21   217
22:3   148
22:15-20   366
22:32   148
23:43   205, 390
24:19ff.   279
24:21   196, 205
24:37   212, 213, 244, 385

John
1:1ff.   53, 210, 221, 382
1:2,3   266
1:11   218
1:14   217, 221, 248, 264
2:11   200
3:3,4   149, 245
3:6,7   264
3:17   149
3:18   46
3:36   157, 398f.
4:19-24   423
4:24   264
4:25f.   204
5:24   217
5:25,28f.   390
5:39   57
6:19   217
6:51b-59   366
6:63   264, 269
8:44   153
9:3   120, 150
9:35ff.   204
11:24ff.   217
11:44   385
14:2,3   217
14:6   46
14:12   411
14:15ff.   218
14:17   264
14:25f.   218
15:1-3   428
15:5   298
15:9ff.   217
15:22   157
15:26   269
16:4b-15   217, 218
18:28   278
18:36   196
20:1   278
20:22f.   350

20:30f. 317
21 280

Acts
1:6-8 280, 281, 283
1:21-26 279
2:4 263
2:5 281
2:12f. 248
2:36 282
2:38 365
2:42-46 281, 295, 373f.
4 297
4:12 46
4:19f. 242, 281
5:29 208
6:1-6 313
8:30 173
8:36,37 362
9:13 282
10:36 281
10:43 57
13:1-3 313
13:15 302
13:47 284
14:22 283
15:13,14 282, 302
17:2f. 55
17:28 89
17:31 94
22:16 362
26:23 213

Romans
1:1 280
1:1-6 218
1:4 209, 382
1:7 282
1:16f. 95
1:18-23 70f.
1:19f. 41
1:20f. 84f., 265, 271
1:25 159
2:14ff. 159, 343
3:21 345
3:25f. 95
3:28 241
5 210, 211, 382
5:12-21 211
5:12 158, 163
5:18f. 159
5:20f. 344
5:21 161

6 211
6:4f. 213, 296, 385
7 160, 211
7:5 160
7:14-18 160
7:24f. 161
8 211
8:4 265
8:9 365
8:19-23 258, 395
8:23ff. 220, 258
8:29 168
8:34 256
8:38f. 300
9:25 301
10:4 220
10:9 209, 251, 282, 362, 382
10:10 250
10:12 304
11:1 282
11:14-26 282
11:32-36 399, 410
12:4-8 305
14:23 155
16:1 299

1 Corinthians
1:2 282, 284, 299
1:9 363
1:22 249
2:7f. 249, 355
2:9 404
2:11f. 249
6:4 299
6:11 363
6:14 213, 385
6:19 161
7:10 53, 55
7:25 55
10:16f. 298
11:23-25 58, 366
11:25 296
12:12 305
12:13-27 298
13 220
13:12 35, 403
15 212, 220, 384
15:3f. 55, 58
15:5 279
15:14 212, 384
15:20 390
15:28 258, 337, 403
15:32 378
15:42-54 387

15:44,45 264
15:50 385
15:52b 387
15:55-58 122, 148, 154, 253, 334
16:22 372, 397

2 Corinthians
1:1 299
3:6 57, 220
3:17 264, 269, 365
3:18 168, 329
4:14 220
5:5 265
5:7 220
5:10 396
5:17-19 49, 95, 252, 257

Galatians
1:8 53, 59
2:20 220
3:3 422
3:13,24 344
3:27f. 304f.
4:4 110
4:22-31 58
5:14 426
6:7 397
6:14f. 257

Ephesians
1:23 299
3:10 299, 300
4:10 402
4:13 292
5:22-33 299

Philippians
2:5-11 209, 219, 382
3:8 288
3:12 258

Colossians
1:15,16 210, 383, 395
1:18 213, 257, 385
2:9 250
2:13f. 252f.
2:19 299
4:16 56

1 Thessalonians
4:13 220, 387

4:15,16 388, 396
5:2 220

1 Timothy
1:3,14 314
1:18 313
2:4 399
3:14 313
4:13 314
5:1f. 314
5:16 299
5:22 314

Titus
3:5 365

Hebrews
1:1f. 47, 55, 110, 172, 211, 342, 383
1:10-12 389
4:13 89
10:31 95
12:2 252, 404

1 Peter
2:9 282
3:15 36
3:19 255

2 Peter
1:1 94
2:17 402
3:2 55
3:4 390
3:10 394
3:15-16 55f.

1 John
2:15,17 149

Revelation
1:18 255
6:9 392
12:10 148
14:11 399
20:12 396
21:3f. 403
21:22-25 340
22:20 372, 397

Apocrypha
Judith 262
Wisdom 262
Sirach 262

Apostolic Fathers
1 Clement 59
Ignatius 221
2 Clement 55f., 265
Hermas 265f.

INDEX OF SUBJECTS

Absolution, 349-352
Accommodation, theory of, 178
Adoptionism, 234
Agnosticism, 26
Ahura Mazda, 145f.
Animals, 124, 127-130, 134-136, 150
Anti-Godly powers, 115, 118, 143, 150-154, 156-158, 253, 275, 324, 326, 328
Antinomies, 45, 79, 85
Apocalyptic, 47f., 109, 113, 178, 180, 203, 212f., 384f., 387, 396-398, 402f.
Apologetics, 19-22, 36-37, 85, 100, 106
Apologists, 19-25, 72, 222f.
Apostasy, 60
Apostles, 53, 55, 59, 177, 277-282, 287
Apostles' Creed, 29f., 97, 176, 241, 254-256, 296, 366, 385, 403
Apostolic fathers, 18, 221f.
Apostolic succession, 293, 313, 316f.
Arianism, 224-229, 232, 258
Ascension, 177, 179, 180, 216, 256f.
Aseity, 88, 92
Atheism, 26f., 31, 41, 72, 96, 104, 105f., 118, 160, 223f., 361
Atonement, theories of, 252-254
Augsburg Confession, 236, 272, 307f., 311, 349, 353, 358f., 367

Babylonian exile, 99f.
Babylonian influences, 145f.
Baptism, 162, 211, 220, 242, 282, 287, 291f., 296, 298, 304f., 306, 312f., 335, 349, 351, 353-366, 374f.
Bible, 22, 28f., 35, 53-63, 178, 288f., 304, 316, 318, 320f.
Birth narratives, 180, 244
Bishops, 59, 287, 293, 308
Body, 125, 262, 264, 380, 385f., 403
Body of Christ, 298f., 306, 353, 365, 371, 373
Book of Concord, 63, 347
Buddhism, 13, 173, 336, 377

Call, 309f., 313f.
Canaanites, 68f.
Canon, 54-63, 318
Catholic(ity), 289, 319
Chalcedon, Council of (A.D. 451), 50f., 232-234
Christ, 27, 29, 61, 111-113, 154, 161, 207-258, 296, 300f., 309f., 326f., 335, 355, 369-372, 383; two natures of, 29, 50-52, 176, 223f., 227, 229-234, 235, 239f., 243, 250-252
Christianity, 13-15, 66, 119, 181, 223, 349, 378
Christocentricity, 29, 31, 62, 237, 246, 286, 300
Christological controversies, 50, 229-234, 250
Christological titles, 202-204, 215
Christology, 30, 180, 207-258, 370-372
Christomonism, 245f.
Church, 25, 27, 35, 53, 58, 61, 110, 215f., 263f., 276-340, 353-355, 365f.
Church and society, 322-329
Church fathers, 59, 61, 356f., 372
Clergy 302-307, 309
Communicatio idiomatum, 239f.
Compassion of God, 49, 93-95, 107, 123, 144, 256, 263, 275, 383
Confession and absolution, 349-352
Confirmation, 287, 375
Conscience, 41, 117, 318
Conscience of society, 322-329
Constantinople, First Council of (A.D. 381), 228f., 269f., 284
Constantinople, Fifth Council of (A.D. 553), 234
Conversion, 171, 329, 335, 348, 362
Cosmic Christ, 254-258
Cosmological argument, 77-79, 81
Covenant, 57f., 93f., 115, 121, 220, 338
Creation, 36f., 43, 83, 96-131, 142, 149, 151f., 209-212, 223, 261f., 268f., 271f., 275, 297, 373, 382f.; priestly account, 99f., 101, 124f.; Yahwistic account 101, 125-128
Creator, 64, 84, 97-102, 105, 124-128, 149, 338, 393
Creatureliness, 124-128
Creed(s), 60, 61, 108f., 209, 226-229, 255, 318, 362
Cross, 26, 174, 237-239, 249, 254, 331, 371
Crucifixion, 213, 244, 248f., 278, 381

Deacon(s), 293, 308, 311f., 330
Death, 122, 125, 143f., 147, 158f., 211, 253, 335, 363f., 377f., 383, 386f., 391, 398
Death-of-God theology, 181, 247
Deception, theory of, 26, 234f.
Deism, 90, 92, 102, 105-108, 113, 211, 383
Demons/demonic, 145, 148, 150, 153, 160
Denominations, 284f., 290, 292, 294, 296, 306, 320f., 337, 358, 365
Descent to the dead, 254-256
Design, 79-81, 90
Determinism, 90
Devil, 26, 154, 234f., 253, 264, 326
Disciples, 278-282, 381
Disobedience, 131, 142
Docetism, 230, 243, 250
Donatism, 24, 358
Doxology, 38, 85, 133, 137f.
Dualism, 100, 132, 146-150, 275

Easter, 48, 177, 204, 207f., 213f., 245, 279, 381
Ecclesiology, 30, 286
Ecological crisis, 126, 131-134, 340
Ecumenism, 36, 62, 285-294, 318f., 333, 368
Ego eimi, 197-199, 204
Emperor(s), 19, 24, 31, 208, 224-226, 228
Empty tomb, 180, 211f., 214, 244, 384
Enlightenment, 42f., 81, 150, 176, 178

445

446 INDEX OF SUBJECTS

Eschatology, 34, 47f., 111, 118, 120-123, 182f., 187-189, 199-206, 220, 278, 283f., 296, 322, 328f., 332, 338-340, 365, 372f., 376-404
Eternal life, 30, 82, 183, 217, 365, 398
Eternity, 88, 92, 389
Ethics, 117, 132, 187f., 328, 349
Ethnology, 71
Ethology, 117, 159, 328
Eucharist, 240f., 291-293, 296, 298, 316, 334, 349, 352-363, 366-375
Evil, 90, 119, 140-154, 163f., 166f., 171, 329
Evolution, 99, 116, 142, 184f., 273f.
Exegesis, 51, 58, 178, 288

Faith, 112f., 241f., 250, 362, 366; Christian, 13, 15f., 17, 20, 34, 53, 63, 174, 275; credible, 36, 175; reasonable, 15, 19, 27, 83; responsible, 9f., 15, 19, 22, 27, 34; seeks understanding 27, 37, 73
Fall, 26, 105, 118, 141-144, 146f., 154, 160, 166f., 210f., 229f., 234, 383
Fate/fatalism, 89, 92, 114, 163
Feeling of absolute dependence, 31, 87, 179
Filioque, 228f., 284f.
First cause, 77-79, 86, 98, 106, 222
Flesh, 160f., 230f., 260f., 264, 385f.
Foreknowledge, 89f.
Forgiveness, 39, 138, 157, 332, 335, 345, 350-352, 363
Freedom, 14, 90f., 220; human, 21, 89, 115, 120, 133, 136, 143, 160-166, 168, 170, 272, 349

Gnosticism, 54, 59, 130, 149, 220, 244, 263, 267, 386
God, 20, 22, 24, 27-29, 32, 38, 41, 43, 64-95, 97-102, 108f., 114-123, 144, 146, 152-154, 172, 182, 221-229, 232, 251f., 399f., 403f.; active in history, 16, 30, 97f., 108-114, 250; attributes of, 41, 49, 73, 75., 85-95; knowledge of, 22, 30, 41-43, 46, 79f., 72-87, 237, 246; proofs of existence, 24, 26, 37, 50, 73-85, 249; self-disclosure of, 40f., 44-53, 63, 72, 84, 87f., 95, 107, 112, 204, 214, 268, 275
Gods, 20, 36, 66-72, 83, 92, 100, 119, 209
Good works, 165, 242
Gospel, 18, 43, 48, 59, 62, 144, 174, 184, 194, 211, 219, 306, 310, 317-319, 342-353, 383
Gospels, 37, 54, 56, 174, 177, 189, 214-218
Grace, 25, 28f., 43, 61f., 95, 120, 144, 161, 164, 166f., 211, 311, 315, 345f., 363f., 397
Greek thought, 18, 20-22, 27, 89, 227f., 386, 389

Healing, 122f., 138f.
Heaven, 35, 217, 390, 401f.
Hell, 254-256, 300, 390, 401-403
Hellenism, 23, 31, 181, 222f., 378
Heretic/heresy, 23, 39, 132, 204, 224, 229, 233f., 285, 316, 319f., 358
Higher dimension, 44-46, 51f., 213f., 244f., 250-254
Historical argument, 83f.
History, 13, 16, 30, 33, 42, 49, 51, 98, 110-114, 119f., 189, 205f., 210, 212, 216, 243, 270-272, 383; goal of in Jesus Christ, 48f., 204-206, 210-213, 383; turning point in Jesus Christ, 48, 111, 205, 216
Holiness, 49, 93-95, 296
Holy Spirit, 20, 112, 157, 218, 228f., 237, 258-276, 296f., 318, 358, 364-366
Homoousios, 225-227, 268-270
Hope, 48-50, 329, 336f., 340, 376-404
Humanity, 85, 92, 94, 117f., 124-139, 153f., 155, 159-171, 247, 251, 262f., 297, 324f., 328, 380

"I am," 197-199, 204
Idolatry, 71f., 156, 159f.
Image of God, 128-134, 154, 166-169, 172
Immortality, 82, 262, 372, 380, 386, 388, 392
Incarnation, 27-29, 217, 239, 243-249, 251, 268
Infallibility, 287, 291f.

Infant Baptism, 359-361, 374
Infant Communion, 374f.
Intermediate state, 388-393
Intertestamental period, 145-147, 262f., 387
Islam, 13, 23, 26f., 66, 132, 173, 233, 236
Israel, 49, 51, 57f., 67-70, 93f., 97, 100, 108f., 177, 179, 194f., 215, 277, 281f., 321f., 399
Jesus, 20, 22, 26, 33, 51f., 110, 122, 147f., 156f., 178-206, 243-247, 276f., 355, 367, 369f., 404; historical, 46, 50f., 53f., 175-191, 207, 250, 381f.
Jesus Christ, 30, 42, 46-53, 63, 84, 95, 111, 123, 172-258, 275f., 296f., 317, 382, 397, 403f.
Jews, 20, 26, 55, 62, 194, 281, 338, 342f., 384, 399
Judaism, 54, 66, 156, 195, 200, 262f., 281-283, 321f., 338, 349
Judgment, 82f., 95, 120, 169, 189, 203, 215, 258, 295, 386, 390-398, 400f.
Justification, 211, 241f., 291, 315, 318, 348
Justice, 327, 329, 399

Kerygma, 18, 54, 63, 190f., 220, 243, 280, 342
Kingdom of evil, 169-171
Kingdom of God, 48, 95, 119, 157, 169-171, 182, 184-188, 200f., 204, 276f., 326f., 329, 335, 365, 400f.
Knowledge, 42, 107, 131, 136

Laity, 35, 287, 301-307
Language, 134, 297
Last Supper, 196, 278, 367, 371f.
Lateran Council, Fourth (1215), 368
Law (Torah), 54, 62, 194f., 343
Law, 29, 43, 82, 211, 220, 342-349
Law and gospel, 121, 342-346, 350, 399
Leaders, 301f., 307-310, 312-314
Liberal theology, 32, 42, 183f., 188f., 245
Liberation theology, 33f., 183, 318, 329
Liturgy, 38, 335, 339, 354

INDEX OF SUBJECTS 447

Logos, 21f., 33, 72, 194, 221-224, 226, 230-232, 248, 266f., 275
Lord, 53, 55, 208f., 250, 282, 321, 326f., 369, 382
Lord's Supper, 312, 349, 367, 369f., 373
Love command, 201f., 347f.
Love of God, 93, 107f., 201f., 345, 347f., 399
Lutheran church/theology, 290-292, 309, 316, 354, 359, 367f.
Lutheran Orthodoxy, 29, 168, 347

Manichaeanism, 24, 160, 275
Marcionism, 54, 56
Marxism, 14, 132, 323, 325, 332, 336, 404
Materialism, 14, 104-106, 288, 378, 404
Means of grace, 341-375
Messiah, 57f., 94, 122, 180, 182, 185f., 189, 195f., 198f., 202f., 205, 209, 219, 244, 277, 281-283, 322
Middle Ages, 14, 24f., 28, 59f., 66, 81, 150, 234f., 295, 375, 393, 397
Ministers/ministry, 293f., 303f., 307, 310-312, 316, 330, 358f.
Miracles, 54, 121-123, 139, 181, 189, 194, 216, 334
Mission(ary), 13f., 29, 290-284, 304, 333, 336f., 362, 364
Monasticism, 304, 332f.
Monophysites, 60, 233
Monotheism, 70f., 146, 223f.
Montanism, 54, 56
Moral argument, 81-83, 85, 104
Moslems, 26f., 66, 336
Mysticism, 25, 28, 247
Myth(ology), 99f., 154, 190

Natural knowledge of God, 72-85, 265
Natural law, 84, 117, 150, 159, 180, 271, 327f., 342-344
Natural theology, 42f., 70f., 84
Nature, 25f., 42, 76, 81-83, 88, 100, 103f., 106, 114-117, 121, 125, 131-134, 144, 164, 273f.
Neo-Platonism, 22, 26, 86, 167, 170
Nestorianism, 60, 232f.

New creation, 118, 120, 168, 211f., 219f., 251, 257f., 263, 271f., 329, 334, 365, 373, 383f., 395
New Testament, 22, 37, 46, 53-58, 93f., 110, 122, 147-150, 156f., 174, 176, 190f., 200, 206, 208, 214-221, 263-265, 298, 309, 316f., 355, 382, 392f., 394-396, 398f., 402f.
Nicea, Council of (A.D. 325), 225-228, 232, 236
Nicene Creed, 226f., 284, 291, 296

Office of the Keys, 349-352
Old Testament, 44, 47, 53-58, 62, 67, 93f., 109, 111, 115, 141-145, 179, 201, 215, 219, 260-262, 270, 321, 338f., 345, 380, 401f.
Omnipotence, 86, 88, 91f., 257
Omnipresence, 86, 88f., 92, 239f., 257
Omniscience, 86, 88, 89-92
Ontological argument, 26, 73-76, 81
Oral tradition, 54f., 58f.
Ordained/ordination, 118, 293, 303, 305, 309, 313-316, 328, 357
Original sin, 167, 170f.
Orthodox Church theology, 24, 284-286, 290, 293, 316, 322, 355f., 368f., 374f.
Overpopulation, 126, 131-134

Pagans/paganism, 20f., 41, 69, 72, 119, 132, 159f., 223, 342f., 349, 356, 364, 378, 399
Pantheism, 83, 89, 102-105, 107f., 113, 132
Papacy/pope, 24, 285, 287, 291
Paradox, 51, 152, 247f.
Parousia, 212f., 205f., 210, 219, 257, 273, 284, 293, 332, 367, 373, 379, 397
Pelagianism, 24, 38f., 162-165, 170
Pentecost, 248, 281, 297f.
People of God, 294-317
Persecution, 19, 31, 282
Person, God as, 92-94, 105
Philosophy, 18-21, 24, 26, 27, 30f., 41, 86f., 104, 151f., 349, 377
Platonism, 21-23, 377

Political messiah(ship), 196, 203, 205, 245f.
Polytheism, 92, 102, 223f.
Prayer, 13, 20, 122f., 137-139, 294, 334f.
Predestination, 24, 89, 164
Preservation, 117f., 271f., 297, 328
Priest(hood), 293, 301-308, 311f., 315f., 357, 374
Process thought, 33, 86f., 90, 107f.
Proclamation, 177, 190-192, 294, 296f., 312, 336, 339, 350f.
Progress, 132, 136, 377, 379
Proleptic anticipation, 48, 120, 204, 212f., 220, 258, 277, 296, 322, 331-334, 365, 379, 385, 390f., 404
Proofs of God's existence, 24, 26, 28, 37, 50, 73-85, 213, 249, 250
Prophets, 54, 109
Protestantism, 284f., 288f., 290-294, 308, 339
Providence, 22, 30, 106, 114-123; general, 114-120; special, 120-123
Punishment, 119, 148, 392, 401

Q source, 54, 202f.
Qumran, 197, 277, 281

Real presence, 240f., 291, 356, 367f.
Reason, 19, 27f., 41, 45f., 50, 72f., 82-85, 91, 104, 106, 150, 176, 223, 249, 271, 275
Redemption, 30f., 47, 58, 97f., 196, 258, 345
Reformation/Reformers, 24, 29, 60, 176, 234, 236-242, 270-272, 285, 307f., 318, 360
Reformed churches/theology, 24, 239, 248f., 290f., 293, 316, 318, 349, 367f.
Religion, 31f., 42, 44, 71, 92, 104, 246, 273, 326
Religions, 13, 20, 32, 41f., 49, 66f., 71f., 97f., 100, 106, 112, 132, 173, 223, 295f., 336, 349, 379
Responsibility, 120, 144f., 161-166
Resurrection of dead, 15, 48, 212, 220, 379-381, 385-393, 403
Resurrection of Jesus Christ, 34, 48, 122, 177, 179, 180, 183, 205, 208-214, 221,

448 INDEX OF SUBJECTS

244, 248, 254, 257f., 278-282, 381-385
Resurrection body, 385-388, 395
Revelation, 17, 32, 40-52, 60, 106, 112, 238
Revolution, 184f., 246
Righteousness of God, 94f., 272
Roman Catholic church, 27f., 35, 103, 229, 285-292, 300f., 308, 312f., 316, 339, 357, 359, 368
Roman Catholic doctrine, 24, 27, 234, 291f., 303f., 351, 354, 367f.
Roman Catholic theologians, 168f., 285, 292, 359, 392
Roman Catholicism, 25, 284, 322, 326
Roman Empire, 66, 226
Rome, 14, 119, 162, 169, 326

Sabbath, 99, 197, 339
Sacrament(s), 27f., 30, 89, 294, 300, 306, 308, 311f., 315, 341, 349, 352-375
Saints, 296, 302, 321
Salvation, 24, 29, 35, 46f., 49, 63, 91, 110, 112f., 119f., 164, 189, 201, 217, 219, 224, 229f., 234-242, 252-258, 272, 283f., 300, 318, 329, 336, 358f., 361, 371, 395, 399
Salvation history (*Heilsgeschichte*), 49, 51f., 58, 108-114, 216, 270-272, 275, 283
Satan, 115, 144-153, 234f., 241, 326
Satisfaction, theory of, 234f., 252f.
Scholasticism, 28, 73, 357
Science, 16, 45, 76, 96f., 99, 121, 124, 151, 181, 214, 389, 394
Scripture, 17, 24, 27, 29, 33f., 53-63, 178, 288f., 316-318, 381
Sectarian/sects, 60, 294, 319f.

Secularity/secularism, 13f., 39, 271, 273, 288, 330, 377-379
Seminal *logos*, 21, 33, 72, 223
Servant role, 329-331, 339
Sexuality, 125f., 129-131, 163, 165
Sickness, 122, 138f., 145, 149
Sin, 26, 29, 64, 120, 131-134, 140-171, 210f., 230, 235, 298, 327, 329, 344
Skepticism, 26f., 175, 243
Small Catechism, 62, 241f., 335, 349, 351, 357, 359, 364, 366-368.
Social Gospel movement, 33, 171, 182-185
Social sin, 169-171
Son of God, 20, 209, 215, 219, 222-229, 237, 266-269, 382
Son of man, 188, 203f., 215
Soul, 125, 262, 380, 386, 391f.
Spirit, 55, 115, 125, 133, 161, 220, 228f., 249, 259-275, 296f., 321, 364f., 372
Spirit, 100, 105f., 125, 260-262, 380
State, 322-329
Stoics, 18, 114, 223
Superstition, 71f.

Teleological argument, 79-81
Temptation, 143-145, 154
Ten Commandments, 62, 108, 166, 343, 347
Theism, 92, 102, 105-108
Theodicy, 26, 90, 119, 152-154
Theology, 17, 18-39, 152, 258, 381
Third use of the law, 346-349, 351
Time, 88f., 388f., 393, 394
Tradition, 55f., 58-63, 288f., 317-321
Transcendence, 43, 274
Transubstantiation, 367-369

Trent, Council of, 59f., 167, 234, 285f., 288, 315, 355, 358f., 368
Trinitarian controversy, 221-229
Trinity, 29f., 221-229, 236f., 258, 265-270, 363, 365
Twelve, 278-281
Two kingdoms doctrine, 326f.

Ubiquity, 240, 368
Unity, 60, 284-294, 297, 300, 302, 316f., 333, 337f.
Universal salvation, 256, 336f., 398-400
Universe, 116, 132, 394f.; theories of its origin, 96f., 99, 151
Utopianism, 328f., 332, 404

Values, 14, 21, 107
Vatican I, 84, 286
Vatican II, 35, 59f., 285-290, 292, 300, 303, 308, 315, 322, 353f., 355, 360

Will of God, 90, 344, 347, 398
Wisdom literature, 97f.
Women's liberation movement, 131
Word of God, 43, 53f., 60, 100, 178, 223, 294, 300, 310f., 317f., 341-352, 357-359, 361
World, 45, 49, 64, 76, 83f., 96, 100, 102-114, 136, 210, 265, 271, 275, 304, 323-329, 334, 393, 394-396
World architect, 81
World Council of Churches, 286, 290, 292-294, 333, 337
Worship, 22, 54, 56, 67, 107f., 295, 302, 333, 339, 343, 353f., 373f.
Wrath of God, 95, 252

Yahweh, 44, 46f., 51, 62, 65, 67-70, 72, 92f., 97, 101, 108, 197, 209, 251, 297, 382

Zealots, 194
Zoroastrianism (Parsiism), 145-147, 402

3 1542 00060 8822

230.
S411r

DATE DUE

WITHDRAWN

**Haas Library
Muhlenberg College**
Allentown, Pennsylvania